OVEN TEMPERATURES

The following chart gives the conversions from degrees Fahrenheit to degrees Celsius (formerly known as Centigrade) recommended by the manufacturers of electric cookers.

Description	Electric setting	Gas mark
very cool	225°F – 110°C	$\frac{1}{4}$
	250°F – 130°C	$\frac{1}{2}$
cool	275°F – 140°C	1
	300°F – 150°C	2
very moderate	325°F – 170°C	3
moderate	350°F – 180°C	4
moderate *to*	375°F – 190°C	5
moderately hot	400°F – 200°C	6
hot	425°F – 220°C	7
	450°F – 230°C	8
very hot	475°F – 240°C	9

NOTE: This table is an approximate guide only. Different makes of cooker vary and if you are in any doubt about the setting it is as well to refer to the manufacturer's temperature chart.

BRITISH MEASURE / AMERICAN EQUIVALENT

BRITISH MEASURE	AMERICAN EQUIVALENT
Flour – plain or self-raising :	*Sifted flour – all-purpose*
4 ounces	1 cup
Cornflour :	*Cornstarch :*
4½ ounces	1 cup
Icing sugar :	*Sifted confectioners' sugar :*
4½ ounces	1 cup
Soft brown sugar :	*Light and dark brown sugar :*
8 ounces	1 cup (firmly packed)
Castor or granulated sugar :	*Granulated sugar :*
7½ ounces	1 cup
Butter, margarine, cooking fat, lard, dripping :	*Butter, shortening, lard, drippings – solid or melted :*
1 ounce	2 tablespoons
8 ounces	1 cup
Grated cheese – Cheddar type :	*Grated cheese – Cheddar type :*
4 ounces	1 cup
Cereals and cereal foods :	
7 ounces pearl barley	1 cup
6 ounces semolina/ground rice/ tapioca	1 cup
2 ounces fresh soft breadcrumbs/ cake crumbs	1 cup
4 ounces dried breadcrumbs	1 cup
3½ ounces rolled oats	1 cup
Vegetables and fruits :	
4 ounces shelled peas	¾ cup
4 ounces cooked sweet corn	1 cup
4 sticks celery	1 cup chopped celery
7 ounces chopped tomatoes	1 cup
3–4 ounces button mushrooms	1 cup
2 ounces chopped pickled beetroot	⅓ cup
4 ounces black/redcurrants/ bilberries	1 cup
5 ounces raspberries/strawberries	1 cup
Preserves :	
12 ounces clear honey/golden syrup/molasses/black treacle	1 cup
11 ounces maple/corn syrup	1 cup
5–6 ounces jam/marmalade/ jelly	½ cup
Dried fruit, nuts :	
5–6 ounces currants/sultanas/ raisins/chopped candied peel	1 cup
8 ounces glacé cherries	1 cup candied cherries
5 ounces whole shelled almonds	1 cup
4 ounces ground almonds	1 cup

BASIC METHODS OF COOKING

Baking – Cooking in dry heat in the oven.

Boiling – Cooking by immersing the food in a pan of liquid, which must be kept boiling gently – all the time.

Braising – Almost a combination of stewing and roasting. Meat is placed on a bed of vegetables with a little liquid surrounding, in a covered vessel, and cooked slowly in the oven.

Casserole – Cooking slowly in the oven in a covered casserole dish – usually meat, rabbit, etc.

Frying – Cooking in a little hot fat in an open pan. Deep frying is cooking by immersion in a deep pan of heated fat.

Grilling – Cooking quickly under a red-hot grill: used for smaller tender pieces of meat, fish, etc.

Poaching – Cooking gently in water which is just below boiling point: usually eggs or fish.

Pressure Cooking – Cooking at higher temperatures than usual, so that food is cooked much more quickly.

Roasting – Cooking with a little fat in a hot oven. Fat is poured from the baking tin over the meat or poultry from time to time, using a long-handled spoon: this is known as basting.

Simmering – The water is kept just below boiling point, ... the side of the pan.

Steaming – Cooking .... of boiling water, or in a b......... boiling water.

Stewing – Cooking slowly until the food is tender. It is done in just enough liquid to cover the food, as the liquid is served with it and should be rich. Stews may be cooked in covered saucepans or casseroles, on a hot-plate or in the oven – but always at a low temperature.

COOKERY
IN
COLOUR

A PICTURE ENCYCLOPEDIA
FOR EVERY OCCASION
EDITED BY
MARGUERITE PATTEN

AND PUBLISHED BY
THE HAMLYN PUBLISHING GROUP LIMITED
LONDON · NEW YORK · SYDNEY · TORONTO

INTRODUCTION

I hope you will enjoy working through this book. A really up-to-the-minute cookery encyclopedia, it contains not only interesting familiar recipes and basic cooking knowledge, but also many very unusual dishes and a host of new ideas for meals of all kinds. There are special chapters on pressure cooking and time-controlled cooking, and you will find instructions for jams, bottling and preserving, making sweetmeats, teatime cookery, how to select and use wines – in fact, COOKERY IN COLOUR is a perfect companion for the busy modern housewife.

All recipes are for four persons unless otherwise stated. Most of the recipes are illustrated with colour or black and white photographs, which I think will be a great help to you, because a large part of the success of a meal lies in its appeal to the eye. Food should both taste and look good.

For quickness of reference the entries have been numbered in order, right through the book, and the comprehensive index at the back refers to these numbers. It is proposed in this country, that in common with many other countries of the world, we use the Metric rather than the Imperial measures. You will find, therefore, that in this revised edition of COOKERY IN COLOUR the weights and measures and oven temperatures are given in every recipe in both Metric and Imperial. At the beginning and end of the book are to be found various tables of weights and measures, oven temperatures, etc.

Mine has been the task of editing COOKERY IN COLOUR, and I should like to thank and pay tribute to all the many people who have gone out of their way to provide what I hope you, the reader, will agree are outstanding cookery pictures. It has been a pleasure to compile this book of over a thousand recipes, and I hope that you will find it a pleasure to use. I also hope that it will provide an incentive to try all sorts of dishes that you haven't met before.

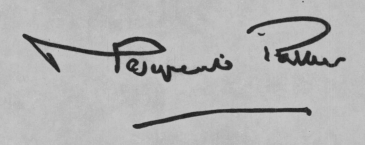

CONTENTS

HORS D'OEUVRE

A good hors d'oeuvre makes a pleasant start to the meal. If you have a substantial course to follow, choose a light hors d'oeuvre such as fruit. If on the other hand, the main part of the meal is light and rather straight forward, a mixed hors d'oeuvre with a wide variety of ingredients makes a very suitable beginning.

1 GRAPEFRUIT

Allow ½ grapefruit for each person. Cut away the pith and skin, loosen each section with a sharp fruit knife so it is easy to eat. Dust lightly with sugar and decorate with Maraschino cherries or sprigs of mint. If using canned instead of fresh grapefruit serve in glasses and decorate with cherries. Grapefruit has a better flavour if served very cold, so if you have a refrigerator chill the grapefruit before serving.

2 GRAPEFRUIT BASKETS

Prepare the grapefruit in the usual way. Mix the sections with other fruit – fresh strawberries, canned mandarin oranges and sliced preserved ginger are some of the most suitable. Make handles of angelica and decorate with sprigs of mint. If time permits serrate the edge of each grapefruit half.

3 HOT GRAPEFRUIT

Halve and prepare the grapefruit in the usual way. Spread just a small amount of butter over the top, add a sprinkling of brown sugar and mixed spice. Heat either in a moderate oven, 360°F, 180°C, Gas Mark 4, or under the grill until the surface of the fruit is golden brown and the juice begins to flow. For special occasions add a little dry sherry as well as butter, spice and sugar.

Melon with Angostura bitters

4 MELON BASKET

Choose a firm melon. Charentais, which come from Spain, Italy and France, or Dutch Cantaloupe melons are considered by some people the best. The Honeydew types of melon, green or yellow, are also excellent. Melon is at its best served slightly iced, so keep for a time in the refrigerator. Cut into slices and serve with castor sugar and ground ginger – or top with slices of preserved ginger. For easy serving cut the slices into sections. For a more impressive hors d'oeuvre cut the top off the melon carefully – this can be serrated – remove the fruit pulp and dice. Mix this with preserved ginger. Sweeten to taste and pile back into the melon case. Top with a mixture of fresh fruits in season. For special occasions pour over a little white wine some time before serving. A pineapple, as illustrated on opposite page, can be used in place of a melon. Top with cream cheese for a light meal.

5 MELON AND SMOKED HAM

An unusual but delicious hors d'oeuvre is to serve a slice of ripe melon with a slice of smoked Parma ham. Cut the melon into slices, scrape off the pips. Roll the slices of ham and place them on the upturned melon slices. When melon is not available use canned or fresh figs or peeled ripe pears with the ham.

6 MELON WITH ANGOSTURA BITTERS

If melon is sliced and just a few dashes of Angostura bitters are put on it, this will appeal very much to people who do not like anything too sweet at the beginning of a meal.

7 MIXED HORS D'OEUVRE
(Illustrated in colour on the opposite page)

This selection of foods will appeal to those people who like a very light dressing and not too much mayonnaise.
Cottage cheese garnished with canned peach slices.
Tomato salad with French dressing (Recipe No. 398) and garnished with sprigs of parsley.
Rollmop herrings (Recipe No. 8) served with thin apple slices tossed in mayonnaise mixed with natural yoghourt.
Thin strips of raw carrot served with watercress.
Slices of lean ham, rolled and filled with cottage cheese, served with shredded lettuce.
Baked herrings, garnished with fresh orange segments.

Mixed hors d'oeuvre

Pineapple basket

8   ROLLMOP HERRINGS

Use large herrings. Clean, take out roes and backbone and cut off heads, divide into two fillets. Make a brine of 50g (2oz) kitchen salt and 568ml (1 pint) water. Soak the herrings in the brine for 2 hours. Lift out of the brine and put into a large shallow dish. Cover with pure malt vinegar and leave for several hours. When ready, take the fish out of the vinegar, lay flat on a wooden board, then roll each fillet round a small tablespoonful finely shredded onion, secure with a small cocktail stick. Put into jars with bay leaves, gherkins and a chilli and cover with cold spiced vinegar (Recipe No. 974). Cover and store in a cool dry place. Prepared in this manner they will keep 3–4 weeks.

9   MIXED HORS D'OEUVRE

When planning a mixed hors d'oeuvre try to have a good variety of different flavours and colouring. Ideally your hors d'oeuvre should consist of:

Something with a fish flavour: sardines, anchovies, rollmop herrings, mussels, prawns, smoked salmon, fresh salmon, fish salads of any kind, cooked cod's roe or other hard roes or smoked cod's roe pâté. Dress the fish with mayonnaise (Recipe No. 408) or oil and vinegar and garnish it with chopped parsley etc.

Salads: selection of potato etc. The salad should be tossed in French dressing (Recipe No. 398) or mixed with mayonnaise.

Meat: diced salami, chopped sausages, small cubes or rolls of ham, tongue, chicken. These can be mixed with sliced tomato for colour or chicken could be tossed in mayonnaise.

Eggs: sliced hard-boiled or hard-boiled and stuffed.

In addition use some of the savoury ingredients which are so excellent and which are a very good stand-by in the store cupboard – pickled gherkins, cocktail onions, olives, pickled walnuts.

Rollmop herrings

10   FRUIT COCKTAIL

This is not only delicious as a sweet but can be served as an hors d'oeuvre if wished. Peel a pineapple carefully, trying to keep its shape intact. Replace leaves, and arrange in a bowl. Put a mixture of diced fresh fruit all round and decorate with sprigs of mint. If serving as a sweet, dust with sugar and moisten with a little fresh orange juice or Curaçao – or soak in a sugar syrup. If serving as an hors d'oeuvre, put on very little sugar and add a small quantity of dry sherry.

Fruit cocktail

PATES

A home-made pâté is a delicious hors d'oeuvre. There are various and quite economical ways of making this.

Chicken liver pâté

20   CHICKEN LIVER PATE

75g/3oz butter
225–300g/9–12oz frozen or fresh chicken livers*
3 tablespoons cream · good pinch mixed herbs
salt and pepper · red pepper, stuffed olives and
watercress to garnish

The equivalent weight in goose, duck or turkey livers could be used instead

Heat the butter in a frying pan and cook the livers gently until just tender. If you have an electric blender put them into this with the cream, herbs and seasonings. Switch on until smooth. Put into a buttered dish and allow to cool. When making a pâté by hand rub the cooked livers through a sieve and then add the hot butter from the pan, cream, seasoning and herbs. Put into a buttered dish and allow to cool. Spoon on to crisp lettuce leaves, or if firm enough cut into slices. Serve with hot toast and butter. For a change finely chopped cocktail onions and gherkins can be added, or substitute some of the cream for sherry or brandy. Garnish with strips of red pepper, stuffed olives and watercress.

21   CALF LIVER PATE

8 rashers long streaky bacon · 50g/2oz butter
25g/1oz flour · 142ml/¼pint milk · ½kg/1lb calves liver
3–4 tablespoons cream or evaporated milk · 1 egg
salt · black pepper · sliced olives and gherkins to garnish

Butter a loaf tin and arrange about 5 of the rashers of bacon at the bottom of this. Heat the butter in a pan, stir in the flour and cook for several minutes, then gradually add the cold milk. Bring to the boil, stirring and cook until thick and smooth. Put the liver and the remainder of the bacon through a mincer twice if possible, until very fine and smooth. Add to the sauce, together with the cream and beaten egg. Season very well. Put into the tin, over the bacon. Cover with foil or buttered paper and stand the tin in a 'bain-marie' – a dish of cold water. Cook for approximately 45 minutes in the centre of a very moderate oven, 325°F, 170°C, Gas Mark 3. Allow to cool. Leave in tin until ready to serve, then turn out and garnish with the sliced stuffed olives and gherkins. Serve with crisp lettuce, hot toast and butter.

22   HOT BACON ROLLS

6 rashers streaky bacon
sage and onion stuffing (Recipe No. 280)
1 small white cabbage · chopped parsley and
bay leaves to garnish

Remove the rind from the bacon rashers. Place a little stuffiing on each rasher. Roll up and secure with a wooden cocktail stick. Place on a baking sheet and cook in a moderate oven, 350°F, 180°C, Gas Mark 4, for 25–30 minutes. Shred the cabbage and cook in boiling salted water until just tender. Drain well and place on a serving dish. Remove the cocktail sticks from the bacon rolls and arrange the rolls on the cabbage. Serve garnished with chopped parsley and bay leaves.
Makes 6 servings.

Hot bacon rolls

Prawn cocktail

26   FISH COCKTAIL

1 *small can tuna fish or flaked salmon*
6 *level tablespoons tomato ketchup* · 2 *tablespoons lemon juice*
½ *level teaspoon salt* · ¼ *teaspoon pepper*
1 *teaspoon finely shredded horseradish*
1 *teaspoon Worcestershire sauce* · *lettuce*
lemon slices to garnish

Remove the tuna from the can and break into pieces. Combine the rest of the ingredients together and mix with the tuna. Line 2 cocktail glasses with lettuce leaves (from the heart if possible) and three-quarters fill with the mixture. Garnish each glass with ½ slice of lemon on the side. Serve with brown bread and butter.

27   PRAWN COCKTAIL WITH SOURED CREAM SAUCE

½ *lettuce, shredded* · 150g/6oz *shelled prawns*
1 *tablespoon tomato ketchup* · *dash Worcestershire sauce*
salt and pepper · 1 *carton soured cream*
whole prawns, lemon wedges and paprika to garnish

Divide lettuce and shelled prawns between 4 glasses. Blend together ketchup, Worcestershire sauce, seasoning and soured cream. Pour over sauce just before serving. Sprinkle with paprika. Garnish with whole prawns and lemon wedges, slit halfway up between the skin and the flesh so that they sit on the edge of the glass. Serve with thinly sliced brown bread and butter.

Prawn cocktail with soured cream sauce

23   PRAWN OR SHRIMP COCKTAIL

lettuce · *generous* ½ *litre/1 pint peeled fresh prawns or shrimps**
cocktail sauce (Recipe No. 25)

**When fresh prawns or shrimps are unobtainable use the excellent frozen or canned variety*

If serving on flat dishes choose small leaves of lettuce. Arrange the prawns or shrimps on these and coat with the sauce. The correct way of serving these cocktails, though, is to use glasses, when the lettuce should be shredded very finely and put at the bottom of the glasses. Cover with the prawns or shrimps and the sauce. Garnish with lemon if wished. Serve as cold as possible; in fact if you can arrange the glass in another container of crushed ice it is an advantage.

24   LOBSTER OR CRAB COCKTAIL

Use the same method as for prawn cocktail – cut the lobster meat finely and garnish with one or two small lobster claws. When serving crab meat arrange light and dark meat neatly on the shredded lettuce. Garnish with small crab claws and lemon.

25   COCKTAIL SAUCE

(For prawn or shrimp cocktail)

5 *tablespoons thick mayonnaise (Recipe No. 408)*
1 *tablespoon tomato ketchup or thick tomato purée*
1 *tablespoon Worcestershire sauce* · 1 *tablespoon lemon juice*
1 *teaspoon finely chopped onion*
1 *teaspoon finely chopped celery when in season or*
¼ *teaspoon celery salt* · *salt to taste*

Mix together all the ingredients.

Ask the fishmonger to open these for you. Serve in one shell, with paprika or cayenne pepper, slices of lemon and brown bread and butter. Some people like a little vinegar with them.

UNUSUAL HORS D'OEUVRE

Cheese and ham rolls

29 CHEESE AND HAM ROLLS

75g/3oz cream cheese or flavoured cheese spread
6 stuffed olives, chopped · 1 teaspoon horseradish
2 tablespoons single cream · seasoning · slices ham
radish roses and hard-boiled egg quarters to garnish

Mix ingredients and spread on thin slices of ham. Roll up, secure with cocktail sticks and serve as cold as possible. Garnish with radish roses and quarters of hard-boiled egg.

30 CHEESE STUFFED APPLES
(Illustrated in colour on the jacket)

Remove a slice from the top of 4 eating apples. Remove the cores and some of the flesh. Mix together a few finely chopped walnuts and cream cheese. Spoon this mixture into the apple cases. Garnish with halved black grapes and glacé cherries.

31 SPANISH SAVOURY RICE

75g/3oz long grain rice · 4 rashers bacon
1 small onion, chopped · ½ green pepper, chopped
250g/10oz can condensed tomato soup · 4 tablespoons water
seasoning · cheese biscuits
sliced stuffed olives and parsley to garnish

Cook the rice in salted water until tender. Drain and rinse. Chop the bacon and fry until crisp. Remove from the pan and fry the onion and pepper until tender. Add bacon, rice, soup, water and seasoning. Heat gently. Pile on cheese biscuits and garnish with sliced stuffed olives and parsley.

Spanish savoury rice

SOUPS

With so many excellent ready prepared soups on the market one often wonders if it is worth while making soup at home. If you have the ingredients you can produce a very economical and interesting home-made variety. In this chapter are some of the most popular soups and some very unusual ones too.

Remember, the good ready prepared soups are wholesome food, but if you wish to give them an individual flavour, extra touches of seasoning and garnish help enormously. Suggestions are also included for making ready prepared soups more individual. Two modern appliances help a great deal in soup making – first, a pressure cooker for stock and cooking the ingredients quickly and secondly, an electric liquidiser, which takes the place of a sieve so excellently.

32 CONSOMME

300g/12oz shin of beef · generous litre/2pints good stock
seasoning · 1 onion · 1 carrot · small piece celery
sprig parsley · bay leaf

Cut the meat into small pieces and put into a saucepan together with the other ingredients. Simmer very gently for 1 hour, then strain through several thicknesses of muslin. Add 1 dessertspoon sherry if desired. To clear a consommé put in a stiffly beaten egg white and clean egg shell, gently simmer for 20 minutes, then re-strain.

33 CONSOMME JULIENNE

To the above quantity allow:
1 good-sized carrot · ½ medium-sized turnip
1 leek or onion · small piece cabbage

Cut the vegetables into thin pieces about the size and thickness of a matchstick. Melt 25g (1oz) margarine in a saucepan and toss the vegetables in this until just turning brown. Add about 4 tablespoons of the consommé and cook gently until quite tender. Discard any fat; add the remaining consommé and reheat gently.

34 CONSOMME JARDINIERE

Use the same vegetables as for consommé julienne but this time cut them either into small cubes or, using a vegetable cutter, shape into tiny rounds the size of a pea. Simmer in the consommé for a good 15 minutes.

35 CONSOMME AU VERMICELLI

To the quantity of consommé given add 2 tablespoons vermicelli. Cook gently for 7 minutes, then serve.

36 CONSOMME ROYALE

In this soup the custard for the garnish is made as follows: Put the yolks of 1 or 2 eggs into a basin, whisk lightly, then add 1 whole egg and 4 tablespoons white stock or milk. Mix together and season well. Cover with greased paper and steam for 20–30 minutes. When quite cold and firm cut into small fancy shapes and serve on top of the consommé.

37 BANQUET CONSOMME

To the quantity of consommé given add julienne (thin strips) of smoked salmon.

38 SUMMER SOUP
(Jellied consommé)

Make consommé as Recipe No. 32 and allow to cool, when it will set into a light jelly. If the weather is hot and you have no refrigerator, dissolve 2 *level* teaspoons powdered gelatine in the consommé. Beat lightly before putting into soup cups. Garnish with slices of cucumber, lemon or smoked salmon.

Brown onion soup (Recipe No. 49)

FISH SOUPS

39   LOBSTER BISQUE

(Thick soup for parties)

½ large lobster or small lobster
generous ½litre/1pint water or fish stock
1 teaspoon lemon juice · 25g/1oz flour · 284ml/½pint milk
50g/2oz margarine or butter · 2 tablespoons cream
seasoning · paprika to garnish

Remove the flesh from the lobster and cut into small pieces. Save a few of the pieces for a garnish. Put the shell – well washed and crushed – into a large saucepan. Cover with the water or stock, add the lemon juice and simmer gently for a good 30 minutes. Strain carefully through a fine sieve and return to the pan together with lobster meat. Blend the flour with the milk and stir this into the soup together with margarine or butter. Bring slowly to the boil and cook, stirring all the time until thickened. Add the cream and seasoning, reheat (but do not allow to boil) and serve. Garnish with paprika pepper and the pieces of lobster.

40 LOBSTER AND ASPARAGUS BISQUE

Use Recipe No. 39 but instead of all fish stock use partly asparagus stock. Garnish with asparagus tips and pieces of lobster.

41   CREAM OF MUSSEL SOUP

generous litre/2pints mussels · 284ml/½pint water
1 onion · seasoning · 1 small bunch parsley
generous ½litre/1pint white sauce – thin consistency*
1 dessertspoon vinegar · 1 tablespoon white wine, optional
chopped parsley to garnish

*Made with 25g (1oz) butter, 25g (1oz) flour, generous ½ litre (1 pint) milk

Scrub the mussels well, discarding any that are open and will not close when sharply tapped. Put into a large saucepan together with water, onion, a good pinch of salt and pepper and the bunch of parsley. Heat slowly until the mussels open. Remove the beards from the mussels. Sometimes you will find a small growth, looking like a weed, in the mussels – this must be taken out. Make the white sauce, strain the liquid in which the mussels have been cooked, add this to the sauce, together with vinegar, wine and any additional seasoning to taste. Lastly add the mussels. These may be removed from the shells or not, as wished. Heat the soup gently and serve sprinkled with chopped parsley.

42   TOMATO CRAB BISQUE

250g/10oz can condensed tomato soup · 284ml/½pint milk
1 teaspoon chopped onion · pinch salt · pinch ground marjoram
1 small can flaked crab meat
142ml/¼pint single cream or evaporated milk

Combine the first 5 ingredients and heat thoroughly. Gradually stir in the crab meat and the cream. Serve hot.

Tomato crab bisque

POTATO SOUPS

43 CREAMY POTATO CHOWDER

5 medium-sized potatoes · 3 medium-sized onions
375g/15oz can mushroom soup · 25g/1oz butter
¾litre/1½pints milk · salt and pepper · grated nutmeg
1 teaspoon made mustard

Dice potatoes and slice the onions. Cook the potatoes and onions in a small amount of water until tender and then rub through a sieve. Add the mushroom soup, butter, milk, salt and pepper to taste, nutmeg and mustard. Heat gently. For colour, a few green peas, sliced carrot or chopped pepper can be added. Serve hot or icy cold.
Makes 6–8 servings.

44 VARIATIONS

Add a dash of Angostura bitters to the soup, whip 142ml (¼ pint) double cream and place a spoonful on top of each serving.
Top with dabs of chive-flavoured cottage cheese.
Season the chowder with a very little curry powder.
Reduce the potatoes by 2 and add 50g (2oz) of cooked long grain rice before serving.

Creamy potato chowder

Potato soup

45 POTATO AND GREEN PEA SOUP

½kg/1lb green peas · good handful young pea pods
300g/12oz potatoes · scant ¾litre/1¼pints white stock or water
seasoning · ½ teaspoon sugar · sprig mint
284ml/½pint milk

Put the peas, the pods – broken into small pieces – the diced potatoes, liquid, seasoning, sugar and mint into a saucepan and simmer gently for about 45 minutes. Discard the mint; rub mixture through a sieve. Reheat with the milk. Garnish with hard-boiled egg if wished.

46 POTATO SOUP WITH CHEESE RUSKS

300g/12oz potatoes · 1 medium-sized onion · 15g/½oz butter
50g/2oz bacon, optional · 1 level teaspoon salt
pinch pepper, nutmeg, thyme
generous litre/2pints hot white stock or water
cheese rusks (Recipe No. 47)

Scrub and peel the potatoes and cut into cubes; slice the onion thinly. Heat the butter in a saucepan and lightly brown the onion (and diced bacon if used). Add the potato cubes, seasoning and flavouring and pour on the stock. Cook gently 15–20 minutes. Serve hot with cheese rusks.

47 CHEESE RUSKS

4 large slices thickly buttered white or brown bread
100g/4oz Cheddar cheese, finely grated

Cover the buttered bread slices with the finely grated cheese, pressing down with a knife. Bake in a moderately hot oven, 400°F, 200°C, Gas Mark 6, for 15–20 minutes until crisp and golden brown. Cut neatly. The soup and cheese rusks together make a nourishing meal.

Cream of mushroom soup

VEGETABLE SOUPS

48   CREAM OF MUSHROOM SOUP

200g/8oz *mushrooms** · 50g/2oz *margarine or butter*
50g/2oz *flour* · generous ½litre/1pint *water or stock*
426ml/¾pint *milk* · *seasoning* · *parsley to garnish*

**The stems of mushrooms could be used if liked and fried whole mushrooms*
added to the soup at the last moment

Chop mushrooms finely unless the soup is to be strained.
Melt margarine or butter in saucepan, fry mushrooms for
5 minutes, stirring from time to time. Stir in the flour and
cook for 3 minutes. Remove the pan from the heat and gradually add water and milk. Bring to the boil and cook until soup
thickens. Season and serve garnished with parsley.

49   BROWN ONION SOUP

(Illustrated in colour at the beginning of this section)

4 *large onions* · 50g/2oz *butter* · 15g/½oz *cornflour*
426ml/¾pint *brown stock* · *seasoning*
few drops Worcestershire sauce · 1 *tablespoon sherry, optional*

Cook the onions in the water until tender, then chop finely.
Melt the butter in a saucepan, stir in the cornflour and cook
for 2–3 minutes. Remove from the heat and gradually stir in
the stock. Bring to the boil, stirring. Add seasoning, Worcestershire sauce and sherry if used. Add onions and serve.

50   LEEK AND POTATO SOUP

3 *good-sized leeks* · 40g/1½oz *margarine or butter*
½kg/1lb *potatoes, sliced* · ¾litre/1½pints *white stock or water*
seasoning   4 *tablespoons milk*
4 *tablespoons single cream or evaporated milk*
parsley to garnish

Slice the leeks – using some of the green part to give a good
colour – then heat the butter in the pan and cook the leeks for
about 5 minutes, taking care they do not discolour. Add the
sliced potatoes, stock and seasoning. Cook steadily for about 30
minutes. Sieve, return to the pan, adding the milk and cream,
and reheat without boiling. Pour into hot soup tureen and
garnish with parsley.

Cream of tomato soup

51   CREAM OF TOMATO SOUP

50g/2oz butter · ½kg/1lb tomatoes, sliced
1 onion, chopped · 2 bay leaves · 4 peppercorns
142ml/¼pint water or white stock · 50g/2oz flour
generous ½litre/1pint milk · seasoning · cream, optional
chopped parsley to garnish

Heat half the butter and fry the sliced tomatoes and chopped onion together with bay leaves and peppercorns. Add water and simmer until vegetables are quite soft. Rub through a hair or nylon sieve. Heat the remaining butter in a pan and stir in the flour. Cook for several minutes and gradually add the milk. Bring to the boil and cook until smooth and thickened; season well. Remember this is a thin white sauce. Reheat the tomato purée. Take both pans off the heat and make sure the contents are not boiling, then, using an egg whisk, whisk together. Add a little cream if wished. This method prevents the soup curdling. Serve garnished with chopped parsley.

Note: 3 teaspoons Angostura bitters added to the soup just before serving will give it a good flavour.

52   CREAM OF TOMATO SOUP WITH CHEESE

Make the above cream of tomato soup, but just before serving put a good layer of grated cheese on top. Dutch Edam or Gouda cheese, with its mild flavour, is a very good accompaniment to this soup.

Clear tomato soup

Green pea soup

53   CLEAR TOMATO SOUP

¾kg/1½lb tomatoes, chopped
generous ½litre/1pint water or white stock
½ small uncooked beetroot · small stick celery
1 small onion, chopped · few drops Worcestershire sauce
1 teaspoon vinegar or lemon juice · seasoning · 2 bay leaves

Put the ingredients all together in a large saucepan and cook gently until the tomatoes are very soft. This should take about 25 minutes. Remove the beetroot and bay leaves; then rub through a sieve and finally strain through muslin. Reheat or serve cold. If a slightly thickened soup is required rub through the sieve, without straining afterwards. If serving hot, top each serving with a knob of butter.

54   GREEN PEA SOUP

200g/8oz dried peas · generous litre/2pints bacon stock★
2 onions, chopped · 1 carrot, chopped · 1 turnip, chopped
seasoning · sprig mint · 1 teaspoon sugar
2 rashers grilled bacon to garnish

★*When you have stock left from boiling a piece of bacon, try to use it in a soup like this, because the flavour is excellent. A lentil or vegetable soup can be made with bacon stock too, with very good result*

Soak the peas overnight in the bacon stock – put into saucepan with the vegetables, seasoning, mint and sugar and simmer gently for 1¼–1½ hours. Either rub through a sieve or beat until very smooth. Taste and re-season. Garnish with crisp pieces of bacon.

Cream of artichoke soup

55   CREAM OF ARTICHOKE SOUP

¾kg/1½lb Jerusalem artichokes
generous ½litre/1pint water or white stock
¼ teaspoon vinegar · seasoning · 50g/2oz butter
15g/½oz flour · 142–284ml/¼–½pint milk
paprika pepper to garnish

Wash and peel the artichokes and, if large, cut into small pieces. Remember to keep the artichokes in cold water, with a tablespoon of lemon juice to keep them a good colour, until ready to cook them. Put into a saucepan with the water or stock, vinegar and seasoning. Simmer gently for a good 30 minutes. Rub through a sieve, then return the purée to the saucepan together with the butter. Blend the flour with the cold milk, stir into the boiling purée and continue cooking, stirring all the time, until you have a smooth thick sauce. Garnish with paprika pepper. If liked a few of the cooked artichokes can be saved, cut into tiny pieces and then put into the soup.

56 CREAM OF VEGETABLE SOUP

Ingredients as cream of artichoke soup (Recipe No. 55), but instead of artichokes use the same weight of mixed vegetables. Have a good proportion of carrots, for they give a more interesting colour, as well as a good flavour.

57 CARAWAY SEED TOAST FINGERS

slices white bread · butter · caraway seeds

Remove the crusts from several fairly thin slices of bread. Butter one side and sprinkle with caraway seeds. Toast the buttered side to a golden brown and cut into fingers. Serve at once.

58 CHEESE SOUP

½ onion, finely chopped · 50g/2oz butter · 40g/1½oz flour
generous ½litre/1pint milk · generous ½litre/1pint stock
2 teaspoons salt · pinch pepper
200g/8oz processed Cheddar cheese, grated
3 carrots, finely chopped or grated
2 sticks celery, finely chopped or grated
caraway seed toast fingers (Recipe No. 57)

Fry the onion in the butter until tender. Add the flour and cook slowly for a minute, stirring. Add the milk and stock gradually, stirring continuously, and bring to the boil. Season. Add the grated cheese and stir until it is melted. Add carrots and celery and cook until the vegetables are tender. Serve with caraway seed toast fingers.

59 WINTER VEGETABLE SOUP

generous litre/2pints chicken stock or water and stock cubes
50g/2oz soft margarine · 1 level teaspoon salt
good shake pepper · 100g/4oz mushrooms · 2 large onions
2 large carrots · 3 sticks celery · 50g/2oz flour
generous ½litre/1pint milk

Put the stock or water and stock cubes and margarine into a large saucepan and bring to the boil. Add most of the salt and the pepper. Meanwhile wash and peel all the vegetables and chop them finely or grate where possible. Put into the boiling stock, lower the heat and cook for 25 minutes. Blend the flour and milk, add to the soup and cook until thickened and smooth, add more salt if necessary.
Makes 7–8 servings.

60 CREAM OF SPINACH SOUP

1 small packet frozen spinach · 25g/1oz butter
1 small onion, sliced · 25g/1oz cornflour · ¾litre/1½pints milk
2 egg yolks · 3 tablespoons single cream · seasoning
croûtons (Recipe No. 61) to garnish

Cook and sieve the spinach. Heat the butter in a saucepan and fry the onion until tender. Add the cornflour, mix well and cook for a few minutes. Add the milk. Stir until boiling and boil for 3 minutes. Strain the sauce on to the spinach, then return to the heat. Mix the egg yolks and cream, add a little of the soup, then return all to the saucepan. Add seasonings and reheat without boiling. Serve garnished with croûtons.

61 CROUTONS

(To serve with soup)

Cut slices of bread into very small dice. Fry in butter until crisp and golden brown. Drain well and sprinkle over soup or serve in a separate bowl.

Winter vegetable soup

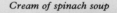

Cream of spinach soup

SOME LESS USUAL SOUPS

62   **SOUR HOT SOUP**

100g/4oz lean pork · 40g/1½oz beancurd*
3 dried mushrooms** · generous ½ litre/1pint stock
pepper and salt to taste · pinch monosodium glutamate***
1 tablespoon vinegar · 2 level teaspoons cornflour
1 tablespoon sherry

*Available in shops specialising in Chinese foods
**6 fresh mushrooms could be used
***Monosodium glutamate (Chinese taste powder) is on sale in many food shops and supermarkets. Ask for 'Ac'cent'

Cut the pork into fine slivers and break the beancurd into small pieces. Bring the stock to the boil, add the pork, beancurd and dried mushrooms and simmer gently for 15–20 minutes, until the pork is tender. Stir in the seasonings and the vinegar. Mix the cornflour to a smooth paste with a little cold water, add to the soup and boil for 3 minutes, stirring constantly. Before serving add the sherry.

63   **CREAM OF APPLE SOUP**

284ml/½pint white sauce (Recipe No. 663)
¾kg/1½lb apples, cut finely · water · sugar · juice 1 lemon
284ml/½pint cider · seasoning

Make the white sauce and keep hot. Simmer the apples, until tender, with water to cover, sugar to taste and lemon juice. Sieve the apple mixture, add to hot sauce with cider; season and whisk together. Serve at once.

64   **CHESTNUT SOUP**

½kg/1lb chestnuts · generous ½litre/1pint water or white stock
50g/2oz margarine or butter · 284ml/½pint milk
good pinch salt, cayenne pepper and sugar (if liked)
croûtons (Recipe No. 61)

Split the skins of the chestnuts; cover with water and cook for 15 minutes. Peel the nuts while still hot; then return to the saucepan with the water or stock. Simmer gently for 45 minutes. Rub the chestnuts through a sieve; then put the purée into the pan, together with the butter or margarine, milk and seasoning. Heat slowly, and serve with crisp pieces of toast or croûtons.

Sour hot soup

Iced tomato soup

COLD SOUPS

65   ICED TOMATO SOUP

Use Recipe No. 53 for clear tomato soup, but when ready pour into freezing tray of refrigerator and leave for a short time, until slightly iced. Serve garnished with chopped parsley.

66   ICED CHERRY SOUP

¾kg/1½lb cherries or can cherries · water · sugar to taste
juice 1 lemon · few whole cherries and
mint leaves to garnish

Cover fruit with water. Simmer gently, adding sugar to taste, and lemon juice. Rub through sieve, pour into freezing trays to lightly freeze. Serve in soup cups and garnish with whole cherries and mint leaves.

67   ICED CUCUMBER SOUP

1 medium-sized cucumber · 1 small onion, chopped
15g/½oz butter · 284ml/½pint stock · seasoning
4 tablespoons milk or evaporated milk · lemon to garnish

Cut cucumber into pieces – leaving on most of the peel. Fry onion in butter, add cucumber, half the stock, seasoning and simmer gently for about 15 minutes. Put through a sieve or into an electric blender. Add milk and rest of stock, and when cold pour into freezing tray and leave until lightly frosted. Serve, garnished with lemon, in cold soup cups.

MEAT SOUPS

68 OXTAIL SOUP

1 *small oxtail* · 50g/2oz *cooking fat or margarine*
1 *small turnip, sliced* · 3 *medium-sized carrots, sliced*
1 *large onion, sliced* · 1½litres/3pints *stock or water*
good pinch mixed herbs · *seasoning* · 50g/2oz *flour*

Soak the cut up oxtail in water for about 1 hour. Throw away
the water. Heat the fat and fry the sliced vegetables for about
5 minutes. Add the stock, oxtail, pinch of herbs and plenty of
seasoning and simmer gently for about 3 hours. Blend the
flour with a little cold stock or water and stir this into the soup.
Bring to the boil and cook for about 10 minutes. Take out the
pieces of oxtail and cut the meat from the bones. Return the
meat to the soup and reheat. There is a fair amount of fat on
this soup, so it is quite a good idea to make it the day before –
allow it to cool and then take the fat from the top.

69 PEPPERPOT SOUP

½kg/1lb *shin or skirt of beef* · 4 teaspoons *Worcestershire sauce*
2 level teaspoons *salt* · scant 1¼litres/2½pints *water*
2 onions, chopped · 2 carrots, quartered · 3 sticks celery, sliced
bouquet garni · 2 tablespoons *tomato purée*
50g/2oz *spaghetti* · 25g/1oz *butter* · 25g/1oz *flour*

Cut beef into cubes. Place in a bowl with Worcestershire
sauce and marinate for 12 hours in a refrigerator, turning
occasionally. Place meat and sauce in a large saucepan, add
salt and water and bring slowly to the boil. Add vegetables,
herbs and tomato purée and simmer for 15 minutes. Add
spaghetti, broken in small pieces and continue cooking for a
further 15 minutes. Remove bouquet garni. Work butter and
flour together. Remove soup from heat. Divide butter mixture
into six and stir in each portion separately until dissolved.
Return to heat and simmer for 5 minutes. Serve with chunks
of French bread and butter.
Makes 6 servings.

70 CHICKEN SOUP

chicken carcass · generous litre/2pints *chicken stock
made from a cube* · about 100g/4oz *cooked chicken meat*
284ml/½pint *milk* · 1 tablespoon *cornflour* · 25g/1oz *butter*
seasoning

Simmer the carcass in the stock for 1 hour, then strain. Add
the cooked chicken meat and milk and cook for a further 15
minutes, then rub through a sieve. Blend with cornflour, add
butter and seasoning. Cook for 10 minutes.

71 USING READY PREPARED SOUPS

The following recipes, as well as others in this section, show
what can be done with the ready prepared soups of today.
You can also make a great deal of difference to your soup by the
flavourings you add and the garnishes you give it.

72 SAVOURY SOUP IN MINUTES

2 rashers bacon, chopped · 1 small onion, chopped
250g/10oz *can condensed mushroom soup*
375g/15oz *can tomato soup* · 375g/15oz *can chicken soup*

Fry bacon until crisp, then transfer to absorbent paper. Fry
onion in the bacon fat until tender. Drain off the excess fat.
Add the soup and heat. Stir in the bacon pieces.
Makes 6 servings.

Pepperpot soup

Savoury soup in minutes

73 QUICK CREAM OF CUCUMBER SOUP

250g/10oz can condensed chicken soup · 284ml/½pint milk
75g/3oz cucumber, peeled and chopped · pinch salt
cucumber slices to garnish

Dilute the soup by adding the milk slowly, stirring. Add the cucumber and salt. Simmer 5 minutes. Serve chilled, garnished with a few slices of cucumber.

74 QUICK MINESTRONE SOUP

1 small onion · 15g/½oz cabbage · 1 medium-sized carrot
¾litre/1½pints water · 1 packet chicken noodle soup
2 tomatoes · grated Parmesan cheese

Chop the onion finely, shred the cabbage and chop or grate the carrot. Bring the water to the boil, add the onion and carrot, and simmer for 5 minutes. Add the chicken noodle soup, the cabbage and skinned and chopped tomatoes; simmer for a further 7 minutes. Serve with finely grated cheese.

Quick minestrone soup

Quick cream of cucumber soup

COLD CANNED SOUPS

75 ICED MULLIGATAWNY SOUP

Open a can of mulligatawny soup, mix with a little single cream or milk. Serve iced with crisp flowerets of cauliflower.

76 MINT PEA SOUP

Add finely chopped mint and a little mayonnaise (Recipe No. 408) to a can of pea soup; thin down with milk.

77 TOMATO AND CHICKEN SOUP

Mix cans of tomato and of chicken soup together. Serve garnished with lemon.

FISH

Always be careful when buying fish to see it is really fresh. The flesh should be firm, eyes bright, and there should be no unpleasant smell. You will find in this section the best methods of cooking a wide variety of fish, as well as some unusual recipes.

78 HOW TO RECOGNISE AND COOK OILY FISH

FISH and when in season	IT LOOKS LIKE THIS	BUY AND COOK IT LIKE THIS
HERRINGS Obtainable from various sources throughout year; from Britain in season June – February		Buy whole, but most fishmongers will bone and fillet if wished. Make sure herrings are very firm and bright-eyed. Can be grilled, fried, baked (with stuffing if wished) or pickled and soused to have with salads. Most economical. 1–2 herrings per person.
MACKEREL March – July		Looks like a larger, more silvery herring. Take great care to see they are fresh, since stale mackerel can be particularly dangerous. Cook as herrings, particularly good served with a thick gooseberry purée as sauce. 1 per person.
MULLET April – October		Both grey and red. Bake or grill with plenty of butter. Red mullet is particularly delicious baked in covered bags of buttered paper. Always retain liver of fish, as this has particularly good flavour. 1 grey or 2 red (smaller) mullet per person.
SALMON March – August		Serve hot or cold. Take great care in cooking not to dry the fish and lose both oily texture and flavour and colour. A substantial fish, allow approximately 150g (6 oz) per person (Recipe No. 80).
SALMON TROUT April – August		Cook as salmon, but generally best to buy a small salmon trout and cook it whole – when buying whole salmon trout allow 200g (8 oz) per person.
SPRATS October – March		These tiny fish can be baked or fried. Remove heads, dust with seasoned flour before cooking. Very easily digested and quite delicious. Allow about 150–200g (6–8 oz) per person.
WHITEBAIT May – August		The tiniest fish used. Do not take off heads, dust well in seasoned flour and cook in deep fat until crisp and tender. Drain well and serve either as a main course or an hors d'oeuvre with cayenne pepper, lemon and brown bread and butter. Allow about 150–200g (6–8 oz) per person.

79 FROZEN FISH

Enormous strides have been made in the freezing of fish. The fish is frozen within a very short time of being caught, which means it reaches the housewife in the very peak of condition. There are no separate recipes for frozen fish in this section, since the fish can be used in all the recipes. It is not a poor substitute for fresh fish.

80 TO COOK SALMON STEAKS

Wrap each piece of fish in well-oiled greaseproof paper or foil. Put a little salt and a squeeze of lemon juice over the fish. Put into a saucepan which has a very well fitting lid, cover the fish with cold water. Bring the water in the pan slowly to the boil and simmer for about 7 minutes. If serving the fish cold remove the pan from the heat and allow the fish to stand in the liquid until quite cold. This gives a beautifully moist fish. This is the easiest and the most satisfactory way of cooking salmon.

Grilled herrings with mustard sauce (Recipe No. 83)

Salmon mayonnaise

81 TO COOK LARGER PIECES OF SALMON

Prepare as Recipe No. 80, allowing just 10 minutes per ½kg (1 lb) when the water has come to the boil. For an impressive *salmon mayonnaise*, serve with mixed vegetable salad, cooked peas, cucumber, lettuce and garnish with a piping of mayonnaise (Recipe No. 408).

Salmon mousse

Trout meunière

82 SALMON MOUSSE

200–300g/8–12oz salmon, canned or fresh*
2 tablespoons vinegar · 15g/½oz butter · 1 dessertspoon flour
2 teaspoons sugar · 1 teaspoon dry mustard · 2 eggs
142ml/¼pint milk · 15g/½oz powdered gelatine
3 tablespoons cold water · salt and pepper
2 tablespoons double cream · lemon and tomato slices,
shrimps and parsley to garnish

*300g (12oz) cooked white fish could be used instead

Drain off liquid from can of salmon (or stock in which fish was cooked) into a measuring jug. Add enough vinegar (preferably 1 tablespoon tarragon and the remainder malt) to bring liquid to 142ml (¼ pint). Add butter and heat until fat has just melted. Allow to cool. Flake the fish. Mix flour, sugar and mustard in top of double boiler, or a basin placed over a pan of hot water. Add eggs, one at a time, and beat well to mix. When smooth gradually stir in fish liquid, followed by the milk. Cook, stirring constantly until mixture is thick, remove from heat. Soften gelatine in cold water, then stir until dissolved in hot mixture. Turn into large bowl and add fish. Set in cool place, stirring occasionally. When cold and thick, season and fold in lightly whipped cream. Turn into a mould, rinsed with cold water. Place in a cold place (refrigerator if possible) until set. When ready to serve, turn out on to a serving dish, and garnish with lemon and tomato slices, shrimps, and parsley.

83 GRILLED HERRINGS WITH MUSTARD SAUCE

(Illustrated in colour at the beginning of this section)

Trim and clean herrings. Brush with melted butter and grill on both sides. Make white sauce (Recipe No. 663) and stir in 2 teaspoons made mustard and 1 teaspoon vinegar. Garnish the herrings with lemon and sprigs of parsley and serve with the mustard sauce.

84 TROUT MEUNIERE

Trout should not be confused with salmon trout. It is a fresh-water fish (see fresh-water table No. 142) and can be grilled, baked or fried.

A simple but delicious way is to serve Trout Meunière. Heat about 50g (2 oz) butter for each 2 fish in a large pan. Fry the fish steadily in this, then when cooked lift on to a hot dish; add a squeeze of lemon juice and seasoning to the butter and cook until golden brown. Pour over the fish. Garnish with lemon wedges.

Baked herrings Provençale

85 BAKED HERRINGS PROVENCALE

4 herrings · 2 small onions · ½kg/1lb tomatoes
25g/1oz melted butter · 1 teaspoon sugar · salt and pepper
2 tablespoons vinegar

Well grease an ovenproof dish. Behead and clean herrings, trimming the fins and tails. Score diagonally on top about ½-cm (¼-inch) deep.
Peel onions and slice into thin wedges. Lightly fry in half the quantity of butter for 5 minutes. Plunge tomatoes in boiling water for a moment, then remove skins and cut into wedges. Make a bed of tomato and fried onion wedges on the bottom of the dish. Sprinkle with sugar, salt, plenty of pepper and vinegar. Arrange herrings on top and brush with melted butter. Cover with foil or lid and bake in a moderately hot oven, 375°F, 190°C, Gas Mark 5, for 45 minutes.

86 STUFFED HERRINGS

4 herrings · oatmeal stuffing (Recipe No. 87)
salt and pepper · quick-cooking rolled oats or oatmeal
lemon to garnish

Clean and split the herrings. Remove the bones by inserting the thumb under the tail end and lifting carefully. Place a portion of the stuffing in each herring and roll up. Place close together in a greased ovenproof dish, sprinkle with salt, pepper and oats or oatmeal. Cover with greased paper and bake for 30 minutes in a moderately hot oven, 375°F, 190°C, Gas Mark 5. Serve with slices of lemon or mustard sauce and creamed potatoes.

87 OATMEAL STUFFING

75g/3oz quick-cooking rolled oats or oatmeal
1 dessertspoon chopped fresh herbs (parsley, sage, etc.)
1 tablespoon grated onion · 50g/2oz butter or margarine
1 egg · little milk · salt and pepper

Mix ingredients together in a bowl.

88 HERRING SALADS

Herrings make wonderful salads, which can be varied in a number of ways. Cook herrings, which should be boned and filleted, by grilling, frying or sousing. This means cooking them very slowly in a well spiced vinegar in the oven. Serve the herrings on a bed of crisp lettuce and garnish with canned or fresh potato and vegetable salads. Onions, gherkins and beetroot can also be added.

89 TO BONE HERRINGS

With a sharp knife cut off the head. With the blade of a knife scrape the fish to remove the scales. Slit the herring down the underside. Place the fish underside downwards, on a working surface. Press firmly with the thumb, along the backbone to loosen it. Turn the fish over, take hold of the bone and pull firmly – the small bones will come with it. Wash and pat fish dry.

To bone herrings

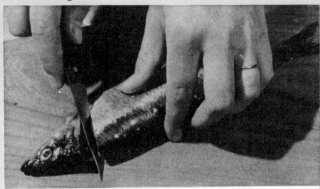

90   TO COOK MACKEREL

Mackerel can be cooked in the same way as herrings (see Recipes Nos. 83, 85–88). They are excellent just baked in the oven or soused, which means cooking very slowly with vinegar, sliced onions, pickling spices and herbs. This keeps them very moist indeed.

Take great care to see that they are fresh, since stale mackerel can be dangerous.

91   TO POACH FISH

Never boil fish rapidly. It is inclined to break and will certainly become very dry. Poaching means just cooking very gently, either in salted water, or in a fish stock made from the bones and skin of the fish and flavoured with a bay leaf, onion and carrot.

92   TO BAKE FISH

When baking fish in the oven keep it well covered with greased paper, or use wine, stock or milk to keep it moist. Do not over-cook.

93   BAKED HALIBUT

about ¾kg/1½lb *halibut · seasoning · little melted butter*
½kg/1lb *leeks · chopped walnuts and lemon to garnish*

Sprinkle the halibut with seasoning and brush with melted butter. Cover with foil and bake in a moderate oven, 375°F, 190°C, Gas Mark 5, for about 35 minutes. Meanwhile wash the leeks well and cook in boiling salted water until tender. Drain and place on a heated serving dish. Place the halibut on top and serve garnished with chopped walnuts and lemon.

Baked halibut

FISH and when in season	IT LOOKS LIKE THIS	BUY AND COOK IT LIKE THIS

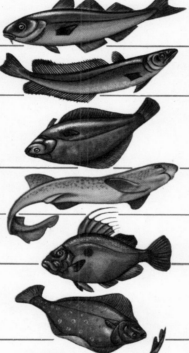

BREAM
July–December

Generally a fresh-water fish. Buy whole or in fillets. Not very plentiful, but a good flavour. Bake with a savoury stuffing or grill. Allow 150–200g (6–8 oz) on bone, 100–150g (4–6 oz) filleted per person.

COD
Throughout year; best October–March

Excellent all-purpose fish because of its definite flavour; particularly good in 'made-up' dishes. Poach, fry, bake or grill. It has large flakes, so when frying it is inclined to break unless floured well before being coated with egg and crumbs or batter.

FLOUNDER
November–March

Not quite such a delicate flavour as sole or plaice, but very much like them. Can be used in just the same way. Allow 200g (8 oz) per person or 1 small fish, or 100–150g (4–6 oz) when filleted.

HADDOCK
October–February

Can be used in every way like cod. Buy fillets, cutlets or whole fish. Can be slightly dry when cooked unless kept well moistened. 200g (8 oz) per person when whole but 100–150g (4–6 oz) when in fillets or steaks.

HAKE
June–January

Again not unlike cod, but a more delicate flavour. Best fried or baked. Buy steaks or fillets. 100–150g (4–6 oz) per person. Good with various sauces.

HALIBUT
July–April

More expensive fish, though generally cheaper than turbot. Excellent poached, grilled or baked. Small halibut under 1½kg (3 lb) should be baked whole. A 'filling' fish, so allow 100–150g (4–6 oz) per person when buying steaks or a good 150g (6 oz) when buying whole.

DOG FISH or HUSS
September–May

Will be skinned and filleted. Not very usual. Best baked or fried. Not very 'fleshy' so allow 150–200g (6–8 oz) per person. Best with a good flavoured sauce.

JOHN DORY or DORY
September–early January

Not very usual – good flavour, but ugly appearance. Buy fillets and cook in any way suitable for sole or turbot. Allow 150g (6 oz) per person.

PLAICE
Late May–December

One of the most popular of fish, easily distinguished from other flat fish by yellow to reddish brown spots on the dark skin. Bake, fry, grill or serve in the same way as sole. Steam or poach for invalids. 1 small fish per person or approximately 150g (6 oz).

SKATE
November–May

An ugly but undoubtedly delicious fish. Generally sold in rather triangular-shaped pieces. Fry, bake or poach or use cold in salads. It is recommended that the fish be steamed a few minutes before being fried. Because of the large heavy bones allow about 250g (10 oz) per person.

SOLE
Some kind available all year

Considered by many people the finest fish of all, and certainly the one that has produced more delicious fish dishes and sauces than any other. Dover sole does not mean it comes from Dover, but is so called to distinguish it as the finest sole. Others, lemon, Torbay, witch, dabs are all good though. Bake, fry, poach, steam, grill and serve just with lemon, melted butter or other sauces. Allow 1 fish or 200g (8 oz) per person.

TURBOT
April–early September

Can be distinguished from halibut by the spots on its skin. Bake, grill, fry or poach and serve with sauce. Excellent cold in fish salads too. It is a substantial and expensive fish. Allow 100–150g (4–6 oz) as fillet or good 150g (6 oz) when in steaks or whole.

WHITING
October–April

An ideal fish for children and invalids since it has a very fine delicate flavour. Much less expensive than sole or plaice, and can be filleted and served in the same way. Poach, bake, grill or fry. Allow 1 fish or 200g (8 oz) per person when filleted.

Baked cod steaks

Creamed cod

95 BAKED COD STEAKS

2 rashers bacon · 1 small onion · chopped parsley
4 cod steaks · little melted butter · juice 1 lemon · seasoning,
including dry mustard · tomato slices to garnish

Chop the bacon and onion and mix together with the parsley. Brush the cod steaks with melted butter, sprinkle with lemon juice and seasoning, including dry mustard. Top each steak with a little of the bacon mixture and bake for 15 minutes in a moderately hot oven, 400°F, 200°C, Gas Mark 6. Serve garnished with tomato slices.

96 CREAMED COD

Place 4 cod steaks in an ovenproof dish. Brush with melted margarine and sprinkle with seasoning. Cover with a lid or foil and cook in a moderate oven, 350°F, 180°C, Gas Mark 4, for about 20 minutes.
Meanwhile make a white sauce (Recipe No. 663). Place the cod steaks on a serving dish and pour over the white sauce. Sprinkle with a little cayenne pepper, if liked, and serve.

97 COD PROVENCALE

1 medium-sized onion · 1 clove garlic · 300g/12oz tomatoes
about ½kg/1lb cod fillet, skinned · 25g/1oz seasoned flour
oil for frying · 1 level teaspoon chopped fresh herbs
as available, (parsley, thyme, sage, etc.) · salt and pepper
sliced stuffed olives, optional

Slice the onion and crush the garlic. Skin the tomatoes, remove pips and slice. Cut the fish into 5-cm (2-inch) squares then roll it in the seasoned flour. In a frying pan heat a little oil then fry the fish quickly until golden brown on both sides, approximately 8 minutes. Drain, arrange in a shallow serving dish and keep hot. Strain off surplus oil leaving 1 good table-spoon in the pan. Fry the onion until tender then add the garlic, tomato and herbs. Toss quickly over a brisk heat for 2–3 minutes. Season to taste and add olives if used. Reheat and pour over the fish, or serve alongside.

Cod Provençale

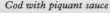
Cod with piquant sauce

98 COD WITH PIQUANT SAUCE

4 cod or haddock cutlets · little melted margarine · seasoning
284ml/½pint milk · 50g/2oz soft margarine
1 onion, chopped · 100g/4oz mushrooms, chopped
1 small green pepper, chopped · 25g/1oz flour
4 tomatoes, skinned and chopped · seasoning
stock, drained from the fish · lemon wedges to garnish

Place the fish in a baking dish. Brush with melted margarine and sprinkle with seasoning. Pour in the milk. Cover with greased paper and bake in a moderate oven, 350°F, 180°C, Gas Mark 4, for 20 minutes. Drain off stock for sauce. Keep fish hot.
Melt the margarine and fry onion, mushrooms and pepper until soft. Stir in flour, tomatoes, seasoning and stock. Bring to the boil and cook for 3 minutes. Pour over the fish. Serve garnished with lemon wedges.

Cheese stuffed haddock curls

Haddock balls

99 CHEESE STUFFED HADDOCK CURLS

4 tail-end pieces of haddock fillet, about 75g/3oz each
1 teaspoon lemon juice · 2 teaspoons seasoned flour
cheese stuffing (Recipe No. 100) · little beaten egg
crisp breadcrumbs · 40g/1½oz butter or margarine
lemon and parsley to garnish
284ml/½pint cheese sauce (Recipe Nos. 660, 665)

Wash the fillets in cold salt water, drain and dry. Sprinkle with lemon juice and dust with seasoned flour. Mix together the stuffing ingredients and divide into 4 equal portions. Stuff each fillet, curl and tie. Brush with beaten egg and dredge with breadcrumbs, shaking off the surplus. Melt the margarine in a baking tin and when hot stand in the fish curls and baste well. Bake in a moderately hot oven, 375°F, 190°C, Gas Mark 5, for 20–25 minutes. Serve hot garnished with lemon twists and parsley sprigs and serve the cheese sauce separately.

100 CHEESE STUFFING

100g/4oz Cheddar cheese, grated · 50g/2oz fresh breadcrumbs
good pinch cayenne pepper · 1 level teaspoon salt
1 tablespoon chopped parsley · 1 egg

Mix all ingredients together.

101 HADDOCK BALLS

1 large smoked haddock · 150g/6oz cold mashed potatoes
pepper · 2 heaped teaspoons chopped parsley · 1 egg
browned crumbs · cooking fat for frying

Cook the haddock, remove skin and bone or use left-over cooked haddock. Flake the flesh finely. Add the potatoes, pepper and chopped parsley; form into 6 balls. Dip in beaten egg and coat with browned crumbs. Fry in deep fat, heated to 350°F, 180°C for 3 minutes, until brown and crisp. Drain on absorbent paper and serve hot or cold with tomatoes and watercress.

102 BAKED STUFFED HADDOCK

Small haddock, like small cod, is excellent if stuffed and served whole. Choose either a veal stuffing (Recipe No. 254), adding plenty of lemon juice to flavour, or a sage and onion stuffing (Recipe No. 280). Bone the fish or ask the fishmonger to bone it for you, insert the stuffing and skewer or tie in place. Allow approximately 12 minutes per ½kg (1 lb) in a moderately hot oven, 400°F, 200°C, Gas Mark 6. Put the fish in a well buttered dish and cover with buttered paper. Serve with whole baked tomatoes and garnish with parsley.

Baked stuffed haddock

Macaroni fish pie

103 MACARONI FISH PIE

½kg/1lb *hake or haddock · seasoning ·* 142ml/¼pint *milk*
25g/1oz *butter ·* 100–150g/4–6oz *quick-cooking macaroni*
284ml/½pint *cheese sauce (Recipe Nos. 660, 665)*
little grated Cheddar cheese · little melted butter
parsley to garnish

Place the fish in a saucepan. Season, add milk and butter and simmer for 8–10 minutes, until fish is just tender. Lift on to a plate, flake with a fork, retain liquid. Meanwhile cook macaroni according to instructions on packet. Strain. To the cheese sauce add flaked fish and macaroni and season to taste. Put into a buttered ovenproof dish. Sprinkle with grated cheese and butter; brown under grill. Garnish with parsley.
If preparing this beforehand heat through in the oven, but use a little more liquid in the sauce so that the dish is not too dry.

104 FRIED FISH AND CHIPS

This is one of the most popular ways of serving any white fish. It is important to remember the following:
1. Dry the fish well and coat very thinly with seasoned flour.
2. Dip in fritter batter (Recipe No. 647) made rather thinner than usual, or in beaten egg and crumbs. Shake off surplus crumbs or allow excess batter to drain away.
3. For shallow frying make sure the fat, which can be butter, or the modern whipped-up cooking fat (vegetable shortening), is hot. Put in the fish, cook steadily until brown, turn and cook on the other side. If using deep fat or oil make sure this is not too hot, so that the outside browns before the fish is cooked. The ideal temperature for frying is 350°F, 180°C.
4. Always drain fried fish. Use kitchen paper. The latest absorbent kitchen rolls are excellent. Never use grease-proof paper.
5. Do not over-cook the fish.
The ideal accompaniment is beautifully fried potato chips (Recipe No. 296). Lemon fans, tomato slices and parsley are good garnishes for fried fish.

Fried fish

105 WHITING

Whiting has a rather delicate flavour and is easily digestible, but it is not a fish which keeps well. Be sure to check that the eyes are bright and the fish silver in colour. Skin the fish before frying, and fasten the tail between the eye-holes.* To remove the backbone slit the fish down the back at each side of the bone, break the bone at either end and carefully lift it out. Whiting can be served in the same ways as sole or plaice. Fried fillets are good served with fried parsley, a thick tomato sauce (Recipe No. 656) or with Béarnaise sauce (Recipe No. 683). Small whiting are delicious baked in the oven with a good mushroom sauce (Recipe No. 681) or cooked with chopped shallots in white wine or cider.
* This is easier if backbone removed as in method and then the fish secured with a wooden cocktail stick.

Stuffed fillets of plaice

Grilled fish

106   STUFFED FILLETS OF PLAICE OR SOLE

1 large jar lobster, crab or shrimp paste
4 large fillets plaice or sole · 2 eating apples
watercress and few green grapes to garnish

Spread the paste on each fillet of plaice or sole. Roll firmly and stand in a buttered ovenproof dish; season well. Cover with well buttered paper and bake for 12–15 minutes in a moderately hot oven, 375°F, 190°C, Gas Mark 5. Meanwhile, core the apples and cut into slices. Brush the slices with melted butter and cook, on each side, under a heated grill for 2–3 minutes. Place the cooked fish rolls on the apple rings and fill the centre with a halved green grape. If liked, serve on a bed of saffron rice (Recipe No. 140). Garnish with a sprig of watercress.
Fruit blends well with many kinds of fish. One of the most famous dishes is Sole Veronique (Recipe No. 121). The above recipe has a refreshing 'bite' with its garnishes of grapes and cooked apple rings; these may be omitted if wished.

107   GRILLED FISH

Most fish, fresh or frozen, is suitable for grilling. Fillets of fish, unless very thick, can be grilled without turning. Whole fish should be turned so that it is cooked on both sides. Make sure that the grill is hot before you begin cooking and keep the fish well brushed with melted butter so that it does not become dry. Never over-cook grilled fish. Serve garnished with lemon wedges and sprigs of parsley. For an unusual accompaniment try very thin cucumber slices mixed with chopped chives.

108   SMOKED FISH – AND HOW TO SERVE IT

COD	This is filleted then cured. Cook as smoked haddock. Allow 200g (8 oz) per person.	**SALMON**	See Recipe Nos. 14, 15, 16.
		SPRATS	Serve like smoked trout or grill or fry. Allow 200g (8 oz) per person.
HADDOCK	Either filleted and smoked or cured whole. Poach in water or milk and serve with butter or a sauce. Top with poached egg if wished. Take care not to over-cook. Excellent as kedgeree (Recipe No. 859). Allow 200–250g (8–10 oz) per person.	**TROUT**	An excellent hors d'oeuvre – serve with horseradish sauce (Recipe No. 662), lemon and brown bread and butter. Allow 1 fish per person.
HERRING	Kippers – these can be fried, grilled, baked or boiled. Bloaters – best grilled or fried. Buckling – serve as smoked trout. Allow 1–2 fish per person.	**WHITING**	Cook as haddock, generally called 'golden fillets'. Allow 2 fillets per person.
		EEL	An unusual, but excellent hors d'oeuvre – serve as smoked trout, removing tough skin. Allow 75–100g (3–4 oz) per person.

The plaice in the picture have been filleted before frying. Many fishmongers will fillet fish for you, but it is quite easy to do it yourself. With a sharp knife make a definite slit down the centre and round the edge of the whole fish. Insert the knife at the tip by the tail and, with your left hand begin to lift the flesh while the knife, held in your right hand, cuts the flesh away from the bones. A little salt on the tip of the knife often helps.

Dip the fillets in batter (Recipe No. 647) and fry in oil heated to 350°F, 180°C until crisp and golden brown. Drain on absorbent paper and serve garnished with lemon slices and sprigs of parsley. Serve with chipped potatoes (Recipe No. 296) and tartare sauce (Recipe No. 661).

Filleting fish

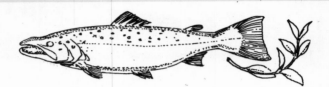

110 COD WITH CHEESE TRIANGLES

4 cod steaks · seasoning · squeeze lemon juice
1 small onion, peeled and chopped
2 tomatoes, skinned and sliced · 100g/4oz mushrooms, sliced
4 tablespoons stock or water
3 slices bread · little grated cheese

Place the cod steaks in an ovenproof dish. Sprinkle with seasoning and add a squeeze of lemon juice. Add the onion, tomatoes and mushrooms. Pour in the stock or water. Cover and cook in a moderate oven, 350°F, 180°C, Gas Mark 4, for about 40 minutes. Lightly toast the bread on both sides, sprinkle with grated cheese and place under a hot grill to melt the cheese. Remove the crusts, cut into triangles and arrange round the edge of the fish.

Cod with cheese triangles

Tomato fish cakes

111 TOMATO FISH CAKES

100g/4oz potatoes · 300g/12oz white fish · seasoning
1 tablespoon chopped parsley · 1 tablespoon tomato ketchup
1 egg, beaten · crisp breadcrumbs · cooking fat for frying
stuffed olives and parsley to garnish

Cook and mash the potatoes. Steam and flake the fish. Mix together and add seasoning, parsley and tomato ketchup. Mix thoroughly together and shape into cakes. Coat with egg and breadcrumbs and fry in shallow or deep fat until golden brown. Drain on absorbent paper and serve garnished with stuffed olives and parsley.

112 FRIDAY FLAN

150g/6oz short crust pastry (Recipe No. 566)
284ml/½pint cheese sauce (Recipe No. 665), coating consistency
200g/8oz cooked white fish · prawns, optional
and bacon rolls to garnish

Line 20-cm (8-inch) flan ring with the pastry and bake 'blind' (Recipe No. 560). Make the cheese sauce and stir in the flaked fish. Leave on a low heat, stirring from time to time, to allow the fish to become hot. Spoon into the flan case. Garnish with prawns, if liked, and bacon rolls.

Friday flan

Scalloped haddock

113 SCALLOPED HADDOCK

1 small onion · 284ml/½pint milk · pinch mace
25g/1oz cooking fat · 25g/1oz flour · seasoning to taste
3 tomatoes, skinned and sliced · ½kg/1lb cooked smoked haddock
browned breadcrumbs · Parmesan cheese, grated

Chop the onion finely. Simmer in the milk with the mace until tender. Melt the cooking fat in a pan, mix in the flour. Pour in the milk gradually, stirring all the time. Bring to the boil, add the seasoning and tomatoes and boil for 2–3 minutes. Add the flaked fish. Divide the mixture between 4 scallop shells. Sprinkle with a mixture of browned crumbs and Parmesan cheese. Bake in a moderately hot oven, 400°F, 200°C, Gas Mark 6, for 5–10 minutes or brown under the grill. Serve with green salad.

114 TUNA SOUFFLE

1 small can tuna fish · 25g/1oz butter or margarine
25g/1oz flour · 142ml/¼pint milk · 3 egg yolks · 4 egg whites
seasoning

Mash tuna fish. Make a thick sauce with the butter or margarine, flour and milk. Add the egg yolks, one at a time, the tuna and seasoning. Lastly fold in the stiffly beaten egg whites and turn the mixture into a buttered 15-cm (6-inch) soufflé dish (or any other ovenproof dish of similar size and shape). Cook for 30 minutes in the centre of a moderately hot oven, 400°F, 200°C, Gas Mark 6. Serve at once otherwise the soufflé will subside.

115 WHITE FISH SOUFFLE

Use the tuna fish soufflé recipe above, but instead of tuna add finely flaked white fish. If liked stir a little anchovy essence into the mixture to give additional flavour. A mixture of flaked smoked haddock and grated Parmesan cheese also makes a very good soufflé.

White fish soufflé

Haddock flan

116   HADDOCK FLAN

150g/6oz short crust pastry (Recipe No. 566)
300g/12oz haddock, poached · 50g/2oz butter
1 onion, chopped · 75g/3oz button mushrooms
2–3 tomatoes, skinned and chopped · 1 rounded tablespoon flour
284ml/½pint fish stock · seasoning · 1 egg yolk
1 tablespoon single cream · tomato slices and chopped
parsley to garnish

Line a 20-cm (8-inch) flan ring with pastry and bake 'blind' (Recipe No. 560). Melt half the butter and fry the chopped onion, chopped mushroom stalks and the tomatoes until cooked. Rub through a sieve. Cook the flour in the remaining butter without browning it. Add to the purée then stir in the strained fish stock. Reheat to thicken and add seasoning to taste. Blend the egg yolk and cream together and stir into sauce. Add the poached fish. Keep hot, but do not boil. Meanwhile, slice the remaining mushrooms and fry in a little butter. Turn the fish mixture into the pastry case. Garnish with sliced tomatoes, mushrooms and chopped parsley. The flan can be served hot ot cold.

CLASSIC RECIPES WITH SOLE
OR OTHER WHITE FISH

117   FISH WITH A SAUCE

An interesting sauce makes a great deal of difference to white fish – add the stock in which fish has been poached or baked to the sauce for additional flavour.

118   FISH AU GRATIN

Coat cooked fish with cheese sauce (Recipe No. 665), cover with grated cheese and breadcrumbs, and brown under the grill. Garnish with tomato, lemon and parsley. A Dutch Gouda gives a pleasantly mild flavour, but other cheeses can be used.

119   SOLE MORNAY

(Also illustrated in colour on the jacket)

Roll fillets of sole and secure with wooden cocktail sticks. Cover and cook in a moderate oven, 350°F, 180°C, Gas Mark 4, for 15 minutes. Remove the cocktail sticks and coat the sole with cheese sauce (Recipe No. 665); sprinkle with grated cheese and brown under a hot grill. If liked, serve garnished with a sprig of watercress.

120   SOLE BONNE FEMME

Prepare the fish as in Recipe No. 119. Cook in the oven in a little white wine. Coat with white sauce (Recipe No. 663), made with the cooking liquor plus milk. Garnish with fried strips of mushroom and piped potatoes.

121   SOLE VERONIQUE

Follow the recipe for sole bonne femme (Recipe No. 120). Garnish the dish with peeled green grapes.

122   SOLE MEUNIERE

Cook the sole in the way described under trout meunière (Recipe No. 84).

123   SOLE WALEWSKA

Follow the recipe for sole bonne femme. Coat with Hollandaise sauce (Recipe No. 682) and top with lobster and mushroom or truffle.

124   SOLE NICOISE

Prepare the fish as in Recipe No. 119. Cook in the oven in milk, white wine or cider. Coat with white sauce (Recipe No. 663) made with the cooking liquor plus milk and flavoured with anchovy essence. Garnish with anchovy butter (butter flavoured with anchovy essence) and serve with well seasoned stewed tomatoes.

Sole mornay

125 SHELLFISH	
FISH and when in season	**COOK IT LIKE THIS**
CRAB May–August	Dress and serve cold as a pilaff (Recipe No. 132). Very good as a cocktail (Recipe No. 24). Can be served hot topped with breadcrumbs and butter and browned under hot grill. Be sure to remove the stomach bag and grey-brown fingers.
LOBSTER February–October	Serve hot or cold (Recipe Nos. 126–129). Take out the narrow intestinal vein. The red coral of a female lobster is delicious; never eat fingers at base of claws.
OYSTERS September–April	See Recipe No. 28.
PRAWNS Small: February–October Large: March–December	Excellent frozen small prawns or large prawns known as scampi (Recipe No. 136) enable you to serve these throughout the year. Delicious hot or cold, in main dishes or with a sauce.
SHRIMPS February–October	See prawns.

Be particularly careful that the fish is really fresh, as stale shellfish can be very harmful.

126   **LOBSTER**

Ask the fishmonger to split the fish and remove the intestinal vein, then remove flesh and dress as desired. There is no dark meat with a lobster, but the bright red 'coral' found in a female lobster is delicious. Serve with mayonnaise (Recipe Nos. 408, 412) and a green salad.

CLASSIC DISHES WITH LOBSTER

127   **LOBSTER THERMIDOR**

Fry a few sliced mushrooms and skinned and chopped tomatoes in hot butter and stir these into a cheese sauce (Recipe Nos. 660, 665). Add the lobster meat, top with grated cheese and brown under the grill.

128   **LOBSTER AMERICAINE**

Fry an onion in hot butter, then add several skinned tomatoes. Simmer gently, add a little white wine and for special occasions a small quantity of brandy. Stir the lobster meat into this hot sauce.

129 LOBSTER A LA CATALANE

*1 large or 2 small lobsters, split and meat removed from
shell as whole as possible · 50g/2oz butter
4 tablespoons tomato ketchup · 1 small onion, finely chopped
1 clove garlic, crushed · pepper and salt
3 tablespoons white wine · 1 dessertspoon chopped parsley
duchesse potatoes (Recipe No. 300)*

Fry the halves of lobsters in heated butter until lightly
browned. Do not over-cook as this toughens flesh. Place on a
hot serving dish. Put tomato ketchup into a pan, add onion
and garlic, pepper and salt and white wine. Stir over heat
until onion is slightly softened, then pour – or strain, if clear
sauce is required – over lobsters before serving. Garnish with
chopped parsley and duchesse potatoes, lightly browned in
a hot oven. Serve wedges of lemon separately.

Lobster à la Catalane

130 COQUILLE ST. JACQUES

*5 medium-sized scallops · 190ml/⅓pint milk
little mashed potato · 50g/2oz butter · 25g/1oz flour
seasoning · small bunch parsley · chopped parsley to garnish
few crisp breadcrumbs · 25g/1oz cheese, grated · lemon wedges*

Simmer the scallops (often called 'escallops') in the milk for
approximately 10 minutes, until quite soft. It is important
that this is done slowly, for too quick cooking makes them
tough. When cooked, put the scallops on to their shells. Pipe
round a border of mashed potato. Melt the butter in the pan,
stir in the flour and cook gently for 3 minutes. Gradually add
the milk. This should be made up again to the 190ml (⅓
pint) as some will have evaporated when cooking the scallops. Cook
the sauce until thick, adding seasoning and the wine. Carefully mask the tops of the scallops with this. Sprinkle with the
crumbs and cheese and either put into a hot oven, 425°F,
220°C, Gas Mark 7, or under the grill until heated through
and crisp and brown on top. Serve with lemon wedges.

Coquilles St. Jacques

Mussels Marinière

131 MUSSELS MARINIERE

*generous litre/2pints mussels · water to cover
1 small onion · 2–3 sticks celery, when available
1 tablespoon tarragon vinegar · little white wine, optional
seasoning · small bunch parsley · chopped parsley to garnish*

Scrub the mussels well, discarding any that are open and will
not close when sharply tapped. Put into a large saucepan
together with water, onion, celery, vinegar and wine if used,
a good pinch of salt and pepper and the parsley. Heat slowly
until the mussels open. Remove the beards from the mussels.
Sometimes you will find a small growth, looking like a weed,
in the mussels – this must be taken out. Leave the mussels
on half the shell. Re-boil the liquid and strain over them.
Garnish with chopped parsley.

132 CRAB PILAFF

One medium-sized crab is enough for 2 people. Feel the crab when you buy it, and if it feels surprisingly light for its size, ask the fishmonger to break it open – for 'lightness' often indicates that it is 'watery' and you are not getting good solid crab meat.

To dress the crab: open the main part of the shell by pulling up the rounded part. Take out the skin-like 'bag' and the greyish brown fingers, both of which should be discarded. Remove all the white meat from the body and claws and mix; take out dark meat. Serve light and dark meat in the shell or on salad or as a *pilaff*. Mix the meat from 2 medium-sized crabs with 100g (4 oz) cooked rice, 2 large tomatoes, skinned and chopped, 75g (3 oz) sultanas and seasoning. Divide the mixture between the 2 shells. Garnish with criss-cross strips of anchovy fillets, lettuce and lemon wedges.

133 TO SERVE HOT CRAB

Crab can be used in the same type of dishes as lobster, but an easy way of serving crab hot is to dress the crab (Recipe No. 132) and cover the top with breadcrumbs and/or grated cheese and a little butter and brown under a hot grill.

134 SHRIMP RICE CUPS

generous ½litre/1pint *water* · 150g/6oz *long grain rice*
1 *level teaspoon salt* · 1 *small green pepper*
175g/7oz *can shrimps* · 6 *level tablespoons mayonnaise*
(*Recipe Nos. 408, 412*) · 1 *tablespoon lemon juice*
seasoning · *oil*

Choose a pan with a well fitting lid, bring water to the boil, add rice and salt, stir. Return to the boil, cover, reduce heat and simmer for about 15 minutes until rice tender but not oversoft. If you wish to cool rice quickly, turn into a sieve and run under cold water. Remove seeds from pepper, reserve a few thinly cut strips and chop remaining flesh. Drain shrimps. Reserve a few for garnish, chop remainder. Blend mayonnaise with the lemon juice and fold through the rice with green pepper and shrimps. Adjust seasoning. Press into lightly oiled cups or other similar shapes such as dariole moulds or individual patty tins. Invert on to individual plates or a large serving dish and remove containers. Garnish with reserved shrimps and strips of green pepper and if liked add curled slices of lemon and parsley.
Makes 6 servings.

135 FISH AND SHRIMP PIE

½kg/1lb *cooked white fish*
284ml/½pint *white sauce (Recipe No. 663)*
100g/4oz *frozen or peeled shrimps* · 1 *hard-boiled egg,*
chopped · *seasoning* · 50g/2oz *margarine or butter*
100g/4oz *flour* · *anchovy fillets to garnish*

Flake the fish and mix with the sauce, shrimps and egg. Season. Put into an ovenproof dish. Rub the fat into the flour to form a crumble mixture. Cover the fish mixture with this. Cook in a very moderate to moderate oven, 350°F, 180°C, Gas Mark 4, for 30–35 minutes. Garnish with anchovy fillets.

136 SCAMPI

These large prawns, which have become very popular, can be served in many ways. The most popular is to coat them in egg and breadcrumbs or batter, fry them in deep hot fat or oil, and serve with tartare sauce (Recipe Nos. 661, 680). They can, however, be served either as scampi meunière (see Recipe No. 84 for trout meunière), or in any way suggested for lobster.

Crab pilaff

Shrimp rice cups

Fish and shrimp pie

Shrimps and savoury rice

RICE MEDLEY

137 SHRIMPS AND SAVOURY RICE

Cook 200g (8 oz) long grain rice in 1½ litres (3 pints) boiling salted water until just tender. Drain and mix with chopped celery and a little finely chopped onion or chives, if available. Place in a serving dish and arrange 50g (2 oz) shrimps round the edge. Garnish with slices of hard-boiled egg and parsley and serve with sweet and sour sauce (Recipe No. 202), made with 284ml (½ pint) stock, etc.

Fried rice with shrimps and peppers

138 FRIED RICE WITH MUSHROOMS

2 tablespoons oil · 1 onion, chopped · 100g/4oz button mushrooms
200g/8oz cooked long grain rice · 1 tablespoon soy sauce
salt and pepper

Heat frying pan, add oil and chopped onion and fry until brown. Then add mushrooms, coarsely chopped and fry until semi-cooked. Add rice and fry gently until the whole begins to brown, stirring occasionally. When mixture is hot, add soy sauce and salt and pepper to taste.

139 FRIED RICE WITH SHRIMPS AND PEPPERS

2 tablespoons oil · 1 apple, peeled and sliced · 1 onion, chopped
100g/4oz shrimps or prawns* · 2 tablespoons chopped red pepper
½ green pepper, sliced · 200g/8oz cooked long grain rice
1 tablespoon soy sauce · 2 eggs, beaten · salt to taste
shrimps or prawns and parsley to garnish

*Use fresh, frozen or canned shrimps or prawns

Heat the oil slowly in the pan and fry apple and onion, coarsely chopped, until brown. Add shrimps, sliced peppers and fry until semi-cooked. Then add rice and fry gently until the whole begins to brown, stirring continuously. When mixture is hot, add soy sauce, then the eggs, beaten with salt to taste, and sauté for about 2 minutes. Turn into a heated serving dish and serve garnished with shrimps or prawns and parsley.

Curried prawns

140 CURRIED PRAWNS

curry sauce (Recipe No. 659) · 200g/8oz frozen or
284ml/½pint fresh shelled prawns

Make the curry sauce, and simmer for about an hour. Add the prawns and cook gently until hot. DO NOT over-cook or you will toughen shellfish.

Serve with long grain rice and interesting side dishes. When cooking rice, wash the uncooked rice in two changes of water, then drain. Cook in a large saucepan with plenty of water. Bring to the boil quickly and simmer for 20 minutes or more until each grain is soft but not mushy. Drain through a colander, rinse in running cold water, then stand colander over a pan of simmering water or put rice in a shallow dish in a cool oven, 275°F, 140°C, Gas Mark 1, to heat through.

SAFFRON RICE

Melt a little butter in a saucepan. Fry a finely chopped onion and a little chopped green pepper (optional). Add 200g (8 oz) long grain rice; stir in ½ teaspoon saffron and generous ½litre (1 pint) hot chicken stock. Bring to the boil, then cover and simmer for about 16 minutes until the stock has been absorbed and the rice is tender.

Serve all or some of the following as accompaniments: currants (washed in boiling water to make them moist and juicy), chutney, shredded coconut, mandarin oranges, apple slices and poppadums, which can be bought in packets in shops specialising in Indian foods. Fry them in fat or grill until crisp.

141 PRAWN AND RICE RING

284ml/½pint tomato sauce (Recipe No. 656)
100g/4oz mushrooms, sliced · little sherry
1–2 tomatoes, chopped
generous ½litre/1pint shelled prawns or shrimps
200g/8oz long grain rice · 25g/1oz butter
1 teaspoon lemon juice · lettuce
few pear slices and an orange slice to garnish

Make the sauce and add the mushrooms, sherry, tomatoes and cook gently until tender, then add most of the shelled prawns. Meanwhile cook the rice; drain, toss in butter and add to the sauce with the lemon juice. Spoon the mixture into a rinsed mould and leave to set. Turn on to a lettuce-lined plate and garnish with reserved prawns, sliced pears and a twist of orange.

Prawn and rice ring

142 HOW TO RECOGNISE AND COOK FRESH-WATER FISH

FISH and when in season	IT LOOKS LIKE THIS	BUY AND COOK IT LIKE THIS
CARP October–February	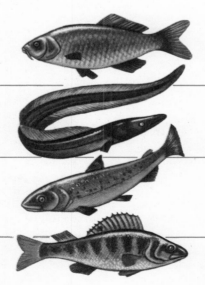	Unless very small, this fish is too tough for grilling or frying – best baked rather slowly, preferably with onions and tomatoes in a covered casserole. Allow 200g (8 oz) per person.
EEL September–May		Must be purchased from a fishmonger who keeps them alive in a tank. He will cut and skin them. Stew or make into a jelly. 150–200g (6–8 oz) per person.
TROUT April–September		Buy whole, grill, fry or bake. Delicious fried and served with brown butter sauce, i.e. meunière (Recipe No. 84). Keep well basted when cooking as the flesh is rather dry. Ideal to cook almost immediately after being caught.
PERCH May–February		Generally small enough to serve 1 fish per person. Be careful of the spikes in the dorsal fin as they are very sharp. This fish is difficult to scale, so plunge it for a minute in boiling water then scale. Delicious flavour. Best fried, poached and served with brown butter sauce i.e. meunière (Recipe No. 84).

BREAM See white fish table (Recipe No. 94)

143 TUNA KEDGEREE

150g/6oz *long grain rice* · 1 *onion, chopped* · 50g/2oz *butter*
2 *hard-boiled eggs* · 175g/7oz *can tuna fish* · *seasoning*
triangles of toast and parsley to garnish

Cook the rice in boiling salted water until just tender. Fry the onion, in the heated butter, until soft. Drain the rice and mix with the onion, chopped egg whites, flaked tuna fish and seasoning. Heat through gently, then spoon on to a serving dish. Serve garnished with triangles of toast, parsley and the sieved egg yolk.

Tuna kedgeree

144 CHOPSTICK TUNA WITH NOODLES

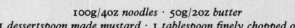

100g/4oz *noodles* · 50g/2oz *butter*
1 *dessertspoon made mustard* · 1 *tablespoon finely chopped onion* ·
6 *tablespoons finely chopped celery* · 25g/1oz *flour*
142ml/¼pint *milk* · 250g/10oz *can mushroom soup*
1 *tablespoon chopped peanuts* · 1 *dessertspoon lemon juice*
175g/7oz *can tuna fish* · *mandarin orange segments to garnish*

Cook the noodles in fast boiling salted water until just tender. Drain and toss in half the butter blended with the made mustard. Lightly cook the chopped onion and celery in the rest of the butter. Stir in the flour; cook for a minute without browning. Stir in the milk and soup and bring to the boil, stirring well. Cook 3 minutes. Lightly fold in the nuts, lemon juice and tuna, divided into chunks, and heat thoroughly. Line a warmed bowl with the hot noodles. Pile the tuna on top. Garnish with mandarin orange segments. Serve with chutney (mango chutney is especially good with this), salted peanuts and tomato and onion salad (Recipe No. 145).
Variation
Omit the noodles. Garnish with cubes of bread fried in butter and a little paprika, if liked.

Chopstick tuna

Tuna casserole

145 TOMATO AND ONION SALAD

Slice onions and tomatoes very thinly. Put into a dish and cover with well seasoned oil and vinegar. Leave for the flavours to blend for as long as possible. Garnish with chopped parsley.

146 TUNA CASSEROLE

200g/8oz *cooked long grain rice* · 175g/7oz *can tuna fish*
1 *small onion, finely chopped* · 2 *sticks celery, finely chopped*
375g/15oz *can mushroom soup* · *seasoning*
1 *dessertspoon made mustard*
75g/3oz *cheese, grated* · *sippets of fried bread and
almonds to garnish*

Mix together the rice, tuna fish, onion, celery, soup, seasoning, mustard and cheese. Place in a casserole and cook in a moderately hot oven, 400°F, 200°C, Gas Mark 6, for 20 minutes. Garnish with sippets of fried bread and split almonds and serve from the casserole dish.
Makes 6 servings.

147   CHAUDFROID OF FISH

½kg/1lb cooked white fish · chaudfroid sauce (Recipe No. 151)
savoury creams (Recipe Nos. 148–150)
· lettuce, watercress, tomato and cucumber to garnish

Arrange fish on wire cooling tray with plate or foil underneath
to catch any drips. Allow chaudfroid sauce to start to thicken
and spread over fish with knife dipped in hot water. When
firm pipe with savoury cream; serve on lettuce and garnish
with watercress, tomato and cucumber.

SAVOURY CREAMS

148   Lemon
Beat little lemon juice and grated rind into creamed soft
margarine or butter.

149   Mustard
Add a little made mustard and finely chopped watercress to
creamed soft margarine or butter.

150   Anchovy
Add anchovy essence and pepper to creamed soft margarine
or butter.

Chaudfroid of fish

151   CHAUDFROID SAUCE

142ml/¼pint aspic jelly (Recipe No. 283)
284ml/½pint thick mayonnaise (Recipe Nos. 408, 412) or
salad dressing (Recipe Nos. 416, 419)

Make aspic jelly, allow to cool and mix with mayonnaise.

152   COTTAGE CHEESE
AND SALMON MOULD

¾ packet aspic jelly
390ml (i.e. ¾pint less 2 tablespoons) water
¼ cucumber, thinly sliced · 2 hard-boiled eggs, sliced
175g/7oz can salmon · 200g/8oz cottage cheese
2 tablespoons mayonnaise (Recipe Nos. 408, 412)
salt and pepper · 1 tablespoon chopped olives or gherkin

Make up the jelly with 390ml (i.e. ¾ pint less 2 tablespoons)
water. Pour ½-cm (¼-inch) layer of aspic jelly into a fairly deep
oval dish. Chill. When set arrange slices of cucumber and
hard-boiled egg on the bottom. Chill. Pour another ½-cm (¼-
inch) layer of jelly on top. Chill. Mix together remaining aspic
jelly, chopped egg, flaked salmon, cottage cheese, mayonnaise, seasoning and chopped olives or gherkin. Turn into
dish and chill. When set turn out on to a dish and serve.

Cottage cheese and salmon mould

Salmon ring

153   SALMON RING

2 eggs, separated · 142ml/¼pint white sauce (Recipe No. 663)
2 level teaspoons powdered gelatine · 1 tablespoon lemon juice
6 tablespoons hot water · 175g/7oz can salmon
2 tablespoons top of the milk · seasoning · salad to garnish

Beat the egg yolks into the cooled white sauce. Soften gelatine
in the lemon juice add the water and stir until dissolved. Add
this to the egg mixture. Fold in the flaked salmon, top of the
milk, seasoning and lastly the stiffly beaten egg whites. Pour
into a rinsed ring mould and leave to set in the refrigerator.
Turn out and serve garnished with salad vegetables.

MEAT

This section contains both unusual dishes and recipes to help you get the best results from roasting, grilling, frying or casserole cooking. Home-killed or imported meat can be used – many of the pictures show New Zealand meat, which is of prime quality and particularly tender.

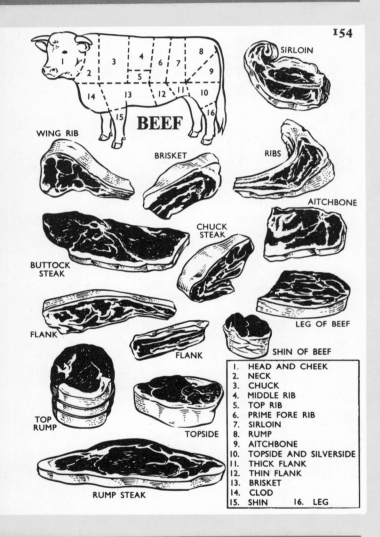

154

- 1. HEAD AND CHEEK
- 2. NECK
- 3. CHUCK
- 4. MIDDLE RIB
- 5. TOP RIB
- 6. PRIME FORE RIB
- 7. SIRLOIN
- 8. RUMP
- 9. AITCHBONE
- 10. TOPSIDE AND SILVERSIDE
- 11. THICK FLANK
- 12. THIN FLANK
- 13. BRISKET
- 14. CLOD
- 15. SHIN   16. LEG

155   **BEEF**

The lean should be a clear bright red, and the fat firm and pale cream in colour. The very best joints MUST have a certain amount of fat on them.

Purpose	Cut to choose	Cooking Time	Accompaniments
Roasting	Sirloin Ribs Fillet Aitch-bone (good quality) Topside Rump	15 minutes per ¼kg (1lb) plus 15 minutes over Well-done, 20 minutes per ¼kg (1lb) plus 20 minutes over, or 40 minutes per ¼kg (1lb) in very slow oven	Mustard Horseradish sauce Yorkshire pudding Roast potatoes Gravy
Grilling or Frying	Rump Fillet Sirloin Entrecôte	5–15 minutes depending on thickness and personal preference	Chipped or mashed potatoes Salad Tomatoes Mushrooms
Stewing or Braising	Skirt or chuck Bladebone 'Leg of Mutton' cut Brisket Flank	1½–3 hours (see also under pressure cooking, Recipe No. 894)	Mixed vegetables Dumplings Thickened gravy Caper or onion sauce
Pickling or Boiling	Brisket Shin or leg Silverside Flank Aitch-bone	1½–3 hours	Vegetables or salad
Stock for soups etc.	Neck Shin or leg Clod Marrow bone Oxtail Flank	1½–3 hours	

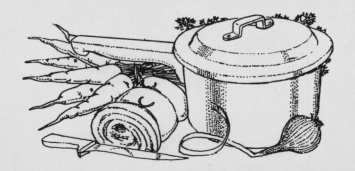

Roast leg of lamb, shoulder of lamb, leg of pork and fore ribs of beef (Recipe No. 167)

156 MUTTON or LAMB

See that the lean is a dull red, but very firm. The fat should be white in colour. You can differentiate between lamb and mutton – lamb is paler in colour.

Purpose	Cut to choose	Cooking Time	Accompaniments

Roasting	Leg
	Loin
	Best end of
	  neck (lamb)
	Shoulder
	Breast, stuffed
	  and rolled
		20 minutes per
		½kg (1lb) plus
		20 minutes over
			Mutton:
			  redcurrant jelly
			Lamb: mint jelly
			  or mint sauce
			Fresh peas

Grilling or Frying	Loin chops Gigot chops Cutlets	10–15 minutes	Chipped potatoes Tomatoes Mushrooms Peas Salad
Stewing, Braising or Boiling	Neck Breast Leg Shoulder	1½–2½ hours	Mixed vegetables Creamed potatoes
Stock for soups etc.	Scrag end of neck Head Trotters	1½–2½ hours	

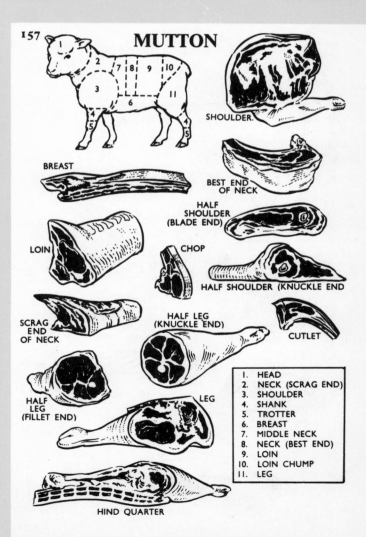

157 MUTTON

SHOULDER

BREAST

BEST END OF NECK

HALF SHOULDER (BLADE END)

LOIN

CHOP

HALF SHOULDER (KNUCKLE END)

SCRAG END OF NECK

HALF LEG (KNUCKLE END)

CUTLET

HALF LEG (FILLET END)

LEG

HIND QUARTER

1. HEAD
2. NECK (SCRAG END)
3. SHOULDER
4. SHANK
5. TROTTER
6. BREAST
7. MIDDLE NECK
8. NECK (BEST END)
9. LOIN
10. LOIN CHUMP
11. LEG

VEAL

Be very critical, particularly in hot weather, as veal does not keep well. There is little fat to see, but what there is should be firm and white; the lean must look dry and be a pale pink.

Purpose	Cut to choose	Cooking Time	Accompaniments

Roasting	Shoulder
	Breast
	Best end of
	   neck
	Loin
	Fillet
	Chump end
	   of loin
		25 minutes per
		½kg (1lb) plus
		25 minutes over
			Sausages
			Veal stuffing or
			  other well
			  flavoured
			  stuffing. Keep
			  well basted
			Thickened gravy

Grilling
or
Frying
	Chops from
	  loin
	Fillet
	Best end of
	  neck chops
		15–20 minutes	Chipped potatoes
			Tomatoes
			Mushrooms

	Thin slices from
	  leg
		5–6 minutes	As escalopes
			  with various
			  garnishes etc.

Stewing or Braising	Breast Fillet Knuckle Middle and scrag end of neck	1½–2½ hours	Mixed vegetables Various sauces
Boiling	Head Feet Breast	1½–2½ hours	Mixed vegetables or salad
Stock for soups etc.	Feet Knuckle	1½–2½ hours	

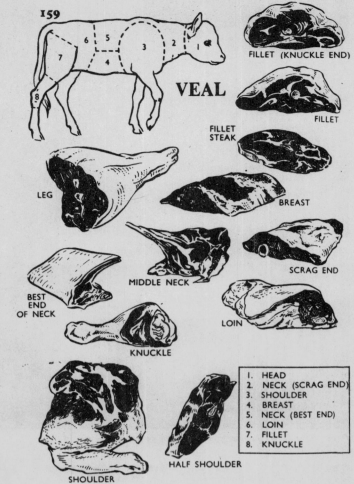

VEAL

FILLET (KNUCKLE END)

FILLET

FILLET STEAK

BREAST

SCRAG END

MIDDLE NECK

BEST END OF NECK

LOIN

KNUCKLE

LEG

SHOULDER

HALF SHOULDER

1. HEAD
2. NECK (SCRAG END)
3. SHOULDER
4. BREAST
5. NECK (BEST END)
6. LOIN
7. FILLET
8. KNUCKLE

PORK

LEG

CHOP

LOIN

BLADE BONE

SPARE RIB

BELLY

HAND AND SPRING

1. HEAD
2. SPARE RIB
3. HAND
4. BELLY
5. LOIN
6. LEG.

PORK

The lean part of the meat must look pale pink, and the fat white and dry. Pork must *never* be served under-done. Try to avoid serving pork in very hot weather.

Purpose	Cut to choose	Cooking Time	Accompaniments
Roasting	Loin Leg Bladebone Spare rib	25 minutes per ½kg (1lb) plus 25 minutes over	Sage and onion stuffing Mustard Apple sauce Orange salad Thickened gravy
Frying	Chops from loin Spare rib chops	15–20 minutes	Apple sauce Apple rings Sage and onion stuffing Tomatoes Mushrooms
Boiling	Head Hand and spring Belly Cuts given for roasting	2½ hours	Salad Mixed vegetables

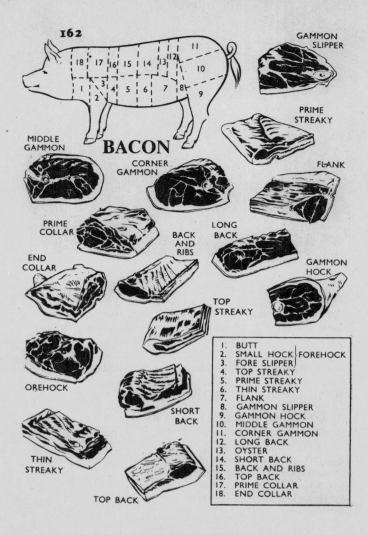

162

BACON

GAMMON SLIPPER

PRIME STREAKY

MIDDLE GAMMON

CORNER GAMMON

FLANK

PRIME COLLAR

BACK AND RIBS

LONG BACK

END COLLAR

GAMMON HOCK

TOP STREAKY

OREHOCK

SHORT BACK

THIN STREAKY

TOP BACK

1. BUTT
2. SMALL HOCK } FOREHOCK
3. FORE SLIPPER }
4. TOP STREAKY
5. PRIME STREAKY
6. THIN STREAKY
7. FLANK
8. GAMMON SLIPPER
9. GAMMON HOCK
10. MIDDLE GAMMON
11. CORNER GAMMON
12. LONG BACK
13. OYSTER
14. SHORT BACK
15. BACK AND RIBS
16. TOP BACK
17. PRIME COLLAR
18. END COLLAR

164   TO BONE MEAT

Carving is much easier if the meat is boned – your butcher will doubtless do this for you, but if he has not done so, it is not difficult. Use a proper boning knife with a slim but firm blade, and feel round the bone with the tip before cutting the meat – work slowly so as to avoid waste.

165   TO CARVE MEAT

GOOD CARVING TAKES PRACTICE but there are certain rules to help you.

1. *Do buy a good knife* – and if you have a large family or entertain a great deal, it is wise to have two knives, since the heat of the meat is inclined to blunt the knife.
2. *To carve beef* – cut long slices across the joint. When carving sirloin on the bone you must, however, first, remove the top bone or chine, cut the first slices along the bone, then turn the joint and cut thick slices at right angles from the bone.
3. *To carve lamb or mutton* – cut rather thicker slices downwards. The shoulder is not easy to carve, but you should follow the formation of the bone, which means carving round it – starting in the centre of the joint and cutting diagonal slices.
4. *To carve pork* – cut downwards as for mutton. Ask the butcher to chine, i.e. cut through bones, on loin.
5. *To carve veal* – most joints as beef, but shoulder as for mutton, loin as for pork.
6. *To carve joints of bacon* – as bacon has been boned, generally cut across. A whole ham on the bone should be carved diagonally – the first cuts if the ham is large should be downwards.

163   **BACON and HAM**

See it looks moist and not too dry, with brightly coloured lean part. Bacon may be blanched to remove excess of salt before adding to other dishes. Do not confuse ham and bacon – they have been cured in entirely different ways, giving quite distinct flavours.

Purpose	Cut to choose	Cooking Time	Accompaniments
Roasting or Baking	Gammon slipper Middle gammon Back and ribs Joint top streaky	20 minutes per ½kg (1lb) and 20 minutes over If well done, cook like pork for 25 minutes per ½kg (1lb)	Mustard Salad Unusual garnishes such as baked apples, halved baked pears filled with red-currant jelly, etc.
Grilling or Frying	Top streaky Prime streaky Thin streaky Gammon slipper Middle gammon Corner gammon Long back Short back Back and ribs Top back Prime collar	Few minutes only for thin rashers, but with thick slices of gammon cook outside fairly quickly, then reduce heat to cook through to the middle. Keep gammon well brushed with fat when grilling	Eggs, tomatoes, mushrooms, etc. for breakfast Vegetables or salad for a main meal
Boiling or Braising	Forehock Prime streaky Flank Gammon slipper Gammon hock Middle gammon Corner gammon Long back Back and ribs Top back Prime collar End of collar Oyster cut	Soak well if you want very mild flavour, then simmer gently for for 20–25 minutes per ½kg (1lb) and 20 to 25 minutes over Do not boil too quickly. A pressure cooker can be used (Recipe No. 896) Ham or bacon stock is excellent for soups	Any vegetables – beans and peas are particularly good with boiled bacon Salad etc. Parsley or other sauces

To bone meat

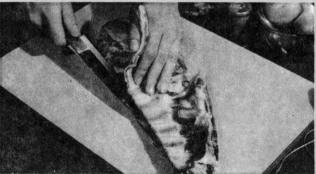

To carve meat

Roast pork with spicy apple sauce

Roast leg of lamb

166 ROAST PORK WITH SPICY APPLE SAUCE

Follow directions in Recipe No. 167 for roasting pork. To make the sauce, peel and core 4 cooking apples. Slice and place in a pan with 2 tablespoons water, 2 cloves, 1 tablespoon sugar and a pinch of cinnamon. Simmer until soft, remove the cloves, whisk in a knob of butter. Stir in 2 tablespoons raisins.

167 TO ROAST MEAT

Roasting must be a form of cooking kept for really prime joints – see the tables for kinds of joints to choose.

Beef takes 15–20 minutes per ½kg (1 lb) according to taste, plus an additional 20 minutes.
Mutton, lamb take 20 minutes per ½kg (1 lb) or even a little longer as people tend to like it well done, plus an additional 20 minutes.
Pork, bacon, veal all need very good cooking, so allow 25 minutes for each ½kg (1 lb) and 25 minutes over. These times are all for a hot oven, or at least a moderately hot oven; but during the past years *slow roasting* has become very popular, and if you have any doubts as to whether the meat is tender then choose this method. Instead of roasting at from 400–450°F, 200–220°C, Gas Mark 6–7, use a very slow oven 275–325°F, 140–170°C, Gas Mark 1–2 and allow twice as long. The meat will not spoil, and will certainly be more tender.

FOR PERFECT ROASTING remember:
1. Do not have too much fat on the joint – otherwise you harden the outside.
   Beef needs little fat.
   Veal needs more fat – or you can do as a French cook would, thread narrow strips of fat bacon through a large-eyed needle and push these through the veal – this produces an excellent flavour and very moist texture.
   Lamb needs a little fat if very lean, but mutton does not.
   Pork; to get a good crackling do not add fat, but brush the skin with melted butter or olive oil.
   Bacon or ham; soak well before roasting – further details in Recipe No. 174.
2. Covering the joint with a lid (in a covered roaster) or foil will not spoil it, and will keep the oven very clean. For crisp joints, particularly pork, remove the foil or lid 30 minutes before serving.
3. Do not over-cook meat; it does not make it more tender, but tends to toughen it.

The picture shows lamb being 'basted' with hot fat from the roasting tin. This is *not* essential but helps to keep meat and poultry moist.

Roast beef

Roast ham

168 ROAST BREAST OF LAMB

Breast of lamb is a particularly economical roasting joint – other recipes are given in this section for cooking this joint. Choose a stuffing that counteracts the rather fatty meat. This has an excellent flavour.

169 ROAST BEEF

Just over 30 minutes before serving the roast beef – for cooking times and oven temperatures see charts (Recipe Nos. 155, 167) – heat a knob of fat in the Yorkshire pudding tin in the oven. Pour in the batter (Recipe No. 636), and cook the pudding at the top of the oven. When cooked cut in small slices and arrange round beef. If preferred bake in separate patty tins, allowing about 15 minutes.

In the picture roast rib of beef is served with duchesse potatoes (Recipe No. 300) and carrots.

170 CROWN ROAST OF LAMB

with mint sauce

To make this impressive dish buy approximately 12–14 small loin chops. Ask the butcher to chine them, and skewer to make a round of meat. Roast for the time given in charts for lamb (Recipe Nos. 156, 167). When cooked top each bone with a cutlet frill. Fill the centre with mixed vegetables, peas, stuffing or creamed potatoes, and garnish with peas, etc. Serve with mint sauce.

171 Mint sauce

Chop mint finely, add sugar to taste, vinegar and if liked a little hot water to melt the sugar.

172 LOIN OF PORK

with apple sauce

To stuff loin, loosen the skin, and press sage and onion stuffing (Recipe No. 280) under the skin. Roast for the time given in charts (Recipe Nos. 161, 167).

173 Apple sauce

Simmer prepared apples with water and sugar to taste. Sieve or beat until smooth – reheat with knob of butter.

174 ROAST HAM

Ham can be roasted as well as being boiled. It must be soaked well in cold water for several hours or overnight. If wished simmer for most of the cooking time – and then remove the skin. Cover with brown sugar, a little spice, halved glacé cherries and cloves, and put into a moderate oven, 375°F, 190°C, Gas Mark 5, for about 45 minutes until crisp and golden brown.

To roast the ham entirely, cover either with foil or with a flour and water crust. Bake for the time given in the roasting charts (Recipe Nos. 163, 167). Remove the skin, and if wished cover with honey or brown sugar, spice or a little fruit juice. If liked baste the ham during cooking with fruit juice or cider.

Roast loin of pork with apricot stuffing

Stuffed breast of veal

175 ROAST LOIN OF PORK WITH APRICOT STUFFING

about 2kg/4lb loin, boned · apricot stuffing (Recipe No. 181)
1 clove garlic · parsley · marjoram · canned apricot halves
to garnish

Stuff the loin, roll up and tie securely. Chop garlic and herbs and rub well into the meat. Place the meat in a roasting tin and cook for 10 minutes in a very moderate oven, 350°F, 180°C, Gas Mark 4. Reduce heat to 300°F, 150°C, Gas Mark 2 and cook for 2½–3 hours. Transfer the pork to a serving dish and serve garnished with canned apricot halves.

176 ROAST MIDDLE GAMMON

middle gammon, weighing not less than 1kg/2lb
Demerara sugar

Soak the gammon in cold water overnight, or at least for some hours. Cover in foil or a crust made from a stiff flour and water paste. Do not roll this out too thinly, it should cover the meat completely to seal in all the juices. Cook for the time given in roasting charts (Recipe Nos. 163, 167), less 30 minutes then remove the foil or crust and press Demerara sugar into the fat. Return to the oven for 30 minutes. Place on a heated serving dish. Garnish with a selection of cooked vegetables in season.

177 STUFFED BREAST OF VEAL

breast of veal, weighing about 1¼–1½kg/2½–3lb
200g/8oz lean minced beef · 1 tablespoon chopped parsley
2 tablespoons breadcrumbs · 6–8 small gherkins
1 hard-boiled egg · seasoning · 1 egg, beaten
75g/3oz butter or bacon fat · few rashers bacon, optional
2–3 large onions · 2 tablespoons tomato ketchup
284ml/½pint brown sauce (Recipe No. 685)

Prepare the meat, either by cutting back the outer skin to make a 'pocket' for the stuffing or better still by having the meat boned, so the stuffing can be spread over this and then the breast rolled and tied.

To prepare the stuffing, mix the minced beef with the parsley, breadcrumbs, chopped gherkins, chopped hard-boiled egg, and seasoning and bind with the beaten egg. Spread inside the 'pocket' or over the meat, and if boned roll firmly, but not too tightly, and tie. Put into roasting tin with the butter or bacon fat, and if wished cover the top of the veal roll with rashers of bacon. Put into a moderate oven, 350°F, 180°C, Gas Mark 4, for about 15 minutes then add the onions cut into rings. Return to the oven for a further 1¾ hours. Remove the bacon for the last 10–15 minutes to enable the top of the veal to brown. Serve with the well drained onion rings round the meat. Stir the tomato ketchup into the brown sauce and serve in a sauce boat.

Roast middle gammon

Cider braised lamb

Roast shoulder with apricot stuffing

178   CIDER BRAISED LAMB

leg of lamb · 2 sprigs rosemary · ½kg/1lb leeks
generous ½ litre/1pint cider · large potatoes

With a sharp knife loosen the skin in two places, to make small pockets, and put a small sprig of rosemary in each. Prepare the leeks, cut into thin slices and put into a meat tin. Place the joint on top and pour the cider over. Season. Prepare potatoes and put them round the joint. Baste with the cider. Cover with foil and cook at 350°F, 180°C, Gas Mark 4, allowing 25 minutes per ½kg (1 lb). Remove cover, baste again and cook, uncovered for a further 25 minutes to brown the lamb. Serve on a hot dish, garnish with potatoes and whole, cooked carrots. Thicken the liquid from the pan, add some of the leeks and serve in a sauce boat.

179   ORANGE CROWN ROAST

12–14 loin chops in 1 or 2 joints (Recipe No. 170)

Orange stuffing

1 medium-sized onion, finely chopped · 50g/2oz butter
200g/8oz white breadcrumbs
1 dessertspoon very finely chopped parsley
grated rind and juice 2 oranges · salt and pepper · 2 egg yolks

Prepare the crown roast as Recipe No. 182. Prepare the stuffing by frying the onion in the butter until soft but not brown, add all other ingredients. Put the meat in the tin, fill centre with the stuffing. Protect stuffing and bones with foil and roast as the charts for lamb (Recipe Nos. 156, 167), but allow extra 25 minutes to compensate for weight of stuffing.

Crown roast of lamb

180   ROAST SHOULDER OF LAMB WITH APRICOT STUFFING

Ask the butcher to bone the shoulder of lamb – or using a very sharp boning knife cut the meat away from the bone. Stuff, roll up and tie securely with fine string or stuff flat and skewer or sew the edges together. Roast in a moderately hot oven, 400°F, 200°C, Gas Mark 6, allowing 30 minutes to the ½kg (1 lb) and 30 minutes over.

181   APRICOT STUFFING

1 tablespoon chopped onion · 25g/1oz butter
4 rounded tablespoons fresh white breadcrumbs
salt and pepper · ½ teaspoon parsley · ½ teaspoon sage
1–2 tablespoons milk · 50g/2oz dried apricots, chopped

Gently fry the onion in butter. Add breadcrumbs, salt, pepper and herbs, mix with milk; finally add apricots.

182   PREPARING CROWN ROAST

2 pieces loin or best end neck of lamb, each with 6 cutlets
corn oil for roasting · celery and onion stuffing (Recipe No. 183)
fresh orange segments to garnish

Ask the butcher to trim the ends of the bones evenly and to chop halfway through the base of each cutlet so that each piece of meat may be shaped into a semi-circle. Remove the skin and any excess fat from the pieces of meat. Cut 3½cm (1½ inches) down from ends of cutlets and scrape the meat away leaving the tips of the bones as clean as possible. Place pieces of meat on either side of a jam jar bending them round the jar to form a circle. Tie meat securely with thin clean string. Cover tips of bones with foil. Place in a roasting tin and baste with corn oil. Make the stuffing. Remove the jam jar from the centre of the crown and fill the crown with the stuffing. Cook in a moderately hot oven, 375°F, 190°C, Gas Mark 5, for 1½–1¾ hours. Place on a warm serving dish, remove the string and garnish the tip of each cutlet with a cutlet frill. Arrange fresh orange segments in the centre. Serve with duchesse potatoes (Recipe No. 300) and Brussels sprouts.

183   CELERY AND ONION STUFFING

1 tablespoon corn oil · 1 small onion, chopped
3 sticks celery, finely chopped
75g/3oz white breadcrumbs · seasoning
1½–2 tablespoons chopped parsley · little beaten egg to bind

Heat the oil and fry onion and celery until soft, but not browned. Add to breadcrumbs, seasoning and parsley and bind with a little beaten egg.

Grilled steak

TO GRILL MEAT

To grill meat make sure the grill is really hot before the food is put underneath; this is important as the heat of the grill seals in the flavour of the meat at once.

Do not try to grill meat which is not a prime cut. If using an infra-red grill follow the directions given by the manufacturer – the times in the meat charts are for an ordinary gas or electric grill.

The picture above shows the attractive effect given by 'scoring' steak with a very hot skewer just before serving. Put the skewer under the grill until red hot, hold carefully and mark 'lines' across the cooked steak.

Pork chops

Brush the grill with plenty of oil or butter.

Brush the steak also with oil or butter. Cook quickly on either side for 2–3 minutes – for an underdone or 'rare' steak that is probably enough and it can be served at once; for a medium steak lower the heat and cook for a further 5–6 minutes; for a well-done steak lower the heat as much as possible to cook steak gently through to the centre, for about 10 minutes taking care not to scorch the outside.

Serve with any of following: grilled mushrooms, grilled tomatoes, fried onions, or to give a pleasant touch of sharpness, with rings of lemon and capers. Many people like a crisp green salad and Béarnaise sauce (Recipe No. 683) with grilled steak. Serve garnished with parsley butter (butter mixed with chopped parsley) and sprigs of watercress.

STEAKS TO CHOOSE

Minute steak – very thin slice of steak, so called because it needs only a minute on either side.

Rump steak – full of flavour, but less tender on the whole than fillet.

Fillet steak – very tender and lean.

Sirloin steak – cut from across the sirloin – excellent proportion of lean and fat.

Entrecôte – cut from middle of ribs or sirloin – tender, very good flavour.

Point steak – cut from the pointed end of the rump and most tender.

Porterhouse – very large sirlion steak, up to 2kg (4 lb).

Planked steak – so called because it is served on wooden plank.

Tournedos – fillet steak tied into circle with string, so looks round; served with various garnishes.

Some favourite garnishes for tournedos are:

Tournedos d'Orsay – steak garnished with olives and mushrooms.

Tournedos Parisienne – steak garnished with asparagus tips and Béarnaise sauce (Recipe No. 683).

Tournedos Pompadour – topped with tomato purée, slice of grilled ham and truffle or mushrooms.

185   PORK AND GAMMON

Pork chops or cutlets (cutlets have the bone trimmed to look more attractive when served – they are always cut from the loin) need little basting with fat, as there is generally a good distribution of fat and lean.

When the outside of the meat has been sealed turn the heat low to make sure they are well cooked through to the centre. Serve with apple sauce (Recipe No. 173), orange salad (Recipe No. 279), sage and onion stuffing (Recipe No. 280) or with grilled tomatoes and mushrooms.

For an unusual accompaniment try jellied apple slices. Cut 2 red-skinned, cored apples into wedges and arrange in a large shallow pan. Dissolve 200g (8 oz) redcurrant or apple jelly in 142ml ($\frac{1}{4}$ pint) boiling water and pour over apples and cook over a low heat until apples are tender and nicely glazed.

Gammon is, however, a very lean part of bacon, so brush well with melted butter. Snip the fat to encourage it to become crisp and brown. Put under a low grill – this prevents the bacon from curling up. Cook steadily to make sure it is tender through to the middle.

If wished glaze by sprinkling a little brown sugar on top and returning to the grill for a minute.

Serve with grilled tomatoes, mushrooms and vegetables, or with glazed pineapple rings or halved peaches or apricots, and a crisp green salad.

Mixed grill

186   MIXED GRILL

A mixed grill can be made from a variety of ingredients, but your grill is made or marred by the way it is served. Have the various foods attractively arranged on the plate, with a suitable garnish to add colour and variety. Watercress is the most usual garnish for a mixed grill, particularly if it includes steak, but try also potato crisps, cucumber slices, green peas, uncooked quartered tomatoes or thinly sliced red pepper. For the grill itself, choose from the following:

loin chops
gigot chops of lamb (gigot chops are not shown on the chart, but they come from where leg joins loin) · lamb cutlets · steak
kidney · bacon · sausages · liver
eggs (these should be fried at the last minute) · tomatoes
mushrooms

There is no reason why veal or pork chops or cutlets, could not be used instead of lamb, but lamb is generally used.
The secret of a good mixed grill is to time the cooking carefully, i.e. do not put all ingredients under the grill at the same time; start with food that takes the longest cooking, then gradually add the other ingredients.
Remember kidneys can easily be over-cooked, so add these towards the end. Sausages on the other hand require a fair amount of cooking.
With most grills tomatoes and mushrooms can be cooked in the grill pan, while the meats are cooked on the grill – it may, however, be advisable to put the pan with mushrooms and tomatoes underneath for a few minutes to give them a 'start', before covering with the grid and meat. Serve with vegetables or a crisp green salad.

187   KEBABS or SKEWER COOKING

This is a most attractive way of serving grilled foods. Arrange a mixture of foods – kidneys, bacon, sausages, cubed steak or tender lamb, mushrooms, tiny onions, tomato halves, pineapple cubes, etc. on metal skewers. Brush with plenty of melted butter and cook under the grill, turning the skewers to make sure that the food is well cooked. The food can be slipped from the skewer quite easily on to serving plates. Serve with vegetables or cooked long grain rice.

188   ROTISSERIE COOKING

Today there are many versions of the old-fashioned spit – modern electric rotisseries, that cook the food on an electric spit. Here you have all the advantages of a grill, but you can cook whole chickens and joints.

Kebabs

189 CHOPS EN PAPILLOTE

2 hard-boiled eggs · 40g/1½oz fresh breadcrumbs · 1 small clove garlic, chopped in little salt · ½ teaspoon salt · pinch pepper 1 tablespoon chopped parsley · 40g/1½oz butter, melted 4 lamb chops

Chop the hard-boiled eggs finely, and mix with the breadcrumbs, garlic, seasoning, parsley and melted butter. Coat each chop with this mixture, wrap in a piece of foil or greaseproof paper, and cook in a hot oven, 400–425°F, 200–220°C, Gas Mark 6–7, for 25–30 minutes. Remove to the grill pan – open the foil and grill the chops until golden brown. Serve with vegetables in season.

Chops en papillote

190 GRILLED PORK CHOPS WITH PINEAPPLE

4 pork chops · 4 pineapple rings

Cook the pork chops under a moderate grill for 15–20 minutes, turning the chops after 10 minutes to ensure steady, even cooking. Brush both sides of the pineapple rings with melted fat from the pork chops, place under the grill with the chops for the last 5 minutes of cooking. Serve with forcemeat balls (Recipe No. 191).

191 FORCEMEAT BALLS

150g/6oz breadcrumbs · salt and pepper 1 teaspoon mixed herbs paprika pepper · 1 teaspoon chopped parsley 50g/2oz butter, melted · 2 teaspoons finely chopped onion 1 clove garlic, crushed · few toasted or browned breadcrumbs fat for frying

Mix the breadcrumbs with rest of the ingredients, bind together with a little milk to a firm consistency; form into balls, roll in toasted breadcrumbs and fry in pork fat.

Grilled pork chops with pineapple

Ginger lamb with rice

192 GINGER LAMB WITH RICE

½kg/1lb lamb, minced · 1 egg, beaten · 1 teaspoon garlic salt pinch pepper · 150g/6oz ginger biscuit crumbs · 1 small can pineapple pieces 1 large green pepper, cut into squares 4–6 tablespoons tomato sauce (Recipe No. 656), fresh purée or ketchup · 2 tablespoons brown sugar 1 teaspoon dry mustard · 1 tablespoon lemon juice pinch ground ginger

Combine lamb, egg, garlic salt, pepper and ginger biscuit crumbs. Mix well, form into small balls. Alternate meat balls, pineapple and green pepper on metal skewers. Brush with a mixture of tomato sauce, brown sugar, mustard, lemon juice and ginger. Grill 7–8 minutes on each side, basting occasionally. Serve on a bed of hot long grain rice.

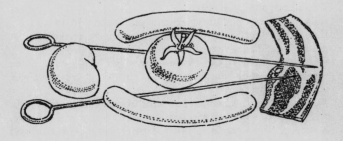

193   GRILLED LAMB CHOPS

4 loin chops lamb · little melted butter
halved tomatoes and sprigs of watercress to garnish

Brush the chops with a little melted butter and put on to the grill pan. Heat grill and cook chops for 5–7 minutes on each side. Arrange on a serving dish and serve garnished with a halved tomatoes and sprigs of watercress.

194   HAGGIS
(An easy to make recipe)

200g/8oz sheep's liver · 2 onions · 100g/4oz beef suet
200g/8oz oatmeal · salt and pepper · ½ teaspoon dried sage

Cover the liver with water and simmer for 40 minutes. Drain and keep the liquid. Mince the liver finely. Parboil the onions then chop with the suet. Brown the oatmeal by tossing quickly in a thick pan over the heat. Combine the minced liver, suet, onions and oatmeal and season with salt and pepper and sage. Moisten with the liquor in which the liver was cooked. Turn into a greased basin, cover with greaseproof paper and steam for 2 hours.

195   NOISETTES OF LAMB GARNI

¾kg/1½lb best end neck of lamb · 4 large firm tomatoes
¾kg/1½lb hot mashed potatoes · 1 small packet frozen peas

Divide the lamb into cutlets and remove the bone. Curl the end around the edge of the cutlet and secure with a small skewer. Cut the tomatoes in half and scoop out the centres, keeping the tomato pulp on one side to use in the gravy. Pipe or spread a layer of potato down the centre of an ovenproof dish, surround with tomato shells and place the dish in a moderate oven, 375°F, 190°C, Gas Mark 5, for about 15 minutes. Fry or grill the noisettes of lamb for 6–8 minutes on each side, drain and arrange on the potato. Meanwhile, cook the peas, drain and use the liquor for the gravy, thickening with flour in the usual way. Add dripping from cooking noisettes and the tomato pulp. Pile the peas into the tomato shells and serve. Serve the gravy separately.

196   HOSTESS PLATTER

4 lamb cutlets from best end of neck
200g/8oz frozen or fresh peas · 1 orange · mint leaves to garnish

Trim the cutlets and fry or grill, for about 8 minutes on each side, until tender. Meanwhile cook the peas; coarsely grate the orange rind, peel the orange and segment it. Arrange the chops on a serving dish. Pile the peas in the centre and sprinkle with the grated orange rind. Garnish with mint leaves and orange segments.

Grilled lamb chops

Noisettes of lamb

Hostess platter

Bacon and vegetable risotto

TO FRY MEAT

197

Do not have the fat too hot in the pan before adding the meat, otherwise the outside will burn.

Veal, particularly fillets, are better fried than grilled, as they have so little fat.

Liver should be fried for the same reason. Take particular care not to over-cook liver – it needs just a few minutes. If liver is over-cooked it becomes very tough and dry. Choose calves or lamb's liver.

Chops of lamb, pork and mutton can be fried instead of grilled – little, if any, fat will be required.

Steak can be fried, but is generally considered better if grilled.

Bacon is considered by many people to have a better flavour if grilled, but that is just a matter of opinion.

Sausages should be fried steadily – and not too much fat used.

Kidneys need frying gently, so that they do not harden on the outside.

Serve fried foods with 'refreshing' accompaniments – tomatoes, mushrooms, a green salad.

Always drain fried foods on absorbent paper before serving. Electric frying pans today mean that food can be fried on the serving table and eaten very freshly cooked.

198 BACON AND VEGETABLE RISOTTO

300g/12oz *thick collar rashers bacon, cubed* · 75g/3oz *butter*
1 *large onion, peeled and chopped* · 1 *clove garlic, crushed*
200g/8oz *long grain rice*
scant ¾litre/1¼pints *stock made from a cube* · *pinch nutmeg*
salt and pepper · 4 *heaped tablespoons cooked peas*
1 *red pepper, chopped and blanched*
200g/8oz *can sweet corn, drained*
75g/3oz *cheese, grated* · *parsley to garnish*

Melt most of the butter in a pan and add the bacon, onion and garlic. Fry until the onion is soft but not coloured. Add rice and continue to stir for 4–5 minutes. Take saucepan off heat and add stock, nutmeg and seasoning. Bring slowly to the boil, stirring all the time. Cover and allow to simmer very gently for about 20 minutes, or until all the liquid has been absorbed. Add vegetables and cook very gently for a further 5 minutes. Just before serving mix in remaining butter and the cheese. Garnish with sprigs of parsley.

199 FRIED GAMMON

Score the edges to encourage the fat to become crisp. Heat a little fat in a pan and cook steadily, turning when the under side is well cooked. Serve with fried pineapple rings. If liked, garnish with potato crisps and tomato baskets – a few cooked peas piled into scooped out tomato halves.

Fried gammon

Back, streaky, collar or gammon rashers are all recommended for frying. If you want thin rashers ask for a No. 3 cut; gammon rashers, however, are usually cut a little thicker. Cut off the rind with kitchen scissors – this is often useful for your stockpot when making soup. When using streaky bacon be sure to cut out the bone. If the bacon is very fat, snip the fat through at intervals so that it lies flat when cooking. To get the best results, put the bacon into a COLD frying pan, and arrange the rashers of bacon so that the lean overlaps the fat. This means that the lean is kept moist and well 'basted' by the fat. There is no need to add fat to the pan unless the bacon is very lean.

201   SWEET AND SOUR PORK

½kg/1lb *lean pork, cubed · seasoning · 1 tablespoon cornflour*
about 2 tablespoons oil for frying

Sprinkle the meat with seasoning. Roll in cornflour and fry in the hot oil for about 10 minutes, until browned on all sides and cook through. Remove the meat to a serving dish and pour the sweet sour sauce over. If liked, serve with cooked long grain rice.

202   SWEET SOUR SAUCE

142ml/¼pint *stock · 1 green pepper · 1 level tablespoon cornflour*
1 tablespoon brown sugar · 2 teaspoons soy sauce
142ml/¼pint *vinegar · 1 eating apple, cored and sliced*
3 canned pineapple rings · 6–8 pieces sweet mustard pickles

Put the stock and the pepper, cut in 6 or 8 large pieces, into the pan and simmer gently for 5 minutes or until the pepper is tender. Mix the cornflour, the brown sugar, soy sauce and vinegar together smoothly and stir into the stock. Add the sliced apple and cook for 3 minutes. Cut the pineapple rings and pickles in small pieces and add to the sauce.

Bacon

Sweet and sour pork

203 PORK CHOPS WITH APPLE RINGS

4 pork chops
2 large cooking apples, peeled, cored and sliced · glacé cherries

Trim the chops and grill for 15–20 minutes, turning frequently. Brush the apple rings with a little melted fat and grill for a few minutes. Arrange the chops on a serving dish. Garnish with apple rings with a glacé cherry in the centre.

204 BACON CHOPS

Bacon chops are back rashers, cut thickly. Allow 1 or 2 per person. Trim off the rind, snip the fat and fry or grill for about 7 minutes each side. See that the fat is browned and crisp. Serve with vegetables for a main meal.

Pork chops with apple rings

Country meat balls

205 COUNTRY MEAT BALLS

½kg/1lb minced beef
75g/3oz fresh breadcrumbs · pinch mixed herbs, optional
1 small onion, sliced · seasoning · 1 egg, beaten
1 tablespoon flour · 25g/1oz margarine or butter
2 rashers streaky bacon, chopped · 1 carrot, chopped
3 tomatoes, skinned and chopped · 375g/15oz can butter beans
parsley to garnish

Mix the minced beef, breadcrumbs, herbs, if used, onion and seasoning together. Bind with the beaten egg. Shape into 12 balls and toss in flour. Heat the margarine in a frying pan and fry the meat balls until browned. Remove from the pan. Fry the bacon, carrots and tomatoes for 2–3 minutes. Add the butter beans plus liquid from the can. Bring to the boil then transfer to casserole with the meat balls. Cover and cook in a moderately hot oven, 375°F, 190°C, Gas Mark 5, for 30 minutes. Garnish with parsley and serve from the casserole dish.

Liver with bacon

206 LIVER WITH BACON

Coat thin slices of lamb's or calves liver in a very little seasoned flour. Fry quickly on both sides in heated butter or oil. Remove to a serving dish and keep hot. In the same pan fry bacon rashers. Place with the liver. Serve at once with Brussels sprouts.

207 TROTTERS IN PARSLEY SAUCE

2 pig's trotters · 1 large onion · little bacon rind · 1 bay leaf
seasoning · 25g/1oz butter or margarine
1 tablespoon cornflour to thicken · chopped parsley
few cooked peas, optional
creamed potato and lemon slices to garnish

Scrub the trotters and place in a saucepan with the coarsely chopped onion and bacon rind. Cover with water, bring to the boil and skim. Add bay leaf and seasoning and simmer until tender. Remove the trotters and keep hot. Strain 284ml (½ pint) of the liquor into another saucepan. Stir in the butter and the cornflour, blended with 3 tablespoons liquid. Bring to the boil and cook until thickened. Add parsley and peas, if used, and pour over the trotters. Garnish with a border of piped potato and lemon slices.

Trotters in parsley sauce

208 PORK AND LIVER MEAT BALLS

½kg/1lb ox liver · 200g/8oz belly of pork · 2 onions, peeled
50g/2oz rolled oats
1 teaspoon fresh basil, chives or parsley · seasoning
142ml/¼pint stock made from a cube · watercress to garnish
savoury tomato sauce (Recipe No. 209)

Put the liver in cold water to cover and bring to the boil. Simmer for 3 minutes, drain and discard water. Mince liver with pork and onions. Add the oats, basil and seasoning. Form the mixture into 8 balls. Place in a casserole dish, pour in the stock, cover and cook in a moderately hot oven, 375°F, 190°C, Gas Mark 5, for about 1 hour. Garnish with sprigs of watercress and serve with savoury tomato sauce.
Makes 6 servings.

209 SAVOURY TOMATO SAUCE

25g/1oz butter · 25g/1oz flour · liquid from cooking liver
2 tablespoons tomato purée or ketchup

Melt butter in pan, stir in the flour, cook for a few minutes. Measure the liver liquid, add sufficient water to give 284ml (½ pint). Stir into the roux, bring to the boil and thicken, then add tomato purée or ketchup.

Pork and liver meat balls

Veal escalopes

210 VEAL ESCALOPES

4 thin slices veal · 1 egg, beaten · 75g/3oz white breadcrumbs
75g/3oz Cheddar cheese, finely grated, optional · pinch salt
dash cayenne pepper · 50g/2oz cooking fat · 50g/2oz butter
4 lemon quarters · 4 stuffed olives · 4 anchovies

Trim the veal slices if necessary to give neat shape, and dip in beaten egg. Mix the breadcrumbs and grated cheese if used, season with salt and cayenne pepper, and use to coat the veal. Prepare the lemon quarters, wrap an anchovy round each olive, and keep on one side for garnish. Fry the veal on both sides in hot fat for about 10 minutes until golden brown. Heat the butter to a light golden brown. Arrange the escalopes slightly overlapping on a hot dish, pour over the browned butter. Garnish with lemon quarters, the olives and anchovies. Serve at once.

STEWING

Beef and vegetable olives

211 CASEROLE AND BRAISED DISHES

Stewing meat is a process that is done gently, so that the less tender pieces of meat (see Recipe No. 155 etc.) are made tender and kept moist during cooking. Unless you are using a pressure cooker this should be done very gently, either in a saucepan or a casserole. The meat and vegetables can be tossed in fat first, but unless recipes state otherwise the meat must NOT be cooked for too long a period in the fat, otherwise it will certainly toughen.

Cut the meat into neat dice, but do not cut it too small or the dish will not look attractive.

Braising is the cooking term used when the meat is cooked all the time in a thick sauce or gravy. When meat is stewed, either in a pan or a casserole, the mixture is generally thickened at the end of the long slow cooking time.

212 BEEF AND VEGETABLE OLIVES

4 large thin slices stewing beef · 25g/1oz fat
1 large can mixed vegetable soup or
284ml/½pint brown sauce (Recipe No. 685)

For the stuffing

100g/4oz breadcrumbs
2 level tablespoons shredded suet · pinch mixed herbs · seasoning
1 level tablespoon chopped parsley · 1 egg
chopped parsley to garnish

Mix all the ingredients for the stuffing together. Spread on the thin slices of meat. Roll these firmly and tie with pieces of cotton. Fry for a few minutes in the hot fat. Put into a casserole, pour over the hot vegetable soup or brown sauce. Cover with a lid and cook in a slow oven, 300°F, 150°C, Gas Mark 2, for 2 hours. Garnish with parsley and serve with mashed potatoes; untie the olives before serving.

Hungarian goulash

213 HUNGARIAN GOULASH

75g/3oz dripping or butter · ½kg/1lb lean beef · ½kg/1lb veal
½kg/1lb onions · 2 tomatoes, quartered · 1 teaspoon salt
2 teaspoons paprika pepper · 2 tablespoons tomato purée
½kg/1lb potatoes · 1 green pepper, sliced
142ml/¼pint single or soured cream

Heat the fat in a pan. Cut meat into neat pieces. Slice the onion thinly. Fry meat and onion until pale golden, add tomatoes, seasonings and tomato purée and simmer gently for 30 minutes. Add sliced potatoes and green pepper, then continue cooking gently for another 1–1½ hours until meat and potatoes are very tender. Just before serving stir in the cream.

214 BEEF WITH GREEN VEGETABLES

200g/8oz lean beef · 2 teaspoons cornflour
4 spring onions or shallots · 1 small cucumber
1 small green pepper · 25g/1oz blanched almonds, halved
2 tablespoons oil for frying · 142ml/¼pint stock
1 dessertspoon soy sauce

Cut the beef in small pieces and coat well with the cornflour. Cut 2 of the onions in small pieces, slice most of the cucumber thinly (do not peel). Remove all seeds from the pepper and cut it in thin strips. Sauté the meat, vegetables and almonds in the oil for about 10 minutes or until the meat is well browned. Put in a casserole. Add the stock to the frying pan, simmer gently for 1 minute, and then pour over the meat, vegetables and almonds in the casserole. Stir in the soy sauce, cover and cook in a moderate oven, 350°F, 180°C, Gas Mark 4, until the meat is tender. Garnish with remaining cucumber, cubed and 'flowers' of onion.

HOT-POTS

215

This is not only a very excellent way of serving stewing meat, but a labour saving one too, as the meat and all the vegetables, including the potatoes, can be cooked and served in the same dish.

Toss meat and any vegetables – carrots, sliced onions, crushed garlic, sliced peppers etc. in a little fat then season well. Put a layer of the meat and vegetable mixture, then a layer of un-cooked sliced potatoes in a casserole, continue like this, seasoning each layer of potatoes well – and end with a layer of potatoes. Pour over a small amount of stock. Put a little fat on top of the potatoes. Cover with the casserole lid or foil and cook slowly for about 2½ hours at 300–325°F, 150–170°C, Gas Mark 2–3. Remove the lid for the last 10 minutes, so that the top layer of potatoes can become crisp and brown. Serve with a green salad or green vegetables.

All stewing pieces of beef, veal, pork or mutton and lamb are suitable. With the fatter meats, i.e. pork and mutton, it is a good idea to trim the surplus fat from the meat at the beginning and use this fat for frying lean meat and vegetables.

Hot-pot

Blanquette of veal

Steak Elizabetta with mustard dumplings

216 BLANQUETTE OF VEAL

15g/½oz *margarine*
½kg/1lb *lean stewing veal, cut into 2½-cm (1-inch) cubes*
426ml/¾pint *water · 1 packet thick onion soup mix*
¼ *teaspoon lemon juice · 2 level teaspoons cornflour*
4 *tablespoons milk · seasoning*
few peas, button mushrooms and slices of lemon to garnish

Melt the fat and lightly fry the veal for a few minutes, add the water, then the soup mix; bring to the boil stirring all the time. Add the lemon juice and cover the pan. Simmer gently for approximately 2 hours, stirring occasionally. Blend the cornflour with the milk and add to the stew; bring to the boil and simmer for a further 5 minutes. Add seasoning to taste and serve the stew in a shallow casserole and garnish with a few cooked peas, button mushrooms and slices of lemon.

217 STEAK ELIZABETTA
with mustard dumplings

1kg/2lb *chuck steak or shin beef, cut into small pieces*
1 *heaped tablespoon flour · ½ teaspoon salt · ¼ teaspoon pepper*
½ *teaspoon dry mustard · 25g/1oz dripping or margarine*
2 *medium-sized onions, peeled and sliced*
3 *medium-sized carrots, sliced · 426ml/¾pint stock or water*
1 *tablespoon vinegar*

Coat the meat in the flour, seasoned with salt, pepper and mustard. Heat the fat in a pan, lightly brown the onions and then the meat. Add the carrots, stir in the water and vinegar and bring to the boil. Turn into a casserole, cover and cook in a very moderate oven, 325°F, 170°C, Gas Mark 3, for 1½–2 hours. 30 minutes before steak is ready place dumplings (Recipe No. 218) on top of meat, cover tightly and cook for a further 30 minutes.
Makes 6 servings.

Variations to the casserole of beef

Add 100g (4 oz) ox kidney or 200g (8 oz) sliced liver . . . . add 100–200g (4–8 oz) mushrooms . . . . omit carrots and add 12 or more oysters in last 10 minutes of cooking . . . . omit onions and add 6 or more shallots each stuck with a clove . . . . add a chopped green pepper . . . . or 6 pickled walnuts . . . . substitute red wine for half or more of the water . . . . or substitute tomato juice for part or all of the water.

218 MUSTARD DUMPLINGS

100g/4oz *self-raising flour · ½ teaspoon salt*
½ *teaspoon dry mustard · 50g/2oz shredded suet or*
25g/1oz *margarine*

Sift together flour, salt and mustard. Add suet or rub in margarine. Mix to a dry dough with 3–4 tablespoons cold water and shape into small balls.
Makes 6 servings.

219 TOMATO STEAK ROLLS

4 *sticks celery*
½kg/1lb *top rump steak, thinly sliced into 8 slices by butcher*
seasoned flour · 25g/1oz dripping or fat
250g/10oz *can tomato or tomato rice soup*
4 *tablespoons cold water*

Cut celery into pieces the same width as the meat slices. Put into boiling salted water. Cook for 3 minutes only, drain and roll each slice of meat round 2 celery sticks and tie with fine string or cotton. Toss the steak rolls in seasoned flour and fry in the heated dripping until browned. Place in a casserole. Blend the soup and water together and pour into the casserole dish. Cover and cook in a very moderate oven, 325°F, 170°C, Gas Mark 3, for about 1¾ hours. Remove string from rolls; arrange on a serving dish and pour over the sauce.

Tomato steak rolls

Veal birds

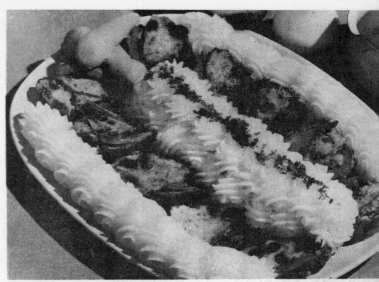

Hearts with walnut stuffing

220   VEAL BIRDS

¾kg/1½lb *veal, cut thinly and pounded · made mustard to taste*
seasoned flour · fat for frying
142ml/¼pint *stock or tomato juice · stuffed olives to garnish*

Orange stuffing

6 tablespoons white breadcrumbs
½ level teaspoon mixed herbs · grated rind 1 small orange
seasoning · 1 egg yolk to bind

Divide the veal into 8 even-sized pieces. Mince any trimmings and add to the stuffing ingredients and bind together with a little beaten egg. Lightly spread the veal with mustard; spread with stuffing, roll up and secure with a wooden cocktail stick or string. Coat with seasoned flour and fry in heated fat until golden brown, then either lower the heat and cook very slowly for 10 minutes turning round several times or transfer to a dish and cook for 25 minutes in a moderate oven. When cooked remove the cocktail sticks or string. Arrange the rolls on a serving dish. Pour the stock and tomato juice into the pan, and, scraping the bottom of the pan, bring to the boil. Spoon over the veal. Garnish the veal with stuffed olives.
For a special occasion add a garnish of pickled walnuts on squares of fried bread and grilled button mushrooms.

221   HEARTS WITH WALNUT STUFFING

4 lamb's hearts · walnut stuffing (Recipe No. 222)
stock · 4 large onions, sliced
creamed potatoes (Recipe No. 303) · chopped parsley
and a few cooked carrots to garnish

Prepare the hearts by cutting away tough skin, etc. Make up the stuffing. Stuff the hearts and skewer or tie the ends to prevent the stuffing escaping. Simmer gently for about 1½ hours in a little well seasoned stock with the onions. Slice the hearts and place on a serving dish. Pipe the potato down the centre and along the edge of the dish. Serve at once, garnished with chopped parsley and a few cooked carrots.

222   WALNUT STUFFING

50g/2oz *fresh breadcrumbs* · 50g/2oz *walnuts, chopped*
50g/2oz *fat bacon, chopped · salt and pepper · pinch mace*
142ml/¼pint *stock or water* · 25g/1oz *butter or margarine*
4 large onions, chopped · egg to bind

Put all the ingredients into a small basin and add sufficient egg to bind.

Salamagundi with pasta shapes

223   SALAMAGUNDI WITH PASTA SHAPES

1 medium-sized onion · few cloves, optional
¾kg/1½lb *neck of lamb* · 100g/4oz *lamb's liver* · 25g/1oz *flour*
1 teaspoon dry mustard · salt and pepper
25g/1oz *lard or dripping · 1 large cooking apple*
100g/4oz *lean bacon · few mushrooms, optional*
generous ½litre/1pint *stock or water · 1 small can butter beans*
6 pickled onions · 200g/8oz *pasta shapes*

Stick onion with a few cloves, if used. Cut the neck of lamb into neat pieces. Toss with the sliced liver in the flour and mustard and season with salt and pepper. Lightly fry meat and sliced onion in the fat. Add sliced apple, chopped bacon, mushrooms if used and water. Turn into a casserole. Cook in a very moderate oven, 325°F, 170°C, Gas Mark 3, for about 1½ hours. Add the beans and pickled onions and return to oven to heat thoroughly. Serve with pasta shapes, cooked in boiling salted water for 12 minutes, then drained.

Casserole of bacon

224 CASSEROLE OF BACON

Choose one of the cuts of bacon suggested in the table (Recipe No. 163). Soak for some hours or overnight in cold water. Put into a casserole with various vegetables, a bay leaf and water, or use cider for an excellent flavour. Cover the casserole with foil or a lid and cook gently allowing 20–25 minutes per ½kg (1 lb) in a moderately hot oven, 375–400°F, 190°C, Gas Mark 5, or 35–40 minutes per ½kg (1 lb) in a very moderate oven, 325–350°F, 150°C, Gas Mark 2–3. Apples, prunes, raisins are some of the more unusual ingredients that can be put into the casserole, as well as vegetables, or instead of them.

Do not thicken the liquid before cooking, but season well with dry mustard.

225 RAGOUT OF VEAL

50g/2oz dripping or fat · ½kg/1lb stewing veal
2 onions, sliced
50g/2oz mushrooms or 2 red or green peppers, sliced
375g/15oz can cream of tomato soup
1 tablespoon paprika pepper, optional
4 tablespoons water · seasoning · parsley to garnish

Heat the fat in a pan and fry the diced veal, sliced onions and mushrooms or peppers for a few minutes. Cover with the tomato soup and water or water blended with paprika. Add seasoning to taste, put the lid on the pan and simmer gently for approximately 1 hour. Garnish with parsley.

Ragoût of veal

Liver with orange slices

227 ## LIVER WITH ORANGE SLICES

$\frac{1}{2}$kg/1lb *lamb's liver* · 1 *tablespoon flour*
pinch salt, pepper, cayenne pepper and dry mustard
25g/1oz *fat* · *spicy sauce (Recipe No. 228)*
creamed potatoes (Recipe No. 303)
fresh orange slices and parsley to garnish

Trim the liver and cut into 4 slices. Dip in flour seasoned with salt, pepper, etc. Heat the fat and fry the liver for a few minutes on each side. Arrange the liver on a serving dish and keep warm. Make the sauce and pour over the liver slices. Pipe a border of creamed potatoes round the edge of the dish. Garnish with fresh orange slices and parsley.

226 ## STEAK AND MACARONI CASSEROLE

300g/12oz *stewing steak* · 1 *onion* · 1 *stick celery*
3 *mushrooms* · 1$\frac{1}{2}$ *tablespoons dripping* · 40g/1$\frac{1}{2}$oz *flour*
$\frac{3}{4}$litre/1$\frac{1}{2}$pints *stock or water* · *seasoning*
75g/3oz *quick-cooking macaroni*
about 50g/2oz *canned or frozen peas*

Cut meat into neat pieces. Peel and chop onion. Prepare celery and mushrooms and cut into fairly large pieces. Melt dripping in a pan and fry onions and meat gently. Remove meat and onion from fat, add flour and cook roux until lightly browned. Add stock gradually and bring to the boil, stir until smooth. Put in meat, onions, celery, mushrooms and seasoning. Cover pan and simmer gently for 2–2$\frac{1}{2}$ hours. 7–10 minutes before serving add the uncooked macaroni. Boil fairly quickly to cook macaroni; add peas a few minutes before serving.

228 ## SPICY SAUCE

25g/1oz *butter* · 1 *onion, peeled and chopped*
2 *cloves garlic, crushed* · 4 *tablespoons stock or water*
2 *tablespoons red wine* · $\frac{1}{4}$ *teaspoon Tabasco sauce*
pinch soft brown sugar · *seasoning*

Heat the butter and fry the onion and garlic until soft. Add the stock and wine. Simmer until it has reduced a little, then add the Tabasco sauce, sugar and seasoning.

229 DEVILLED PORK CHOPS

4 pork chops · 25g/1oz dripping or margarine
2 small onions, peeled and chopped · few mushrooms
1 small green pepper · 1 rounded tablespoon flour
2 teaspoons dry mustard · 284ml/½pint stock or water
2 teaspoons Worcestershire sauce · 1 tablespoon tomato ketchup
2–3 cloves · salt to taste · chopped parsley to garnish

Trim the chops and lightly brown them in hot fat in a heavy pan. Remove to a casserole. Fry the onion in the fat until golden. Add chopped mushrooms and pepper. Stir in flour and mustard; cook, stirring, until lightly browned and remove from heat. Gradually add the stock, Worcestershire sauce, tomato ketchup, cloves and salt to taste. Stirring, bring to the boil and pour into the casserole. Cover and cook in a very moderate oven, 325°F, 170°C, Gas Mark 3, for 45 minutes. Serve, garnished with parsley, from casserole dish. Devilled celery (Recipe No. 230) goes well with this dish.

Devilled pork chops

230 DEVILLED CELERY

2 teaspoons made mustard · 25g/1oz butter
½kg/1lb cooked celery

Blend mustard with butter and toss hot celery in this.

231 HARICOT MUTTON
(Quick recipe)

½kg/1lb scrag end of mutton, minced
25g/1oz dripping or cooking fat · 375g/15oz can baked beans
125g/5oz can condensed tomato soup · 1 clove garlic
1 green pepper · 1 teaspoon mixed herbs · salt and pepper

Fry the meat in the heated fat until lightly brown. Mix together the contents of the cans, and the garlic and the finely chopped green pepper, the herbs and the seasoning. Finally add the meat, place in a casserole, cover and cook in a slow oven, 300°F, 150°C, Gas Mark 2, for 1–1¼ hours.

Haricot mutton

232 PORK OLIVES

½kg/1lb lean pork · 200g/8oz pork sausage meat
seasoned flour · 25g/1oz butter · 1 small onion, chopped
284ml/½pint stock or red wine sauce (Recipe No. 233)
salt and pepper · creamed potatoes (Recipe No. 303)

Trim all fat off the meat and cut into oblongs 10-cm (4-inches) long and 5-cm (2-inches) wide. Flatten the slices by beating with a wooden spoon, spread with sausage meat, roll up and secure with a small skewer. Roll in seasoned flour and fry in melted butter until golden brown, then add the chopped onion. Put the pork olives, onion and stock or red wine sauce into a casserole dish. Season. Cover and cook in a very moderate oven, 325°F, 170°C, Gas Mark 3, for about 1½ hours. Remove the skewers; place the pork olives and cooking liquor in a serving dish. Pipe a border of hot creamed potatoes round the edge of the dish.

233 RED WINE SAUCE

1 onion, finely chopped · 50g/2oz butter
1 teaspoon Worcestershire sauce · 284ml/½pint red wine
salt and paprika pepper

Fry the chopped onion in butter until golden brown and soft, add the other ingredients, simmer for 10 minutes.

Pork olives

Irish hot-pot

Bacon with lentils

234 IRISH HOT-POT

about 1¼kg/2½lb *middle neck of mutton*
about 1¼kg/2½lb *potatoes* · 1 *large onion* · 2 *carrots, sliced*
plenty of black pepper, salt and chopped parsley
generous ½litre/1pint water · *tomato ketchup, optional*

Trim meat and cut into pieces, rejecting excessive fat. Peel and slice potatoes. Peel and slice onion. Line a casserole with sliced potatoes, then cover with a layer of meat (dusted with pepper and salt), a sprinkling of chopped parsley, sliced onions and carrots. Fill up dish with further layers of potatoes and meat etc., finishing with a layer of potatoes, neatly overlapping. Boil water and add carefully to casserole. For additional flavouring add 2 tablespoons tomato ketchup to water when boiling. Cover and place in a very moderate oven, 325°F, 170°C, Gas Mark 3, until contents begin to simmer. Lower heat to 300°F, 150°C, Gas Mark 2, and cook gently for about 1½ hours. Cook, uncovered, for the last 15 minutes to brown the potatoes.

235 BACON WITH LENTILS
(A famous French luncheon dish)

about ¾kg/1½lb *collar of bacon* · 50g/2oz *dripping*
12 *small onions* · *black pepper* · ½kg/1lb *brown lentils*
1 *stick celery* · 2 *carrots* · *fresh herbs* · 2–3 *cloves garlic*
25g/1oz *butter* · *parsley to garnish*

For this recipe you require a lean cut of bacon, but with plenty of fat on the edge to counteract the dryness of lentils. Prime collar bacon is excellent and very good value. Place bacon in a saucepan, cover with cold water, bring slowly to boiling point, then strain and rinse in cold water. Melt a little dripping in a deep casserole. Dry the bacon and put it in the casserole dish with the small onions and black pepper. When the onions begin to brown, add lentils, celery, carrots, cut lengthways, a bunch of fresh herbs (tied), and crushed cloves of garlic. Cover with cold water, and cook very slowly with the lid on for about 2 hours. Test lentils to see if they are cooked. Take out bacon, carrots and herbs, strain the lentils. Stir in the butter with the lentils, arrange them round a serving dish with more onions if liked; slice the bacon, and arrange the slices in the middle of the dish. Garnish with parsley.
Makes 6 servings.

Lamb goulash

236 LAMB GOULASH

¾kg/1½lb *boned shoulder of lamb, cut into cubes*
40g/1½oz *dripping* · 1 *packet (½litre/1pint size) onion soup*
1 *level dessertspoon paprika pepper*
284ml/½pint *dry red wine* · 426ml/¾pint *water*
2–3 *sticks celery, cut into strips*
1 *red pepper, seeded and sliced*
142ml/¼pint *soured cream, or fresh cream soured with*
lemon juice · *salt and pepper* · *cooked long grain rice*
little chopped green pepper · *parsley to garnish*

Brown the lamb quickly in the dripping in a large saucepan. Remove from the heat, stir in the soup mix, paprika, wine and water and add the celery and red pepper. Bring to the boil, stirring continuously, cover and simmer about 1 hour or until tender. Remove from the heat, stir in the cream, reheat but do not boil. Adjust seasoning. Arrange cooked rice mixed with a little chopped green pepper, in a border on a heated serving dish. Spoon the goulash in the centre. Garnish with parsley.
Makes 5–6 servings.

Corned beef loaf

QUICKLY PREPARED MEAT DISHES

237   CORNED BEEF LOAF

25g/1oz dripping or fat · 1 onion · 300g/12oz can corned beef
100g/4oz breadcrumbs · pinch sage · seasoning · 1 egg
200g/8oz can red cherries · lettuce to garnish

Heat the dripping and fry the chopped onion. Mix with flaked corned beef, breadcrumbs, sage, seasoning, egg and enough syrup from the cherries to give sticky consistency. Grease a loaf tin and arrange the drained cherries in the bottom. Put in the corned beef mixture and cover with greased paper. Cook for 45 minutes in a moderately hot oven, 375°F, 190°C, Gas Mark 5. Turn out and serve on a bed of lettuce.

CORNED BEEF HASH

300g/12oz can corned beef · 200g/8oz mashed potatoes
1 egg · seasoning · 25g/1oz dripping or fat for frying
sliced beetroot and parsley to garnish

Flake the corned beef and mix with the potatoes and beaten egg. Season well. Heat the dripping in a pan and put in the mixture. Spread this evenly and allow to cook slowly until the underside is golden brown and the mixture really hot. Fold like an omelette and turn on to a hot dish. Serve garnished with beetroot and parsley.

239 STUFFED BAKED MARROW

375g/15oz can stewed steak and onions* · 50g/2oz breadcrumbs
good pinch sage · seasoning · 1 medium-sized marrow
50g/2oz dripping or fat

*Or use 300g (12 oz) cooked minced beef and 2 onions, chopped and fried

Place the stewed steak and onions in a basin. Add the breadcrumbs, sage and a little seasoning. Cut the end off the marrow and peel unless very young; scoop out seeds. Fill the marrow with the meat mixture, replace the cut end in position, securing this with a skewer. Heat the fat in a meat tin and turn marrow round in this. Then cook for 1 hour in a moderately hot oven, 400°F, 200°C, Gas Mark 6. Cut into slices to serve and garnish with baked tomatoes, peas and creamed potatoes.

240 MOUSSAKA

300g/12oz cooked potatoes, sliced
½kg/1lb cooked neck or shoulder of lamb, minced
4 tomatoes, skinned and sliced · little chopped parsley
284ml/½pint white sauce (Recipe No. 663)
100g/4oz cheese, grated · watercress to garnish

Arrange half the potatoes in layers in greased ovenproof dish. Put the meat, sliced tomatoes and parsley on top of the potatoes. Cover with remaining potatoes. Make the white sauce and stir in most of the cheese and pour over potatoes. Sprinkle with remaining cheese. Cook for 25 minutes in a moderately hot oven, 400°F, 200°C, Gas Mark 6. Garnish with watercress.

241 SAVOURY SHEPHERD'S PIE

2 375g/15oz cans minced steak · 1 tablespoon Angostura bitters
seasoning · ½kg/1lb freshly cooked potatoes
little melted margarine

Place the minced beef in an ovenproof dish. Mix in Angostura and seasoning. Mash the potatoes and smooth over the top of the meat. Mark with a fork, brush with a little melted margarine and cook in a moderate oven, 375°F, 190°C, Gas Mark 5, for 30–35 minutes.
Makes 5–6 servings.

Moussaka

Savoury shepherd's pie

TOMATO MINCE

25g/1oz lard · 1 medium-sized onion, finely chopped
½kg/1lb minced beef · seasoning, including cayenne pepper
250g/10oz can condensed tomato soup · 6 tablespoons water
1 rounded tablespoon oatmeal
creamed potatoes (Recipe No. 303)

Melt the lard and fry the onion until tender. Add the minced beef, seasoning, soup, water and oatmeal. Bring slowly to the boil, stir well, cover and simmer for 30–40 minutes. Spoon into a serving dish and pipe the creamed potatoes round the edge.

Tomato mince

243 ECONOMICAL SPANISH SAUCE

25g/1oz dripping or fat · 1 onion, sliced · 25g/1oz flour
generous ½litre/1pint stock or water · 1 carrot, sliced
50g/2oz mushroom stalks
pinch ground mace, celery salt and pepper
1 tablespoon tomato ketchup

Melt the dripping and fry the onion slowly to a golden brown, add the flour and cook until lightly browned, stirring occasionally. Pour in the stock and bring to the boil stirring, add the carrot, mushroom stalks and seasoning; cover and simmer for 30–40 minutes, stirring occasionally. Strain the sauce, stir in the tomato ketchup and reheat. Serve with liver loaf (Recipe No. 247).

Beef scone pie.

Lamb in mint jelly

244 BEEF SCONE PIE

1 onion, finely chopped · 25g/1oz lard · ¾kg/1½lb minced beef
250g/10oz can condensed oxtail soup · seasoning
150g/6oz self-raising flour · pinch salt
50g/2oz margarine · milk

Fry the onion in the heated lard until tender. Add the minced beef and stirring, cook until browned. Mix in the soup and seasoning and simmer gently for 15 minutes. Meanwhile sieve the flour and salt into a mixing bowl. Rub in the fat and mix to a fairly soft dough with milk. Roll out on a floured board and cut into rounds. Spoon the mixture into a deep casserole and place the scone rounds on top and cook in a hot oven, 425°F, 220°C, Gas Mark 7, for 20–25 minutes until scones are golden brown. Makes 6 servings.

Variation
Instead of using canned oxtail soup try this with economical Spanish sauce (Recipe No. 243).

245 LAMB IN MINT JELLY

1 carrot · 1 onion · bunch fresh mint
generous ½litre/1pint stock · 1 level teaspoon salt
15g/½oz powdered gelatine · 200g/8oz cold cooked lamb, cubed
onion rings and parsley to garnish

Simmer carrot, onion and mint together in the stock for approximately 30 minutes. Strain and add salt. Dissolve the gelatine in 2 tablespoons of warm water and add to the stock and allow to cool. As the jelly begins to set add the diced meat and pour into a loaf tin and allow to set. Turn out and garnish with onion rings and parsley. Serve with a salad.

246 · CHEESE SHEPHERD'S PIE

1 medium-sized onion, chopped · 25g/1oz fat
250g/10oz cold cooked meat, minced
2 level tablespoons tomato ketchup
3 tablespoons water or stock · seasoning
½kg/1lb cooked mashed potato
200g/8oz Cheddar cheese, grated · 3–4 tablespoons milk
parsley to garnish

Fry the onion in fat until cooked but not brown. Mix onion, meat, tomato ketchup, water and seasoning together. Divide between four individual dishes. Make topping by mixing potato and cheese together; add milk. Divide potato mixture and spread over meat mixture, mark with a fork into swirls. Place dishes on a baking sheet, and bake in a moderate oven, 375°F, 190°C, Gas Mark 5, for 30 minutes. Garnish with parsley.

Cheese shepherd's pie

247 LIVER LOAF

good ½kg/1¼lb calves or pig's liver
100g/4oz fat salt pork or bacon · 3–4 anchovy fillets
1 level teaspoon salt · ¼ teaspoon black pepper
1 tablespoon grated onion · 1 clove garlic, crushed
50g/2oz stale breadcrumbs · 1 egg and extra yolk or 2 small eggs
8–10 rashers thinly cut streaky bacon
bay leaf and salad vegetables to garnish

Slice liver and put through mincer with pork and anchovies. Add seasoning, grated onion and crushed garlic. Put through mincer twice. Blend with breadcrumbs (soaked with eggs). Line a buttered loaf tin or oblong mould with bacon rashers and pack in mixture, spreading evenly. Cover with extra rashers of streaky bacon. Stand container in pan half filled with hot water. Cook in moderate oven, 325–350°F, 170°C, Gas Mark 3, for about 1½ hours. Place greaseproof paper over plate and weight down and leave until cool. Turn out and serve garnished with a bay leaf and salad vegetables.
This loaf can also be served as an hors d'oeuvre before the main course of a meal.

Liver loaf

248 BACON LOAF

300g/12oz bacon · 1 small can pineapple pieces
100g/4oz fine breadcrumbs · salt and pepper · pinch mixed herbs
1 large egg · tomato halves and parsley to garnish

Mince or chop both the bacon and well drained pineapple. Mix with breadcrumbs, seasoning, herbs, and egg and 1 tablespoon pineapple syrup from can. Blend well and put into a well greased loaf tin. Cover with greased paper and cook for about 1¼ hours in the centre of a moderate oven, 350°F, 180°C, Gas Mark 4. Turn out carefully and garnish with tomato halves and parsley. If liked, serve with quick asparagus sauce (Recipe No. 249).

Bacon loaf

249 QUICK ASPARAGUS SAUCE

250g/10oz can asparagus soup
2 tablespoons mayonnaise (Recipe No. 408)

Heat asparagus soup, remove from the heat and stir in mayonnaise.

POULTRY & GAME

Poultry when young and tender should not be over-cooked, as it is spoiled in flavour and difficult to carve. Allow plenty of time for frozen poultry to defrost before cooking. Older poultry and game is better cooked slowly unless you are using a pressure cooker.

250	Type	How to cook	Accompaniments
CHICKEN		Weigh with stuffing, allow 15 minutes per ½kg (1 lb) and 15 minutes over. Roast young fowls in hot oven for 15 minutes, lower heat to moderately hot for remainder of time	Veal stuffing (Recipe No. 254), bread sauce (Recipe No. 255), sausages and bacon rolls, green salad, thickened gravy
		Older birds should be boiled or steamed, allowing 30 minutes per ½kg (1 lb)	Coat with white sauce (Recipe No. 663) and serve with creamed potatoes
		Spring chickens can be jointed and fried or grilled. For small broilers see Recipe No. 261	Grilled or fried tomatoes, mushrooms, salads, tartare sauce (Recipe No. 680)
DUCK AND GOOSE		Roasted – 15 minutes per ½kg (1 lb) and 15 minutes over. Start in a hot oven then reduce to moderate	Sage and onion stuffing (Recipe No. 280), apple sauce, thick brown gravy or orange sauce with port wine (Recipe No. 252), orange salad
GROUSE		Temperatures and timing as chicken. Cover well and put knob butter inside. Excellent in pie (Recipe No. 281)	Bread sauce (Recipe No. 255), or redcurrant jelly, fried breadcrumbs, game chips and a green salad
GUINEA FOWL		As for chicken or grouse	As for chicken or grouse
HARE		Cook in a casserole or if young, roast as duck	Mixed vegetables, forcemeat balls, red-currant jelly
PIGEON		If very young roast for about 25–35 minutes in hot oven. Cover with greased paper or foil. Excellent in raised pie or braised (Recipe No. 282)	As for chicken or grouse
PARTRIDGE		As for grouse	As for grouse
PHEASANT		Cover with fat bacon. Roast for 45–60 minutes. Baste well during cooking	Bread sauce (Recipe No. 255), clear gravy with squeeze of lemon juice in it, fried bread-crumbs, game chips (Recipe No. 302), chestnuts
RABBIT		Braised or in fricassée. Roasted allow 20 minutes per ½kg (1 lb) and 20 minutes over, cover well to prevent becoming dry	Sage and onion stuffing (Recipe No. 280), apple sauce
TURKEY		Weigh with stuffing, allow *minimum* 15 minutes per ½kg (1 lb) and 15 minutes over up to a total weight of 5½kg (12 lb). For every ½kg (1 lb) over this weight allow 12 minutes only. Roast in a hot oven for first hour then lower heat to moderately hot. See Recipe No. 262	Veal stuffing, bread sauce (Recipe No. 255), sausages, salads, thickened gravy
VENISON		As veal (Recipe No. 158)	As veal

251   DUCK WITH ORANGE

(Illustrated in colour on the opposite page)

Roast duck as described in Recipe No. 250 but prick skin after first 30 minutes so that the fat can run out and give a crisp outside. If wished brush with little melted honey to aid crispness. Garnish with slices of orange and a sprig of watercress and serve with orange sauce (Recipe No. 252).

252   ORANGE SAUCE WITH PORT WINE

Peel 2 oranges, remove white pith and cut peel into very narrow ribbons. Simmer in a little water until tender. Make brown sauce (Recipe No. 685) with stock from giblets. Add a little port wine, the orange strips and some of the orange stock. If liked, add a pinch sugar.

Duck with orange (Recipe No. 251)

253   ROAST CHICKEN

Cover breast of chicken with fat bacon, butter or cooking fat. If wished turn the bird during cooking so that the breast is downwards and so is automatically 'basted' by fat dripping from legs. Stuffing should be put in at the neck end of the bird. Use a veal stuffing (Recipe No. 254) or a forcemeat stuffing (Recipe No. 257). Push this under the flap of skin and secure with a skewer if wished.

· 254   VEAL STUFFING

100g/4oz *breadcrumbs* · 1 *egg*
50g/2oz *shredded suet or melted margarine*
2–3 *teaspoons chopped parsley* · ½ *teaspoon mixed herbs*
grated rind and juice ½ *lemon*

Mix all the ingredients thoroughly together. The cooked meat from the giblets can be chopped and added to make a rich 'meaty' stuffing if liked.

255   BREAD SAUCE

1 *small onion* · 2–3 *cloves, optional* · 284ml/½pint *milk*
50g/2oz *breadcrumbs* · 25–50g/1–2oz *margarine*
salt, pepper

Peel the onion and if using cloves stick these firmly into the onion. Put this into the milk together with the other ingredients. Slowly bring the milk to the boil. Remove from the heat and stand in a warm place for as long as possible. Just before the meal is ready, remove the onion, heat the sauce gently, beating with a wooden spoon. Serve in a sauce boat.

256   BRAISED CHICKEN

generous ½litre/1pint *water* · 1 *fowl or roasting chicken*
forcemeat stuffing (Recipe No. 257) or 200g/8oz *sausage meat*
75g/3oz *butter* · about 12 *small onions* · 40g/1½oz *flour*
seasoning · about 12 *button mushrooms*
4 *tablespoons single cream*

Simmer giblets in water to obtain generous ½litre (1 pint) stock. Stuff chicken with forcemeat or sausage meat. Brown the chicken in the butter until golden brown. Lift out, and brown the onions. Lift out onions and stir flour into fat, cooking until golden brown, then gradually add the stock. Bring to the boil and cook for a few minutes. If using a young roasting chicken the onions can be put into casserole with this – with a boiling fowl it is advisable to add them later in the cooking period. Cover chicken with sauce, season, put lid on casserole and allow approximately 20 minutes per ½kg (1 lb) and 20 minutes over in a moderate oven, 350–375°F, 180°C, Gas Mark 4. With an older boiling fowl allow 30 minutes per ½kg (1 lb) and 30 minutes over in a very moderate oven, 325–350°F, 170°C, Gas Mark 3. Add onions 1 hour before serving and add mushrooms 30 minutes before serving. Just before serving, stir in the single cream.

257   FORCEMEAT STUFFING

200g/8oz *sausage meat* · *chopped parsley* · 1 *egg*
pinch mixed herbs

Mix all ingredients thoroughly. If liked the finely chopped cooked giblets of the poultry can be added.

258   CELERY AND RAISIN FORCEMEAT

Chop 3–4 sticks celery finely. Add to the ingredients in the forcemeat stuffing above together with 3 tablespoons seedless raisins. This stuffing is excellent with chicken or veal.

259   GRILLED CHICKEN

1 *small broiler chicken* · 4 *tablespoons cooking oil*
1 *tablespoon lemon juice* · *salt and pepper*
grilled mushrooms, bacon rolls and sprigs of watercress to garnish

Cut the chicken into four joints – the two legs and two joints of breast and wing. Put into the grill pan. Mix the oil, lemon juice and seasoning together. Pour over the chicken and leave to stand for 1–2 hours, turning occasionally. Cook under a medium hot grill for about 20 minutes, turning and basting with the oil mixture. Serve with the juices from the grill pan. Garnish with grilled mushrooms, bacon rolls and sprigs of watercress.

Grilled chicken

Braised chicken

260   TO CARVE A CHICKEN

A good-sized chicken can be carved into 6–8 portions; remove the leg, and divide in two and cut the breast and wings into 2 or 4 joints. A very small spring chicken is divided in halves or 4 joints, but a very large chicken can be carved like a turkey (Recipe No. 260).

261   TO CARVE A GOOSE

Carve as turkey – giving slices of breast and leg meat.

262   ROAST TURKEY

This is stuffed and roasted like a chicken; it is quite a good idea to have two kinds of stuffing, putting them at either end of bird. Keep breast well covered in fat, baste during cooking with hot fat. If wished wrap bird entirely in foil and allow at least 20 minutes extra cooking time. If using foil remove this for last 20–30 minutes of cooking time to brown skin. Use veal or forcemeat stuffings (Recipe Nos. 254, 257) or for a change try rolled oat or chestnut stuffings (Recipe Nos. 265, 264). Serve with bread sauce (Recipe No. 255) or cranberry sauce (Recipe No. 263) and surround with cooked sausages and bacon rolls. Modern very broad breasted turkeys may need longer cooking than in Recipe No. 250 (allow 20 minutes per ½kg (1 lb). If liked, duchesse potatoes (Recipe No. 300) can be served in place of roast potatoes. Recipe No. 268 gives another method of roasting turkey or other poultry.

263   CRANBERRY SAUCE

200–300g/8–12oz *cranberries* · 142ml/¼pint *water*
50–75g/2–3oz *sugar* · *knob butter*

Simmer the cranberries in the water. Rub through a sieve, add sugar to taste and a little knob of butter. For an unsieved sauce, make a syrup of water and sugar. Add the cranberries; cook until a thick mixture, add butter.

264   CHESTNUT STUFFING

½kg/1lb *chestnuts*
200g/8oz *chopped cooked ham, optional* · *little milk*
50g/2oz *breadcrumbs* · 50g/2oz *butter*

Split the chestnuts and boil for about 10 minutes in water. Remove the skins, and simmer the nuts in stock until very tender. Rub through a sieve and add to the other ingredients. This stuffing can be varied by adding chopped onion, mixed herbs or parsley, but do not use strong flavours to obscure the delicious chestnut taste.

265   OAT STUFFING

100g/4oz *breadcrumbs* · 100g/4oz *margarine*
100g/4oz *quick-cooking rolled oats* · *seasoning*
4 *teaspoons mixed herbs* · 8 *tablespoons stock or water*

Fry breadcrumbs in margarine until golden brown. Add oats, seasoning and herbs. Moisten with stock or water.

266   TO CARVE A TURKEY

Remove leg on to side of dish or separate dish. Cut long thin slices of breast meat and slices off leg. Serve each portion with both light (breast) and dark (leg) meat.

267   TO CARVE A DUCK

Cut into 4 joints – legs are 1 joint each and the breast and wing another.

Roast turkey

Turkey pilaff

268   VERY SLOW ROASTING POULTRY INCLUDING TURKEY

Allow 1¼ hours for first ½kg (1lb) and then 25 minutes over up to 3kg (7lb) and 20 minutes to a ½kg (1lb) after that. A 2½kg (5lb) bird takes 2 hours 55 minutes, but a 5kg (10lb) bird takes 4 hours 45 minutes. Roast in a very slow oven. To brown bird raise the temperature of oven for the last 25 minutes. This is an excellent way of cooking if in doubt as to tenderness of bird.

269   TURKEY PILAFF
(An ideal way to use up Christmas turkey)

50g/2oz *butter* · 1 *large onion, finely chopped*
200g/8oz *long grain rice* · *generous* ½litre/1pint *stock or water*
salt and pepper · 150g/6oz *cold cooked turkey, chopped**
50g/2oz *seedless raisins* · ½kg/1lb *pork sausages*
little fat for frying · *grilled mushrooms and*
chopped parsley to garnish

**Left-over goose, duck or chicken can be used in same way*

Melt 25g (1 oz) butter and gently fry the onion until soft but not browned. Add rice, stir and fry for several minutes, add stock and seasoning, bring to the boil then cover and cook gently for about 15 minutes; by this time the rice should be just cooked and all the liquid absorbed. Add the turkey, raisins and the remaining butter, stir well and keep hot. While the pilaff is cooking, prick the sausages and fry slowly in a little hot fat until cooked, about 15 minutes. Pile the pilaff in the centre of a hot dish, arrange the sausages around it and garnish with grilled mushrooms and chopped parsley. If preferred garnish with fried chopped almonds.

Paella

270   PAELLA

4 pieces cooked or raw chicken* · 1 onion · 1 clove garlic
2 tablespoons olive oil
generous litre/2pints water · 2 medium-sized tomatoes
100g/4oz long grain rice · 1 chicken stock cube
little saffron, if possible · 1 small cooked lobster or can lobster
4 Dublin Bay prawns or 8–10 large prawns · 6–8 mussels
few canned pimentos or red peppers · 200g/8oz frozen peas
asparagus spears, optional and slices of lemon to garnish

*If using raw, chicken should be jointed young frying chicken

Cut up chicken, onion and garlic and fry in the oil until
golden. Add half the water and simmer for 15 minutes. Add
tomatoes, skinned and diced, rice and remaining water and
stock cube. Simmer 5 minutes, stir in saffron. Add the lobster
pieces, prawns, mussels, pimentos and peas. Continue cooking
until rice has absorbed most of the liquid, 15–20 minutes.
Garnish with asparagus spears, if liked and slices of lemon.
The above is a true paella. Many of the ingredients can be
omitted, but to keep the interest of the dish you MUST mix
some shellfish with the chicken.

271   POULTRY OR GAME SALAD

Any cold poultry or game is delicious with salad. Include
oranges, nuts, etc. in the salad, particularly with richer poultry
such as duck or goose.

272   ROAST GUINEA FOWL

This is cooked and carved like chicken, but if not stuffed put a
good piece of butter inside to keep flesh moist. Serve with
bread sauce (Recipe No. 255). *Fried crumbs* can also be
served. Make rather large crumbs, and fry in hot butter until
they are crisp and golden brown. Garnish with watercress.

273   CHAUDFROID OF CHICKEN

142ml/¼pint aspic jelly (Recipe No. 283)
joints cooked chicken · 142ml/¼pint mayonnaise
small pieces of radish and green or red pepper to garnish

Make the aspic jelly and when it is cool, but not set, add the
mayonnaise. Coat the chicken joints and when firm garnish
with small pieces of radish, green or red pepper, etc. Serve on
a bed of shredded lettuce and radishes.

Chaudfroid of chicken

Chicken with cider

274   CHICKEN WITH CIDER

3 tablespoons oil for frying · 1 roasting chicken
1 onion, chopped or a few button onions · 1 green pepper, sliced
2 tomatoes, skinned and quartered · 1 tablespoon flour
seasoning · ½ level teaspoon ground ginger
1 level teaspoon paprika · 426ml/¾pint cider
1 tablespoon tomato purée · pinch sugar
chopped parsley to garnish

Heat the oil in a very large pan and fry the chicken until
browned. Remove the chicken and add the vegetables and
fry for 3–4 minutes. Work in the flour, seasoning, ginger and
paprika. Stir in the cider and cook until thickened. Add the
purée and sugar. Replace the chicken. Cover and simmer for
1–1½ hours. Serve garnished with chopped parsley, with a
green salad and new or creamed potatoes.

Chicken noodle ring

276 CHICKEN NOODLE RING

100g/4oz *noodles* · ¾litre/1½pints *chicken stock made from a cube*
1½ tablespoons gelatine · 300g/12oz *cooked chicken, chopped*
3 *tomatoes, skinned and chopped*
lettuce and watercress to garnish

Cook the noodles in the stock until just tender. Dissolve the gelatine in a little cold water, then carefully stir into the noodles and stock. Allow to cool, but not set, then stir in the chicken and tomatoes. Pour into a rinsed ring mould and leave to set. When set turn on to a serving plate; arrange lettuce leaves round the edge and fill the centre with sprigs of watercress.

277 GOLDEN CHICKEN WITH PEPPERS

(Illustrated in colour on the jacket)

4 *chicken joints* · *seasoned flour* · 100g/4oz *butter*
12 *tiny onions* · 12 *button mushrooms* · 2 *sticks celery, chopped*
1 *red pepper, sliced* · *seasoning* · 142ml/¼pint *chicken stock*
142ml/¼pint *dry white wine* · 1 *small packet frozen peas*
25g/1oz *fat* · 25g/1oz *flour* · 142ml/¼pint *single cream*

Coat the chicken joints in seasoned flour. Heat the butter in a saucepan and fry the joints until browned. Add the onions, mushrooms, celery and pepper and fry for 2–3 minutes. Add seasoning, chicken stock and dry white wine. Cover and simmer for a bout 40 minutes. Add the peas and cook for a further 10 minutes. Drain the chicken and vegetables and place in a heated serving dish. Bring the sauce to the boil and thicken by whisking fat and flour worked together, into the sauce. Remove from the heat and stir in the cream (do not re-boil). Pour over the chicken and vegetables and serve.

278 FRIED CHICKEN JOINTS

4 *chicken joints* · 1 *egg* · 50g/2oz *breadcrumbs*
fat for frying · 4 *small bananas* · *bacon rolls to garnish*

Coat the chicken joints in beaten egg and breadcrumbs. Fry in shallow fat until crisp and brown. Peel and fry the bananas. Drain the fried chicken and bananas and serve garnished with bacon rolls.

275 LEMON CHICKEN

1 *lemon* · 1 *large boiling fowl* · 2 *sticks celery*
200g/8oz *button onions* · 2 *carrots* · 3 *bay leaves*
3 *white peppercorns* · *seasoning* · 100g/4oz *mushrooms, sliced*
50g/2oz *butter* · 1 *egg* · 4 *tablespoons single cream*
2 *tablespoons sherry* · 100g/4oz *blanched almonds*

Squeeze the lemon all over the outside of the bird, remove any pips and put the skin inside. Put the chicken with the diced vegetables (leave the onions whole), bay leaves and peppercorns into a casserole and add water to cover. Season lightly. Put the lid on and cook for 3–4 hours in a slow oven, 300°F, 150°C, Gas Mark 2. When tender remove chicken from liquid and keep warm. Fry mushrooms in butter. Beat the egg and cream in a basin, gradually add 284ml (½ pint) of the boiling stock, stirring all the time until smooth and thick. Add mushrooms, sherry and blanched almonds. Replace chicken, pour over the sauce and serve.

Fried chicken joints

279 ORANGE SALAD FOR DUCK

This picture shows how to cut off the peel and divide the sections of orange for orange salad. Choose large, juicy fruit – *cut* away the peel with all the pith, then cut sections leaving skin behind. For a change sprinkle with a little cinnamon and sugar before putting on a bed of lettuce.

Orange salad for duck

280 SAGE AND ONION STUFFING

2 large onions, peeled · 50g/2oz breadcrumbs
25g/1oz shredded suet · 1 teaspoon dried sage · 1 egg*
good pinch salt and pepper

*Some of the onion stock may be used instead. This makes a less firm stuffing which many people prefer

Put the onions into a saucepan, and add about 284ml (½ pint) water. Simmer steadily for about 20 minutes, when the onions will be partly cooked. Remove from the water and chop up into small pieces. Transfer to a basin, then add all the other ingredients.

Grouse or pigeon pie

281 GROUSE OR PIGEON PIE

1 grouse or 2 or 3 pigeons · 1–2 hard-boiled eggs
2 rashers bacon · 1 small onion, finely chopped
100g/4oz mushrooms, chopped · seasoning
284ml/½pint stock · 150g/6oz flaky pastry (Recipe No. 604)

Cut the uncooked grouse into neat pieces and flour slightly. Slice the egg and cut the bacon into neat strips. Arrange with the onion and mushrooms in a deep pie dish. Season well; pour in stock. Cover with the pastry and cook in the centre of a very hot oven, 450°F, 230°C, Gas Mark 8, for 15 minutes. Put a piece of paper over the pastry, lower the heat to 375°F, 190°C, Gas Mark 5, for a further 1¼ hours. This is an economical way of serving grouse. A small quantity of steak can also be included.

282 BRAISED PIGEONS WITH PEAS

2 large or 4 small pigeons · 1 large onion · 2 rashers bacon
75g/3oz margarine · 40g/1½oz flour · ¾litre/1½pints water*
1 heaped teaspoon meat or vegetable extract*
salt and pepper to taste · 200g/8oz frozen or fresh peas
carrots to garnish

*Stock may be used instead of these ingredients

Wash the pigeons well, dry, and, if large, cut in halves lengthways. Peel and chop onion. Cut up bacon, removing rind, and fry until beginning to brown. Remove. Add margarine to pan, heat, add pigeons and fry until nicely browned. Remove. Add onion and fry until beginning to brown, turning over frequently. Add flour and stir until bubbling. Add water, and stir until boiling. Cook for 3 minutes, stirring continuously. Stir in meat or vegetable extract and seasoning, then return pigeons and bacon to the pan, cover, and cook for 1½–2 hours in the centre of a moderate oven, 325°F, 170°C, Gas Mark 3. Add the peas and cook for a further 30 minutes. Serve the pigeons on a bed of braised vegetables and garnish with a few cooked carrots.

Braised pigeons with peas

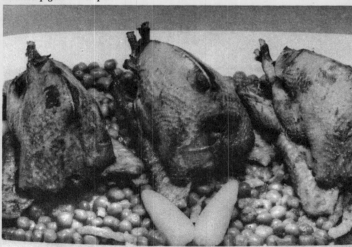

283 CHICKEN AND HAM MOUSSE

1 *packet aspic jelly* · generous ½litre/1pint *hot water*
25g/1oz *powdered gelatine* · 2 *tablespoons hot water*
1 *firm tomato* · *capers* · 1 *hard-boiled egg, sliced*
50g/2oz *butter* · 50g/2oz *flour* · 1 *small can evaporated milk*
chicken stock, see method · 300g/12oz *cooked chicken, minced*
100g/4oz *cooked ham, minced* · *seasoning* · 4 *egg whites*
cucumber slices and parsley to garnish

First make a *standard aspic jelly* by dissolving the aspic jelly powder in the hot water. Spoon 6 tablespoons into the bottom of a round mould or cake tin (without a loose bottom). Dip pieces of tomato, capers and egg slices in liquid aspic, arrange in a pattern on top of the set aspic. Allow to set firmly. Pour 6 tablespoons of liquid aspic on top of decorations, allow to set. Meanwhile dissolve the gelatine in hot water, add to the remaining aspic jelly and stir until dissolved. Melt the butter in a saucepan, add the flour and cook gently for a few minutes. Make milk up to generous ½litre (1 pint) with chicken stock and add to the saucepan, stirring all the time. Bring to the boil and cook over a gentle heat for 3 minutes. Add the chicken and ham and cool. Add seasoning and remaining liquid aspic. Allow to cool and begin to stiffen very slightly. Whisk egg whites until stiff and fold into the chicken mixture. When cold, but not set, pour into tin and leave to set. Turn out and garnish with cucumber slices and sprigs of parsley.
Makes 6 servings.

284 DEVILLED RABBIT

1 *small rabbit* · *seasoning* · *dry mustard* · 1 *large onion*
25g/1oz *bacon* · 1 *bay leaf* · 4 *tablespoons stock or water*
284ml/½pint *milk* · 25g/1oz *cooking fat* · 25g/1oz *flour*
¾kg/1½lb *mashed potatoes*

Soak the jointed rabbit in cold salted water for at least 1 hour. Remove and dry on a clean cloth. Season well and coat with mustard. Slice the onion thinly and cut up the bacon. Lay the rabbit joints in a casserole and add the bacon, onion, bay leaf and stock. Cover and bake on the middle shelf of a moderately hot oven, 400°F, 200°C, Gas Mark 6, for 1 hour or until rabbit is tender. Strain off liquid and make up to 284ml (½ pint) with milk. Melt the fat in a pan, add flour and gradually add liquor. Bring to the boil, cook for 3 minutes, stirring continuously. Serve rabbit joints, onion and bacon on a meat dish, coat with the sauce and surround with a border of piped mashed potatoes.

Chicken and ham mousse

Fricassée of chicken

285 FRICASSEE OF CHICKEN

75g/3oz *butter* · 40g/1½oz *flour* · 284ml/½pint *chicken stock*
142ml/¼pint *milk* · 100g/4oz *mushrooms, sliced*
½kg/1lb *cooked chicken* · *little single cream* · *seasoning*
triangles of toast to garnish

Heat half the butter in a pan, stir in the flour and cook the roux gently for a few minutes. Add stock and milk and stir until smooth. Put in diced chicken and heat gently for about 20 minutes. Meanwhile fry the sliced mushrooms in the remaining butter. Stir the cream, mushrooms and seasoning into the chicken mixture. Spoon into a serving dish and garnish with triangles of toast.

286 GRILLED PIGEONS MERCURY

Young tender pigeons can be grilled if kept well basted. Put a small knob of butter inside birds to keep them moist. Brush birds with melted butter and cook under moderately hot grill – putting in extra butter from time to time. For the last 5 minutes of cooking add button mushrooms. Garnish with watercress and rice moulds.

Grilled pigeons Mercury

VEGETABLES

HOW TO PREPARE AND SERVE VEGETABLES

ARTICHOKES, GLOBE Cook steadily in boiling salted water for about 30 minutes. Serve with a little melted butter or white, cheese or Hollandaise sauce.

ARTICHOKES, JERUSALEM Scrub well and peel or scrape. Soak in a little cold water, adding a few drops of vinegar. Cook for about 30 minutes in boiling salted water, adding a few drops of vinegar. Serve with melted butter, white, cheese or Hollandaise sauce.

ASPARAGUS Wash carefully, then cut off a little of the thick white base of stalks. Either steam or boil the bunch in salted water in a tall pan for 20–25 minutes. Serve with melted butter or Mousseline sauce.

BEANS, BROAD Shell and wash, unless very young, when they can be cooked whole. Cook in boiling salted water for about 20 minutes. Serve with a little melted butter and chopped parsley.

BEANS, FRENCH or RUNNER Wash and string. French beans can be left whole, but runner beans are better thinly sliced. Cook steadily in boiling salted water for about 15 minutes.

BEETROOT Wash carefully and cook in boiling salted water until soft; time will vary according to size, but test by pressing gently. Generally served cold with salads, but delicious hot with parsley or Hollandaise sauce.

BRUSSELS SPROUTS Mark a cross with a sharp knife at the base of each sprout. Boil rapidly like cabbage. For a change, try a garnish of finely grated lemon rind (*Illustrated in colour on the opposite page*).

CABBAGE, SPRING, SUMMER or SAVOY Shred finely with sharp knife and boil rapidly for about 10 minutes in salted water. Serve raw in salads.

CARROTS Scrub well or scrape, cook in boiling salted water until soft.

CAULIFLOWER Cut off thick stalks and outer leaves, divide head into small sprigs, cook rapidly in boiling salted water. Serve with white, parsley or cheese sauce.

CELERY, CELERIAC and CHICORY Generally eaten raw and in salads, but very good cooked. Divide into neat pieces and cook in boiling salted water for about 20 minutes. Serve with white, parsley or cheese sauce.

CORN ON THE COB Wash corn cob, strip off outer green leaves and silks, and boil in salted water for about 20 minutes, until the corn feels soft. Serve with a little melted butter. Do not boil too quickly or for too long, otherwise the corn will be tough.

CUCUMBER Generally served with vinegar, but can be boiled in pieces in salted water or braised.

EGGPLANT or AUBERGINE Wash and remove any hard stalk. Cook in a casserole dish with knob of margarine and little milk for 30 minutes. Can be stuffed (Recipe No. 330) or fried like potatoes.

ENDIVE Shred and serve in salads.

FENNEL A little, cut finely, flavours a salad, but it can be cooked like other vegetables in boiling salted water and served with a white sauce. Particularly good served with fish.

HARICOT BEANS Dried haricot beans require soaking for 48 hours, then simmer in the water in which they were soaked for about $1\frac{1}{2}$ hours. Serve with cheese sauce or include in casserole dishes.

LEEKS Cut off roots and outer leaves, split down the middle so they can be thoroughly washed. Use in place of onions in soups and stews, or boil for 15–20 minutes in salted water. Serve with white or cheese sauce.

LETTUCE Although normally served in salads, lettuce can be cooked like cabbage or in a little butter in a covered pan until soft, or braised.

MUSHROOMS Can be fried or grilled in butter or baked in a covered casserole for about 30 minutes. Mushrooms can also be stewed in milk, then remaining liquid thickened with a little flour or cornflour.

ONIONS Put into soups and stews, fry with meat or savoury dishes. As a separate vegetable boil for a good hour in salted water and serve with white sauce.

PARSNIPS Put into soups and stews, but do not have too large a proportion of parsnips as their flavour is very strong and will dominate the dish. Very good baked round meat.

PEAS Shell and cook steadily in boiling salted water for 10–15 minutes. Serve with a little melted butter. Mint and a teaspoon of sugar improve the flavour.

PEPPERS, GREEN or RED Shred and serve in salads. Can be baked and stuffed (Recipe Nos. 325, 326, 333).

POTATOES Always put into boiling salted water and cook steadily until soft. Can also be fried, roasted, baked in their jackets or steamed.

SALSIFY Wash or scrape well, then cook as for Jerusalem artichokes. Serve with a little melted butter and chopped parsley.

SPINACH Wash leaves in several changes of water. There is no need to add water to spinach, so just put into a strong pan with a little salt and boil rapidly until tender – about 15 minutes. Either rub through a sieve or turn on to a board and chop finely, then return to the pan with a little milk and butter and reheat.

TOMATOES Delicious raw, or can be used in every way cooked; they add flavour to all savoury dishes.

TURNIPS Put into soups and stews. When young they are delicious cooked in boiling salted water, then mashed.

VEGETABLE MARROW Peel, cut into neat pieces and either steam over boiling water, adding a little salt, or bake, stuffed or boil in salted water until tender. Serve with cheese or white sauce. Small marrows, called **courgettes** or **zucchini**, can be cut in half, stuffed and cooked in the oven (*Illustrated in colour on the opposite page*). For other stuffed marrow recipes see Recipe Nos. 239, 331.

Stuffed vegetable marrow, carrots Vichy, mixed vegetables and Brussels sprouts

288 CAULIFLOWER NOISETTE

1 *large cauliflower* · 100g/4oz *Cheddar cheese, grated*
salt and pepper · *nutmeg* · 50g/2oz *butter*
chopped parsley to garnish

Cook the prepared cauliflower in boiling salted water until
just tender. Drain well. Grease an ovenproof dish and cover
the bottom with a layer of grated cheese. Break up the cauliflower carefully and distribute over the dish. Season well and
sprinkle over the remainder of the cheese. Heat the butter until
it browns and pour over the cauliflower. Brown under a grill.
Garnish with chopped parsley and serve.

Cauliflower noisette

289 CAULIFLOWER CHEESE

1 *medium-sized cauliflower* · 284ml/½pint *cheese sauce**
(Recipe Nos. 660, 665)
25g/1oz *Cheddar cheese, grated* · 1 *tablespoon crisp or soft*
breadcrumbs · *grilled bacon rolls, tomato slices and*
chopped parsley to garnish

*If liked use half milk and half cauliflower stock

Soak the cauliflower in cold water for about 15 minutes, then
break into flowerets. Cook in a little boiling salted water in a
covered pan until tender and arrange neatly in an ovenproof
dish. Make the cheese sauce. Coat the cauliflower with the
cheese sauce. Sprinkle with the grated cheese and crumbs and
brown under a hot grill. Garnish with bacon rolls, tomato
slices and chopped parsley.

Cauliflower cheese

Tomato and courgette rice

290 TOMATO AND COURGETTE RICE

50g/2oz *long grain rice* · ½kg/1lb *courgettes, washed*
6 *large tomatoes, skinned* · 25g/1oz *butter*
142ml/¼pint *stock or water* · *seasoning*

Sprinkle the rice in the bottom of an ovenproof dish. Place
the courgettes, whole and unpeeled, on top. Then add the
skinned tomatoes. Dot with butter, pour in the stock and add
the seasoning. Cover and cook in a moderate oven, 350°F,
180°C, Gas Mark 4, for 1¼–1½ hours, until the courgettes are
tender.
Makes 6 servings.

291 CABBAGE WITH MUSTARD DRESSING

1 *medium-sized cabbage* · 25g/1oz *butter*
2 *teaspoons mustard mixed with vinegar*

Cut the cabbage in strips and cook it in as little salted water as
possible without letting it burn. Drain well and then toss with
two forks, while still hot, in a dressing made by blending
butter with made mustard. If you mix the cabbage and
dressing quickly it is hot enough to serve at once.

292 CAULIFLOWER AU GRATIN
(With mushroom sauce)

1 cauliflower · 250g/10oz can condensed mushroom soup
25g/1oz cheese, grated · 25g/1oz browned breadcrumbs
chives or parsley to garnish

Cook the cauliflower whole in boiling salted water. While the cauliflower is cooking, mix the soup and the cheese together in a saucepan, and then heat, stirring constantly, until the cheese has melted and the sauce is very hot. Pour the sauce over the cauliflower, then sprinkle with the breadcrumbs. Brown under a hot grill. Garnish with chopped chives or parsley.

293 STUFFED CABBAGE LEAVES

5–6 large cabbage leaves · 200g/8oz cooked pork or beef, minced
1 small onion, chopped · 1 egg
40g/1½oz quick-cooking rolled oats
1 dessertspoon Worcestershire sauce · little milk if necessary
seasoning to taste · little stock or water
brown or tomato sauce (Recipe Nos. 685, 656, 657)

Wash the cabbage leaves and drain. Mix together all the other ingredients, except the stock and sauce. Place this filling on the cabbage leaves and roll up. Arrange in a greased ovenproof dish and pour on a little stock. Cover dish. Cook in centre of a moderate oven, 325°F, 170°C, Gas Mark 3, for 50–60 minutes until tender. Drain and serve with brown or tomato sauce. If liked a border of cooked rice can be arranged round the edge of the dish.

294 PIQUANT CABBAGE

3 rashers streaky bacon, chopped · 1 small onion, sliced
1 tablespoon oil · 1 medium-sized cabbage, shredded
284ml/½pint boiling water · 1 cooking apple, peeled and chopped
seasoning · pinch brown sugar
½kg/1lb tomatoes, skinned and quartered
2 frankfurter sausages, sliced

Fry the bacon and onion in the heated oil. Add the cabbage and water. Cover and simmer for 20–25 minutes, until the cabbage is just tender. Add the remaining ingredients and cook, uncovered, for a further 10 minutes. Spoon on to a heated dish and serve.

Cabbage au gratin

Stuffed cabbage leaves

Piquant cabbage

295 CABBAGE AU GRATIN

1 medium-sized Savoy cabbage · white sauce (Recipe No. 663)
seasoning, including nutmeg and dry mustard
50g/2oz cheese, grated · 25–50g/1–2oz breadcrumbs
watercress to garnish

Quarter the cabbage and cook in boiling salted water until just tender. Drain well and chop finely. Place in an ovenproof dish. Make the white sauce and stir in the seasoning. Pour over the cabbage; sprinkle with grated cheese and breadcrumbs and brown under a hot grill. Serve at once, garnished with sprigs of watercress.

Chipped potatoes

POTATOES

296 CHIPPED POTATOES

Peel potatoes, then cut into long fingers. Wash these, then dry well. Heat fat or oil to 350°F, 180°C. Test temperature by adding 1 chip. If it sinks to the bottom and there is no movement of the fat it is not sufficiently hot. If, however, the fat bubbles immediately the chip is put in, and the chip stays at the top of the fat, then the fat is the right heat. Put enough chips into the frying basket to about a quarter full. Lower carefully into the fat, watching to see there is no danger of it overflowing. Cook the potatoes for about 3 minutes. Remove the potatoes with the basket and stand on a plate. Just before serving the chips, reheat the fat, test to make sure it is hot enough, and fry the chips rapidly for about 2 minutes until crisp and brown. Drain on crumpled tissue paper or absorbent kitchen roll. Serve at once.

297 POTATO CROQUETTES

mashed potatoes · flour · egg · breadcrumbs
deep fat for frying

Form mashed potatoes, which should be smooth, but firm, into required shapes. Coat with little flour, then with beaten egg and breadcrumbs. Heat fat to 350°F, 180°C (see instructions for chipped potatoes, Recipe No. 296) and put the croquettes carefully into frying basket. Fry for several minutes and drain well on absorbent paper. Serve at once.

298 SAUTE POTATOES

Cut par-boiled or cooked potatoes into rounds. Heat butter or fat in a frying pan and fry the potatoes until crisp and brown. Drain on absorbent paper and serve at once.

Bacon stuffed potatoes

300   DUCHESSE POTATOES

1–2 eggs, beaten · 50g/2oz butter
good ½kg/1¼lb potatoes, well mashed

Mix the beaten egg and butter with the potatoes, pipe on to greased baking sheets and cook for about 25 minutes in a moderately hot oven, 375–400°F, 190°C, Gas Mark 5. Serve with meat, fish or cheese dishes.

301   ROAST POTATOES

Peel the potatoes, dry them well in a cloth. Put into hot fat in a roasting tin; spoon the fat over them so that they are evenly coated. Cook for about 1 hour in a hot oven or roast in the fat round the joint.

302   GAME CHIPS

Cut wafer thin slices of potato; an electric slicer or mandolin is ideal for this. Dry well and fry in deep fat or oil heated to 350°F, 180°C for about 1 minute. Lift out; reheat fat and fry again for ½ minute. Drain on absorbent paper. Serve with game.

303   CREAMED POTATOES

Boil potatoes. Drain and beat until soft and smooth. Add a little hot milk and beat with a wooden spoon until the potatoes are very white and fluffy. Add margarine or butter and seasoning.

299   BACON STUFFED POTATOES

Bake potatoes in their jackets, see Recipe No. 340. Cut a thin slice from the top of each and scoop out the cooked potato. Mash with seasoning, including paprika, and a little single cream. Mix with fried chopped bacon and a little chopped onion or chives. Spoon into the potato cases and serve garnished with grilled bacon rolls and a sprig of parsley.

Boiled potatoes (Recipe No. 306)

Baked corn potatoes

304 BAKED CORN POTATOES

4 large potatoes · butter or margarine · seasoning
2 eggs, separated · 275g/11oz can sweet corn, drained
50g/2oz cheese, grated

Bake the potatoes in their jackets until tender. Halve, remove all centre pulp. Mash well, adding butter, seasoning, egg yolks and sweet corn. Whisk egg whites until very stiff, fold into potato mixture. Pile back in cases and cook for approximately 20 minutes in centre of a moderate oven, 375°F, 190°C, Gas Mark 5. Sprinkle with grated cheese and serve.

Cheese scalloped potatoes

305 CHEESE SCALLOPED POTATOES

about ¾kg/1½lb potatoes · seasoning
250g/10oz can condensed mushroom soup · 284ml/½pint milk
little butter · 100g/4oz Gouda cheese, grated

Slice potatoes very thinly. Arrange in an ovenproof dish, seasoning well. Mix soup and milk. Pour over potatoes; dot with butter and sprinkle with cheese. Cook in centre of very moderate oven, 325°F, 170°C, Gas Mark 3, for 1½–2 hours.

Boiled potatoes

306 BOILED OR STEAMED POTATOES

(Also illustrated in colour on the preceding page)

They can either be cooked steadily in salted water, or if a firm potato is required for potato salad it is a good idea to use a steamer. Remember *never* to boil potatoes too quickly otherwise you will find they break on the outside. Garnish with chopped parsley.

Potatoes Macain

307 POTATOES MACAIN

4 rashers bacon, chopped · 1 onion, chopped
¾kg/1½lb mashed potatoes* · 25g/1oz butter
142ml/¼pint milk · salt · pepper · chopped parsley
parsley to garnish

*Instant potato, made according to packet instructions, could be used for this recipe

Fry the bacon, put to drain. Then fry the onion in the bacon fat. Combine the mashed potato, butter, milk, seasoning, parsley and bacon with the onion; form into cakes and brown, in the bacon fat, on both sides. Drain on absorbent paper and serve garnished with parsley.

308 POTATO NESTS

50g/2oz *soft margarine* · 1kg/2lb *mashed potatoes* · 1 *egg*
seasoning
Filling
1 *teaspoon chopped onion* · 50g/2oz *soft margarine*
40g/1½oz *flour* · 284ml/½pint *milk*
75g/3oz *cheese, grated* · 200g/8oz *lean ham, cubed*
seasoning · *watercress and cooked peas to garnish*

Beat the margarine into the potatoes. Add egg and seasoning. Pipe or spoon mixture on to a greased baking sheet into nest shapes. Brush with melted margarine and cook in a hot oven, 425°F, 220°C, Gas Mark 7, for 15 minutes. Fry the onion in heated margarine until soft. Stir in the flour and cook for 1 minute. Gradually add the milk, stirring all the time and cook for 2 minutes. Stir in cheese, ham and seasoning. Spoon into hot potato cases and serve garnished with watercress and cooked peas.

Potato nests

Carrots Vichy

309 CARROTS VICHY

(Also illustrated in colour at the beginning of this section)

½kg/1lb *young carrots* · 50g/2oz *margarine* · *salt and pepper*
2 *tablespoons single cream or milk* · *chopped parsley to garnish*

Slice the carrots thinly (if small, leave whole); toss in hot margarine, until well coated, put into a covered dish with plenty of seasoning and cream or milk. Cook for approximately 30 minutes in a moderately hot oven, 400°F, 200°C, Gas Mark 6. Serve garnished with chopped parsley.

310 POTATOES ANNA

dripping · ½kg/1lb *potatoes* · *margarine*

Grease an ovenproof dish or tin liberally with well clarified dripping and heat this until the dripping begins to smoke slightly. Arrange well dried slices of potatoes (the thickness of a penny) in the dish, just letting them overlap. Season each layer and brush the top with margarine. Cook for about 1 hour on the bottom shelf of a moderately hot oven, 400°F, 200°C, Gas Mark 6, until the potatoes are tender and the top layer brown. Serve in the dish or turn out on to a serving dish.

Potatoes Anna

Potatoes Parisienne

311 POTATOES PARISIENNE

These are small balls of raw potato, roasted in hot fat or oil in the oven. To make potatoes Parisienne you need a potato baller, like the one illustrated (it can also be used to make melon balls etc.). Insert the scoop into the potato and push firmly at the same time; turn the scoop to get a ball shape. Dry well and roast in a moderately hot oven, 400°F, 200°C, Gas Mark 6, for 40 minutes. Drain on absorbent paper and serve.

Vegetable and cheese pie

312   VEGETABLE AND CHEESE PIE

½kg/1lb mixed cooked vegetables
284ml/½pint cheese sauce (Recipe No. 665)
½kg/1lb creamed potatoes (Recipe No. 303)
butter or margarine · little grated cheese, optional
chopped parsley to garnish

Mix well drained vegetables with the sauce. Put into a pie dish, cover with creamed potatoes. Pipe border of potato if wished. Put small pieces of butter or margarine on top, plus a little grated cheese if used. Cook for approximately 25 minutes in moderately hot oven, 400°F, 200°C, Gas Mark 6. Serve garnished with chopped parsley.

313   CREAMED VEGETABLES

200g/8oz frozen mixed vegetables
284ml/½pint white sauce (Recipe No. 663)
2 hard-boiled eggs, quartered · 2 tomatoes, quartered
rashers grilled bacon

Cook the frozen vegetables, drain and stir into the hot sauce, together with the quartered hard-boiled eggs and tomatoes. Arrange in a hot dish and top with cooked bacon.

314   CHEESE AND VEGETABLE CASSEROLE

Arrange layers of cooked mixed vegetables and grated Gouda cheese in an ovenproof dish. Season each layer and top with par-boiled sliced potatoes. Brush with melted butter and cook in a moderately hot oven, 400°F, 200°C, Gas Mark 6, for about 35 minutes.

Cheese and vegetable casserole

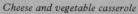

Sweet corn pie

315   SWEET CORN PIE

200g/8oz frozen corn off the cob or 275g/11oz can sweet corn*
284ml/½pint milk · salt and pepper · 2 eggs · 50g/2oz butter
75g/3oz cheese, grated · parsley to garnish

*Fresh corn on the cob can be used. Cook the corn and remove from the cob when tender

If using frozen corn cook this until just tender, then mix with the milk. Season well and bring just to the boil. Beat the eggs, pour over the milk, whisking well. Add the butter and cheese and mix thoroughly. Turn into an ovenproof dish and cook in the centre of a very moderate oven, 325°F, 170°C, Gas Mark 3, for about 1 hour, until golden brown. Garnish with parsley.

316   VEGETABLE PIE

Use the same method as sweet corn pie (Recipe No. 315), but substitute cooked diced mixed vegetables for the sweet corn. Carrots and peas are an excellent mixture, and so are mushrooms and new potatoes. Asparagus makes a more luxurious dish for special occasions.

Apple sauerkraut

317 APPLE SAUERKRAUT

½kg/1lb *sauerkraut* · 50g/2oz *pork fat or butter*
3 *tart eating apples* · 2 *onions, sliced* · 4 *sausages*
2 *rashers bacon, chopped* · 2 *tomatoes, skinned and quartered*
2 *bay leaves* · *salt and pepper* · *caraway seeds, optional*

Put sauerkraut in a casserole with pork fat or butter. Core and
quarter apples, but do not peel, and add them to sauerkraut,
together with onions, sausages, bacon, tomatoes, bay leaves
and a little water. Cook in a moderately hot oven, 375°F,
190°C, Gas Mark 5, for about 45 minutes; add seasoning and
caraway seeds, if used. Cook in a moderate oven for a few
minutes longer.

Ratatouille

318 RATATOUILLE

2 *onions* · ½kg/1lb *tomatoes* · 1 *medium-sized marrow* or
½kg/1lb *courgettes* · 4 *small aubergines* · 1 *red or green pepper*
little bacon fat or rind from gammon · 1–2 *cloves garlic*
seasoning

Chop the onions. Skin the tomatoes, then cut them in half,
sprinkle with salt and leave upturned to drain. Peel the
marrow, cut in large chunks (or slice courgettes), remove the
stalks from the aubergines, cut in half, scoop out slightly and
cut into chunks. Seed and slice the pepper. Heat the fat or
rind in a strong pan and gently fry the onions and the crushed
garlic. Add the aubergines, marrow, tomatoes and pepper.
Season well and simmer, with well-fitting lid on the pan,
until the vegetables are tender.
Makes 6 servings.

Corn toasties

319 CORN TOASTIES

75g/3oz *butter* · 1 *small onion, chopped* · 2 *tomatoes, chopped*
50g/2oz *mushrooms, chopped*
275g/11oz *can corn and sweet pepper mixed*
50g/2oz *ham, chopped* · 25g/1oz *cheese, grated*
2 *slices toast* · *chopped parsley to garnish*

Heat the butter in a pan and fry the finely chopped onion,
tomatoes and mushrooms. Mix in the drained corn and
pepper. Heat gently and stir in the chopped ham and grated
cheese. Garnish with triangles of toast and chopped parsley.

320 STUFFED ONIONS

4 large onions, weighing about 200g/8oz each
3 rashers bacon, chopped · 40g/1½oz quick-cooking rolled oats
1 teaspoon Worcestershire sauce
15g/½oz stale Danish blue or Gorgonzola cheese, grated
50g/2oz Cheshire or Cheddar cheese, grated
pinch mixed herbs · salt and pepper · 2–4 tablespoons stock*
mushrooms and tomato slices to garnish

*Or water flavoured with meat or vegetable extract

Peel the onions then make 2 cross cuts about 1½-cm (¾-inch) deep over top of each one. Cook in boiling salted water for 20–25 minutes, then drain and leave until cold; with very sharp knife, cut slice from top of each onion, about 1-cm (½-inch) down. Prise out onion centres and the trimmings from the top. Fry bacon until crisp. Remove from heat and stir in oats followed by chopped onion, Worcestershire sauce, cheese, herbs and seasoning to taste. Mix thoroughly then pack stuffing into onions. Put onions in greased casserole. Pour in just enough stock to cover the bottom of the dish. Put lid on and cook in a moderate oven, 325°F, 170°C, Gas Mark 3, for 1½ hours, until onions are tender. Transfer to a heated serving dish and garnish with mushrooms, baked in butter in the oven and tomato slices.

Stuffed onions

321 BEANS AND MACARONI

3 tomatoes · 75g/3oz quick-cooking macaroni · 50g/2oz butter
100g/4oz cheese, grated · seasoning · ½kg/1lb runner beans,
stringed and sliced or 1 large packet frozen beans

Skin and chop the tomatoes. Cook the macaroni according to the instructions on the packet. Melt half the butter and fry the tomatoes for about 4 minutes. Add the drained macaroni, reheat, then stir in the cheese and seasoning. Meanwhile cook the beans. Drain and toss in the remaining butter. Arrange the beans down the centre of a heated serving dish and place the macaroni mixture on either side.

Beans and macaroni

Leek, bean and bacon savoury

322 LEEK, BEAN AND BACON SAVOURY

6 rashers bacon · 4 medium-sized leeks · 50g/2oz butter
1 medium-sized can baked beans
hard-boiled egg quarters and parsley to garnish

Cut bacon rashers in halves. Roll up pieces and thread on to thin skewers. Fry in a large pan until lightly crisped. Remove bacon to a dish and keep hot. Cut well washed and drained leeks into 1-cm (½-inch) slices. Add butter to bacon fat in pan and when hot put in sliced leeks and fry until tender, keeping slices as whole as possible. Take up slices with a draining spoon and put in dish with bacon. Stir baked beans into residual fat in pan and make piping hot. To serve, spoon beans into middle of serving dish and top with the bacon rolls; arrange leeks around. Garnish with quarters of hard-boiled egg and parsley.

Savoury tomatoes

Peppers and tomatoes au gratin

323   SAVOURY TOMATOES

Cut firm tomatoes into 5 sections, but not right through at the bottom, to form 'petals'. Gently pull these sections outwards and fill with cooked, chopped vegetables, potato or vegetable salad or drained canned vegetables. Place a little mayonnaise (Recipe No. 408) in the centre of each tomato and garnish, as liked, with prawns, cooked peas etc. Serve the tomatoes on thin slices of cucumber.

324   PEPPERS OR CAPSICUMS

These red and green peppers add flavour to soups and stews, are excellent shredded in salads, or can be stuffed (Recipe Nos. 333, 325) and eaten as a main dish.

Vegetable salad

325   PEPPERS AND TOMATOES AU GRATIN

Cut 2 green peppers in half and remove the seeds. Cook in boiling water for 3 minutes. Cut a slice from the top of 4 tomatoes and scoop out the centres. Leave upside down to drain. Fill the pepper and tomato cases with sage and onion stuffing (Recipe No. 280), mixed with the tomato pulp. Sprinkle with grated cheese and cook in a moderate oven, 350°F, 180°C, Gas Mark 4, for 30 minutes. Serve garnished with chopped parsley.

326   VEGETABLE SALADS

A complete and satisfying meal can be made of vegetables. Remember to include some of each of the following groups:

Beans	
Peas	which provide proteins
Lentils	
Carrots	which are satisfying
Potatoes	

Tomatoes and green vegetables to give vitamins

Try to include something really unusual and interesting e.g. a globe artichoke as a centre piece.

The picture shows chopped pears and walnuts, mixed with mayonnaise (Recipe Nos. 408, 412), arranged on a bed of lettuce. The salad is garnished with chopped celery and tomato slices.

For a change try chopped apple, tossed in lemon juice, mixed with chopped green pepper, arranged on a bed of lettuce. Serve garnished with sliced stuffed olives.

With a little imagination a variety of very satisfying vegetable dishes can be created. For example, try the delicious and economical French country stew, ratatouille (Recipe No. 318), or the ever popular cauliflower cheese (Recipe No. 289), or stuffed aubergines (Recipe No. 330).

327 FROZEN VEGETABLES

Frozen vegetables have become extremely popular during the past years and for a very good reason: their flavour is excellent and there is a very large variety from which to choose. Take care not to over-cook frozen vegetables. Cooking times are given and should be followed carefully. In this chapter no particular reference is made to frozen vegetables, but they can be used in suitable recipes in place of fresh vegetables.

328 FRIED AUBERGINES OR EGGPLANT

Halve aubergines. Scoop out the hard centre core and fry the aubergine cases until just tender. Fill the cases with sage and onion stuffing (Recipe No. 280) and cook in a moderate oven, 350°F, 180°C, Gas Mark 4, for 30 minutes. Serve garnished with parsley.

329 VEGETABLE CURRY

50g/2oz margarine · 1 onion, chopped · 1 apple, chopped
1 tablespoon curry powder · 1 tablespoon flour
generous ½litre/1pint stock
½kg/1lb mixed vegetables (onions, carrots, celery), chopped
squeeze lemon juice · 1 dessertspoon desiccated coconut
1 tablespoon sultanas · 1 teaspoon soft brown sugar
1 dessertspoon chutney · seasoning · 100g/4oz mushrooms, sliced
cooked long grain rice · parsley to garnish

Heat the margarine and fry the onion and apple until soft. Stir in the curry powder and flour and cook for 3–4 minutes. Gradually add the stock and bring to the boil. Add the mixed vegetables, lemon juice, coconut, sultanas, brown sugar, chutney and seasoning. Cover and simmer for about 35 minutes. Add the mushrooms and simmer for a further 15 minutes. Spoon into a serving dish, arrange a border of rice round the edge of the dish and serve garnished with a sprig of parsley.

Vegetable curry

330 STUFFED AUBERGINES

2 medium-sized aubergines · ½ teaspoon salt
2 teaspoons olive oil or melted butter
50g/2oz cooked bacon, chopped · 1 tablespoon chopped parsley
1 tomato, skinned and chopped · 50g/2oz fresh breadcrumbs
salt and pepper · 100g/4oz Cheddar cheese, grated
1 tablespoon finely chopped cooked onion · parsley to garnish

Wash aubergines, remove stalk, and cut in half lengthways.
Cut round each half aubergine ½-cm (¼-inch) from the skin and
then score the surface lightly to ensure even cooking. Sprinkle
with salt and olive oil or melted butter. Put on a greased baking
tin in a moderately hot oven, 400°F, 200°C, Gas Mark 5,
until the centre is nearly cooked, 15–20 minutes. Make stuffing
by mixing all the ingredients together. Scoop out about half
the flesh from the centre of the cooked aubergines, chop up
and add to stuffing. Fill aubergine cases with stuffing; return
to the oven for 15 minutes. Serve hot with tomato or cheese
sauce (Recipe Nos. 656, 657, 660, 665). Garnish with parsley.

Stuffed aubergines

331 STUFFED VEGETABLE MARROW

½ small green pepper · 1 medium-sized marrow
250g/10oz can condensed Scotch broth · seasoning
150g/6oz cooked lamb, cubed · 1 teaspoon Worcestershire sauce
tomato slices and parsley to garnish

Put green pepper into boiling water for 3 minutes. Drain,
remove seeds and chop flesh. Peel the marrow, but if young
the skin can be left on. Slice off the top to give a boat shape and
remove the seeds. Mix the Scotch broth with seasoning, lamb
and Worcestershire sauce. Stuff the marrow with this mixture
and replace the top. Wrap in foil and place in a roasting tin.
Cook in a moderately hot oven, 375°F, 190°C, Gas Mark 5,
for 1½–1¾ hours. Serve garnished with tomato slices and
parsley.

Stuffed vegetable marrow

Cheese stuffed peppers

332 CHEESE AND ONION SAUCE

1 onion, finely chopped · 25g/1oz butter · 25g/1oz flour
284ml/½pint milk · salt, pepper and nutmeg
100g/4oz Cheddar cheese, grated

Toss onion in heated butter for a few minutes, taking care it
does not brown. Stir in the flour and cook for 2 minutes then
gradually add the milk. Bring to boil and cook until thickened.
Add seasoning and cheese and heat without boiling again.

333 CHEESE STUFFED PEPPERS

4 large green peppers · 150g/6oz white bread
4 tablespoons milk · 1 tablespoon chopped parsley
2 tablespoons tomato chutney · salt and pepper to taste
100g/4oz cream cheese or cheese spread · cooked long grain rice
cheese and onion sauce (Recipe No. 332), optional

Cut off the tops of the peppers, scoop out core and seeds and
wash peppers. Drop into boiling water and cook for 3 minutes.
Crumble the bread and soften with milk, mix in the parsley,
tomato chutney, seasoning and warmed cream cheese or
cheese spread. Fill peppers with this mixture, replace the
caps and put into a baking tin with a little water. Cook in a
moderately hot oven, 375°F, 190°C, Gas Mark 5, for 30–35
minutes until soft. Serve on a bed of rice. If liked, serve cheese
and onion sauce separately.

Mushroom stuffed tomatoes

334 MUSHROOMS WITH CHEESE FILLINGS

½ teaspoon dry mustard · 1 egg yolk
200g/8oz medium-sized mushrooms, skinned and with stalks
removed · 142ml/¼pint milk · 1 tablespoon fried chopped onion
4 rashers streaky bacon, roughly chopped and fried
1 tablespoon fresh breadcrumbs
1 teaspoon finely chopped parsley
50g/2oz Cheddar or Parmesan cheese, finely grated
salt and pepper · thick slices fried tomato
parsley to garnish

Mix mustard with little water and blend with egg yolk.
Lightly poach the mushrooms and trimmed stalks in the milk.
Remove and drain. Mix together the onion, bacon, breadcrumbs, chopped parsley, grated cheese and seasoning to
taste. Bind with the beaten egg and mustard then put the
mixture, in teaspoonfuls, on to the poached mushrooms. Top
each with a stalk and grill for 3–5 minutes and place on to the
tomato slices. Transfer to a serving dish and garnish with
parsley.

335 MUSHROOM STUFFED TOMATOES

6 large firm tomatoes · 50g/2oz mushrooms, sliced
2 tablespoons oil · 100g/4oz cooked long grain rice
seasoning, including pinch thyme
2 tablespoons chopped chives · parsley to garnish

Cut the tops off the tomatoes, scoop out and chop the pulp.
Fry the mushrooms in oil then add the rice and fry for about
5 minutes. Add the seasoning and chives. Spoon the rice
mixture into the tomato cases. Replace the tops and place in an
ovenproof dish. Cook in a moderately hot oven, 375°F, 190°C,
Gas Mark 5, for 20 minutes. Serve garnished with parsley.
Makes 6 servings.

336 CREAMED MUSHROOMS

Simmer mushrooms in milk until just tender. Blend a little
cornflour or flour with cold milk, add to the milk and cook
until thickened, put in a good knob of butter and a little single
cream, season well; add a squeeze of lemon. Serve garnished
with chopped parsley.

Creamed mushrooms

EGG & CHEESE DISHES

Cheese and eggs are a first-class food. A meal containing cheese or eggs is every bit as nutritious as one with meat or fish. There are so many different cheeses to choose from that dishes need never be monotonous.

Cheese and vegetable savoury

Egg and avocado salad

337 CHEESE AND VEGETABLE SAVOURY

Fill a casserole with layers of heated canned vegetables or freshly cooked vegetables. Cover each layer with grated cheese and top with cheese sauce (Recipe Nos. 660, 665). Sprinkle with browned crumbs and place under a hot grill for 3–4 minutes.

338 EGG PIE WITH BACON

Mix together heated canned or cooked vegetables, diced hard-boiled eggs and diced cooked bacon. Bind with white sauce (Recipe No. 663). Arrange in a shallow dish and garnish with strips of grilled bacon.

339 EGG AND AVOCADO SALAD

Arrange washed and drained endive on a serving dish. Place tomato slices round the edge of the dish and slices of hard-boiled egg and avocado pear, sprinkled with lemon juice, down the centre. Garnish with chopped parsley and radish 'roses'.

340 CHEESE STUFFED POTATOES
(Illustrated in colour on the opposite page)

4 really large potatoes · margarine or butter · seasoning grated cheese · parsley to garnish

Cook the potatoes in their jackets in the oven until tender. The time will depend on how quickly you wish to do them, but the best result is obtained by cooking fairly steadily for about 1½ hours in the centre of a very moderate oven, 325°F, 170°C, Gas Mark 3. Cut the potatoes in half, scoop out the pulp and put it into a basin. Mash well, add margarine or butter, seasoning and as much grated cheese as you like. Pile back into the potato cases; sprinkle with grated cheese and return to the oven or place under a hot grill to brown. Serve garnished with parsley.

Other recipes for baked potatoes will be found in the vegetable section

There are many more cheese recipes throughout this book, particularly in the sections on pastry, entertaining, salads and vegetables

Cheese stuffed potatoes

341 TEN MINUTE CHEESE SOUFFLES

2 eggs, separated · cayenne pepper, salt, little dry mustard
2 heaped dessertspoons grated Cheddar cheese
little extra grated Cheddar cheese

Whip the yolks and seasoning, mix in grated cheese, fold in stiffly beaten egg whites. Two-thirds fill lightly greased individual soufflé or ovenproof dishes. Sprinkle with a little grated Cheddar cheese, and cook in a hot oven, 425°F, 220°C, Gas Mark 7, for 6–8 minutes until well risen and golden brown. Serve at once.

Ten minute cheese soufflés

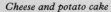
Cheese and potato cake

Camembert mousse

342 CHEESE AND POTATO CAKE

25g/1oz breadcrumbs · 1kg/2lb cooked potatoes, mashed
25g/1oz unsalted butter · 2 tablespoons milk
200g/8oz Gouda cheese, grated · 3 eggs, separated
salt, pepper and nutmeg to season
bacon rolls, parsley and tomato slices to garnish

Butter a soufflé or ovenproof dish and sprinkle bottom and sides with breadcrumbs. Place the mashed potatoes in a mixing bowl and add the butter, milk, cheese and egg yolks. Beat well with a wooden spoon and add the seasonings. Fold the stiffly beaten egg whites into the potato mixture and place in the prepared dish. Place dish on a baking sheet. Cook the cheese and potato cake on the top shelf of a moderately hot oven, 400°F, 200°C, Gas Mark 6, for 30 minutes. When cooked, turn out on to a serving dish. Serve garnished with bacon rolls, parsley and tomato slices.
Makes 8 servings.

343 CAMEMBERT MOUSSE

25g/1oz soft margarine · 25g/1oz flour · 284ml/½pint milk
50g/2oz Camembert cheese, weight without rind
25g/1oz grated Parmesan cheese
1 heaped teaspoon tomato purée
1 heaped teaspoon French mustard · salt and cayenne pepper
1 heaped teaspoon powdered gelatine · 2 eggs, separated
gherkins · stuffed olives and cucumber slices to garnish

Tie a wide band of double greaseproof paper round the outside of a 13-cm (5-inch) soufflé or ovenproof dish, extending above the rim. Melt the margarine, stir in the flour and cook for a minute. Add the milk gradually, bring to the boil and boil a minute, stirring. Add the creamed Camembert, grated Parmesan and seasonings and stir until smooth. Soften the gelatine in 1 tablespoon cold water and dissolve in 2 tablespoons boiling water. Add egg yolks and dissolved gelatine to the cheese sauce, stirring over gentle heat until it thickens. Cool, stirring occasionally, and when almost set fold in the stiffly beaten egg whites. Pour into the prepared dish and leave to set. Remove paper carefully and garnish the mousse with gherkins, stuffed olives and cucumber slices.

344 POTATO CHEESE CAKES

½kg/1lb *mashed potatoes* · 100g/4oz *cheese, grated*
1 *egg yolk* · 1 *teaspoon chopped chives or spring onions*
salt and pepper to taste · *flour or egg and crumbs for coating*
fat or oil for frying

Blend cooked potatoes with 75g (3 oz) of the grated cheese and stir in egg yolk, chives and seasonings. Mix well and divide into small portions with floured hands. Use flour or egg and breadcrumbs for coating shapes, and shallow fry in heated fat or oil until golden brown on both sides. Drain on absorbent paper, sprinkle with remaining cheese and serve with fried bacon rashers.

Potato cheese cakes

345 TOMATO AND CHEESE SURPRISES

8 *small firm tomatoes* · 50g/2oz *cheese, grated* · *salt*
cayenne pepper · *seasoned flour* · 1 *egg* · *brown breadcrumbs*
fat for frying · *parsley to garnish*

Skin the tomatoes and remove the cores. Stuff tightly with the grated cheese seasoned well with salt and cayenne. Roll in seasoned flour. Dip in egg and coat well with breadcrumbs. Fry in fat heated to 350°F, 180°C, for 2–3 minutes until a golden brown. Drain on absorbent paper and serve with salad. Garnish with parsley.

Tomato and cheese surprises

Hot cheese soufflé

346 HOT CHEESE SOUFFLE

3 *eggs* · 25g/1oz *butter* · 15g/½oz *flour* · 142ml/¼pint *milk*
75g/3oz *cheese, grated** · *seasoning, including dry mustard*

**New Zealand Cheddar cheese gives a very good texture in this soufflé*

Separate the eggs. Melt the butter and stir in the flour, gradually add the milk and bring to the boil, stirring until smooth. Cool slightly; add cheese, seasoning and egg yolks one by one, beating well. Fold in the stiffly beaten egg whites and put into a greased ovenproof dish or soufflé dish. Cook in centre of a moderately hot oven, 400°F, 200°C, Gas Mark 6, for about 20 minutes, till well risen and brown. Serve at once.

CLASSIC CHEESE DISHES

Fondue

348   CHEESE ON TOAST

Arrange thin slices of Cheddar cheese on hot buttered toast and put under a hot grill to melt the cheese. Do not over-cook as the cheese will become tough. Serve with chutney.

349   CHEESE PUDDING

100g/4oz *white bread* · 50g/2oz *butter* · 426ml/¾pint *milk*
2 *eggs* · 100–125g/4–5oz *cheese, grated**

**Use Cheddar or Edam cheese*

Cut the bread into cubes and put into a basin. Heat the butter with the milk, pour over the bread. Allow to cool slightly, then add the beaten eggs and most of the grated cheese. Season well. Pour into an ovenproof dish and cover the top with the remainder of the cheese. Cook for 30–40 minutes in the centre of moderate oven, 350°F, 180°C, Gas Mark 4, until firm.

350   WELSH RAREBIT

25g/1oz *butter* · 25g/1oz *flour* · 142ml/¼pint *milk**
1 *teaspoon made mustard* · *salt* · *pepper*
1 *tablespoon beer, ale or Worcestershire sauce*
200g/8oz *cheese, grated* · 4 *slices buttered toast*
parsley to garnish

**If liked, use 2 level tablespoons instant milk, blended with 4 tablespoons cold water, in place of the fresh milk*

Heat the butter in a saucepan, stir in the flour and cook steadily for several minutes, then gradually add the cold milk. Bring to the boil and cook until smooth and thick. Add the mustard, salt, pepper, beer and most of the cheese. Heat steadily, without boiling too quickly, until the cheese has melted. Spread over the hot buttered toast, sprinkle with the remainder of the cheese and brown under a hot grill. Serve at once, garnished with parsley.

This Welsh rarebit mixture can be stored in covered jars for a few days in a refrigerator.

Welsh rarebit

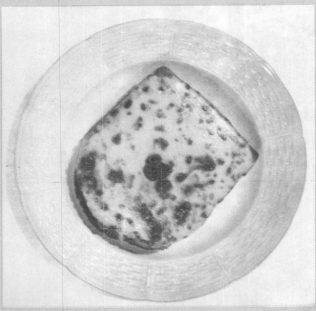

347   FONDUE

This famous Swiss delicacy has become very popular. There are quite a number of variations of it, but this is the classic way to make it.

½kg/1lb *Gruyère cheese, grated* · *seasoning*
284ml/½pint *dry white wine, Graves is ideal*

Butter the bottom and sides of an earthenware casserole or ovenproof dish. An unsalted butter is best for this. Add the Gruyère cheese, or for a milder flavour use a Dutch Gouda. Add seasoning and the white wine. Keep warm over a gentle heat and stir from time to time. If liked a little brandy or Curaçao can be added. Some people use cornflour, which prevents the possibility of the mixture curdling. Details of blending this are in the Cheddar fondue (Recipe No. 358). Serve the fondue with toasted or untoasted bread. This is cut into squares and using a fork, or the fingers, dipped in the cheese mixture, and eaten at once. Under no circumstances let the cheese mixture boil quickly, otherwise it becomes tough and is spoilt.

351 HAWAIIAN SANDWICHES

4 slices bread · butter · 4 slices ham · 4 pineapple rings
4 slices Gouda cheese · paprika pepper and parsley to garnish

Toast bread and spread with butter; then cover with ham, pineapple and lastly the cheese. Brown under the grill until the cheese begins to melt. Serve garnished with paprika pepper and parsley.

352 MACARONI CHEESE

75g/3oz macaroni · 284ml/½pint cheese sauce
(Recipe No. 665)*
50g/2oz cheese, grated · 1 tablespoon crisp breadcrumbs
25g/1oz margarine or butter
triangles of toast and parsley to garnish

*For a more moist macaroni cheese, use 426ml (¾pint) cheese sauce to the same quantity of cooked macaroni

Put the macaroni into about ¾ litre (1½ pints) boiling salted water. Cook steadily until the macaroni is just tender. Do not over-cook; elbow-length quick-cooking macaroni takes only 7 minutes. Drain in a colander, place in a hot dish and pour over the cheese sauce. Sprinkle cheese and breadcrumbs on top and dot with margarine or butter. Either cook for about 25 minutes near the top of a moderately hot oven, 375°F, 190°C, Gas Mark 5, until crisp and brown, or put under a hot grill. Garnish with triangles of toast and parsley.

Macaroni cheese

353   MACARONI CHEESE WITH BACON AND ONION

100g/4oz *short-cut macaroni* · 8 *rashers back bacon, chopped*
2 *medium-sized onions, thinly sliced*
284ml/½pint *rich cheese sauce (Recipe No. 354)*
50g/2oz *cheese, grated*

Cook macaroni as directed on packet. Drain. Fry bacon lightly, remove from the pan and drain. Fry the onions in bacon fat until lightly browned. Make the cheese sauce, stir in the drained macaroni, onions and half the bacon. Turn into an ovenproof dish, sprinkle with the grated cheese and remaining bacon and brown under the grill.

Macaroni cheese with bacon and onion

Garnishes for Welsh rarebit

354   RICH CHEESE SAUCE

15g/½oz *butter or margarine* · 15g/½oz *flour*
284ml/½pint *milk* · *good pinch salt* · 1 *teaspoon made mustard*
150g/6oz *Cheddar cheese, grated*

To make this sauce use method for ordinary cheese sauce (Recipe No. 665) but because of the higher proportion of cheese, less flour and butter are required.

355   GARNISHES FOR WELSH RAREBIT

This picture shows various garnishes for Welsh rarebit. Try grilled bacon rashers, a few stewed prunes, a canned pineapple ring, sliced grilled mushrooms, a sardine or tomato slices.

356   TOMATO RAREBIT

Instead of using milk and beer in Recipe No. 350 use the contents of a 250g (10oz) can condensed tomato soup. Garnish with grated cheese but do NOT brown under the grill.

Cheese casserole

357   CHEESE CASSEROLE

200g/8oz *Continental (Vienna) sausages*
generous ½litre/1pint *white sauce (Recipe No. 663)*
3 *teaspoons made mustard* · 100g/4oz *strong cheese, finely grated*
100g/4oz *cooked macaroni* · *seasoning to taste*
cooked sliced mushrooms to garnish

Stand the sausages in boiling water for 10 minutes, then remove and cut into fairly thick slices. Make the white sauce and add the mustard, cheese (reserve some for garnish), sausage slices, cooked macaroni and seasoning to taste. Reheat gently and turn the mixture into a serving dish. Garnish with remaining cheese and the sliced mushrooms.

358 CHEDDAR FONDUE

2 cloves garlic · ½kg/1lb *Cheddar cheese, grated*
284ml/½pint *white wine* · 1 tablespoon cornflour
1 tablespoon Kirsch · 375g/15oz *can cream of celery soup*
pieces French bread

Rub round the inside of an earthenware casserole or fondue
dish with the cut clove of garlic, then crush the garlic. Place the
cheese and crushed garlic in the dish and add the wine.
Slowly melt the cheese over a low heat. Blend the cornflour
and Kirsch together and add to the melted cheese. Bring to
the boil to thicken the mixture, cook for a few minutes then
lower the heat. Add the soup gradually, stirring well between
additions. This can be kept warm over a low heat but should
not be allowed to boil again. To serve, dip pieces of bread on
long handled forks into the hot fondue.
Makes 6–8 servings.

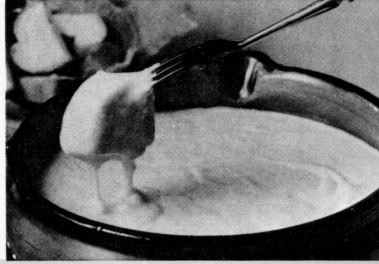

Cheddar fondue

Tomato fondue

Cheese scone rings

359 TOMATO FONDUE

142ml/¼pint *inexpensive white wine* · 1 *small clove garlic*
250g/10oz *can condensed tomato soup* · 150g/6oz *cheese, grated*
2 eggs · *salt to taste* · *little ground black pepper*

Put wine with crushed clove of garlic into a small pan and cook
until wine is well reduced. Strain into a bowl and add the
condensed soup, grated cheese, beaten eggs and seasoning.
Mix well, then return the mixture to rinsed pan and stir over
low heat until blended. Do not allow the mixture to boil.
To serve, dip pieces of bread on long handled forks into the
hot fondue.

360 CHEESE SCONE RINGS

200g/8oz *plain flour* · ½ *level teaspoon salt*
pinch dry mustard · 4 *level teaspoons baking powder*
50g/2oz *butter* · 125g/5oz *Dunlop or Cheddar cheese, grated*
about 142ml/¼pint *milk*

Sieve the flour, salt, mustard and baking powder together,
and rub in the butter. Add most of the grated cheese and
sufficient milk to make a soft dough. Knead lightly and roll out
to 2½-cm (1-inch) thickness and cut out rounds with a 5-cm
(2-inch) plain cutter. Arrange the scones in 2 rings of 8, on a
lightly floured baking sheet and brush with milk. Sprinkle the
remaining grated cheese on top and cook in a hot oven, 425°F,
220°C, Gas Mark 7, for 10–15 minutes, until well risen and
golden brown. Serve hot or cold at any meal; they make a
pleasant change from bread rolls with soup or the main course.

361 CHEESE AND TUNA MEDLEY

175g/7oz *can tuna fish* · 100g/4oz *potato crisps*
1 *small packet frozen peas* · 50g/2oz *mushrooms, sliced*
1 *onion, chopped* · 150g/6oz *Cheddar cheese, grated*
salt and pepper · 3 *eggs* · 284ml/½pint *milk*
few peas to garnish

Flake tuna fish in a mixing bowl, crush potato crisps and mix in. Add peas, mushrooms, onion, most of the cheese, seasoning, and mix well together. Beat eggs lightly and add milk. Pour into fish mixture. Put into a buttered ovenproof dish and sprinkle on remaining cheese. Cook in a moderate oven, 350°F, 170°C, Gas Mark 4, for 30–40 minutes. Serve hot, garnished with a few peas.

362 CHEESE QUICKIE

50g/2oz *butter* · 1kg/2lb *boiled potatoes* · *salt and pepper*
12 *spring onions or* 1 *onion* · 100g/4oz *cooked peas*
200g/8oz *Cheddar cheese, cut into cubes*
1 *level teaspoon dry mustard* · 2 *tomatoes, sliced*
little chopped onion to garnish, optional

Heat butter in a large frying pan, slice potatoes and fry until golden brown on underside. Season well. Chop onions and spoon on to potatoes with the peas. Toss cheese in the seasoning and sprinkle on to vegetables. Arrange tomato slices on top. Cover with a lid or foil and heat through gently until cheese begins to melt. If liked, garnish with a little chopped onion.

Cheese and tuna medley

Cheese quickie

363   RICH CHEESE SCONES

*200g/8oz flour (with plain flour use 3 level teaspoons
baking powder) · ¼ teaspoon salt · 50g/2oz butter
100g/4oz cheese, grated · milk to mix
beaten egg or milk to glaze, optional*

Sift together the flour, baking powder (if used) and salt. Rub in the butter and add the grated cheese. Gradually stir in enough milk to give a soft dough. Turn out on to a floured board, knead lightly, then roll out to about 1½-cm (¾-inch) thickness. Cut into rounds, put on to a baking sheet and brush with beaten egg or milk, if liked. Bake near the top of a hot oven, 425°F, 220°C, Gas Mark 7, for 7–10 minutes.

Cheese scones

364   CHEESE TARTLETS

*175g/6oz flaky pastry (Recipe No. 604) · 25g/1oz butter
2 eggs · 100g/4oz cheese, grated · 3 tablespoons soft breadcrumbs
3 tablespoons milk or single cream · salt and pepper*

Roll out the pastry thinly, and line patty tins with this. Bake 'blind' (Recipe No. 560) for 10 minutes only, in a hot oven, 450°F, 230°C, Gas Mark 8. Meanwhile prepare the filling by melting the butter and mixing this with all the other ingredients. Put a small quantity of the filling into the half baked pastry cases and return to the oven; lower the heat to 375°F, 190°C, Gas Mark 5 and cook until the pastry is cooked and filling set.

Other cheese flan recipes will be found in the pastry section

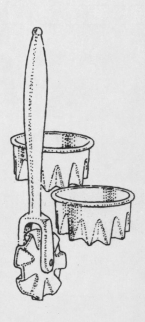

365   EGG AND VEGETABLE CUTLETS

*25g/1oz margarine · 25g/1oz flour
142ml/¼pint milk or milk and vegetable stock
250g/10oz can mixed vegetables · 3 hard-boiled eggs
seasoning · 1 egg, beaten · crisp breadcrumbs
fat or oil for frying · parsley and tomato slices to garnish*

Heat the margarine in a pan, stir in flour, and cook for several minutes. Gradually add milk. Bring to boil and cook until thickened. Add well drained vegetables, chopped hard-boiled eggs and seasoning. Form into cutlet shapes, brush with beaten egg, roll in breadcrumbs and fry until golden brown. Drain on absorbent paper. Garnish with parsley and tomato slices.

Blackcurrant cheesecake

Pineapple cheesecake

Coral island eggs

Quick devilled eggs

366   BLACKCURRANT CHEESECAKE

1 blackcurrant-flavoured jelly · 375g/15oz can blackcurrants
½kg/1lb cottage cheese, sieved · 25g/1oz castor sugar
142ml/¼pint double cream, lightly whipped
8 digestive biscuits, crushed with a rolling pin
25g/1oz Demerara sugar · 50g/2oz butter, melted
grapes to decorate

Measure the blackcurrant juice and make up to 284ml (½ pint) with hot water. Dissolve jelly in this liquid. Blend together sieved blackcurrants, sieved cottage cheese and castor sugar, then stir in cooled jelly. Fold in lightly whipped cream. Turn into a lightly greased 20-cm (8-inch) round cake tin and chill until set.
Place biscuits, Demerara sugar and melted butter in a bowl. Mix well with a fork. Sprinkle over cheesecake mixture, press down lightly. Return to the refrigerator until firm. Turn out and decorate with halved grapes.
Makes 8–10 servings.

367   PINEAPPLE CHEESECAKE

125g/5oz butter · 25g/1oz castor sugar · 200g/8oz flour
pinch salt · 1 egg yolk · 1–2 tablespoons water
2 pineapple rings · 50g/2oz seedless raisins
200g/8oz cottage cheese · 2 cartons soured cream
50g/2oz castor sugar · 2 eggs and 1 egg white
1 teaspoon grated lemon rind

Well grease a 20-cm (8-inch) flan ring and baking sheet. Cream together butter and sugar, then work in flour and salt. Bind together with egg yolk blended with water. Roll out pastry and line flan ring. Chill. Save trimmings, roll out and cut narrow strips for lattice.
Put drained chopped pineapple and raisins on bottom of pastry case. Sieve cottage cheese. Beat in remaining ingredients. Pour into pastry case. Bake in a moderately hot oven, 400°F, 200°C, Gas Mark 6, for 20 minutes. Remove from oven, lattice top with strips and return to oven, 325°F, 170°C, Gas Mark 3, for a further 35 minutes.
Makes 8 servings.

368   CORAL ISLAND EGGS

200g/8oz peeled shrimps · 50g/2oz butter · 2 egg whites
2 teaspoons sherry, optional · seasoning
8 slices white bread · 4 hard-boiled eggs
fat or oil for frying · parsley to garnish

Finely chop shrimps and mix well with butter. Add 1 egg white and mix in sherry (if used) and seasoning. Cut bread into diamond-shaped pieces and place a small mound of the mixture on each piece. Halve hard-boiled eggs lengthways and place one half, flat side down, on each mound, pressing mixture together firmly round base of egg. Brush all over with remaining egg white. Fry in deep fat or oil heated to 350°F, 180°C, with egg side downwards, then turn over and continue cooking until bread is golden brown. Drain on absorbent paper and serve at once garnished with parsley.

369   QUICK DEVILLED EGGS

4 hard-boiled eggs · 2 tablespoons sandwich spread
seasoning · few drops Worcestershire sauce
few prawns and capers · parsley to garnish

Cut the eggs in half lengthways. Remove the yolks and mix well with the sandwich spread, seasoning and sauce. Spoon or pipe the mixture into the whites and top with a few prawns and a caper. Garnish with parsley.

HOT DEVILLED EGGS

6 hard-boiled eggs · 4 tablespoons sandwich spread
1 dessertspoon Worcestershire sauce
1 dessertspoon made mustard · 1 teaspoon salt · pinch pepper
mushroom sauce (Recipe Nos. 371, 674)
mixed vegetables, tomato slices and parsley to garnish

Shell hard-boiled eggs and cut in halves lengthways. Remove yolks and mash. Mix the sandwich spread, Worcestershire sauce, mustard and seasonings. Refill egg white cases with mixture and place in buttered ovenproof dish. Cover with buttered paper and heat through in moderate oven, 350°F, 180°C, Gas Mark 4. Make quick or ordinary mushroom sauce and cook for several minutes, until thickened and flour cooked. Remove eggs to a heated serving dish and pour the sauce over. Garnish with mixed vegetables, tomato slices and parsley.

371 QUICK MUSHROOM SAUCE

25g/1oz butter · 25g/1oz flour · 375g/15oz can mushroom soup
1 dessertspoon Worcestershire sauce

Melt the butter, add the flour, and stir until blended. Add the soup and cook until thickened. Add the Worcestershire sauce.

372 STUFFED EGGS WITH ASPIC

284ml–generous ¼litre/½–1pint aspic jelly (Recipe No. 283)
6 large eggs · 1 small can sardines
4–8 tablespoons mayonnaise (Recipe Nos. 408, 412)
2–3 teaspoons lemon juice · salt and pepper
2 teaspoons chopped parsley or pinch powdered tarragon
gherkins and parsley to garnish

Make the aspic jelly and pour into a shallow dish and leave to set. Hard-boil the eggs, shell, cut in half lengthways, then carefully remove yolks from whites. Mash yolks with sardines, drained of oil, and stir in enough mayonnaise to make a smooth, creamy mixture. Beat in lemon juice, season with salt and pepper, then add the chopped parsley or tarragon. Pile or pipe mixture into the egg whites. When ready to serve, turn aspic jelly on to a double thickness of greaseproof paper that has been lightly brushed or sprinkled with water. Chop the aspic quickly with a sharp knife. Arrange egg halves in serving dish, pile aspic in centre then garnish with gherkins and parsley.

Hot devilled eggs

Stuffed eggs with aspic

Egg and ham bake

373   EGG AND HAM BAKE

100g/4oz lean uncooked pork · 50g/2oz cooked ham
50g/2oz butter · 1 small onion, peeled and sliced
25g/1oz flour · 142ml/¼pint stock or water
300g/12oz tomatoes · 4 eggs

Slice the pork and ham into strips. Melt the butter in a frying pan and fry the onion and pork for about 5 minutes. Stir in the flour and cook for 2–3 minutes. Add the stock and stirring, bring to the boil. Skin and halve the tomatoes and add all but 5 halves to the mixture. Simmer for 15–20 minutes; add the ham towards the end of the cooking time. Transfer to an ovenproof dish and break the eggs over the surface and arrange the remaining tomatoes between them. Cook in a moderately hot oven, 375°F, 190°C, Gas Mark 5, for about 20 minutes, until the eggs are set.

OMELETTES

374   CHOOSING AN OMELETTE PAN

If possible a pan should be kept exclusively for cooking omelettes. It should be made of thick iron or aluminium and have sloping sides and rounded corners so that the omelette can be easily removed when cooked. The correct pan is essential for cooking perfect omelettes.

375   LOOKING AFTER YOUR OMELETTE PAN

An omelette pan should not be washed after use, but wiped clean with soft paper (kitchen rolls are ideal for this). Never get the butter so hot that there is a possibility of anything burning in it. If the pan is treated well it should last for years.

376

Omelettes must be eaten as soon as they are cooked.
Allow 1½–2 eggs per person. Beat the eggs in a basin. Do not
forget to break them separately into a cup, in case one should
be bad, before transferring them to the basin. Add a good pinch
salt and pepper, and for every 2 eggs a tablespoon water. Put
a knob of butter into the pan. When hot pour in the eggs.
Leave for about a minute over a high heat, when the bottom
will have set, then loosen the egg mixture from the sides of the
pan and cook rapidly, tipping the pan from side to side, so
that the liquid egg flows underneath and cooks quickly. When
the egg is as set as you like it, for taste varies, slip a palette
knife under the omelette and fold it away from the handle.
Grasp the handle firmly and tip the omelette on to a hot plate
or dish. Garnish with parsley.
Do not cook more than 4 eggs in a 16-cm (6-inch) pan, otherwise cooking will take too long and the omelette will become
dry.

Spanish omelette (Recipe No. 389)

FILLINGS FOR OMELETTES

An omelette can be varied in a number of ways.

377 MIXED HERB OMELETTE

Add finely chopped herbs to the beaten eggs.

378 CHEESE OMELETTE

Grated cheese should be either mixed with the beaten eggs, or
better still, put over the eggs just before they have set.

379 MACARONI OMELETTE

50g (2 oz) cooked macaroni, mixed with 3 beaten eggs and,
just before folding, grated cheese put in the middle.

380 HAM OMELETTE

Either mix finely chopped ham with the beaten eggs, or put
ham in a little white sauce (Recipe No. 663) in the middle as a
filling.

381 CHICKEN OMELETTE

Either mix finely chopped cooked chicken with the beaten
eggs, or put chicken in a little white sauce (Recipe No. 663) in
the middle as a filling.

382 MUSHROOM OMELETTE

Cook mushrooms and mix with the beaten eggs, or put in the
middle in a little white sauce (Recipe No. 663).

383 TOMATO OMELETTE

Simmer skinned and sliced tomatoes in butter or margarine,
until tender, season well and use as a filling.

384 SOUFFLE OMELETTES

A soufflé omelette is a very much thicker omelette with a very
light, but to some people, slightly drier, texture. It is not
difficult to make. Beat the egg yolks with seasoning (for a sweet
omelette with a little sugar – see Recipe Nos. 386–8), then
fold in the stiffly beaten egg whites. Heat the butter in the pan
in exactly the same way, pour in the egg mixture and cook
steadily. Because this is so thick it is difficult to get it cooking
quickly enough from the bottom, so put the soufflé omelette
under a moderate grill or in the oven, when it is reasonably set
at the bottom. In this way it will cook quickly without tough-
ening the eggs.

385 CHEESE SOUFFLE OMELETTE

2 eggs · pinch salt and cayenne pepper
15g/½oz Cheddar cheese, finely grated
2 tablespoons milk or single cream · 15g/½oz butter

Filling

2 tablespoons thick cheese sauce (Recipe No. 665)
1 tablespoon finely grated Cheddar cheese

Make the cheese sauce for the filling and keep warm. Separate the yolks from the whites. Add the seasoning, grated cheese and milk or cream to the yolks; mix well. Whisk the whites stiffly. Fold the whites into the yolk and cheese mixture. Heat the butter in an omelette pan, pour in the egg mixture and cook over the gentle heat until golden brown and set underneath. Cook the top surface under a fairly hot grill for 2 minutes until golden brown or in a moderately hot oven, 400°F, 200°C, Gas Mark 6, for 5–6 minutes. Turn on to greaseproof paper sprinkled with finely grated Cheddar cheese, mark across the centre with the back of a knife, spread with the cheese sauce, fold in half and serve at once.

SWEET OMELETTES

The soufflé omelette mixture is ideal as a sweet. The following are excellent:

386 APRICOT SOUFFLE OMELETTE

3 eggs · 25g/1oz sugar · 25g/1oz butter
2 tablespoons milk or single cream
a few cooked or canned apricots

Prepare the eggs as described under soufflé omelettes (Recipe No. 384), adding cream and sugar to the egg yolks. Cook as described, then fill with the apricots and serve.

387 JAM OMELETTE

Make as above, with hot jam sauce for a filling.

388 RUM OR BRANDY OMELETTE

Flavour the yolks with rum or brandy. If liked, pour over a little heated spirit before serving and ignite it.

Cheese soufflé omelette

Other omelette recipes are given in the breakfast section.

Apricot soufflé omelette

Spanish baked eggs

Scotch eggs

389 SPANISH OMELETTE
(Tortilla)
(Also illustrated in colour on the preceding page)

This is an ideal omelette for 'using up' savoury ingredients. Fry a little chopped onion or chives and add cooked or canned peas, red or green peppers, chopped shrimps or prawns or cooked or canned meat. When piping hot tip into the beaten eggs, season well (if liked, add a dash of Tabasco sauce) and cook as directed for a plain omelette. If the omelette is very 'fat' do not attempt to fold it but serve it flat on the plate.
Variation: Add whole eggs to fried mixture, cook until set.

390 SCOTCH EGGS

4 eggs · 2 tablespoons flour · 200g/8oz sausage meat
breadcrumbs · 1 egg and 4 tablespoons milk for coating
deep fat or oil for frying · tomato and cucumber slices to garnish

Hard-boil the eggs, shell and cool them then roll lightly in flour. Divide the sausage meat into four, fold evenly and smoothly round the lightly floured eggs. Coat these with the beaten egg and milk blended together; roll each firmly in breadcrumbs. Fry in fat or oil heated to 350°F, 180°C, and drain on absorbent paper. Remember that the sausage meat has to cook through so do not rush the frying process. Halve each egg with a sharp knife dipped in hot water. Serve hot or cold garnished with tomato and cucumber slices.

391 BAKED EGGS

Heat oven to 375°F, 190°C, Gas Mark 5. Warm 4 small ovenproof dishes and brush all round inside with melted butter. Break 2 eggs into each dish and top with a piece of butter. Place dishes in a baking dish half filled with hot (not boiling) water. Cook in the oven for about 8 minutes, until the whites are just set. Serve at once in the dishes.

Baked eggs

Eggs and rice supreme

392 EGGS AND RICE SUPREME

300g/12oz hot cooked long grain rice · 4 hard-boiled eggs
25g/1oz butter or margarine · dash Worcestershire sauce
seasoning · white sauce (Recipe No. 663)
½ teaspoon made mustard
100g/4oz cheese, grated

Divide rice between 4 individual ovenproof dishes. Cut eggs in half lengthways. Remove yolks and blend with butter, Worcestershire sauce and seasoning. Stuff the egg whites with the yolk mixture. Arrange 2 halves on rice in each dish. Stir mustard into white sauce and spoon over eggs. Sprinkle with cheese and place under a hot grill for about 3 minutes.

SALADS *and how to prepare them*

Salads are becoming more and more popular. We realise their value in providing vitamins, also their eye appeal which is important. Try to be adventurous with salads because there is a surprising variety of vegetables, fruit, etc. which can be served. Lettuce is first choice as a basis for a salad, but do not ignore shredded cabbage, endive, shredded sprouts, sprigs of cauliflower, etc., which are often more economical when lettuce is out of season, and are very delicious. The root vegetables, turnip, swede and carrot, when grated, add crispness and interest to your salad. Nuts provide excellent protein and tomatoes add vitamins. Always wash salad vegetables well, lift out of bowl and shake it reasonably dry in a cloth or salad shaker. Do not cut lettuce with an ordinary knife. Use a stainless one or better still, shred it with your fingers as this prevents discolouration.

To skin tomatoes either lower them in very hot water, or put a fine skewer through the centre and hold them over a gas-flame or electric plate until the skin bursts. You will find it comes off very easily. Radishes can be shaped like roses if you cut them down and leave in cold water for about 10 minutes.

Bowl of salad; poached eggs Alexandra (Recipe No. 855)

393 HAM AND APPLE SALAD
(Illustrated in colour on opposite page)

Mix together cooked long grain rice (Recipe No. 140), cubed ham, a little onion, fried in oil and 1 eating apple, cored and chopped. Serve in a bowl lined with lettuce leaves.

394 FRUIT IN SALADS

Fruit seems to some people to be incongruous in a salad, but this is quite wrong. The sharp fruits like orange and grapefruit make a salad most refreshing and counteract any richness in meat. Duck needs an orange salad. For a change try crisp apples, pineapple, sliced banana, strawberries with a cheese salad, and for children add some of the dried fruits, such as dates or soaked prunes, as well. The picture on the left shows sliced apples (tossed in lemon juice) mixed with chopped ham, celery and radishes. The dish is garnished with chopped parsley.

Fruit in salads

Ham and apple salad (Recipe No. 393)

Cheese and beetroot salad

396 CHEESE AND BEETROOT SALAD

200g/8oz *Cheddar cheese, cubed*
200g/8oz *cooked beetroot, cubed*
French dressing (Recipe No. 398)
1 *small green pepper, seeds removed and sliced*
1 *small onion, peeled and sliced · 2 tomatoes, skinned and sliced*
chicory to garnish

Arrange cubes of cheese at either end of a flat serving dish, then cubes of beetroot, tossed in French dressing. Next to the beetroot arrange the slices of pepper, also tossed in dressing. Down the centre of the dish arrange alternate slices of onion and tomato. Garnish the dish with chicory.

395 JAMBALAYA

A savoury rice and meat salad

100g/4oz *long grain rice*
300g/12oz *can pork luncheon meat or cooked meat, finely chopped*
50g/2oz *quick-cooking rolled oats · 4 tablespoons milk*
2 *tablespoons tomato ketchup · 1 teaspoon made mustard*
fat for frying · few green peas · lettuce to garnish

Cook rice in boiling salted water for 10–15 minutes until tender. Drain, rinse under cold water and dry off for a short time in a cool oven. Mix luncheon meat with quick-cooking oats, milk, tomato ketchup and mustard. Shape into a large patty, cut in cubes, fry quickly in hot fat, drain and cool. Fold the cubes into the rice with the peas. Serve on a bed of lettuce.

397 CHICKEN PLATTER

This is a good way of transforming cold chicken into an exciting meal.
Mix chopped cold chicken with a little mayonnaise (Recipe Nos. 408, 412) and place in a bowl. Stand the bowl in the centre of a round bread board or large plate. Surround with slices of salami or liver sausage, frankfurters and a selection of vegetables. Serve with French bread or rolls.

398 FRENCH DRESSING

1 *dessertspoon vinegar*
1 *tablespoon finely chopped parsley or chives*
1 *tablespoon salad oil · pinch sugar, salt and pepper*

Mix all the ingredients together. Before using, mix again.

Chicken platter

Corn and ham cornets

399 CORN AND HAM CORNETS

1 large packet frozen sweet corn · 1 hard-boiled egg
1 tablespoon chopped parsley · 3 dessertspoons salad cream
little milk · 4 slices lean ham · lettuce
tomato wedges to garnish

Cook the sweet corn according to the instructions on the packet. Drain and allow to cool. When cold, add half the egg, chopped, the parsley, salad cream and milk. Mix well together and roll each slice of ham into a cornet shape by twisting firmly or rolling round the outside of a cream horn tin. Arrange on a serving plate lined with lettuce leaves. Fill each ham cornet with a little of the corn mixture and put the remainder in the centre. Garnish with remaining egg, quartered and the tomato wedges.

400 POINSETTIA TOMATOES

Cheese balls

200g/8oz Cheddar cheese, grated · 4 tablespoons sultanas
½ level teaspoon salt · 4 large tomatoes · salt and pepper
pinch cayenne pepper · ½ teaspoon Worcestershire sauce
4 tablespoons salad cream · lettuce
French dressing (Recipe No. 398)

Mix together all the ingredients for the cheese balls. Divide into 8 portions and with wet hands roll into balls. With a sharp knife cut the tomatoes down into one-sixths, leaving the sections attached at the base. Sprinkle with salt and pepper and place a cheese ball in the centre of each tomato. Arrange the tomatoes on a bed of lettuce; garnish with the remaining cheese balls and serve with French dressing.

COTTAGE CHEESE SALADS

401 Cottage cheese and tomato salad Spoon cottage cheese into the centre of a serving dish. Arrange prawns and tomato slices round the edge of the dish. Garnish with endive and chicory.

402 Tuna fish and cheese salad Mix together equal quantities of flaked tuna fish and cottage cheese. Season with salt, pepper and mustard. Arrange on a slice of pineapple.

403 Ham and pineapple salad Mix cottage cheese with chopped ham and pineapple chunks. Serve on a bed of lettuce.

404 Peach cheese salad Spoon chive-flavoured cottage cheese into peach halves. Arrange on a bed of lettuce.

405 Apricot cheese salad Mix together cottage cheese and chopped peanuts. Spoon into apricot halves and serve on a bed of cress. If liked garnish with preserved or stem ginger.

406 Banana split salad Halve a banana lengthways, sprinkle with lemon juice or French dressing; spoon cottage cheese along the centre. Garnish with fresh fruit in season or chopped nuts.

Cottage cheese and tomato salad

407 SALAD PLATTER

A variety of foods can be included in a salad platter to form a well balanced meal.

Include plenty of lettuce, shredded cabbage and/or endive.
Beetroot and grapes add sweetness to the salad.
Nuts, carrots, cucumber, chicory and celery add crispness and flavour.
Tomatoes and parsley provide valuable vitamins.
Peas, nuts and cheese provide protein.

The picture on the right shows shredded cabbage and grated carrot mixed with sliced green pepper and radishes. The vegetables are tossed in mayonnaise (Recipe No. 408). The dish is garnished with sliced carrots.

Salad platter

408 CLASSIC MAYONNAISE

1 egg yolk · good pinch salt, pepper and mustard
about 142ml/¼pint *olive oil or corn oil*
1 dessertspoon vinegar · 1 dessertspoon warm water

Put the egg yolk and seasonings into a basin. *Gradually* beat in the oil, drop by drop, stirring all the time until the mixture is thick. When thick and creamy do not add any more oil, for too much will make the mixture curdle. Beat in the vinegar gradually, then the warm water. Use when fresh.

If using a liquidiser put egg, seasoning and vinegar into goblet. Switch on for a few seconds, then pour oil in steadily (with the speed on medium setting) through the hole left by the 'cap' of the liquidiser lid or with the lid tilted to avoid splashing.

409 Green mayonnaise Add finely chopped parsley, chives, sage and thyme to mayonnaise.

410 Curried mayonnaise Add a little curry powder and paste to mayonnaise.

411 Tomato mayonnaise Add tomato purée or pulp and a few drops of Tabasco or Worcestershire sauce to mayonnaise.

412 MAYONNAISE WITHOUT EGGS

1 level teaspoon mustard* · 1 teaspoon sugar
½ teaspoon salt · pinch pepper
1 small can evaporated milk · 142ml/¼pint *olive oil*
2–3 tablespoons vinegar**

*French or English mustard may be used
**Wine vinegar gives an excellent flavour

Put the mustard into a bowl with sugar, salt and a pinch of pepper. Add the evaporated milk. Mix and gradually beat in the olive oil. Add the vinegar, to thicken the mixture. Season to taste.

This is a quick and easy way of making mayonnaise as there is no danger of it curdling.

413 PIQUANT EGG SALAD

Line a serving dish with lettuce leaves. Mix together chopped celery and cored and sliced eating apples, tossed in lemon juice. If liked, add a little cooked chopped chicken. Spoon into the dish. Arrange quarters of hard-boiled egg around the edge and garnish with chopped parsley and gherkins. Serve with mayonnaise (Recipe Nos. 408, 412).

Piquant egg salad

French loaf salad

414   ORANGE SALAD

Arrange washed and dried lettuce leaves on a serving dish. With a sharp knife, peel an orange and cut away the pith. Cut into segments and arrange on the lettuce. Serve with French dressing (Recipe No. 398) or vinaigrette dressing (Recipe No. 419).

415   ORANGE AND PINEAPPLE SALAD

Follow the recipe, above, for orange salad. Garnish with pineapple cubes and finely chopped egg white. These salads are excellent with duck and rich meats.

416   ECONOMICAL SALAD DRESSING

1 small can full cream condensed milk · ½ teaspoon salt
142ml/¼pint vinegar · 1 teaspoon dry mustard

Mix all the ingredients and beat well. Chill before serving.

417   FRENCH LOAF SALAD

Cut a French loaf along the centre, but not right through, and spread with butter. Line the loaf with small lettuce leaves and arrange slices of cucumber, tomato and hard-boiled egg on the lettuce. Place sardines along the centre and garnish with sprigs of parsley.

418   MAGIC MAYONNAISE

1 small can full cream condensed milk
142ml/¼pint salad oil or melted butter · 2 egg yolks
½ teaspoon salt · 1 teaspoon dry mustard
pinch cayenne pepper · 142ml/¼pint vinegar or lemon juice

Place all the ingredients in a bowl and beat well with a whisk until the mixture thickens. This mayonnaise can be stored in a covered container in the refrigerator for a very long time.

419   VINAIGRETTE DRESSING

2 dessertspoons vinegar★ · 5 dessertspoons olive oil
good pinch salt · pepper to taste

★Use wine, cider or tarragon vinegar

Mix all ingredients in bowl. Before serving mix again.

420   HARD-BOILED EGG SALAD

Arrange 2 rows of hard-boiled egg slices down the centre of an oval serving dish. Either side of the egg slices arrange slices of tomato. Garnish with sprigs of watercress. Spoon mayonnaise (Recipe Nos. 408, 412) over the eggs and sprinkle with a little paprika.

Hard-boiled egg salad

421 CUCUMBER CANDLESTICKS WITH SEAFOOD FILLING

2 straight cucumbers · 1 small can crabmeat or fresh crabmeat
salt and pepper · mayonnaise (Recipe Nos. 408, 412)
juice ½ lemon · 5–6 medium-sized firm tomatoes
few crisp lettuce leaves · about 284ml/½pint fresh shrimps*

*Or 100g/4oz frozen shrimps

Wipe cucumbers and cut off thin seedless end and tip of thick end to leave straight-sided lengths. Cut these into about 4 pieces. With potato peeler, pare off strips of skin along the length of the pieces to give a striped green and white look. With a small spoon, scoop out the seeds, leaving a firm wall of cucumber all round and a piece at base of each length. Sprinkle with salt inside and turn upside-down to drain. Flake crabmeat, season to taste and mix with a little mayonnaise and lemon juice. Fill cucumber candlesticks with the mixture and stand on thick slices of tomato. Arrange on a bed of lettuce. Garnish with shrimps. This salad can also be made with any cooked white fish, boned, flaked and well seasoned. If liked, add a dash of paprika pepper and a few chopped capers.

Butter bean and sardine salad

423 BUTTER BEAN AND SARDINE SALAD

1 large can butter beans · 2 tomatoes, skinned and sliced
2 tablespoons chopped parsley · 2 teaspoons vinegar
1 can sardines · 1 small packet potato crisps

Place the beans, tomatoes, half the parsley and the vinegar in a bowl. Add sufficient oil from the sardines to moisten, and mix together. To serve, spoon the bean mixture into a flat serving dish, sprinkle with the remaining parsley and arrange the sardines down either side. Arrange the crisps in the centre.

422 TUNA AND EGG SALAD

2 hard-boiled eggs · lettuce · 1 small can tuna fish
275g/11oz can mandarin oranges
1 tablespoon mayonnaise (Recipe Nos. 408, 412) · radishes
1 green pepper · chopped parsley to garnish

Shell the eggs and cut into slices. Arrange the lettuce on a flat serving dish. Flake the tuna fish and mix with the well drained mandarin oranges. Pile into the centre of the dish and spoon over the mayonnaise. Arrange hard-boiled eggs and radish slices along each side of the dish. Arrange rings of green pepper on the lettuce. Garnish with chopped parsley.

424 TUNA WHIP AND SALAD

1 small can tuna fish · 6 tablespoons salad cream
1 dessertspoon lemon juice
2 tablespoons single cream or top of milk · good pinch pepper
endive, tomato and hard-boiled egg slices to garnish

Remove tuna from can and mash very finely. Mix with salad cream, lemon juice, cream or top of milk and the pepper. Beat well and if possible, chill before using. Serve garnished with endive, tomato and hard-boiled egg slices.

Tuna and egg salad

425 ORANGE AND TOMATO SALAD

Have you ever eaten oranges and tomatoes together? They make a colourful combination which is delicious. To make the salad, simply alternate sections of peeled orange with slices of firm tomatoes on a bed of lettuce and watercress. Sprinkle with chopped mint and a slightly sweet, tangy French dressing (Recipe No. 426). You will find that this salad makes a wonderful light but satisfying luncheon or high tea dish with bread and cheese. It is also perfect with roast duck, pork or goose.

426 SWEET FRENCH DRESSING

1 teaspoon sugar · ½ teaspoon salt · pinch paprika
3 dessertspoons olive oil
1 dessertspoon white wine vinegar or 1½ dessertspoons lemon juice

Shake all the ingredients together and pour the dressing over a salad just before serving.

427 COLE SLAW

1 small Savoy cabbage · 2 dessertspoons olive oil
1 dessertspoon vinegar · salt and pepper
1–2 tablespoons mayonnaise (Recipe Nos. 408, 412)

Shred the cabbage finely and place in a serving bowl. Mix the remaining ingredients together; toss the cabbage in the mayonnaise mixture. Leave in a cool place for about 15 minutes before serving to allow the flavours to blend.

428 APPLE COLE SLAW

Mix 2 eating apples, cored and grated or chopped with the cabbage. If liked, add a few drained canned pineapple pieces. Serve in a bowl lined with lettuce leaves and garnish with walnut halves, black olives and a sprig of parsley.

Apple cole slaw

429 APPLE AND CELERY COLE SLAW

Mix 1 eating apple, cored and grated or chopped and 2 sticks celery, finely chopped, with the cabbage.

430 SPICED COLE SLAW

Mix 1 eating apple, cored and grated or chopped and 1–2 sticks celery, finely chopped, with the cabbage. Soak 50g (2 oz) seedless raisins in the oil and vinegar mixture. Add a pinch of mixed spice.

431 ORANGE AND CHEESE SALAD FLAN

2½ tablespoons orange juice · finely grated rind 1 orange
90g*/3½oz whipped-up cooking fat · 1 dessertspoon castor sugar
225g*/8oz plain flour · pinch salt · 100g/4oz cream cheese
lettuce, cucumber slices, radishes, orange slices and walnuts
to garnish

*Although not the usual metric conversion gives best result and correct quantity for amount of liquid

Bring orange juice and rind to the boil, add to cooking fat and sugar. Stir in 1 tablespoon flour and whisk until light and creamy. Sieve the rest of the flour and salt together and mix with the orange juice, etc., to form a firm dough. Roll out thinly and line a Swiss roll tin. Prick the bottom, and bake in a moderately hot oven, 400°F, 200°C, Gas Mark 6, for 15–20 minutes. When cool spread with cheese, and garnish with lettuce, cucumber slices, radishes, orange slices and walnuts. Makes 6 servings.

432 MANDARIN RICE SALAD

200g/8oz cooked ham · 1 small green pepper
150g/6oz cooked long grain rice
1 tablespoon finely chopped onion
2 tablespoons French dressing (Recipe No. 398)
275g/11oz can mandarin oranges

Cut the ham into strips. Remove the seeds from the pepper and chop the flesh. Mix together the rice, pepper and onion and toss in the French dressing. Spoon the rice mixture in the centre of a serving dish and arrange the drained mandarin oranges and ham at either end.

Mandarin rice salad

Potato salad

POTATO SALADS

433 **POTATO SALAD**

½kg/1lb *potatoes*
8 tablespoons mayonnaise or salad dressing
(Recipe Nos. 408, 412, 416)
2 teaspoons finely chopped onion · 3 teaspoons chopped parsley
seasoning · slices of cucumber and red pepper to garnish

The secret of a good potato salad is to mix it when hot, and
eat it when cold. Cook the potatoes in salted water until just
cooked – be careful they do not become too soft. Strain and
leave until just cool enough to handle. Cut into cubes and toss
in the mayonnaise, adding onion, parsley and seasoning.
Leave until cold then spoon into a serving dish. Arrange
slices of cucumber around the edge of the dish and garnish
with strips of red pepper. If preferred toss in oil and vinegar
instead of mayonnaise.

434 **POTATO AND CELERY SALAD**

Make as for potato salad, but add 2 sticks of celery, cut into
strips.

435 **SPICED POTATO SALAD**

Make as for potato salad but add capers, chopped gherkins
and a little paprika pepper.

436 **MUSHROOM SALAD**

*200g/8oz button mushrooms · 3 peppers ***
French dressing (Recipe No. 398) · lettuce to garnish

*The salad will look attractive if a red, green and yellow pepper are used

Wash and slice the mushrooms and place in a bowl. Halve the
peppers, remove the seeds and slice thinly. Toss mushrooms
and peppers in the French dressing. Serve garnished with
lettuce.
Raw mushrooms are excellent in any mixed salads, and they
are particularly good served with fish, cheese or egg dishes.

437 **DUTCH MEDLEY SALAD**

2 large apples · 150g/6oz Gouda cheese
100g/4oz cooked ham, sausage or other meat · French mustard
paprika pepper · mayonnaise (Recipe Nos. 408, 412)
3 gherkins, chopped · spring onions · lettuce
capers and tomato slices to garnish

Peel, core and chop the apples. Cube the cheese and ham, etc.
Blend a little French mustard and paprika pepper with the
mayonnaise. Toss the apples, cheese, gherkins, ham and
onion in this. If the mayonnaise is rather thick, thin with some
of the liquid from the jar of gherkins. Serve on a bed of lettuce
and garnish with capers and tomato slices.
This mixture makes a very good filling for stuffed tomatoes,
in which case mix the pulp from tomatoes with the cheese, etc.

438 RUSSIAN SALAD

100g/4oz *cooked potato* · 100g/4oz *cooked carrots* *
100g/4oz *cooked peas**
100g/4oz *cooked runner or French beans* *
50g/2oz *cooked turnip* * · 2 *tablespoons oil*
1 *tablespoon vinegar* · *seasoning*
mayonnaise (Recipe Nos. 408, 412)

Or use cooked mixed frozen vegetables

Cut all the vegetables into small cubes. Put into a large bowl and pour over the oil and vinegar, then season well. Leave for several hours, turning round in the dressing from time to time. Do this gently so the vegetables are not broken. When ready to serve spoon into a lettuce-lined serving dish and coat with mayonnaise.

439 APPLE MOULD WITH CHEESE BALLS

8 *eating apples* · *generous* ½litre/1pint *water*
grated rind and juice 2 lemons · 50g/2oz *sugar*
2 *packets lemon-flavoured jelly* · 200g/8oz *cream cheese*
75g/3oz *blanched almonds, browned*
lettuce and radishes to garnish

Peel the apples thinly, reserve some of the peel and cover this in cold water. Cut the peeled fruit into quarters and remove cores. Put the water, lemon rind, juice and sugar into a saucepan. Bring to the boil and put in the apple quarters. Poach very gently for 10 minutes. Lift out the apples and strain the syrup. Make the syrup up to ¾litre (1½ pints) with water. Reheat and dissolve the jellies in the syrup. Pour a thin layer of jelly into the mould, allow to set; arrange some apple pieces and thin strips of well drained peel on this and cover with cold liquid jelly. Leave to set. Continue in this way until the mould is filled. Leave to set. Meanwhile form the cream cheese into small balls and toss in browned almonds. Turn the mould on to a serving dish. Fill the centre with cheese balls and garnish with lettuce and radishes.
Makes 6–8 servings.

Apple mould with cheese balls

Tomato rice cups

440 TOMATO RICE CUPS

150g/6oz long grain rice · 1 level teaspoon salt
6 tablespoons French dressing (Recipe No. 398)
1 clove garlic, peeled and crushed
2 tablespoons chopped parsley · 4 tomatoes
black olives and mint leaves to garnish

Cook the rice in boiling salted water until just tender, about
15 minutes. Drain in a sieve and run under cold water; shake
to dry slightly but mix while the rice is warm. In a lidded
container shake together the French dressing and garlic. Add
parsley. Before skinning tomatoes, reserve a few strips and
use to garnish. Cut skinned tomatoes in half, discard seeds
and dice flesh. Mix together rice, dressing and tomatoes.
Press into oiled cups or other similar shapes such as dariole
moulds or individual loaf tins. Turn out on to a serving dish.
Garnish with reserved tomato and the black olives and mint
leaves. Serve with a salad.
Makes 4–6 servings.

441 WINTER SALAD

2 hard-boiled eggs · 2 small cans baked beans with sausages★
15g/½oz powdered gelatine · 3 tablespoons cold water
1 medium-sized can tomato juice · 1 tablespoon tomato ketchup
salt · pinch cayenne pepper · few drops Tabasco sauce
little vinegar, optional · 1 lettuce · little shredded horseradish,
moistened with salad cream or mayonnaise
(Recipe Nos. 408, 412)
chicory to garnish

★Or open 1 can baked beans and cook 4–5 small pork sausages

Arrange a slice of hard-boiled egg at the bottom of about 8
lightly oiled dariole moulds. Slice small sausages and set round
sides, adding a few baked beans. Soften the gelatine in 3
tablespoons cold water and add to heated tomato juice. Stir in
tomato ketchup, seasonings to taste and a few drops of Tabasco
sauce. Make slightly more piquant with a little vinegar if liked.
Pour into the moulds, chill until shapes are set. Turn out on
to lettuce-lined dish. Surround with small heaps of baked
beans and top with the shredded horseradish. Garnish with
chicory.

Cucumber and pilchard ring

442 CUCUMBER AND PILCHARD RING

25g/1oz powdered gelatine★ · 3 tablespoons cold water
1 medium-sized can tomato juice · 1 cucumber
200g/8oz can pilchards · 2 tablespoons salad cream

★Relatively high amount due to the water content of cucumber

Soften the gelatine in the cold water. Heat the tomato juice
and dissolve gelatine in this. Allow to cool. Peel and chop ¾
of the cucumber. Slice the remainder thinly and use to
garnish. Stir the chopped cucumber into the cooled tomato
juice and pour into a rinsed ring mould and leave to set.
Meanwhile mix the pilchards with the salad cream. Turn the
cucumber mould on to a serving dish. Fill the centre with
the pilchards and garnish with the cucumber slices. Serve
with a salad.

443 **STUFFED TOMATOES PROVENCALE**

4 tomatoes · 200g/8oz can pilchards
1 clove garlic, chopped · seasoning
chopped chives and watercress to garnish

With a sharp knife, cut a slice from the top of each tomato. Scoop out the pulp and mix with the mashed pilchards. Add the garlic and seasoning. Spoon the mixture into the tomato cases, place the lids at an angle and sprinkle chopped chives on the pilchards. Place the tomatoes on a serving dish and garnish with sprigs of watercress.

444 **HAM ROLLS**

Place chopped green pepper on slices of ham, roll up. Secure with a cocktail stick. Serve with potato salad (Recipe No. 433) and garnish with olives, pickles and radishes.

Stuffed tomatoes Provençale

445 **HAM MOULD**

15g/½oz powdered gelatine · generous ½litre/1pint consommé
1 tablespoon grated horseradish · 2 teaspoons made mustard
1 tablespoon minced onion · pepper
½kg/1lb cooked ham, minced

Soak the gelatine in a little cold water. Heat the consommé, add gelatine and stir until dissolved. Cool. Then add grated horseradish, mustard, onion and a dash of pepper. Place in the refrigerator or cool place for the mixture to begin to thicken. At this stage stir in the ham. Pour into an oiled ring mould or other decorative mould. Allow to set and turn out when required.
Makes 6 servings.

446 **LUNCHEON MEAT AND APRICOT SALAD**

1 Savoy cabbage · 1 medium-sized can apricots
8 slices luncheon meat · little made mustard
parsley and stuffed olives to garnish

Shred the cabbage finely. Drain the apricots and chop most of them and mix with the cabbage. Place in a serving dish. Top with the reserved apricot halves and the slices of luncheon meat, spread with a little mustard and rolled up. Garnish with parsley and stuffed olives.

Luncheon meat and apricot salad

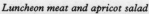

HOT PUDDINGS

A hot pudding makes a good ending to a meal and there is a great variety to choose from – light sponge puddings, including upside-down puddings, fruit tarts (many more pastry sweets will be found in the pastry section) or egg custards of various kinds.

All metric quantities are given in strictly correct proportions but where 25g = 1oz has been used you will find the completed pudding is smaller in quantity. If this would be too little for your family then increase ALL ingredients slightly to give a larger pudding that is the same as that made when following Imperial measurements.

The terms soft and superfine margarines indicate the luxury types of margarine.

447 EXTRA CREAMY MILK PUDDINGS

Mix a large can full cream condensed milk with water to make 852ml – this is a generous ¾litre – 1½pints. Pour into an oven-proof dish. Add 75g (3 oz) washed rice or tapioca or 100g (4 oz) quick-cooking macaroni. Sprinkle top with nutmeg. Cook in a cool oven, 300°F, 150°C, Gas Mark 2, for 2½ hours. For a smaller pudding use a small can full cream condensed milk, made up to just under 568ml i.e. a generous ½litre – 1 pint with water and add 50g (2 oz) rice.

Honey baked apples

448 MILK PUDDING VARIATIONS

Add 50g (2 oz) cleaned dried fruit, 50g (2 oz) grated chocolate or stir in 1 level tablespoon instant coffee powder, blended with a little water.

Remember whenever you are making a milk pudding that a little evaporated or full cream condensed milk improves the flavour.

449 ORANGE MERINGUE PUDDING
(Illustrated in colour on the jacket)

1 large orange · 75g/3oz loaf sugar · ½ lemon
45g/1¾oz cornflour · 284ml/½pint milk
1 egg, separated · 25g/1oz butter · pinch salt
25g/1oz castor sugar · 1 heaped teaspoon cornflour
glacé cherries and angelica to decorate

Rub the zest from the orange on to sugar cubes. Squeeze the juice from the orange and lemon and make the quantity up to 142ml (¼ pint) with water if necessary. Mix the 45g (1¾ oz) cornflour smoothly with a little of the cold milk. Put the rest on to heat with sugar cubes. When the sugar has dissolved, add the mixed cornflour, stir till boiling. Boil for 1 minute; remove from the heat and cool for a few seconds; add the egg yolk, butter and fruit juice. Return to the heat and cook for 1 minute without allowing to boil. Pour into a lightly greased ovenproof dish and cool slightly.

Add a pinch of salt to the egg white and whisk into stiff peaks. Fold in the castor sugar and the cornflour. Pile meringue on top of the orange pudding. Bake in a moderate oven 350–375°F, 180°C, Gas Mark 4, for 15–20 minutes, until meringue has set. Decorate with glacé cherries and angelica.

450 HONEY BAKED APPLES

4 large cooking apples · 100g/4oz cake crumbs
25g/1oz walnuts, chopped · 50g/2oz glacé cherries, chopped
50g/2oz sultanas · 1 tablespoon honey
1 tablespoon golden syrup · 1 teaspoon lemon juice

Core the apples, and slightly hollow the centre opening. Mix the cake crumbs, walnuts, cherries and sultanas together. Melt the honey with the syrup and lemon juice, and mix with the other ingredients. Slit the apple skins either from top to bottom or round the centre. Fill each apple with this mixture, pressing well into the centre. Make sure that some filling shows above the apple. Bake in a moderately hot oven, 400°F, 200°C, Gas Mark 6, for 45 minutes–1 hour, until the apples are tender.

Variation

In place of the above filling use 2 teaspoons mincemeat for each apple.

Caramel topped pudding (Recipe No. 469)

451 APPLE DUMPLINGS

300g/12oz short crust pastry (Recipe No. 566)
4 medium-sized cooking apples · 50g/2oz Demerara sugar
½ teaspoon mixed spice

Make the pastry and roll out thinly; cut into 4 squares, large enough to wrap round the apples. Peel and core the apples and place each in the centre of a pastry square. Mix the sugar and spice together and spoon into the centre of the apples. Dampen the edges of the pastry; pull the corners of the squares to the top of the apples and press edges firmly together. Decorate the tops with leaves made from the pastry trimmings. Place on a baking sheet and bake in a hot oven, 425–450°F, 220–230°C, Gas Mark 6–7, for 15–20 minutes, then lower oven to moderate and bake for 35–40 minutes. Sprinkle with sugar and serve.

Apple dumplings

452 TO CORE APPLES

A good apple corer is essential – this one both peels apples (and vegetables) and removes core. Find centre of apple and push corer through firmly.

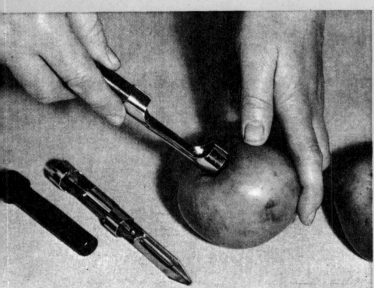

To core apples

453 DANISH APPLE PUDDING

2 fairly large cooking apples · lemon juice
100g/4oz butter · 100g/4oz sugar · 1 egg
200g/8oz flour (with plain flour use 1 teaspoon baking powder)
¼ teaspoon salt · 50g/2oz sultanas · 25g/1oz peanuts
½ teaspoon ground ginger · 2 dessertspoons brown sugar

Peel, core and slice apples thinly. Sprinkle with a little lemon juice. Melt the butter and mix with sugar. Add the egg and beat lightly. Gradually add the sieved flour, salt and baking powder, if used. Grease 20 or 23-cm (8 or 9-inch) shallow cake tin (the pudding is easier to turn out if cooked in a tin with a loose base) and spread two-thirds of the mixture over the bottom of the tin. Mix the apples and sultanas and spread over the mixture; sprinkle over the peanuts, ginger and brown sugar. Place the remaining cake mixture in spoonfuls on the top. Bake in centre of a very moderate to moderate oven, 350°F, 180°C, Gas Mark 4, for 50–55 minutes. Serve hot or cold.

454 BREAD AND BUTTER PUDDING

2 eggs · 1 level teaspoon sugar · 426ml/¾pint milk
2 large slices bread and butter · 50g/2oz currants
little extra sugar

Beat the eggs with a fork, add the sugar and milk. Remove the crusts from the bread and butter and cut into squares. Place in an ovenproof dish, sprinkle over the currants. Pour in the beaten egg mixture. Sprinkle a little sugar over the top. Allow to stand, if possible, for 30 minutes. Bake in a very moderate oven, 325°F, 170°C, Gas Mark 3, for about 1 hour.

Bread and butter pudding

Lemon pudding

455   LEMON PUDDING

¾litre/1½pints *milk* · 200g/8oz *breadcrumbs* · 50g/2oz *butter*
100g/4oz *sugar* · 4 *egg yolks, lightly beaten*
grated rind 1 lemon · 1 *teaspoon vanilla essence*

Topping

juice 1½ *lemons with* 75g/3oz *sugar dissolved in it*
4 *egg whites* · ½ *teaspoon salt* · 4 *level dessertspoons sugar*

Heat the milk and add breadcrumbs and butter; leave to cool.
Add sugar, egg yolks, grated lemon rind and vanilla essence.
Pour into an ovenproof dish and cook in a moderate oven
325°F, 170°C, Gas Mark 2–3 for 35–40 minutes, until just set.
Pour over the lemon juice in which the sugar has been dissolved. Then whisk the egg whites and salt until stiff. Add half
the sugar and whisk again. Finally fold in remaining sugar.
Spread the meringue over the pudding and return it to a hot
oven, 425–450°F, 200°C, Gas Mark 6–7, for 5 minutes, until
the meringue is lightly browned.

456   APRICOT SOUFFLE

1 *medium-sized can apricots, drained*★· 25g/1oz *butter*
15g/½oz *flour* · 25–50g/1–2oz *sugar* · 3 *large eggs*
25g/1oz *almonds, chopped* · *apricot sauce (Recipe No. 457)*

★*Use the juice to make the sauce*

Rub the apricots through a sieve to make a purée. Heat the
butter in a pan, stir in the flour and cook for 1–2 minutes. Add
the apricot purée and sugar; remove from the heat and stir in
the egg yolks. Fold in the stiffly beaten egg whites. Put into a
greased soufflé or ovenproof dish, and sprinkle the nuts over
the top. Bake for about 30 minutes in the centre of a moderately
hot oven, 400°F, 200°C, Gas Mark 6. Serve at once with
apricot sauce.

457   APRICOT SAUCE

If necessary make the juice up to 142ml (¼ pint) with water.
Blend with 1 teaspoon arrowroot or cornflour. Put into a
saucepan with 2 tablespoons apricot jam. Stirring, bring to the
boil and cook until clear.

458   GINGER PUDDING

100g/4oz *self-raising flour (with plain flour use 1 level
teaspoon baking powder)* · 1 *level teaspoon ground ginger*
75g/3oz *margarine* · 75g/3oz *castor sugar* · 2 *eggs*
1 *tablespoon milk*
50g/2oz *crystallised ginger, optional* · *orange sauce
(Recipe No. 459)*

Sieve the flour, baking powder, if used, and ginger together.
Cream the margarine and sugar together until light and fluffy.
Beat in the eggs, one at a time, adding a little of the sieved
flour mixture with the second. Fold in the remaining flour
mixture, the milk and the crystallised ginger, if used. Spoon the
mixture into a greased mould or pudding basin. Cover with
greaseproof paper or foil and steam for 1½ hours. Turn on to a
serving dish and pour over the orange sauce.

Ginger pudding

Orange soufflé

You will find a choice of metric equivalents for flour, etc., and completed pastry, for if you use 25g = 1oz your pie or tart will be perfect BUT you will have smaller quantity than usual which might prove inadequate to cover a favourite dish. If you select the smaller quantity of flour then you should use the smaller quantity of fat so your pastry has the correct proportion.

These are favourite puddings throughout the year and need never become monotonous. Vary the fillings and the type of pastry you use, but remember the following:

1. Always cook a double layer tart in the centre of the oven. If it is cooked towards the top of the oven, the top pastry becomes crisp and brown but the bottom is underdone.
2. Put little if any moisture with the fruit – it will make its own juice.
3. To help to keep the bottom pastry crisp sprinkle with either a little flour and sugar or semolina before arranging fruit on top.

459   ORANGE SAUCE

2 oranges · 100g/4oz castor sugar

Peel the oranges and cut the rind into thin strips. Simmer in a little water until soft. Squeeze the juice from the oranges and make up to 284ml (½ pint) with water. Place the juice in a small saucepan. Add the sugar and dissolve over a low heat. Bring to the boil and add the orange rind and simmer for 2–3 minutes.

460   ORANGE SOUFFLE

25g/1oz butter · 25g/1oz flour · 142ml/¼pint milk
juice 1 orange · 50g/2oz castor sugar · 3 egg yolks
4 egg whites · grated orange rind to decorate

Melt the butter in a saucepan. Stir in the flour and cook for 1–2 minutes. Gradually add the milk and stirring, bring to the boil and cook for 1–2 minutes. Remove from the heat and stir in the orange juice and castor sugar. Allow the mixture to cool slightly, then beat in the egg yolks. Whisk the egg whites until stiff, then fold them gently into the yolk mixture. Spoon the mixture into a greased ovenproof dish or 4 individual greased ovenproof dishes. Bake in a moderate oven, 350–375°F, 180°C, Gas Mark 4, for 15–25 minutes, until well risen and set. (Do not open the oven door until towards end of baking time, as this could cause the soufflé to collapse). Serve at once, decorated with grated orange rind.

462   DOUBLE-CRUST FRUIT TARTS

200 or 225g/8oz plain flour · pinch salt
100 or 110g/4oz soft margarine or butter · 1 egg yolk
about 1 tablespoon cold water

Sieve together the flour and salt. Cut margarine into small pieces and rub into flour. Stir the egg yolk and the cold water into the rubbed in mixture with the blade of a knife. Roll out and use half to line flat plate. Arrange the fruit and sugar over this and cover with the rest of the pastry. Flute edges. Bake in the centre of a hot oven, 425–450°F, 220–230°C, Gas Mark 6–7, for about 35 minutes; reduce heat if necessary after 20 minutes.

Hints for Double-Crust Fruit Tarts

1. To give an attractive glaze brush top with little egg white and sprinkle very lightly with sugar before cooking.
2. Try various fillings – some interesting mixtures are:
   cherries and apricots, canned or fresh
   rhubarb and dried figs
   apple, dates and preserved ginger
   mincemeat and chopped pineapple

463 CHOCOLATE APRICOT SPONGE

125g/5oz self-raising flour (with plain flour use 1¼ level
teaspoons baking powder)
25g/1oz cocoa · 75g/3oz margarine · 75g/3oz castor sugar
1 egg · milk to mix · 1 can apricot pie filling

Sieve the flour, baking powder, if used and cocoa into a
mixing bowl. Rub in the margarine, until the mixture looks
like fine breadcrumbs. Stir in the sugar. Add the egg and
sufficient milk to give a soft consistency. Place half the apricot
pie filling in the bottom of a greased pudding basin; cover
with the chocolate mixture, (allow room for the pudding to
rise). Cover with greased foil or greaseproof paper and steam
for 1½ hours. Meanwhile, heat the remaining pie filling in a
small saucepan. To serve, turn on to a serving dish and top
with remaining pie filling.

Chocolate apricot sponge

464 STEAMED SPONGE WITH CHOCOLATE SAUCE

100g/4oz butter or margarine · 100g/4oz castor sugar
2 eggs
150g/6oz self-raising flour (with plain flour use 1½ level
teaspoons baking powder)
little milk or water · chocolate sauce (Recipe No. 465)

Cream the margarine and sugar. Add the eggs and fold in the
sieved flour. Mix to a soft dropping consistency with a little
milk or water. Spoon the mixture into a greased pudding
basin, cover with greaseproof paper and steam for about 1½
hours. Serve with chocolate sauce.

465 CHOCOLATE SAUCE

1 dessertspoon cornflour · 1 dessertspoon cocoa
284ml/½pint milk · 1 tablespoon sugar · knob butter
vanilla essence

Blend the cornflour and cocoa with a little milk. Heat the
remainder of the milk, and when nearly boiling pour on to the
blended mixture. Return to the heat and cook for 2 minutes,
stirring continuously. Add sugar, a few drops of vanilla
essence and the butter.

466 GOLDEN CAP PUDDING

Use Recipe No. 464 for steamed sponge. Put a layer of golden
syrup in the bottom of the pudding basin. If liked, add 1
teaspoon ground ginger with the flour.

467 BLACK CAP PUDDING

Use Recipe No. 464 for steamed sponge pudding. Put a good
layer of stoned prunes or blackcurrant jam in the bottom of
the pudding basin.

468 APRICOT CASTLE PUDDINGS

Use Recipe No. 464 for steamed sponge pudding. Put a few
chopped almonds in the bottom of 6 greased dariole moulds,
and half fill with the sponge mixture. Cover and steam for
25–30 minutes. Serve with canned apricots.

469 CARAMEL TOPPED PUDDING

(Illustrated in colour at the beginning of this section)

Use Recipe No. 464 for steamed sponge pudding and steam
in a greased pudding basin or fluted mould. When cooked,
turn on to a serving dish and top with a mixture of chopped
fresh fruits. Spoon over caramel syrup made by dissolving
40g (1½ oz) Demerara sugar in a heavy saucepan. Add 142ml
(¼ pint) boiling water and stir until caramel has dissolved. Add
a further 75g (3 oz) sugar and cook gently until the mixture
forms a syrup.

CHRISTMAS PUDDING recipes will be found
in the pressure cooking section (Recipe No. 889) and in the
entertaining section (Recipe No. 1017).

Apricot castle puddings

Baked blackberry roly-poly

Harlequin sponge pudding

470 HARLEQUIN SPONGE PUDDING

100g/4oz *self-raising flour (with plain flour use* 1½ *level teaspoons baking powder)*
pinch salt · 75g/3oz *butter or margarine* · 75g/3oz *castor sugar*
2 *eggs* · 1 *dessertspoon cocoa* · *red colouring*

Brush a medium-sized pudding basin with melted fat. Have ready a steamer or saucepan half filled with boiling water. Sieve together flour, baking powder, if used and salt. Cream together margarine and sugar until light and fluffy. Add eggs, one at a time, and beat in thoroughly. Add flour and fold in with a metal spoon. Divide mixture into three, colouring one with cocoa, one red and leaving the third portion plain. Place the mixtures, in alternate spoonfuls into the basin; cover with greased foil or greaseproof paper and steam for 1½–1¾ hours.

471 CINNAMON AND PLUM SPONGE

100g/4oz *cooking fat* · 100g/4oz *castor sugar* · 2 *eggs*
100g/4oz *self-raising (with plain flour use* 1½ *level teaspoons baking powder)*
½ *level teaspoon cinnamon* · *pinch salt* · ½kg/1lb *stewed plums*

Brush a medium-sized pudding basin with melted fat. Cream the fat and sugar together until light and fluffy Beat in the eggs, one at a time. Sieve the flour, baking powder, if used, cinnamon and salt and fold in gently. Arrange the sponge mixture and drained stoned plums in alternate layers in the basin, beginning with the plums and finishing with the sponge mixture (making three layers of each). Cover with greased foil or greaseproof paper and steam for 1¼–1½ hours. For a special occasion decorate with whipped double cream. Serve with a sauce made from the plum juice.

472 BAKED BLACKBERRY ROLY-POLY

200g/8oz *self-raising flour (with plain flour use* 2 *level teaspoons baking powder)*
pinch salt · 75g/3oz *butter or suet* · 25g/1oz *castor sugar*
2 *teaspoons grated lemon rind* · *about* 4 *tablespoons milk to mix*
300g/12oz *fresh blackberries* · *milk and castor sugar to glaze*
3 *tablespoons water*

Sieve the flour, baking powder, if used, and salt together. Rub in the butter and mix in sugar and lemon rind. Mix to a soft dough with the milk. Roll out, on a floured board, to a rectangle. Cover with most of the fruit, leaving a margin all round. Moisten the edges with water, then roll up like a Swiss roll. Press joins together to seal. Lift on to an ovenproof dish. Make 3 slits on top of the roll, brush with milk and sprinkle with castor sugar. Pour about 3 tablespoons water into the dish and bake in a moderately hot oven, 400°F, 200°C, Gas Mark 6, for 15 minutes. Spoon the remaining blackberries on top of the slits. Reduce oven temperature to 350°F, 180°C, Gas Mark 4 and cook for a further 25–30 minutes.

473 PINEAPPLE UPSIDE-DOWN PUDDING

25g/1oz *butter* · 25g/1oz *brown sugar*
1 *small can pineapple rings* · *glacé cherries*
sponge mixture (Recipe No. 464)
blanched almonds to decorate

Spread the bottom of an ovenproof dish or tin with the butter and sprinkle with the sugar. Arrange the well drained pineapple and glacé cherries on top. Cover with the sponge mixture and bake in the centre of a very moderate oven, 325°F, 170°C, Gas Mark 3, for 50–60 minutes. Turn out and decorate with blanched almonds.

474 APRICOT UPSIDE-DOWN PUDDING

Follow the recipe above for pineapple upside-down pudding, but place drained canned apricot halves in the bottom of the ovenproof dish or tin. Serve with ice cream.

475 BAKED EGG CUSTARD

generous ½litre/1pint *milk* · 2 *eggs* · 25g/1oz *sugar*
nutmeg

Heat the milk but do not let it boil. Beat eggs and sugar together, then add the hot milk, stirring all the time. Strain into a greased ovenproof dish, and grate a little nutmeg on top. Stand the dish in a 'bain-marie', i.e. another dish containing cold water, and bake in a slow oven, 275–300°F, 140–150°C, Gas Mark 1–2, for 45 minutes to 1 hour, until set. Serve from the dish.
For a firmer custard use 3–4 eggs to the same quantity of milk or use just egg yolks instead of whole eggs.

476 COCONUT BAKED CUSTARD

Add 25g (1 oz) desiccated coconut to the custard; sprinkle with coconut and top with halved glacé cherries when cooked.

477 COFFEE BAKED CUSTARD

Use 142ml (¼ pint) strong coffee and 426ml (¾ pint) milk instead of generous ½ litre (1 pint) milk. Add a little extra sugar.

Pineapple upside-down pudding

478   SPONGE FRUIT PUDDING

½kg/1lb fruit in season, stewed · 75g/3oz butter
75g/3oz castor sugar
100g/4oz self-raising flour (with plain flour use 1 level
teaspoon baking powder)
4 tablespoons milk · 3 egg whites · sieved icing sugar

Place the cooked fruit in the bottom of an ovenproof dish; add
a little juice. Cream the butter and sugar together until light
and fluffy. Fold in the sieved flour and baking powder, if used
and the milk. Whisk the egg whites until stiff and gently fold
into the creamed mixture. Spread over the fruit and bake in a
moderate oven, 350°F, 180°C, Gas Mark 4, for about 1 hour
until firm to touch. Serve sprinkled with icing sugar.

Sponge fruit pudding

DESSERTS

What is the secret of a good dessert? It is that it should form a light refreshing end to a good meal. In this chapter you will find a really interesting selection of desserts – jellied sweets, sponge flans, iced sweets – all simple to make and delicious.

Fruit salad

479 PREPARING FRUIT FOR DESSERTS AND FRUIT SALADS

Always remove white pith from oranges and grapefruit, pips and stones from other fruit. Oranges and grapefruit are best peeled with a sharp fruit knife, so that the pith is removed at the same time. Special cherry stoners can be bought, or you can use the bent end of a fine new hairpin. To cut a pineapple make slanting cuts downwards, between the eyes. Remove eyes and skin, then slice across with a stainless steel knife and remove the core with an apple corer. To peel fresh peaches place in a bowl and pour boiling water over them. Leave for a minute; then the skin can be peeled away easily.

480 FRUIT SALAD

The flavour of a fruit salad is much improved if it is made an hour or two before serving. Marinate the fruit in a sprinkling of sugar syrup – and for a special occasion add wine, cider or ginger ale. A dash or two of Angostura bitters is a chef's trick to develop the fruit flavour; it peps up a weather-wilted appetite as well. For the sugar syrup simmer 100g (4 oz) sugar in 142ml (¼ pint) water for 2–3 minutes. Add a few drops of Angostura bitters. The thinly peeled rind of a lemon can also be added. Pour over the fruit and chill.

If bananas, apples or pears are to be included add 1 tablespoon lemon juice to the syrup or prepare and add to the fruit salad at the last minute.

These fruits pair deliciously – grapefruit and pineapple – orange and raspberries – plums and bananas – apricots with dates and coconut – canned apple sauce with mandarin sections and chopped ginger.

Sprigs of mint and the leaves and blue flowers of borage make fragrant decorations. Small clusters of frosted grapes with the salad add a party air.

481 ORANGE SEMOLINA CAKE

100g/4oz *butter* · 100g/4oz *castor sugar*
grated rind 1 orange · *3 eggs*
100g/4oz *self-raising flour* · 100g/4oz *semolina*
2 tablespoons fresh orange juice · *sieved icing sugar*

This is the type of cake, plain, fragrantly flavoured and not too sweet, which is first choice for summer tea or supper. It is specially delicious with fruit salad or ice cream.

Cream butter and sugar and orange rind until light and fluffy. Beat in eggs one at a time. Fold in sieved flour and semolina and then orange juice. Turn into a greased cake tin and bake in centre of a moderate oven, 370°F, 180°C, Gas Mark 4, for 1–1¼ hours. Dust with icing sugar before serving.

482 AUTUMN PUDDING
(Illustrated in colour on opposite page)

½kg/1lb *cooking apples, peeled, cored and sliced*
300g/12oz *fresh blackberries* · 150g/6oz *granulated sugar*
142ml/¼pint *water* · *1 dessertspoon gelatine*
½ *large sliced white loaf, crusts removed*
castor sugar to sprinkle

Cook apple slices with most of the blackberries, sugar and half the water until soft and tender. Dissolve gelatine in remaining hot water and add to cooled fruit mixture. Line a pudding basin with bread and pour in fruit mixture. Cover with a circle of bread, a saucer and a weight on top. Leave to set overnight. Turn out, sprinkle with castor sugar and decorate with blackberries, serve with whipped double cream or custard sauce (Recipe No. 692).

Makes 6 servings.

Autumn pudding (Recipe No. 482)

SPONGE FLANS

Blackberry meringue flan

483 BLACKBERRY MERINGUE FLAN

50g/2oz self-raising flour · 50g/2oz castor sugar
2 eggs · 200g/8oz blackberries · 2 egg whites
100g/4oz castor sugar

Grease and flour a 20-cm (8-inch) sponge flan tin. Sieve flour. Whisk sugar and eggs until thick and creamy. Lightly fold in the flour with a metal spoon. Pour into prepared tin. Bake in a moderately hot oven, 400°F, 200°C, Gas Mark 6, for 7–10 minutes, until golden brown and firm. Turn out and cool on a wire tray. Place the blackberries in the flan case (reserve a few for decoration), whisk the egg whites until stiff, add half the sugar and whisk again, until stiff. Using a metal tablespoon, fold in the remaining sugar. Pipe or spread the meringue over the blackberries. Decorate the top of the meringue with the reserved blackberries. Return to a cool oven, 275°F, 140°C, Gas Mark 1, for 30–35 minutes. Serve cold.

484 CHOCOLATE SPONGE WITH LIME MOUSSE FILLING

100g/4oz self-raising flour · 15g/½oz cocoa
75g/3oz butter or margarine · 75g/3oz castor sugar
2 eggs, beaten with a few drops vanilla essence and
1 tablespoon milk · lime mousse (Recipe No. 485)
glacé cherries to decorate

Sieve together flour and cocoa. Cream fat and sugar until light and fluffy and add eggs and milk alternately with flour and cocoa powder. Turn into well greased 20-cm (8-inch) sponge flan tin and cook in moderately hot oven, 375°F, 190°C, Gas Mark 5, for 20 minutes. Cool, then fill with lime mousse mixture. Decorate with glacé cherries and chill before serving.

485 LIME MOUSSE

1 small can evaporated milk
½ packet lime-flavoured jelly · 1 tablespoon lemon juice

Boil the evaporated milk in the unopened can for 15 minutes. Cool, then open. Make up jelly with 142ml (¼ pint) boiling water only. Leave the jelly in a cold place to thicken slightly. Whisk the evaporated milk until it doubles in volume, and add lemon juice. Whisk the jelly till light and frothy then carefully combine with the milk. Lemon jelly could be used instead.

486 CHOCOLATE PEAR DELIGHT

100g/4oz self-raising flour · 15g/½oz cocoa
75g/3oz butter or margarine · 75g/3oz castor sugar
2 eggs · 1 tablespoon milk · 1 medium-sized can pear halves
1 teaspoon arrowroot · double cream, whipped
and glacé cherries to decorate

Sieve together flour and cocoa. Cream fat and sugar until light and fluffy. Add eggs and milk alternately with flour and cocoa powder. Turn into a well greased 20-cm (8-inch) sponge flan tin and bake in a moderately hot oven, 375°F, 190°C, Gas Mark 5, for 20 minutes. Cool on a wire tray. Drain the pears and arrange in the flan case. Thicken the pear juice with arrowroot (1 teaspoon arrowroot to 142ml (¼ pint) juice). When cool, pour over the fruit. Decorate with whipped double cream and glacé cherries.

Chocolate pear delight

MOULDED DESSERTS

Summer pudding

487 SUMMER PUDDING

about 5 *large thin slices bread*
1 *medium-sized can raspberries*

Cut the crusts off the bread, cut into fingers and line bottom and sides of a pudding basin with this. Drain syrup from fruit and put fruit into the basin. Cover with the rest of the bread. Put a layer of greaseproof paper on top and a weight and leave overnight. Turn out and serve syrup from canned raspberries as a sauce. There are many variations of this recipe (see Recipe No. 482). If wished sponge cake can be used instead of bread. Any fruit can be used. Fresh fruit should be simmered until soft then strained.

488 ORANGE AND PEACH RUSSE

18 *sponge fingers · apricot jam*
50g/2oz *custard powder · ¾litre/1¼pints milk*
50g/2oz *sugar · grated rind 1 orange*
4 *tablespoons orange juice · 25g/1oz powdered gelatine*
284ml/½pint *double cream · 2 egg whites*
1 *small can peach slices · angelica*

Trim the sponge fingers and place them round the edge of an 18-cm (7-inch) cake tin with a removable base, sticking the edges together with jam. Blend the custard powder with 3 tablespoons of milk in a basin. Boil the rest of the milk with the sugar and pour over the blended custard powder. Return to saucepan and cook for 3 minutes. Stir in the grated orange rind. Pour into a basin and stir occasionally until cool. Add the orange juice to the gelatine, and melt in a basin over a saucepan of boiling water. When the custard mixture has cooled, pour in the dissolved gelatine. Whip the cream lightly and fold most of it in with the stiffly beaten egg whites. Pour the thickened mixture into the tin, and leave to set for 3–4 hours. Turn out onto a plate, and decorate with peach slices, the remaining cream and angelica.
Makes 6–8 servings.

489 PEACH AND STRAWBERRY DELIGHT

1 *medium-sized can peaches · 2 lemon-flavoured jellies*
scant ¾litre/1¼pints *milk*
142ml/¼pint *double cream, whipped*
strawberries to decorate

Drain and sieve the peaches (reserve a few for decoration) to make a purée. Measure the juice from the can to give just under 284ml (½ pint); if necessary add a little water to the syrup to give this amount. Heat thoroughly, pour over the jellies and stir until dissolved. Cool, then add the cold milk. Allow to stiffen slightly then fold in the cream and the peach purée. Pour into a rinsed mould and allow to set. Turn out the mould and decorate with the remaining peaches and the strawberries. Makes 6–8 servings.

Peach and strawberry delight

EASY PARTY SWEETS

490   STRAWBERRY CREAM PIE

150–175g/6oz *short crust pastry (Recipe No. 566)*
1 *packet strawberry-flavoured blancmange powder*
generous ½litre/1pint *milk* · 50g/2oz *sugar*
142ml/¼pint *double cream, whipped*
300g–½kg/12oz–1lb *strawberries*

Roll out pastry, line flan ring or pie plate and bake 'blind' (Recipe No. 560). Allow to cool. Blend blancmange powder with little cold milk. Bring rest of milk to the boil, pour over blancmange and return to pan with sugar. Cook until thick. Cool slightly, stirring from time to time, then add most of the whipped cream. Put a layer of sliced strawberries at the bottom of the cooked flan. Cover with strawberry mixture and when firm decorate with remaining strawberries and cream.

491   JELLIED MELON

1 *lemon-flavoured jelly* · 1 *melon*
200g/8oz *can cherries or jar Maraschino cherries*

Make jelly and allow to cool and begin to thicken. Cut the melon into a basket shape. To do this leave strip along the top, as a handle, and cut away pulp. Scoop out centre pulp and chop neatly. Mix drained cherries and diced melon with most of the jelly and put into melon basket. Spread the top with a layer of remaining jelly. Allow to set.

492   APRICOT TRIFLE
(Illustrated in colour on opposite page)

1 *small can apricots* · 1 *orange-flavoured jelly*
4 *sponge cakes* · *little apricot jam*
50g/2oz *almonds, chopped* · 50g/2oz *glacé cherries, chopped*
2½ *level tablespoons custard powder* · 426ml/¾pint *milk*
50g/2oz *sugar* · *double cream, whipped*
angelica to decorate

Drain and chop the apricots. Make the juice up to generous ½litre (1 pint) with water and use to make the jelly. Split the sponges in half and spread with apricot jam. Put into a serving dish and cover with chopped apricots, almonds and cherries (reserve a glacé cherry for decoration). Allow to set. Make the custard with the powder, milk and sugar. Allow to cool, whisking from time to time to prevent a skin forming. When cold pour over the jelly. Decorate with whipped cream, angelica and the reserved cherry.

493   STRAWBERRY ORANGE MOUSSE
(Illustrated in colour on opposite page)

1 *small can strawberries* · 1 *orange-flavoured jelly*
1 *tablespoon concentrated orange squash*
generous 142ml/¼pint *evaporated milk* · *fresh strawberries, castor sugar to decorate*

Drain strawberries and dissolve jelly in the juice over low heat. Rub strawberries through sieve, add to jelly with orange squash and allow to cool until almost setting. Whip the evaporated milk either by the method described in Recipe No. 485 or by chilling the can of milk, then opening the can, pouring the milk into a large bowl and whisking sharply until thick. Slowly add fruit jelly and whisk until almost set. Pour into a rinsed ring mould. Leave to set. When set turn on to a serving plate and decorate with fresh strawberries, sprinkled with castor sugar.

494   HARLEQUIN JELLY

1 *small can pineapple*
1 *small can cherries or Maraschino cherries*
1 *pineapple-flavoured jelly* · 50g/2oz *marshmallows*

Drain the juice from the pineapple and cherries. Add enough water to make up to generous ½litre (1 pint). Make up the jelly with this liquid and pour a thin layer into a rinsed mould and allow to set. Add a layer of chopped cherries, pineapple and marshmallows, then pour in another layer of jelly. Continue to fill the mould like this, allowing each layer to set before adding the next and ending with a layer of jelly. When set, turn on to a serving dish.

495   MANDARIN ORANGE DELIGHTS

1 *small can mandarin oranges* · 1 *orange-flavoured jelly*
1 *egg* · 142ml/¼pint *double cream or evaporated milk, whipped*

Drain the mandarin oranges and reserve a few for decoration. Chop the remainder. Make the juice up to 426ml (¾ pint) with water and use to make the jelly. Allow to cool and pour on to the beaten egg and whisk well. When cold, but not set fold in the chopped mandarin oranges and half the cream or evaporated milk. Pour into individual glasses and leave to set. Decorate with the orange segments and remaining cream.

Apricot trifle

Strawberry orange mousse

Lemon mousse

496 LEMON MOUSSE

6 eggs · 25g/1oz icing sugar, sieved
142ml/¼pint double cream · 15g/½oz powdered gelatine
1 tablespoon water · juice 2 small lemons
glacé cherries to decorate

Separate the eggs. Beat the yolks and sugar together until thick and creamy. Whip the cream until just thick. Soak the gelatine in cold water and lemon juice, then dissolve in a basin over boiling water. Stir into the egg yolk mixture and, when beginning to set, fold in the stiffly beaten egg whites. Fold in half the cream. Turn the mixture into individual dishes or a serving dish and leave to set. Decorate with the remaining cream and glacé cherries.

497 BLACKCURRANT SOUFFLE

1 small can blackcurrants · 1 blackcurrant-flavoured jelly
2 eggs · 50g/2oz sugar
angelica and double cream, whipped, to decorate

This is a very refreshing soufflé mixture, as there is no cream in it.
Strain syrup from the blackcurrants. Add enough hot water to give 426ml (¾ pint), and dissolve jelly in this. Rub black-currants through a sieve to give a purée (or put in a liquidiser). Add to jelly. Beat egg yolks and sugar well and pour black-currant mixture over this. Allow to cool and begin to thicken, then fold in stiffly whisked egg whites and pour into a soufflé dish (Recipe No. 499) or individual dishes. When set decorate with angelica and cream.

498 OAT CRISP

40g/1½oz margarine or butter · 50g/2oz brown sugar
100g/4oz quick-cooking rolled oats

Melt fat in a saucepan over a very gentle heat. Add sugar and oats and mix well. Spread mixture lightly over a flat baking tin, but do not press down. Cook in a very moderate oven, 325°F, 170°C, Gas Mark 3, for about 10 minutes until golden brown. Toss mixture with a fork occasionally during cooking. Remove from the oven and leave to cool, stirring the mixture from time to time to form into crumbs. When quite cold use as required or store in a screw top jar. Excellent to sprinkle over fruit salads; as a topping for trifles, etc.

499 MILANAISE SOUFFLE

3 eggs, separated · 200g/8oz castor sugar · 2½ lemons
15g/½oz powdered gelatine · 4 tablespoons hot water
284ml/½pint double cream · grated chocolate to decorate

Place the egg yolks, sugar, grated lemon rind and juice into a basin. Stand the basin over hot water but do not allow the water to touch the basin. Whisk the mixture until it is thick and creamy. Dissolve the gelatine thoroughly in the hot water, strain if necessary and fold it into the mixture. Allow to cool. Half whip the cream and fold it into the egg yolk mixture. Stiffly whisk the whites of egg and fold in. When it is thick, pour into a soufflé dish with a band of paper tied round the outside (the mixture should come above the top of the dish). Put in a cool place to set; when firm remove the paper and press grated chocolate into the sides.

Orange fruit delights

500   ORANGE FRUIT DELIGHTS

5 oranges · fresh or canned fruit salad
oat crisp (Recipe No. 498) · double cream, whipped,
glacé cherries to decorate

Cut off the tops of the oranges to form a water lily pattern. Do this by inserting a sharp pointed knife into the centre of the orange, cutting first one way and then the other to form the petals of the water lily. With a teaspoon scoop out the orange sections and juice. Mix this with the fruit salad, sprinkle the oat crisp into the bottom, pile the fruit on top. Decorate with a rosette of whipped cream and half a glacé cherry.
Makes 5 servings.

Criss-cross trifle

501   CRISS-CROSS TRIFLE

4 sponge cakes · apricot jam · 1–2 tablespoons sherry, optional
1 small can pears · custard sauce (Recipe No. 692) or
made from custard powder · 25g/1oz blanched almonds, chopped
100g/4oz plain or milk chocolate

Split the sponge cakes, spread with the jam and put into a shallow bowl. Add sherry, if used. Chop pears, put over sponge cakes; add almonds and soak in the pear syrup. Pour custard over sponge cakes. Allow to cool and set. Cover with a plate to prevent a skin forming. Melt the chocolate in a basin over a pan of hot water. Put into a paper piping bag with a hole at the bottom, or an icing syringe with a writing pipe. Pipe criss-cross lines of chocolate across the top of trifle.

Milanaise soufflé

Sherry whirl

502 SEMOLINA MOUSSELINE

284ml/½pint *red or white wine or milk or fruit juice*
284ml/½pint *water* · 100g/4oz *sugar*
100g/4oz *semolina* · 4 *egg whites*
canned or fresh fruit to decorate

Heat liquid and sugar and stir in semolina. Bring to the boil, stirring, and cook gently for 3 minutes. Remove from heat, whisk in 2 unbeaten egg whites and then fold in 2 stiffly whisked egg whites. Pour into a mould and place in baking tin half filled with water and cook in a moderate oven, 350°F, 180°C, Gas Mark 4, for 40 minutes. Chill and turn out. Decorate with canned or fresh fruit. It is worth while trying this recipe with several variations, for each tastes quite different. 284ml (½ pint) milk with 284ml (½ pint) water gives a soft, light creamy mould which blends beautifully with all fruit. 284ml (½ pint) wine with 284ml (½ pint) water gives a piquant 'bite' for a party and by using fruit juice instead of wine you make an excellent children's sweet.

503 DANISH CREME BRULEE

3 *egg yolks* · 1 *egg* · 1 *large can evaporated milk*
2 *heaped teaspoons castor sugar*
castor sugar for topping

Whisk egg yolks with a teaspoon cold water. Add whole egg and whisk together. Rinse a strong saucepan with cold water and put in evaporated milk. Heat to boiling point and take from heat at once. After a moment or so stir milk gradually into well whisked egg and yolks, mixing briskly all the time. Return mixture to pan, add sugar and whisk together over low heat until blended, but do not boil. Draw pan from heat and whisk well until cooled. Pour into an ovenproof serving dish and place in the refrigerator until chilled. Sprinkle thickly with castor sugar and put under hot grill for 2–3 minutes until caramel coloured. Serve at once.

504 SHERRY WHIRL

(Illustrated in colour on opposite page)

1 *orange-flavoured jelly* · 1 *tablespoon dry sherry*
Swiss roll (Recipe No. 730) · 50g/2oz *almonds, chopped*
double cream, whipped, to decorate

Make the jelly in the usual way; add the sherry. Cut the Swiss roll in slices. Pour a layer of jelly into the bottom of a rinsed plain mould and allow to set. Arrange slices of Swiss roll and a few almonds on the jelly and round the sides of the mould. Pour the remaining jelly into the mould. Add remaining almonds and leave to set. When set, turn on to a serving plate and decorate the top with whipped double cream.

505 CHOCOLATE MOUSSE

50g/2oz *plain chocolate* · 2 *eggs* · *double cream, whipped*
chocolate to decorate

Melt the chocolate in a bowl over hot water. Separate the egg whites from the yolks, and stir the yolks into the melted chocolate. Beat the whites until stiff and fold into the mixture. Pour into individual dishes and leave to set. Decorate with whipped double cream and chocolate and serve.

506 LEMON CREAM PIE

biscuit crumb pastry (Recipe No. 507)
½ *lemon-flavoured jelly* · 1 *small can evaporated milk*
grated rind and juice ½ *lemon*
glacé cherries, angelica and chocolate vermicelli to decorate

Make biscuit crumb pastry and line a deep pie plate. Meanwhile dissolve jelly in 142ml (¼ pint) hot water. Leave in a cool place. When cold, whisk in the evaporated milk, lemon juice and rind. Pour into biscuit case and leave to set. Decorate with glacé cherries, angelica and chocolate vermicelli.

507 BISCUIT CRUMB PASTRY

150–175g/6oz *sweet wholemeal biscuits*
75–85g/3oz *butter, melted*

Place biscuits between folded greaseproof paper and crush into crumbs with a rolling pin. Put into a basin. Add the melted butter and bind the crumbs together. Line bottom and sides of deep pie plate or sandwich cake tin with mixture. Leave in a cool place until firm. Other sweet biscuit crumbs or ginger nuts can be used instead of digestive biscuits.
Makes 6–8 servings.

Chocolate mousse

508 LEMON FRUIT MERINGUE BASKET

4 egg whites · 1 teaspoon vanilla essence
225g*/8oz castor sugar · vanilla ice cream
cherries to decorate
Filling
6 tablespoons lemon curd · 1 tablespoon lemon juice
2 egg yolks · 142ml/¼pint double cream, whipped
*You need this amount

Beat egg whites until very stiff, add vanilla essence. Sprinkle in half the sugar and whisk for a second time, then fold in rest of the sugar. Pipe with a 1-cm (½-inch) meringue pipe on to oiled, greaseproof paper placed on a baking sheet, to form round base. Pipe fairly large stars round the edge. Bake in a very cool oven, 200–250°F, 100–110°C, Gas Mark 0–1½, for 1–2 hours until dry and crisp. Remove from the paper and cool. Prepare the filling: put the curd, lemon juice and beaten egg yolks into a basin over a pan of very hot water and cook until thick. Cool, stirring from time to time, then blend with the whipped cream. Fill the meringue case with this mixture and just before serving top with vanilla ice cream, decorate with cherries and more cream if wished. The meringue case can be made beforehand and stored in an airtight tin.

Lemon fruit meringue basket

509 SUMMER CLOUD MOUSSE

1 medium-sized can fruit salad or fresh fruit salad
1 strawberry or raspberry-flavoured jelly
142ml/¼pint double cream · 2 egg whites
wafers or glacé cherries to decorate

Arrange fruit in glasses. Dissolve half the jelly in 284ml (½ pint) water. Cool and pour over fruit in glasses and leave to set. Dissolve the second half of the jelly in 142ml (¼ pint) water only. Cool and fold in lightly whipped cream and stiffly whipped egg whites. Pile on to the set jelly and leave in a cool place. Decorate with wafers or cherries.
Makes 5 servings.

Summer cloud mousse

Strawberry gâteau

510 STRAWBERRY GATEAU

100g/4oz margarine · 100g/4oz castor sugar · 2 eggs
100g/4oz self-raising flour (with plain flour use 1 teaspoon
baking powder)
284ml/½pint double cream, whipped · fresh strawberries

Cream together the margarine and sugar until light and fluffy. Gradually beat in the eggs. Fold in the flour and baking powder, if used. Divide the mixture between two greased sandwich cake tins, with a round of greaseproof paper at the bottom and bake in a moderately hot oven, 375°F, 190°C, Gas Mark 5, for 20–25 minutes. Turn out carefully and cool on a wire tray. Sandwich the two cakes together with whipped cream and strawberries and decorate the top with cream and strawberries.

Rolled oat gâteau

A very crisp 'nutty' flavour is given if 25g (1 oz) quick-cooking rolled oats are used in place of the same amount of flour. Prepare and bake as above.

Frosted banana mousse

Strawberry parfait

FROSTED SWEETS

511   FROSTED BANANA MOUSSE

4 large bananas · pinch salt · 75–100g/3–4oz sugar
1½ tablespoons lemon juice
50g/2oz oat crisp (Recipe No. 500)
284ml/½ pint double cream or evaporated milk
glacé cherries and angelica to decorate

Line a freezing tray with waxed or greaseproof paper. Mash the bananas, then add the salt, sugar, lemon juice and oat crisp, and mix thoroughly. Fold in most of the lightly whipped cream or evaporated milk and freeze the mixture in the usual way. Decorate with remainder of cream, the cherries and angelica.

For instructions on correct freezing of ices see Recipe No. 546.

512   STRAWBERRY PARFAIT

pinch salt · 2 egg whites · 75–100g/3–4oz sugar
3 dessertspoons lemon juice · 284ml/½pint double cream
150–200g/6–8oz fresh or frozen strawberries

Add salt to egg whites and beat till foamy. Gradually beat in sugar, add lemon juice and beat until stiff and glossy. Whip the cream lightly and add this and most of the strawberries, sliced, to the mixture. Pour into freezing trays, and place in refrigerator with controls set at very cold. When firm, turn freezing control back to normal until serving time. Serve in sundae glasses and decorate with whole strawberries.

For instructions on correct freezing of ices see Recipe No. 546. Makes 6 servings.

Raspberry baskets

513   RASPBERRY BASKETS

block vanilla ice cream · 12 ice cream wafers
200g/8oz fresh raspberries ·*
*whipped double cream and angelica** to decorate*

*Frozen raspberries can be used. Defrost before using
**Soak angelica in a little warm water to make it pliable

Cut ice cream into 4 oblongs and press wafers against the sides to give a basket shape. The wafers at either end must be cut. Pile raspberries on top and decorate with cream and handles of angelica.

Pear chocolate sundae

514   STRAWBERRY MELBA

strawberries · ice cream · Melba sauce (Recipe Nos. 516, 517)
double cream, whipped · blanched almonds, chopped

Arrange the fruit and ice cream in individual glasses. Top with Melba sauce, rosettes of whipped cream and blanched almonds.

515   PEACH MELBA

Follow the recipe for strawberry Melba above, but use peeled fresh or canned peaches in place of the strawberries.

516   MELBA SAUCE

1 teaspoon cornflour · 2 tablespoons water · 1 tablespoon sugar
100–125g/4–5oz raspberries*
3–4 tablespoons redcurrant or apple jelly

*Fresh, frozen or canned – omit sugar with latter

Blend cornflour with water. Put all ingredients into pan and cook gently until thickened. If a smooth sauce is required, rub through a sieve. Cool and use as required.

517   ECONOMICAL MELBA SAUCE

½ teaspoon arrowroot or cornflour · 4 tablespoons water
3–4 tablespoons raspberry jam
3–4 tablespoons redcurrant jelly

Blend the arrowroot or cornflour with the water and put into a saucepan with the other ingredients. Cook, stirring, until clear and slightly thickened. Cool before using.

518   PEAR CHOCOLATE SUNDAE

vanilla ice cream
drained canned or cooked pear halves or halved ripe dessert pears
chocolate sauce (Recipe No. 519)
toasted almonds, chopped to decorate

Fill individual glasses with vanilla ice cream and pear halves. Pour over chocolate sauce and decorate with chopped toasted almonds.

Note : This dish is often called pear Hélène.

Pear and shortbread layer

519 CHOCOLATE SAUCE

25g/1oz margarine or butter · 25g/1oz cocoa
½ teaspoon vanilla essence · 2 tablespoons water
50g/2oz sugar or
25g/1oz sugar and 1 tablespoon golden syrup

Put all the ingredients into a saucepan and heat gently until the cocoa has dissolved. Do not boil this sauce as it will lose the shiny appearance.

520 COUPE JACQUES
Mixed fruit sundae

blanched almonds · fruit salad, fresh or canned · ice cream
Melba sauce (Recipe Nos. 516, 517)
double cream, whipped · canned or Maraschino cherries

Chop and brown the almonds lightly under the grill. Arrange the fruit and ice cream in individual glasses. Pour over Melba sauce and decorate with nuts, cream and cherries.

521 PEAR AND SHORTBREAD LAYER

shortbread (Recipe No. 801)
1 medium-sized can pears, drained or cooked fresh pears
100g/4oz apricot jam · 1 tablespoon water · glacé cherries

Make the shortbread, cut into rounds and bake for 20 minutes. Cool on a wire tray. Drain and slice the pears. Bring the apricot jam and water to the boil, then sieve. Place some biscuits on a serving plate, cover with pear slices, then another (smaller) layer of biscuits and pears. Top with shortbread biscuits. Decorate with glacé cherries and pour over the apricot sauce.

MORE ICE CREAM SWEETS

522   **GINGER SUNDAE**

Place vanilla ice cream in a sundae glass. Decorate with crystallised ginger and serve with a wafer.
A delicious variation is to top the ice cream with canned chestnut purée and a marron glacé.

Ginger sundae

523   **WALNUT AND FUDGE PARFAIT**

Arrange ice cream, fudge sauce and chopped walnuts in a sundae glass. For a quick fudge sauce melt fudge in a basin over hot water, adding a little milk so it does not stiffen too much when used, and taking off the heat just *before* mixture reaches 115°C (238°F).

524   **PLUM WHIP**

300g/12oz *plums** · 142ml/¼pint *water*
sugar · generous ½litre/1pint *jelly***
1 *block vanilla and/or strawberry ice cream*

*Other fruit could be used instead
**Raspberry or orange-flavoured jelly for red plums; lemon or greengage-flavoured jelly for golden plums

Stew plums in the water and sweeten to taste, reserve a few whole ones for decoration. Sieve the remainder into a measure. Dissolve the jelly in water so that the jelly, purée and water will together make up generous ½litre (1 pint). Mix together and leave until beginning to set. Whisk vigorously before pouring the mixture into individual serving dishes. To serve, top with portions of ice cream, and decorate with reserved plums.

Plum whip

525   **BANANA AND WALNUT
ICE CREAM**

Arrange portions of ice cream in a serving dish. On each portion place a thick banana slice, sprinkled with lemon juice, and a walnut half.

Banana and walnut ice cream

Baked Alaska

526 BAKED ALASKA
also known as
NORWEGIAN OMELETTE
or
OMELETTE SURPRISE

sponge cake or a cooked pastry flan case (Recipe No. 587)
1 block ice cream · fresh or canned fruit · 5 egg whites
150–250g/6–10oz castor sugar

Place the sponge cake or pastry flan case on an ovenproof serving dish. Cover with fresh or canned drained fruit; place the block of ice cream on top of the fruit. Whisk the egg whites until very stiff. Add half the sugar and whisk until as stiff as before. Gently fold in the remaining sugar. Pile or pipe the meringue over the ice cream. Put in a very hot oven 475–500°F, 240–250°C, Gas Mark 8–9 for 3–5 minutes. Serve at once. The secret of baked Alaska is to cover the ice cream completely with the meringue and to have the oven very hot. Another method of making this dish is to use 5 eggs and beat the egg yolks and sugar together until *very thick*, then fold in the stiffly beaten egg whites. This is then used and baked instead of plain meringue.

527 RATAFIA AND SHERRY DELICE

50g/2oz ratafias · 2–3 tablespoons sherry
1 block vanilla ice cream · double cream, whipped, to decorate

Soak the ratafias in the sherry. Pile the ice cream into individual dishes. Sprinkle with ratafias and top with whipped double cream.

528 APPLES IN HOT CHERRY SAUCE

50g/2oz sugar · 284ml/½pint water
3 medium-sized cooking apples · 1 block vanilla ice cream
cherry sauce (Recipe No. 529)

Place the sugar and water in a wide saucepan and heat gently until the sugar dissolves. Core and peel the apples, then cut in half and place them, flat side down, in the syrup. Cover pan and poach gently for about 10 minutes, until the apples are tender but not broken. Carefully lift on to a plate. Make sauce with the fruit syrup. To serve, cut the ice cream into 6 slices and place in individual dishes. Arrange an apple half on each slice of ice cream and coat with the hot cherry sauce.
Makes 6 servings.

Ratafia and sherry délice

529 HOT CHERRY SAUCE

2½ level teaspoons arrowroot or cornflour · 2 tablespoons water
12 tablespoons fruit syrup · drop red colouring
25g/1oz glacé cherries, chopped · 1–2 tablespoons lemon juice

Blend the arrowroot or cornflour with the water and add to the syrup, bring to the boil, stirring, and simmer for 1 minute. Colour pale pink and mix in the cherries and lemon juice.

Apples in hot cherry sauce

530 YOGHOURT WITH VANILLA CUSTARD

284ml/½pint *yoghourt*
284ml/½pint *thick custard sauce (Recipe No. 692)* · *sugar*
chopped nuts · chopped glacé fruits · wafers

Mix the yoghourt and cooled custard, add sugar to taste. Serve in glasses and top with chopped nuts and chopped glacé fruits. Serve with crisp wafers.

531 ICE CREAM CRUNCH

300–350g/12–14oz *ginger biscuits*
75–90g/3–3½oz *butter* · 125–150g/5–6oz *chocolate*
3 *ripe bananas* · *juice* ½ *lemon* · 1 *block vanilla ice cream*
3 *teaspoons maple syrup**

*A mock maple syrup can be made by heating 2 teaspoons brown sugar and 2 teaspoons golden syrup

Crush the ginger biscuits finely. Melt the butter and chocolate over a low heat. Remove from the heat and mix in the crushed biscuit crumbs; press the mixture into a shallow pie dish and harden slightly for about 1 hour in the refrigerator. Peel and slice the bananas and dip in the lemon juice. Line the base and sides of the biscuit crumb case with banana slices. Fill with spoonfuls of ice cream. Pour over the maple syrup and serve at once.
Makes 6 servings.

Ice cream crunch

532 YOGHOURT MOULD

25g/1oz *raisins* · 12 *tablespoons water*
50g/2oz *Demerara sugar* · 15g/½oz *powdered gelatine**
426ml/¾pint *yoghourt* · 75g/3oz *mixed glacé fruits*
juice 1 *lemon* · *double cream, whipped*

*Enough to set generous ½litre (1pint) of liquid – this varies slightly with make

Simmer the raisins in 142ml (¼ pint) of the water and 3 tablespoons sugar for about 10 minutes. Remove from heat, add the gelatine, softened in remaining water, and stir until the gelatine has thoroughly dissolved. Leave to cool a little and mix in yoghourt with Demerara sugar, half the glacé fruits, chopped finely, and the lemon juice. When the mixture begins to set, stir just once in order to prevent the fruit from sinking to the bottom and turn into a buttered mould. Leave to set and turn out. Decorate with whipped cream and the remaining glacé fruits.

Pear gâteau

CAKES USED AS DESSERTS

533 PEACH AND GRAPE GATEAU

(Illustrated in colour on the jacket)

Make Victoria sandwich as Recipe No. 700. When cold sandwich together with lightly whipped double cream. Smooth cream round the sides and decorate the sides with halved grapes and a piping of cream. Smooth some cream over the top of the gâteau and decorate with drained canned peach slices. Pipe remaining cream round the edge.

534 PEAR GATEAU

Make Victoria sandwich as Recipe No. 700. When cold sandwich together with drained sliced canned pears. Spread the top with sieved raspberry jam. Place 4 pear halves, sprinkled with desiccated coconut, on the jam. Decorate with fresh raspberries, if available and leaves of angelica.

535 CHOCOLATE SPONGE FLAN

Make sponge flan as Recipe No. 483. When cold fill with chocolate blancmange mixed with a little single cream. Decorate with toasted almonds.

536 PARAME MOUSSE

Make up a lemon-flavoured jelly using just under generous ½litre (1 pint) water. Allow to cool. When beginning to set, whisk in 100g (4 oz) cake crumbs, 50g (1 oz) chopped crystallised ginger and 2 stiffly beaten egg whites. Decorate with crystallised ginger and pistachio nuts.

537　KENTISH DELIGHTS

generous ½litre/1pint *milk* · 3 *level tablespoons sugar*
3 *rounded tablespoons finest semolina* · 1 *egg*
8 *glacé cherries, chopped* · *few drops almond essence*
canned or stewed cherries
whipped double or clotted cream to serve

Heat milk in rinsed pan and before it reaches boiling point, gradually add sugar and semolina stirring until thickened. Cook for several minutes. Draw pan from heat and mix in the beaten egg. Heat again, but do not boil. Stir in chopped glacé cherries and almond essence. Divide mixture between lightly buttered castle pudding moulds, and leave until set. Turn out on to serving dish and serve with canned or stewed cherries and whipped double or clotted cream.

Kentish delights

538　LEMON AND MANDARIN FOAM

275g/11oz *can mandarin oranges* · ½ *lemon-flavoured jelly*
284ml/½pint *milk* · 2 *tablespoons semolina*
50g/2oz *castor sugar* · 142ml/¼pint *double cream, whipped*
1 *egg white*

Drain mandarin oranges, measure syrup and add enough water to give just under 284ml (½ pint). Heat and dissolve the lemon jelly in this. When cool and beginning to thicken, whisk well and divide between 4–6 sundae glasses depending on their size. Leave until set. Chop or sieve most of the mandarin oranges to give a purée. Meanwhile heat milk and stir in the semolina and cook for 4–5 minutes. Stir in sugar and fruit purée. Leave until cold. Fold in about a third of the whipped cream and stiffly whisked egg white. Divide between the sweet glasses, filling to the brim. Set in a cool place. Decorate with remaining whipped cream and mandarin oranges.

Lemon and mandarin foam

Orange semolina chantilly

539　ORANGE SEMOLINA CHANTILLY

2 *eggs* · 3 *rounded tablespoons semolina*
generous ½litre/1pint *milk* · *pinch salt*
finely grated rind 1 orange · 50g/2oz *castor sugar*
1 *packet chocolate finger biscuits* · *double cream, whipped*
a glacé cherry and angelica to decorate

Separate the whites and yolks of the eggs. Blend the semolina with a little cold milk. Heat remaining milk with salt, orange rind and sugar. Add the semolina, bring to the boil and cook gently for a minute, stirring carefully all the time with a wooden spoon. Remove from heat, cool slightly, then beat in egg yolks thoroughly. Cook over very low heat, do not allow to boil, for a minute. Remove from heat. Fold in stiffly whisked egg whites. Pour into a rinsed mould or round dish and leave in a cool place. When firm and set, turn out on to a serving dish and place chocolate finger biscuits round the sides. Decorate the top with cream, a cherry and angelica. (It is important to fill the dish in which the custard is baked quite full or it may break when it is turned out).

540 CREME CARAMEL

75g/3oz castor sugar · 3 tablespoons water
squeeze lemon juice · 2 whole eggs* · 2 egg yolks
2 tablespoons sugar · generous ½litre/1pint milk

*If liked use all egg yolks and no whites – this gives a very rich custard

First make the caramel sauce. To do this put the 75g (3 oz) sugar, water and lemon juice into a small heavy pan, place over a low heat and allow to melt, stirring until the sugar has dissolved – do not allow the syrup to come to the boil until all the sugar is melted. Increase the heat and cook, stirring occasionally, until it is a deep golden colour. Remove from heat and pour into a warmed buttered soufflé dish, cake tin or dariole moulds, turning to coat the sides and the bottom evenly with the caramel. Beat the eggs and sugar with a fork, heat the milk to just under boiling point and pour on to the beaten eggs. Stir and strain on to the caramel. Stand in a baking tin with enough hot water round it to come half way up the sides, cover with a piece of buttered paper or foil and bake in a slow oven, 300°F, 150°C, Gas Mark 2, for about 1 hour until quite set. Let the custard get cool before turning it out.

Crème caramel

541 PRETTY MAIDS

50g/2oz milk chocolate · generous ½litre/1pint milk
2 tablespoons semolina · 1 egg
1–2 tablespoons sugar · few drops vanilla essence
double cream, whipped, glacé cherries and chopped nuts to decorate

Break up the chocolate and melt slowly in the milk. Stir in the semolina and bring to the boil. Continue to stir and cook for 3 minutes; remove from the heat, mix in the egg yolk and sugar. Cover (to prevent a skin forming on the top) and leave to cool. Beat egg white until stiff then fold into the semolina mixture together with the vanilla essence. Turn into sundae glasses and decorate with whipped cream, glacé cherries and chopped nuts.

Pretty maids

542 CHOCOLATE FLOATING ISLANDS

75g/3oz plain chocolate · 426ml/¾pint milk · 3 eggs
100g/4oz castor sugar · 1 level teaspoon cornflour
coarsely grated chocolate to decorate

Break up the chocolate and place it in a saucepan with the milk. Place over a low heat to melt the chocolate. In a basin beat the egg yolks, half the sugar and cornflour together. Gradually whisk in the chocolate milk. Return to the saucepan and heat slowly until thickened. Do not allow the mixture to boil. Pour into a serving dish and leave to cool. Meanwhile whisk the egg whites until stiff and fold in the remaining sugar. Drop tablespoonfuls of the egg white mixture into a saucepan of hot water and poach for 1–2 minutes, until firm. Drain and place on the chocolate custard. Decorate with grated chocolate and serve.

The classic dessert, often known as Oeufs à la Neige is made by poaching the meringue mixture in a generous ½litre (1 pint) hot milk, to which is added a little vanilla. When the meringues are firm, see above, drain. Blend the strained milk with the egg yolks and 25g (1 oz) sugar and simmer gently until a smooth egg custard sauce. Pour into a shallow dish to cool, then put the meringues on top.

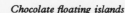
Chocolate floating islands

543 CHOCOLATE PUDDING

1 rounded tablespoon cornflour · 25g/1oz chocolate powder
50g/2oz sugar · generous ½litre/1pint milk
double cream, whipped and walnut halves to decorate

Mix cornflour, chocolate powder and sugar with a little cold milk, stir until smooth. Bring remainder of the milk to the boil. Pour on to the blended cornflour mixture and mix well. Return to the saucepan and to a slow heat to thicken. Pour into a rinsed mould and leave to set. Turn out and decorate with whipped cream and walnuts.

544 APPLE RUSSE

Savoy fingers · 284ml/½pint double cream · 1 egg white
2 level teaspoons powdered gelatine ·
284ml/½pint sweet white wine or mix white wine and
maraschino
75g/3oz sugar · 2 eating apples, peeled, cored and sliced
little sieved apricot jam · double cream, whipped to decorate

Line the sides of a Charlotte mould or plain tin with the Savoy fingers. Whip the cream and then the egg white until stiff; fold together. Dissolve the gelatine in the hot wine and mix in the sugar. Cool, then stir into the whipped cream. As soon as the mixture starts to set fill the mould. Leave to set, turn out and tie with a ribbon. Arrange the apple slices around the edge of the russe; brush with apricot jam. Decorate the centre with whipped cream.

545 LEMON CREAM MOULD

15g/½oz powdered gelatine · 75g/3oz sugar
8 tablespoons hot water · 426ml/¾pint milk · juice 2 lemons
grated rind 1 lemon
double cream, whipped and a glacé cherry to decorate

Dissolve the gelatine with the sugar in the hot water. Cool slightly and mix in to the milk. Whisk in the lemon juice and the grated lemon rind. As soon as the mixture starts to set, pour into a mould, previously rinsed with cold water. When set turn out and decorate with whipped double cream and a glacé cherry.

546 HOME-MADE ICE CREAM

It is not difficult to make ice cream at home, and although the commercially prepared products are excellent there may be occasions when you like to make your own.
Remember:
1. Use a good recipe, i.e. one with sufficient fat content. This is obtained by using canned or fresh cream, full cream condensed milk or evaporated milk.
2. With most recipes it is advisable to freeze very quickly. A home freezer or the type of refrigerator with 2 stars (**) or 3 stars (***) markings freeze very quickly so no adjustment is necessary. If using a refrigerator with no star markings or 1 star (*) only turn the indicator to the coldest position 30 minutes before starting to freeze the mixture.
3. With most recipes it is advisable to beat at least once, to give a light texture.
4. When ice cream has frozen, return indicator to normal position.

Apple russe

Ice cream and raspberry tartlets

547 ONE-WHIP ICE CREAM

1 teaspoon powdered gelatine · 1 tablespoon hot water
3 tablespoons castor sugar · 1 large can evaporated milk
1 teaspoon vanilla essence

Dissolve the gelatine in the hot water. Mix with sugar and evaporated milk. Pour into the freezing tray. Chill until mixture starts to freeze round the edge. Pour into cold bowl, add vanilla essence and whisk until thick and creamy. Return to freezing tray until firm.

548 ICE CREAM MADE WITH EVAPORATED AND CONDENSED MILK

1 small can full cream condensed milk · 142ml/¼pint water
284ml/½pint evaporated milk · flavouring (Recipe No. 550)

Mix the condensed milk with the water and chill. Whip the evaporated milk, as in Recipe Nos. 485 or 493, until thick. Fold into the condensed milk, add flavouring (see Recipe No. 550). Freeze until thick, turn into bowl and beat until very smooth. Replace in the trays and freeze again.
This recipe can be frozen quickly or, if more convenient it can be frozen with the indicator set at normal.

549 STRAWBERRY ICE CREAM

Follow Recipe No. 547 above, but instead of vanilla essence fold in 142ml (¼ pint) strawberry purée – made from fresh, or well drained frozen or canned strawberries. This should be added when beating the frozen mixture in the bowl.
For an attractive dessert, serve strawberry and vanilla ice cream in tall glasses (*Illustrated in colour on the jacket*).

550 ICE CREAM FLAVOURINGS

1. Dissolve 1½ dessertspoons instant coffee powder in the 142ml (¼ pint) water in Recipe No. 548.
2. Melt 100g (4 oz) plain chocolate with the 142ml (¼ pint) water in Recipe No. 548.
3. Stir 284ml (½ pint) thick fruit purée to Recipe No. 548.
4. Use less sugar and add 100g (4 oz) jam to Recipe No. 548.

551 ICE CREAM AND RASPBERRY TARTLETS

200g/8oz rich flan pastry (Recipe No. 576) · 50g/2oz sugar
1½ tablespoons cornflour · scant 284ml/½pint milk
3 egg yolks · ½ teaspoon vanilla essence
home-made ice cream or 1 block raspberry ice cream
100g/4oz fresh or frozen raspberries
double cream, whipped to decorate

Make the pastry, roll out thinly and line fairly deep patty tins. Bake 'blind' (Recipe No. 560) then cool on a wire tray. Blend the sugar, cornflour and a little cold milk in a basin. Bring the rest of the milk to the boil and pour on to the cornflour, stir well, then pour into the saucepan and cook until a smooth thick sauce. Beat the egg yolks and vanilla essence, add the cornflour sauce, then stand the basin over a pan of hot, but NOT boiling, water. Cook gently for 5–10 minutes. Leave to cool, covered, to prevent a skin forming. When cold, half fill each pastry case. Put a spoonful of ice cream in the centre of each tartlet; surround with raspberries, pipe a rosette of cream on top of the ice cream and decorate with a raspberry. Serve at once.

Grape baskets

555   GRAPE BASKETS

100g/4oz *self-raising flour (with plain flour use 1 teaspoon baking powder)*
50g/2oz *butter or soft margarine* · 50g/2oz *castor sugar*
2 eggs · 2 *heaped tablespoons apricot jam, sieved*
1 *tablespoon water* · 50g/2oz *chopped nuts*
few green and black grapes · *angelica**

**Soften in hot water to make it pliable*

Sieve flour. Cream fat and sugar until light and fluffy. Beat in eggs and fold in flour. Spread evenly in medium-sized Swiss roll tin, previously lined in bottom with greaseproof paper, and brushed all round inside with melted fat. Bake on the middle shelf of a moderate oven, 350°F, 180°C, Gas Mark 4, for 20–30 minutes. Turn out, remove paper, and cool on a wire tray. When cold cut out rounds with cutters (the remaining cake can be used in a trifle). Boil jam with water for 2–3 minutes until syrupy, stirring all the time. Spread the jam round the sides and roll in the nuts. Decorate the tops with halved green and black grapes. Make handles with the angelica.

552   MARSHMALLOW ICE CREAM

100g/4oz *marshmallows* · 142ml/¼pint *milk*
142ml/¼pint *double cream, whipped*
50g/2oz *Maraschino cherries, chopped*
50g/2oz *pineapple, chopped* · 25g/1oz *walnuts, chopped*
1 *dessertspoon sugar*

Chop the marshmallows, put about 75g (3 oz) with the milk and allow to melt. Cool, then add the rest of the marshmallows and the remaining ingredients. Pour into a freezing tray and freeze as quickly as possible in the refrigerator. When firm return the indicator on the refrigerator to the normal position to store.

553   STORING COMMERCIALLY-MADE ICE CREAM

Commercially-made ice cream will keep about 2 hours wrapped in several layers of newspaper or in a wide-topped vacuum flask if you have no refrigerator. Always put into the freezing compartment of the refrigerator. Makes vary, so check on the packet how long it will keep in perfect condition.

554   STORING HOME-MADE ICE CREAM

When the ice cream has frozen, return indicator to normal position to store. In a 3 star (***) refrigerator you do not change setting to freeze therefore you do not need to change setting to store. Freeze and store. It is advisable to cover freezing tray with foil or waxed paper. Unless stored in a deep freezer, home-made ice cream should be used quickly, because of the fat content.

556   STRAWBERRY CHIFFON CUPS

200g/8oz *plain flour* · *pinch salt*
1 *teaspoon castor sugar* · 125g/5oz *pure cooking fat*
1–2 *tablespoons cold water* · 100g/4oz *sugar*
2 *teaspoons lemon juice* · 2 eggs · 200g/8oz *strawberries*
142ml/¼pint *double cream or evaporated milk, whipped*
15g/½oz *powdered gelatine* · 4 *tablespoons hot water*

Sieve flour, salt and the teaspoon sugar. Rub in the fat and bind with the cold water. Roll out thinly and line deep patty tins. Bake 'blind' (Recipe No. 560) in a moderately hot oven, 400°F, 200°C, Gas Mark 6, until crisp and golden brown. Add the sugar and lemon juice to the egg yolks, beat well over a pan of hot water until very thick and creamy. Crush most of the strawberries, but keep about 8 for decoration. Fold into egg yolk mixture, together with half the whipped cream. Dissolve the gelatine in the very hot water and add to the strawberry mixture. When cool and beginning to set, fold in the stiffly beaten egg whites. Pile into the pastry cases, decorate with half a strawberry and remaining whipped cream.

557   THE NEW LOOK FOR BANANAS AND CREAM

6 *firm bananas* · *squeeze lemon juice*
50–75g/2–3oz *soft brown sugar* · 40g/1½oz *butter*
2–3 *tablespoons desiccated coconut*
about 142ml/¼pint *double cream, lightly whipped*

Peel the bananas and place in an ovenproof dish; squeeze over lemon juice, sprinkle with brown sugar. Dot with butter and sprinkle over the coconut. Bake in a moderately hot oven, 375°F, 190°C, Gas Mark 5, for about 20 minutes, until the bananas are soft but not mushy. Just before serving, spoon over the very cold cream.

Strawberry chiffon cups

Coffee gâteau suprême

559 COFFEE GATEAU SUPREME

Victoria sandwich cake (Recipe No. 700) *

*Beat 1 tablespoon coffee essence into the creamed fat and sugar. Bake the mixture in two 20-cm (8-inch) sandwich tins

Coffee butter cream

100g/4oz *butter or margarine* · 200g/8oz *icing sugar, sieved*
4 *teaspoons coffee essence* · 100g/4oz *hazel nuts to decorate*

Soften the butter and beat in the icing sugar and coffee essence. Cut the sandwich cakes across in halves and sandwich all four together with some of the coffee butter cream. Very finely chop all but 10 of the hazel nuts. Smooth more of the butter cream round the sides of the cake. Roll the sides in the chopped nuts. Pipe the remainder of the butter cream over the top of the cake. Decorate with the reserved hazel nuts.

558 PAVLOVA

4 *egg whites* · 200g/8oz *sugar* · *ice cream*
pineapple rings and glacé cherries to decorate

Whisk egg whites until very stiff (use an electric mixer if you have one) add sugar as described in meringues (Recipe No. 759). Spread about one-third of the mixture on to a well oiled tin, in a circular shape. Put the remainder of the mixture into a piping bag and pipe a border round the edge. Bake in a very slow oven, 250–275°F, 130–140°C, Gas Mark 0–¼, for about 3 hours, until firm. Cool and store in an airtight tin until ready to use. Fill with ice cream and decorate with pineapple rings and glacé cherries.

The new look for bananas and cream

Pavlova

PASTRY & PANCAKES

560 CERTAIN SUCCESS WITH PASTRY

1. Keep ingredients, utensils and hands as cool as possible.
2. Use a large bowl rather than a small one for short pastry, so that air can be incorporated when rubbing the fat into the flour.
3. When rubbing fat into flour, lift hands as high as possible so that air can be introduced into dough.
4. Rub in fat only with forefinger and thumb. Too much pressure when rubbing in will make pastry too sticky.
5. Sieve flour before mixing. This lightens the dough.
6. It is undoubtedly better to use plain flour for all pastry. Many people however prefer self-raising flour for short pastry, especially when the proportion of fat is decreased, so if successful with self-raising flour do not change. For richer pastry, i.e. flaky or puff pastry, plain flour is better.
7. The consistency of the dough is very important. Be careful not to make it too wet, as this produces a hard pastry. If the dough is too dry, it will be difficult to roll out. Generally speaking the dough is the right texture when it forms a ball, with very little handling.
8. Pastry should be baked quickly.
9. When using very hard fat (perhaps straight from the refrigerator) which is almost impossible to rub into the flour, you will find it helpful to grate it on a coarse grater or to soften it by working with a knife. When making flan pastry the fat can be slightly warmed first.
10. When making short pastry oil can be used instead of fat. For each 25g (1 oz) of fat substitute a scant tablespoon of oil. This will give the pastry a very crisp crust.
11. When rolling out pastry remember never to roll the rolling pin backwards and forwards. It should roll one way only – straight ahead. The pastry should be turned at right angles to obtain the required shape.
12. When rolling the pastry, lift rolling pin from time to time. This helps to keep the dough light.
13. When a recipe says that the pastry case should be baked 'blind' it means empty. To prevent the bottom of the tart or flan rising, fill case with crusts of stale bread or haricot beans on a piece of greased greaseproof paper during the baking. Remove for the last 5 minutes of cooking time.

561   CHOOSING FAT FOR PASTRY

There have been many developments in fats for pastry making and so you will find with most of the basic recipes a list of the fats you can use. They are all good and each give excellent results and a slightly different taste and texture – so you can vary your pastry.

562 AMOUNT OF PASTRY IN RECIPES

When a recipe directs 'use 100g (4 oz) short crust pastry (or puff)' it means pastry made with 100g (4 oz) flour etc. – not a total weight of 100g (4 oz).

Metric conversion for pastry. The *accurate* conversion of 1 oz is 28·35g but the *accepted* conversion is 25g. This means that short crust pastry made with 200g flour and 100g fat has the *correct proportions* but produces a *smaller* total weight than if 8 oz flour and 4 oz fat are used. If you wish to make *exactly* the same amount of pastry by metric weight all you need to do is to increase the flour from 200 to 225g and the fat from 100 to 112g. Where a recipe simply states . . . rolled oat pastry (Recipe No. 632) it means quantity as given in that recipe.

563   DANISH APPLE FLAN
(Illustrated in colour on the opposite page)

200g/8oz short crust pastry (Recipe No. 566)
1 can apple pie filling or ½kg/1lb sweetened THICK apple pulp
50g/2oz sultanas · grated rind 1 orange
4 teaspoons Angostura bitters · 1 tablespoon apricot jam

Make the pastry and line a 20-cm (8-inch) flan ring placed on an upturned baking sheet or tin. Reserve the pastry trimmings. Bake the pastry 'blind' (Recipe No. 560) in a moderately hot oven, 400°F, 200°C, Gas Mark 6, for 20 minutes. Mix together the apple pie filling, sultanas, orange rind, Angostura and apricot jam. Smooth into the partly baked flan case. Roll out the pastry trimmings and cut into strips; use to make a lattice work on top of the apple flan. Return to the oven and cook for a further 15–20 minutes. Serve either hot or cold.

Danish apple flan (Recipe No. 563)

564   MINCE PIES

To make mince pies use biscuit pie crust (Recipe No. 565), for extra shortness or short, flaky or puff pastry (Recipe Nos. 566, 604, 588). If making mince pies in patty tins, cut the bottom round slightly larger than the top lid, so that it forms a neat fitting edge. Always cut 1 or 2 slits on top to allow steam to escape when cooking. If making a lot of mince pies and you run short of patty tins, cook them on baking sheets; when using this method cut both top and bottom rounds the same size.

565   BISCUIT PIE CRUST

250g/10oz plain flour · 50g/2oz cornflour · 150g/6oz butter
2 teaspoons castor sugar · 1 egg yolk · water to mix

Sieve flour and cornflour together. Rub in the butter lightly. Add sugar and mix with egg yolk and water. Knead very lightly on floured board and use as required.

566   SHORT CRUST PASTRY
(For all general purposes)

200g/8oz flour · good pinch salt · 100g/4oz fat*
about 2 tablespoons cold water to mix

*There are many fats and combinations of fats which give a first class short crust pastry. Choose between: Whipped-up cooking fat – use 90g (3½ oz) only as it is very rich pure cooking fat
Margarine – for best results use a table margarine, a superfine or soft margarine
Butter or perhaps the favourite of all, 50g (2 oz) margarine and 50g (2 oz) cooking fat

Sieve flour and salt and rub in fat until mixture looks like fine breadcrumbs. Using first a knife and then the fingertips to feel the pastry, gradually add enough cold water to make the dough into a rolling consistency. Lightly flour the rolling pin and pastry board. If a great deal of flour is necessary to roll out the pastry then you have undoubtedly made it too wet. Roll pastry to required thickness and shape, lifting and turning it to keep it light. Exact cooking times for pastry are given in the recipes but as a general rule it should be baked in a hot oven 425–450°F, 220–230°C, Gas Mark 6–7.

567   RASPBERRY TURNOVERS

200g/8oz short crust pastry (Recipe No. 566)
little flour or semolina
1 medium-sized can raspberries or fresh raspberries
sugar

Make the pastry, roll out thinly and cut into large rounds and place on baking sheets. Dust pastry rounds with a little flour or semolina to prevent fruit making it soggy. Cover half the pastry with well drained canned fruit and sprinkle with sugar. Fold over the rest of the pastry and seal edges; bake in centre of a moderately hot oven, 400°F, 200°C, Gas Mark 6, for about 25 minutes. Dredge with sugar before serving.
Note: Any fruit can be used instead of raspberries. Slice apples very thinly to make sure they are cooked, or cook until thick purée before putting into pastry. Halve plums or apricots and half cook if under-ripe.

Mince pies

568   MALLOW MINCE PIES

100g/4oz short crust pastry (Recipe No. 566)
200g/8oz mincemeat · 1 tablespoon rum
1 rounded tablespoon cornflour · marshmallows

Make the short crust pastry, roll out thinly and line 14–16 deep patty tins. Put mincemeat, rum and cornflour in a saucepan. Bring to the boil and cook for 2–3 minutes, stirring all the time. Place teaspoonfuls of the mixture in each tartlet and bake near the top of a moderately hot oven, 400°F, 200°C, Gas Mark 6, for 15 minutes. Place a marshmallow on the top of each tartlet and return to the oven for a further 10 minutes.

569   CRUNCHY COCONUT PIE

225g*/8oz short crust pastry (Recipe No. 566)
2 large eggs · pinch salt · 100g/4oz sugar · 142ml/¼pint milk
25g/1oz whipped-up cooking fat · ¼ teaspoon almond essence
¼ teaspoon lemon essence · 75g/3oz desiccated coconut

*You require this amount

Make the pastry, roll out and line a large pie plate. Roll out pastry trimmings and cut out a star and leaves. Separate the eggs. Mix egg yolks, salt and sugar together. Add milk, cooking fat, almond and lemon essences. Fold in coconut and whisked egg whites. Pour into the pastry case. Decorate the top with the pastry star and leaves. Bake in the centre of a moderately hot oven, 400°F, 200°C, Gas Mark 6, for 25–30 minutes, until a knife comes out clean when inserted in the filling. Serve cold – the filling of this pie forms two layers, custard on the bottom and a coconut topping.

Crunchy coconut pie

Mallow mince pies

570   LEMON MERINGUE PIE

150g/6oz *short crust pastry (Recipe No. 566)*
4 *level tablespoons cornflour* · 284ml/½pint *water*
25g/1oz *butter or margarine* · *grated rind and juice 2 lemons*
200g/8oz *castor sugar* · 2 *eggs*
glacé cherries and blanched almonds to decorate

Make the pastry and roll out on a lightly floured board; line a deep 18-cm (7-inch) flan case and bake 'blind' (Recipe No. 560). Leave to cool. Blend the cornflour to a smooth paste with a little of the cold water. Bring the fat and rest of the water to the boil, pour over the blended cornflour, stirring well. Pour this liquid into a saucepan and cook for 3 minutes, stirring all the time. Remove from the heat and stir in the lemon rind and juice and half the sugar. Separate the yolks from the whites of the eggs. Stir the yolks into the cooled mixture and pour into the flan case. Whisk the egg whites very stiffly, add 50g (2 oz) sugar and again whisk until stiff. Fold in the remaining sugar. Pile·on top of the lemon mixture, making sure that the meringue touches the edge of the pastry all round. Place in the middle of a slow oven, 300°F, 150°F, Gas Mark 2, for 20–30 minutes until the meringue is firm and only lightly browned. If serving cold then bake pie for about 45 minutes in a cool oven to make sure meringue is really firm. Decorate the meringue with glacé cherries and blanched almonds.

Lemon meringue pie

Syrup tart

571   SYRUP TART

150g/6oz *short crust pastry (Recipe No. 566)*
4 *tablespoons golden syrup* · 50g/2oz *white breadcrumbs*
grated rind and juice 1 lemon

Make the pastry, roll out and line a large pie plate. Reserve pastry trimmings. Make decoration by slitting the pastry from the outside rim at intervals. Moisten the edge with water and fold one corner of cut pastry diagonally over and press down firmly. Continue like this round the plate. Mix the golden syrup, breadcrumbs, grated lemon rind and juice. Spread this mixture over the pastry. Roll out the pastry and cut into narrow strips and place in a criss-cross pattern on top of the filling. Bake in the centre of a hot oven, 425–450°F, 220–230°C, Gas Mark 6–7, for 20–25 minutes, lowering the heat after 15 minutes to make sure the filling does not burn.

572 BELGIAN APPLE PIE

1kg/2lb *cooking apples*
225g*/8oz *short crust or flan pastry (Recipe Nos. 566, 587)*
150g/6oz *brown or white sugar* · 2 *teaspoons cinnamon*
50–75g/2–3oz *sultanas* · *grated rind* 1 *lemon*
castor sugar to sprinkle

*You require this amount

Peel, core and slice apples. Make the pastry and roll out about ½-cm (¼-inch) thick. Damp the edge of a round shallow pie dish and grease the bottom lightly. Line the dish with half the pastry; prick the base. Mix together the sugar, cinnamon, sultanas and lemon rind and fill the dish with layers of apple sprinkled with this mixture. Damp the pastry edge and cover with remaining dough. Be careful not to stretch it. Press the two edges of pastry firmly together, trim neatly and crimp the edge all round the dish with finger and thumb. Slit the top to allow the steam to escape. Bake in centre of hot oven, 425°F, 220°C, Gas Mark 7, for 20 minutes until golden brown. Lower the heat to 350°F, 180°C, Gas Mark 4, and continue cooking for a further 15–20 minutes to cook the apple. Sprinkle with castor sugar and serve with cream or custard.

573 FRENCH APPLE FLAN

(Also illustrated in colour on the jacket)

6 *cooking apples* · 100g/4oz *sugar*
142ml/¼pint *water* · 25g/1oz *butter*
150g/6oz *short crust or rich flan pastry (Recipe Nos. 566, 576)*
4 *eating apples* · *sugar to taste*
apricot glaze (Recipe No. 578)

Peel, core and quarter cooking apples and put them in a saucepan with sugar, water and butter. Cover the saucepan tightly and cook the apples over moderate heat until they are tender. Press the apples through a fine sieve or purée them in a liquidiser; leave to cool. Line a greased flan ring with the pastry and half-fill with the apple purée. Then peel, core and slice finely the eating apples and arrange the slices over the apple purée in a spiral, starting at the centre and working out, the slices overlapping. Sprinkle fruit with sugar and bake in centre of a moderately hot oven, 400°F, 200°C, Gas Mark 6, for 20–30 minutes, until the apples are tender and the crust is golden. It may be necessary to reduce the temperature after first 15 minutes. Brush with apricot glaze and serve hot or cold with cream.
Makes 6 servings.

574 CREAM CHEESE AND APPLE FLAN

150g/6oz *short crust or flan pastry (Recipe Nos. 566, 587)*
3 *eating apples* · 200g/8oz *cream cheese* · 50g/2oz *sugar*
284ml/½pint *syrup** · *redcurrant glaze (Recipe No. 575)*
angelica leaves to decorate

*Made with 284ml (½ pint) water, 50g (2 oz) sugar and a little lemon rind to flavour

Make the pastry, roll out and line a 20-cm (8-inch) flan case. Bake 'blind' (Recipe No. 560) in a moderately hot oven, 400°F, 200°C, Gas Mark 6, until crisp and golden brown. Halve, core and peel the apples. Poach in boiling syrup until just tender. Drain well. Mix the cream cheese and sugar together. Spread evenly on the bottom of the flan case. Arrange the halved apples on top, cut side downwards. Coat carefully with the redcurrant glaze and decorate with angelica leaves. Serve cold.

French apple flan

575 REDCURRANT GLAZE

4 dessertspoons redcurrant jelly · 1 dessertspoon water
2 dessertspoons lemon juice

Put jelly, water and lemon juice into a small, thick saucepan and stir over gentle heat until dissolved. Boil briskly until slightly tacky but do not overboil or the glaze will be of a toffee consistency. Spoon the glaze very carefully over the fruit.

576 RICH FLAN PASTRY
Also known as
FLEUR PASTRY

125g/5oz butter* · 50g/2oz sugar · 200g/8oz flour
pinch salt · 1 egg yolk to bind

*Table, soft or superfine margarine can be used

Cream the fat and sugar together until light in colour. Sieve flour and salt together and add to the creamed mixture, mixing with a knife. Add egg yolk to make a firm dough. Roll out and use as required. To line a flan ring put pastry over case and press down base and sides firmly. Roll over the top with a rolling pin to neaten edge. Flute edges if liked.

577 GLAZED PEAR FLAN

150g/6oz rich flan pastry (Recipe No. 576)
2 level tablespoons cornflour · 25g/1oz sugar · 1 egg
284ml/½pint milk · vanilla essence or sherry to taste
6–8 canned or cooked pear halves
apricot glaze (Recipe No. 578)
25–50g/1–2oz toasted almonds, chopped
and a glacé cherry to decorate

Make the pastry, roll out and line a 20-cm (8-inch) pie plate. Flute edges and bake 'blind' (Recipe No. 560). Allow to cool. Mix the cornflour, sugar and a little of the milk together smoothly. Put the rest of the milk on to heat, add the mixed cornflour and cook for 3 minutes stirring constantly. Remove from the heat, add the beaten egg yolk and vanilla essence or sherry to taste. Return to the heat and cook gently for 2–3 minutes, do not allow to boil. Cool slightly, stirring once or twice, then fold in the stiffly beaten egg white. When the cornflour sauce is nearly cold spoon into the baked pastry case. Arrange the well drained pears on top. Make the glaze and spoon over the pears. Decorate with the almonds and the cherry.

578 APRICOT GLAZE

2 tablespoons apricot jam · 1 tablespoon water

Boil the jam and water together for 2 minutes; strain, cool and use as required.

Glazed pear flan

579   RASPBERRY MERINGUE PIE

125g/5oz short crust pastry (Recipe No. 566)
200g/8oz raspberries, sieved to a purée and made up to
284ml (½ pint) with water · 2 tablespoons cornflour
2–4 tablespoons sugar · 2 eggs · grated lemon rind
100g/4oz castor sugar

Make the pastry, roll out and line a pie dish. Bake 'blind' (Recipe No. 560) in hot oven, 425–450°F, 220–230°C, Gas Mark 6–7, until firm and golden brown. Cool. Gently heat the raspberry purée and water. Mix the cornflour to a thin paste with a little water, then add the raspberry mixture. Return to pan and cook till mixture thickens, stirring all the time. Remove from heat and cool slightly. Add the 2 tablespoons sugar, the egg yolks and lemon rind; reheat gently, but do not boil. Cool, then transfer to cooked pastry case. Make the meringue by whisking the egg whites until stiff, then gradually beat in half the castor sugar and fold in the rest. Pipe the meringue in a criss-cross pattern over the filling and place in a very hot oven, 475°F, 240°C, Gas Mark 9, for 2–3 minutes. Serve hot or cold.

580   HOT APPLE BASKETS

150g/6oz short crust pastry (Recipe No. 566)
½kg/1lb cooking apples · 75g/3oz sugar
3 tablespoons water · 25g/1oz table margarine
25g/1oz plain chocolate · 6–8 glacé cherries

Make the pastry, roll out and line 6–8 deep patty tins. Bake 'blind' (Recipe No. 560) for 10–15 minutes in hot oven, 425–450°F, 220–230°C, Gas Mark 6–7. Peel, core and slice apples. Cook with sugar, water and table margarine until soft. Simmer gently for 5–10 minutes longer until very thick. Keep hot. Grate chocolate coarsely and slice cherries. Remove pastry cases from oven, lift out carefully, and place on hot dish. Fill with the apple filling and decorate with grated chocolate and glacé cherries. The apple baskets may also be served cold.

581   FRUIT CUPS

Pastry recipe as hot apple baskets, above; fill with drained canned fruit cocktail or fresh fruit. Cover with redcurrant glaze (Recipe No. 575), or use same method with sieved apricot jam.

Raspberry meringue pie

Orange tart

ORANGE TART

150g/6oz *short crust pastry (Recipe No. 566)*
3 *tablespoons black treacle* · 75g/3oz *margarine*
75g/3oz *castor sugar* · *grated rind 1 orange* · *1 egg*
25g/1oz *ground almonds* · 100g/4oz *self-raising flour*
(*with plain flour use 1 level teaspoon baking powder*)
juice 1 orange · *halved almonds to decorate*

Make the pastry, roll out and line a pie plate. Spread with black treacle. Cream the fat and sugar together until light and fluffy. Beat in the grated orange rind and egg. Stir in the ground almonds. Fold in the flour alternately with the orange juice. Spread the mixture over the treacle. Bake in a hot oven, 425°F, 220°C, Gas Mark 7, for 15 minutes. Decorate the top with halved almonds; reduce the oven temperature to moderate, 350°F, 180°C, Gas Mark 4, and bake for a further 20–25 minutes. Serve hot or cold.

583 CRANBERRY AND SULTANA FLAN

150g/6oz *short crust or flan pastry (Recipe Nos. 566, 576)*
6 *tablespoons cranberry, redcurrant or apple jelly*
50g/2oz *sultanas* · 142ml/¼pint *double cream*

Make the pastry, roll out and line a flan ring. Bake 'blind' (Recipe No. 560) in a moderately hot oven, 400°F, 200°C, Gas Mark 6, for 20–25 minutes. Leave to cool. Heat the jelly and mix with the sultanas. Smooth into the flan case and allow to cool. Whip the cream until fairly stiff. Put into a piping bag, fitted with a large star tube and pipe rosettes of cream round the edge of the flan. Serve cold.

584 TANGY CHEESE BLOSSOM CREAM

flan pastry case (Recipe No. 587)
6 *tablespoons lemon juice* · 4 *tablespoons orange juice*
2 *tablespoons sugar* · 25g/1oz *butter* · 2 *egg yolks*
1 *level tablespoon powdered gelatine*
2 *tablespoons boiling water* · 200g/8oz *cottage cheese*
2 *tablespoons whipped double cream** · 2 *egg whites*
2 *extra tablespoons sugar* · *fruit to decorate*

*Or omit this and use an extra egg

Make the flan pastry case and bake for 20–25 minutes. Mix fruit juice, sugar and butter. Beat in the egg yolks and stir over low heat (double pan is best) until the mixture begins to thicken. Do not boil. Dissolve the gelatine in the boiling water and add to the fruit juice mixture. Allow to cool. Sieve the cottage cheese and mix with the cream, if used. Combine this with the fruit juice mixture, blending thoroughly. Fold in the egg whites, whisked to a stiff froth with the extra sugar. Pour into flan pastry case, chill and then decorate with fresh fruit in season or canned apricots or peach slices. Alternatively the cheese blossom cream can be served in individual glass dishes; chill, decorate with fruit and serve with shortbread biscuits.
Makes 6–8 servings.

585 STRAWBERRY CUSTARD FLAN

150g/6oz *rich flan pastry (Recipe No. 576)*
2 *level tablespoons custard powder* · 426ml/¾pint *milk*
2 *level tablespoons sugar* · *knob butter*
300g/12oz *strawberries*
redcurrant glaze (Recipe No. 575)

Make pastry, roll out and line a 20-cm (8-inch) fluted flan ring placed on a baking sheet. Bake in a moderately hot oven, 400°F, 200°C, Gas Mark 6, for 20–25 minutes. Leave to cool. Blend the custard powder with 2 tablespoons milk from the 426ml (¾ pint), bring the rest to the boil with the sugar; pour the hot milk over the blended custard powder. Return to the saucepan and bring to the boil. Stir in the butter. Cool, stirring occasionally to prevent a skin forming. Mark the pastry case into 8 portions and fill with alternate sections of cold custard and strawberries. Make the glaze, cool, then spoon over the fruit.

Cranberry and sultana flan

Strawberry custard flan

Custard pear flan

586 CUSTARD PEAR FLAN

150g/6oz *flan pastry (Recipe No. 587)* · 284ml/½pint *milk*
2 eggs · 1 tablespoon sugar · 1 medium-sized can pear halves
*little grated nutmeg · angelica leaves
and grated orange rind to decorate*

Make the pastry, roll out and line a 20-cm (8-inch) flan ring
or a fluted flan dish. Bake the pastry 'blind' (Recipe No. 560)
in a moderately hot oven, 400°F, 200°C, Gas Mark 6, for 10
minutes.
Heat the milk (do not boil); beat the eggs and sugar together
and pour over the heated milk. Pour into the pastry case.
Arrange the well drained pear halves in the custard. Sprinkle
with a little grated nutmeg and bake in a moderate oven, 325°F,
170°C, Gas Mark 3, for a further 45 minutes. When cooked
decorate the top with angelica leaves and grated orange rind.

587 FLAN PASTRY

(For sweet flans and fruit tarts)

100g/4oz *fat** · 2 dessertspoons sugar
200g/8oz *flour* · pinch salt · *egg yolk and cold water
to bind*

**Table, soft or superfine margarine or butter or whipped-up cooking fat
(vegetable shortening) is excellent for this pastry*

Cream fat and sugar together until light in colour. Sieve flour
and salt together and add to creamed fat, mixing with a knife.
Gradually add the egg yolk and enough water to make a firm
rolling consistency. Use fingertips to feel the pastry. To line
a flan ring, roll out the pastry; put pastry over flan ring and
press down base and sides firmly then roll over top with rolling
pin for a good edge. Decorate edge as wished. Bake in a moderately hot oven, 400°F, 200°C, Gas Mark 6. For cooking times,
see individual recipes.

588 PUFF PASTRY

(For vol-au-vent cases, vanilla slices, cream horns, etc.)

200g/8oz *plain flour · good pinch salt · cold water to mix
few drops lemon juice* · 175–200g/7–8oz *fat**

**Use butter, table or soft margarine or ⅔ table margarine and ⅓ whipped-
up cooking fat*

Sieve flour and salt together. Mix to rolling consistency with
cold water and lemon juice. Roll to oblong shape. Make fat
into neat block and place in centre of pastry and fold over it
first the bottom section of pastry, and then the top section, so
that fat is quite covered. Turn the dough at right angles, seal
edges and 'rib' carefully (see Recipe No. 604, flaky pastry)
and roll out. Fold dough into 'envelope', turn it, seal edges,
'rib' and fold again. Repeat five times, so making seven rollings
and seven foldings in all. It will be necessary to put pastry to
rest in cold place once or twice between rollings to prevent it
becoming sticky and soft. Always put it to rest before rolling it
for the last time, and before cooking. Bake in a very hot oven
to make it rise and keep in the fat. Bake for the first 10–15
minutes at 475–500°F, 240–250°C, Gas Mark 8–9, then lower
to Gas Mark 5 or 6 or turn electric oven right out or re-set to
400°F, 200°C to finish cooking. Well made puff pastry should
rise to 4–5 times its original thickness. When making vol-au-
vent cases it may be necessary to remove a little soft dough in
the middle and return the cases to oven to dry out.

Cream horns

591 MILLE FEUILLES

200g/8oz *puff pastry (Recipe No. 588)* · *jam*
double cream, whipped · 50–75g/2–3oz *chopped nuts*
glacé icing (Recipe No. 747)

The puff pastry can either be cut into fingers or into 2 large rounds, about 1-cm (½-inch) thick. If baking as a whole cake, put the two rounds of pastry into a very hot oven, 475°F, 240°C, Gas Mark 8, for 10 minutes, then lower to moderately hot oven and bake until pastry is firm and pale brown in colour. Allow the pastry to get quite cold, then sandwich the 2 layers together with jam and cream. Coat the outside with more cream, and cover with chopped nuts. Cover the top with icing and nuts. For individual slices cut pastry into fingers and bake for about 13 minutes. Decorate as large cake.

592 JALOUSIE

200g/8oz *flaky pastry (Recipe No. 604)* · *jam*
1 *egg white* · *castor sugar*

Make the pastry and roll out to a 20-cm (8-inch) square. Trim the edges and cut in half. Put one half on a baking sheet and spread with jam, leaving a border round the edges. Brush the edges with lightly beaten egg white. Sprinkle the second half of pastry lightly with flour. Make a series of cuts every ½-cm (¼-inch), starting 1½-cm (¾-inch) down from the top of the pastry. Lift the cut portion of pastry on to the jam covered pastry; try not to stretch this. If you lift with a broad-bladed palette knife or fish slice you will find it easier. Brush with remaining egg white and bake in a hot oven, 425°F, 220°C, Gas Mark 7, for 20 minutes. Dredge with castor sugar and cool on a wire tray.

589 CREAM HORNS

200g/8oz *flaky or puff pastry (Recipe Nos. 604, 588)*
1 *egg white* · 2 *teaspoons castor sugar* · 2 *tablespoons jam*
double cream or evaporated milk, whipped
flake bars to decorate

Make the horn cases with the pastry as described in Recipe No. 607, but brush with lightly beaten egg white and dust with a very little castor sugar before cooking. When cold put a small amount of jam at the bottom, then fill with whipped cream and decorate with halved flake bars.

Jalousie

590 ECCLES CAKES

200g/8oz *puff or flaky pastry (Recipe Nos. 588, 604)*
50g/2oz *butter or margarine* · 50g/2oz *sugar*
50g/2oz *sultanas* · 50g/2oz *currants* · 50g/2oz *candied peel*
grated rind and juice 1 *lemon* · *pinch mixed spice*
2 *tablespoons milk* · 2 *teaspoons castor sugar*

Make the pastry and roll it out thinly. Cut into large round shapes. Cream the margarine and sugar together, then work in the remaining ingredients. Put a spoonful of this mixture on 1 half of the pastry. Dampen the edges and fold over, then press together to seal. Shape with a rolling pin and your fingers until you have rounds. Make 2 or 3 splits on the top of each cake. Brush lightly with milk and castor sugar. Bake in the centre of a hot oven, 425°F, 220°C, Gas Mark 7, for about 20 minutes. After 15 minutes the heat can be reduced if the cakes are becoming too brown.

593   CREAM BUNS

choux pastry (Recipe No. 617)
142–284ml/¼–½pint double cream, whipped
25g/1oz icing sugar or chocolate
glacé icing (Recipe No. 747)

There are several ways of making the shape of cream buns. The most simple is to grease and flour individual patty tins and put in a spoonful of the mixture; or pile some of the mixture on to well greased and floured baking sheets. The correct method, however, is to pipe the mixture on to floured and greased baking sheets, allowing room to swell. If you have a deep tin which can be put over the cakes while in the oven, use this, for it helps to give a better shape to them. The tin should be light in weight and allow several inches in height, for the buns will rise considerably as they cook. It is possible to cook the buns without the tin. Put the baking sheet into the centre of a hot oven, 425°F, 220°C, Gas Mark 7, for 35 minutes (allow a good 5 minutes extra cooking time if they are covered). For the last 20 minutes reduce the heat to 375°F, 190°C, Gas Mark 5. At the end of this time the buns should be pale golden in colour, but feel very firm and crisp. Cool away from a draught. You may sometimes find that when you split the buns there is a little uncooked pastry left in the centre. This should be taken out carefully, and if you feel it necessary, the buns returned for a few minutes to a cool oven to dry.
When the buns are cold split them and fill with cream. Sprinkle with sieved icing sugar or coat with chocolate glacé icing.

594   ECLAIRS

choux pastry (Recipe No. 617)
142–284ml/¼–½pint double cream, whipped
chocolate or coffee glacé icing (Recipe No. 747)

Make the pastry and pipe the mixture into finger shapes on to well greased and floured baking sheets, or put into greased and floured finger tins. Bake without covering, in a hot oven, 425°F, 220°C, Gas Mark 7, for 25 minutes. Cool, then split, fill with cream and cover with chocolate or coffee glacé icing.

Profiteroles

595   PROFITEROLES

Make choux pastry (Recipe No. 617) and either pipe or spoon the mixture into rounds the size of hazel nuts; allow room for them to swell. Bake in a hot oven for 10 minutes only; cool, split and fill with whipped cream. Pile into pyramid shape in one dish or individual dishes and serve with hot or cold chocolate sauce (Recipe No. 597).

SOME UNUSUAL PASTRIES

Chocolate coconut ice cream pie

596   CHOCOLATE COCONUT ICE CREAM PIE

90g/3½oz plain flour · 50g/2oz castor sugar
25g/1oz drinking chocolate · 65g/2½oz desiccated coconut
100g/4oz butter · 1 large block ice cream
chocolate sauce (Recipe No. 597) · coconut to decorate

Sieve together the flour, sugar and drinking chocolate; add the coconut, then knead the butter into these ingredients. When the mixture binds together turn on to a lightly floured board, and roll out and line a 20-cm (8-inch) flan case or sandwich tin. When fitting into the tin work the dough about 1 cm (½ inch) up the sides of the tin to form a rim. Prick the bottom. Bake in a moderate oven, 350°F, 180°C, Gas Mark 4, for about 40 minutes. Allow to cool in the tin for a little while before transferring to a wire tray. Immediately before serving pile the ice cream into the flan case, pour over the hot chocolate sauce and decorate with a little coconut.
Makes 6 servings.

597 CHOCOLATE SAUCE

50g/2oz *plain chocolate* · *knob butter*
2–3 *tablespoons water*

Break the chocolate into small pieces and put with the butter and water in a small basin over hot water; stir occasionally until the chocolate has melted.

598 CHOCOLATE, CARAMEL AND WALNUT FLAN

chocolate pastry (Recipe No. 599)
3 *rounded tablespoons sugar* · 3 *tablespoons water*
4 *level tablespoons cornflour* · 426ml/¾pint *milk*
25–50g/1–2oz *walnuts, chopped*

Make the pastry, roll out on a lightly floured board and line a 20-cm (8-inch) fluted flan ring. Prick with a fork and place a round of greaseproof paper in the bottom; fill with baking beans. Bake near the top of a moderately hot oven, 400°F, 200°C, Gas Mark 6, for 10–15 minutes; remove beans and replace in the oven for a further 10–15 minutes. Remove and cool. Bring 2 tablespoons of the sugar with 1 tablespoon of the water to the boil. Allow to boil without stirring until a pale golden brown, then immediately add the remaining water and allow the caramel to dissolve. Blend the cornflour with a little of the milk, bring remaining milk to the boil, then pour over the blended mixture. Return to the pan and cook for 3 minutes, stirring all the time. Add the dissolved caramel and remaining tablespoon of sugar. Pour into the flan case. Sprinkle the top with chopped walnuts. Serve cold.

599 CHOCOLATE PASTRY

3 *tablespoons boiling water* · 90g/3½oz *whipped-up cooking fat*
50g/2oz *drinking chocolate* · 225g*/8oz *flour*
pinch salt

*This gives best result

Add the boiling water to the cooking fat and drinking chocolate in a basin. Add 1 rounded tablespoon of the flour and whisk together with a fork until smooth and creamy. Mix in the rest of the sieved flour and salt to form a firm dough. Use as directed in the individual recipes.

600 BUTTERSCOTCH PIE

crunchy cereal crust (Recipe No. 601) or use
125g/5oz *short crust pastry*
150g/6oz *brown sugar* · 2 *tablespoons cornflour*
3 *tablespoons flour* · ½ *teaspoon salt*
generous ½litre/1pint *milk* · 2 *large eggs*
40g/1½oz *butter* · 1 *teaspoon vanilla essence*
40g/1½oz *castor sugar* · *cherries and angelica to decorate*

Make the cereal crust, cook and cool. Place the brown sugar, cornflour, flour and salt in a heavy saucepan or double boiler. Blend in the milk gradually, stirring constantly. Cook slowly, stirring well, until thickened. Cover and continue to cook very slowly, stirring now and again, for a further 15 minutes. Stir a little of the hot (not boiling) liquid into the beaten egg yolks and then add this to the mixture in the saucepan. Cook for 2 minutes stirring constantly. (Do not allow to boil). Remove from heat, add butter; cool; add vanilla essence. Pour into the

pastry crust. Whisk the egg whites until stiff, fold in the castor sugar. Pipe or spread over the filling and put in a moderately hot oven, 400°F, 200°C, Gas Mark 6, for 8–10 minutes. Decorate with cherries and angelica and serve hot.

601 CRUNCHY CEREAL CRUST

100g/4oz *quick-cooking rolled oats* · 50g/2oz *sugar*
¼ *teaspoon salt* · 2 *tablespoons finely chopped nuts*
50g/2oz *butter or margarine, melted*
little cold water

Mix together the rolled oats, sugar, salt and nuts. Add melted fat. Mix well. Sprinkle with water and stir until blended. Spread over the bottom and sides of a 20-cm (8-inch) pie plate. Press down firmly with the back of a spoon. Bake in a moderate oven, 375°F, 190°C, Gas Mark 4, for 15 minutes

602 CHOCOLATE MERINGUE TARTLETS

100g/4oz *rolled oat pastry (Recipe No. 632)*
generous ½litre/1pint *chocolate blancmange*
1 *egg yolk, optional* · 2 *egg whites*
75g/3oz *castor sugar*

Make the pastry, roll out and line tartlet tins. Bake 'blind' (Recipe No. 560) in a hot oven, 425°F, 220°C, Gas Mark 7, for 10–15 minutes. Allow to cool and fill with warm chocolate blancmange, mixed with the egg yolk, if used. Whisk the egg whites until stiff and fold in the castor sugar. Pipe or pile the meringue on to the blancmange and bake in centre of a moderate oven, 350°F, 180°C, Gas Mark 4, for about 15 minutes until the meringue is set and a pale golden brown. These tartlets may be eaten hot or cold.

Butterscotch pie

Chocolate meringue tartlets

Blackberry layer pudding

603 BLACKBERRY LAYER PUDDING

Suet crust pastry
200g/8oz *self-raising flour*
(with plain flour use 2 level teaspoons baking powder)
pinch salt · 75–100g/3–4oz shredded suet · water to mix
Filling
½kg/1lb *blackberries · sugar*

Sieve the flour, baking powder, if used, and salt into a mixing bowl. Mix in the suet and enough water to make a fairly soft consistency. Roll out thinly and cut a round to fit the bottom of a small pudding basin. Grease the basin well and put the pastry in the bottom. Cover with a layer of blackberries and sprinkle with sugar. Cover with a slightly larger round of pastry and another layer of blackberries, sprinkled with sugar. Continue in this way until all the pastry is used up, ending with a layer of pastry. Sprinkle the top of the pudding with flour and cover securely with foil or greased greaseproof paper. Steam for 2½–3 hours. Turn on to a serving dish, sprinkle the top with sugar and serve. For a good result, make sure that the water is boiling rapidly when the pudding goes on, and always replenish with boiling water.

To make a richer crust (as shown in the picture) bind the suet crust with an egg and water instead of water. Coat the basin evenly with butter, sprinkle with approximately 25g (1oz) sugar, then fill and cook as above.

604 FLAKY PASTRY
(For sausage rolls, mince pies, etc.)

200g/8oz *plain flour · pinch salt · 150g/6oz fat**
water to mix

**Use any of the following : all butter, table, superfine or soft margarine,
⅓ table margarine and ⅔ whipped-up cooking fat or pure cooking fat*

Sieve flour with salt. Divide fat into 3 portions. Rub 1 portion into flour in the usual way and mix to rolling consistency with cold water. Roll out to oblong shape. Take the second portion of fat, divide it into small pieces and lay them on surface of ⅔ of dough. Leave remaining ⅓ without fat. Take its 2 corners and fold back over second ⅓ so that the dough looks like an envelope with its flap open. Fold over top end of pastry, so closing the 'envelope'. Turn pastry at right angles, seal open ends of pastry and 'rib' it. This means depressing it with the rolling pin at intervals, so giving a corrugated effect and equalising the pressure of air. This ensures that the pastry will rise evenly. Repeat the process again using the remaining fat and turning pastry in the same way. Roll out pastry once more, but should it begin to feel very soft and sticky put it into a cold place for 30 minutes to become firm before rolling out. Fold pastry as before, turn it, seal edges and rib it. Altogether the pastry should have 3 foldings and 3 rollings. It is then ready to stand in a cold place for a little while before cooking, as the contrast between the cold and the heat of the oven makes the pastry rise better.

To cook, use a very hot oven, 450–475°F, 230–240°C, Gas Mark 8–9, for the first 15 minutes, after this lower the Gas Mark to 6, or turn the electric oven off, to finish cooking for remaining time at a lower temperature.

605   RICH CHEESE PASTRY

100g/4oz plain flour · salt · cayenne pepper
pinch dry mustard · 65g/2½oz butter
50g/2oz cheese, grated · 1 egg yolk

Sieve the flour and seasoning together, rub in the butter, add the cheese and bind with the egg yolk. If necessary add a little water. Roll out and use for savoury flan or tartlet cases or to make economical cheese biscuits or straws. If cooking by itself, use a hot oven, 425°F, 220°C, Gas Mark 7.

606   CHEESE CUSTARD FLAN

100g/4oz cheese pastry (Recipe No. 605)
1 egg · generous 142ml/¼pint milk · 75g/3oz cheese, grated
salt · cayenne pepper

Make the pastry, roll out and line a fairly deep 18-cm (7-inch) flan ring. Beat the egg, milk, cheese and seasonings together. Pour carefully into the flan case. Bake in the centre of a hot oven, 450°F, 230°C, Gas Mark 7, for 10 minutes, then lower the heat to moderately hot, 375–400°F, 190–200°C, Gas Mark 5–6, for 15–20 minutes, until the filling is firm.

607   SAVOURY CREAM HORNS

200g/8oz flaky pastry (Recipe No. 604)
cheese cream (Recipe No. 608) · egg or milk to glaze
parsley and paprika to garnish

Make the pastry, roll out on a lightly floured board, and cut into long 1-cm (½-inch) strips. In order not to stretch the pastry, it is better to cut these strips on the cross. Grease metal horn tins and wind the pastry carefully round these, allowing it to overlap slightly, and at no time pulling the pastry out of shape. Put on to baking sheet, brush with a little beaten egg or milk to glaze, and cook in a hot oven, 425°F, 220°C, Gas Mark 7, for 10–15 minutes. Remove the metal horns very carefully and if necessary return the cases to the oven, lowering the heat, to dry out. When cold, fill with cheese cream and serve garnished with parsley and paprika.

608   CHEESE CREAM

15g/½oz cornflour · 284ml/½pint milk · 1 egg
75g/3oz cheese, grated · salt and pepper
1–2 tablespoons double cream, whipped

Blend the cornflour with a little cold milk. Bring the rest of the milk to the boil, pour over the cornflour and return to the pan and cook until smooth and thick, stirring well. Continue cooking for 3 minutes, then remove from the heat and allow to cool slightly, add the egg, grated cheese and seasoning. Allow to cool, stirring from time to time to keep mixture smooth and when cool add the cream.

Savoury cream horns

Cornish pasties

Crusty top lamb stew

609   CORNISH PASTIES

300–350g*/approx. 12oz short crust pastry (Recipe No. 566)
150–200g/6–8oz good quality stewing steak or rump
2 medium-sized potatoes · 1 large onion · salt and pepper
pinch dry mustard · 3 tablespoons stock
little milk or beaten egg to glaze
parsley to garnish, optional

*Depending on thickness of pastry

Make the pastry, roll out thinly and cut into rounds, about the size of a tea plate. Cut the meat into small cubes or tiny pieces; chop the potatoes and onion finely. Mix the meat, vegetables and seasonings together. Put a pile in the centre of each pastry round and moisten with a little stock. Brush the pastry edges with the water, then bring them together in the centre. Press the edges together to seal, then flute. Place on a baking sheet, brush with a little milk or beaten egg and bake in the centre of a hot oven, 425°F, 220°C, Gas Mark 7, for 25 minutes. Lower the heat to 350°F, 180°C, Gas Mark 4, and cook for a further 30–35 minutes to ensure that the meat is cooked. Serve hot or cold, garnished with parsley.

610   BEEF AND CHEESE TURNOVERS

2 tablespoons oil · 2 onions, chopped finely
½kg/1lb minced beef · 25g/1oz fresh breadcrumbs
¼ teaspoon dry mustard · ¼ teaspoon garlic · salt
¼ teaspoon basil · ¼ teaspoon paprika
1 tablespoon Worcestershire sauce · 100g/4oz Danish blue cheese
1–2 tablespoons soured cream
250–300g/approx. 10oz short crust pastry (Recipe No. 566)

Heat oil in a pan. Cook onions until light brown. Add beef, breadcrumbs and seasonings and fry gently until beef is cooked. Allow mixture to cool. Add the crumbled cheese and cream. Make pastry and divide into eight equal parts. Roll out each piece into a circle and place spoonfuls of mixture on each. Dampen the edges, then bring together in the centre. Press and flute the edges. Place on a baking sheet and bake in a hot oven, 425–450°F, 220–230°C, Gas Mark 6–7, for about 40 minutes, until crust is golden brown and filling cooked.

611   CRUSTY TOP LAMB STEW

1kg/2lb meat from shoulder or leg · 25g/1oz seasoned flour
2 onions · 25g/1oz lard or dripping · 2 sticks celery, chopped
426ml/¾pint water · 2 level tablespoons tomato purée
seasoning
Topping
200g/8oz plain flour
4 level teaspoons baking powder · ½ level teaspoon salt
50g/2oz butter or margarine · ½ teaspoon dried sage
6 tablespoons milk or 1 egg and 4 tablespoons milk

Trim the meat, cut into cubes and coat in seasoned flour. Slice the onions. Melt the fat and fry the vegetables for 3–4 minutes. Remove and fry the meat. Transfer meat and vegetables to a casserole and add water, blended with tomato purée, and the seasoning. Cover and bake in a very moderate oven, 325°F, 170°C, Gas Mark 3, for 2 hours. Sieve the flour, baking powder and salt. Rub in the fat, add the sage and mix to a soft dough with the milk or egg and milk. Turn on to a floured board and knead lightly. Roll into a round, about 1-cm (½-inch) thick. Cut into 6 equal-sized triangles. Remove casserole from the oven and arrange scone triangles on top of the meat. Brush with milk and return to a moderately hot oven, 400°F, 200°C, Gas Mark 6, for 20 minutes.
Makes 5–6 servings.

Family harvest pie

612 FAMILY HARVEST PIE

1 *bacon joint, forehock or collar*, about good ½kg/approx 1¼lb*
1 *bay leaf* · 1 *blade mace* · 3 *peppercorns* · 25g/1oz *butter*
1 *small onion, peeled and chopped* · 25g/1oz *flour*
142ml/¼pint *bacon stock* · 142ml/¼pint *milk*
2 *hard-boiled eggs, chopped* · 100g/4oz *cooked peas*
150g/6oz *cooked carrots, sliced* · *seasoning*
200g/8oz *short crust pastry (Recipe No. 566)* · *milk to glaze*

* *Smoked bacon needs soaking overnight in cold water*
If sweetcure or green bacon there is no need to soak

Put bacon joint in a pan of cold water with bay leaf, mace and peppercorns, bring to the boil and simmer gently for about 45 minutes until tender. Remove skin and excess fat from bacon; cut the bacon into large cubes – ½-cm (¼-inch) in thickness. Melt butter in a pan, fry the onion for 2–3 minutes, add flour and cook a minute without browning. Remove from heat and gradually add bacon stock and milk. Taste the bacon stock first, if it is too salty use 284ml (½ pint) milk only. Return pan to heat and bring to the boil to thicken, stirring all the time. Remove from heat and add remaining ingredients. Turn into a pie dish. Leave to cool.
Make the pastry. Roll out to a ½-cm (¼-inch) thick and cover dish. Use trimmings to decorate top of pie. Brush with a little milk. Bake in a hot oven, 425–450°F, 220–230°C, Gas Mark 6–7, then lower heat after 20 minutes to moderate and continue cooking for a further 25 minutes.
Makes 4–6 servings.

613 TUNA PIE

1 *small onion, chopped* · 50g/2oz *chopped green pepper*
40g/1½oz *flour* · 284ml/½pint *milk*
250g/10oz *can condensed mushroom soup* · *salt*
1 *small can tuna fish, flaked*
savoury onion pastry (Recipe No. 614)

Cook the onion and pepper in boiling salted water until tender then drain. Meanwhile, blend the flour with some of the milk – add the soup and finally the salt and the rest of the milk. Heat until it has thickened. Add the vegetables and fish and pour into a greased ovenproof dish.

614 SAVOURY ONION PASTRY

100g/4oz *plain flour* · *pinch salt* · 40g/1½oz *margarine*
50g/2oz *cheese, grated*
2 *tablespoons finely chopped or grated onion*

Sieve the flour and salt into a mixing bowl. Rub in the margarine, add half the cheese and mix to a dough with water. Roll out into an oblong, trim the edges and sprinkle on the remainder of the cheese and onion. Roll up like a Swiss roll and cut into thin slices. Place these on top of the fish and bake in centre of a hot oven, 425–450°F, 220–230°C, Gas Mark 6–7, for 20–25 minutes until the pastry is firm and golden brown.

615 PRAWN AND EGG VOL-AU-VENT

200g/8oz *puff pastry (Recipe No. 588)* · 1 *egg, beaten*
1 *small can evaporated milk* · 25g/1oz *butter* · 25g/1oz *flour*
dash Worcestershire sauce · *seasoning*
2 *hard-boiled eggs, chopped*
100g/4oz *peeled prawns* · *watercress to garnish*

Make the pastry and roll out, thinly, to a square. Cut out a circle, using a dinner plate as a guide. Place pastry on a damp baking sheet and with a knife carefully mark an inner circle 3½ cm (1½ inches) in from the edge. Take care not to cut right through the pastry. Brush with beaten egg to glaze and bake in hot oven, 450°F, 230°C, Gas Mark 8, for 12–15 minutes. Carefully lift off lid and remove any uncooked pastry from centre. Return case to oven for 4–5 minutes to dry out. Make the evaporated milk up to 284ml (½ pint) with water. Melt the butter in a saucepan. Add the flour and cook for 1–2 minutes. Gradually add the evaporated milk and stirring, bring to the boil and cook for 3–4 minutes. Add Worcestershire sauce and seasoning; fold in eggs and prawns and pile into pastry case. Top with pastry lid. Garnish with watercress and serve either hot or cold.
More vol-au-vent recipes can be found under Recipe Nos. 624–626.

Prawn and egg vol-au-vent

Mushroom and cheese quiche

616 MUSHROOM AND CHEESE QUICHE

100g/4oz *cheese pastry (Recipe No. 605)*
1 *small onion, chopped* · 100g/4oz *mushrooms, sliced*
50g/2oz *butter* · *generous 12 tablespoons milk*
2 *eggs, beaten* · 75g/3oz *cheese, grated* · *salt and pepper*

Make the pastry, roll out and line a deep flan ring or dish. Fry the onion and mushrooms in the butter. Drain and place in the pastry case. Pour the milk over the beaten eggs, add most of the cheese and the seasoning; pour carefully into the flan case. Sprinkle the remaining grated cheese over the top. Bake in the centre of a moderate oven, 350°F, 180°C, Gas Mark 4, for about 40 minutes, until firm. Serve hot or cold.
For a deeper Quiche (the name given to flans filled with a savoury custard) use double the amounts of pastry and filling. Line a 23-cm (9-inch) really deep flan with the pastry, bake 'blind' (Recipe No. 560) for approximately 20–25 minutes in the centre of a hot oven. Fill with the custard mixture and bake for 1 hour in a very moderate oven, 325°F, 170°C, Gas Mark 3.

617 CHOUX PASTRY

142ml/¼pint *water* · 25g/1oz *margarine or butter*
pinch sugar · 75g/3oz *flour*
2 *whole eggs and 1 egg yolk or 3 small eggs*

Put the water, margarine or butter and sugar into a saucepan. Heat gently until the fat has melted. Remove from the heat and stir in the flour. Return the pan to a low heat and cook very gently but thoroughly, stirring all the time, until the mixture is dry enough to form a ball and leave the pan clean. Once again remove the pan from the heat and gradually add the well beaten eggs. Do this slowly to produce a perfectly smooth mixture. Allow to cool, then use for cream buns and éclairs.

618 HOT WATER CRUST PASTRY

(For raised pies)

375g/12oz *flour*, preferably plain* · *pinch salt*
100g/4oz *fat*** · 142ml/¼pint *warm water*

*Gives better result
**Whipped-up cooking fat is excellent for this pastry. Clarified dripping or lard or pure cooking fat can also be used

Sieve flour and salt together. Melt fat in warm water and add to flour. Mix with knife and knead gently with fingers. Unlike other pastry this should be moulded when warm. Bake in moderately hot oven, 375°F, 190°C, Gas Mark 5.

619 AMERICAN BAKING POWDER PASTRY OR AMERICAN BISCUIT CRUST

200g/8oz *flour*
4 *level teaspoons baking powder (or 2 level teaspoons with self-raising flour)* · *good pinch salt*
25–50g/1–2oz *fat, preferably vegetable shortening*
1 *dessertspoon sugar (if using pastry for a sweet dish)*
·*water or milk to mix*

This recipe is very economical in its use of fat. If it is eaten the day it is cooked and preferably hot, it is very good. Sieve flour, baking powder and salt together. Rub in fat. Add sugar, if used and mix to rolling consistency with cold water or milk. Roll out rather thinly as this pastry will rise a great deal. *Never keep this pastry standing before it is cooked.* Bake in a hot to very hot oven, 450–475°F, 230–240°C, Gas Mark 7–8.

620   POTATO PASTRY

seasoning · 100g/4oz flour · 75g/3oz cooking fat
100g/4oz mashed potatoes · very little water

Add seasoning to flour. Rub in cooking fat, then add the potatoes. Knead firmly and add the water to give firm dough. This
is an excellent pastry for hot savoury dishes; use and bake as
short crust pastry.

621   CHEESE ECLAIRS

choux pastry (Recipe No. 617) · 100g/4oz cream cheese
little double cream, whipped · salt · cayenne pepper
yeast extract

Make éclairs in the usual way (Recipe No. 594) with the choux
pastry and when cold fill with cream cheese, blended with a
little cream and seasoning. Brush the tops of the savoury
éclairs with softened yeast extract. If liked the éclairs can be
filled with cheese cream (Recipe No. 608).

622   BACON AND APPLE TRIANGLES

200g/8oz short crust pastry (Recipe No. 566)
50g/2oz cooking fat · 100g/4oz bacon, chopped
2 tomatoes, quartered · 1 onion, peeled and sliced
1 eating apple, peeled and sliced · seasoning · little beaten egg
to glaze · endive to garnish

Make the pastry, roll out thinly and cut into 4 circles, using a
tea plate as a guide. Place the pastry circles on a baking sheet.
Melt the fat in a frying pan and fry the chopped bacon for 2–3
minutes. Add the tomatoes, onion, eating apple and seasoning.
Cook for 2–3 minutes. Allow the filling to cool and place
tablespoonfuls in the centre of each pastry circle. Brush the
edges with water and bring together as shown in the picture.
Press the edges to seal. Brush with beaten egg to give a glaze
and bake in a moderately hot oven, 400°F, 200°C, Gas Mark
6, for 30–35 minutes. Serve hot or cold garnished with endive.

Bacon and apple triangles

Veal and ham pie

624 VOL-AU-VENT CASES

Method 1

Roll out puff pastry (Recipe No. 588) until just under 1-cm (½-inch) thick. Cut into rounds. From half the rounds make a circle by cutting out centre. Place circle on top of complete round. Seal edges and put on to damp baking sheets. Glaze with beaten egg.

Method 2

Roll out puff pastry until about 2½-cm (1-inch) thick. Cut into rounds or required shape. Put on to damp baking sheets. With a smaller cutter press halfway through pastry. Glaze with beaten egg.

Cook in a very hot oven, 475°F, 240°C, Gas Mark 9, until well risen and brown, then reduce heat slightly to make sure pastry is cooked.

With Method 2, lift out the centre portion – this is quite easy to do with the point of a sharp knife, and return to oven for a short time to dry out.

625 FILLINGS FOR VOL-AU-VENT CASES

Minced or chopped cooked chicken in a creamy white sauce
Cooked mushrooms in a thick sauce
Shellfish in a creamy white sauce, mayonnaise or mixed with lightly scrambled eggs
Thick cheese sauce
Cream cheese and chopped cucumber
Thick meat or vegetable creamy mixture
Steak and kidney

If serving cold allow pastry to cool before adding filling. If serving hot put hot filling into hot pastry at the last minute.

623 VEAL AND HAM PIE

340g*/12oz *hot water crust pastry (Recipe No. 618)*
½kg/1lb *fillet veal* · 150g/6oz *ham* · *seasoning*
½ *level teaspoon grated lemon rind* · 2 *hard-boiled eggs*
7 *tablespoons water or stock* · *beaten egg to glaze*
1 *level teaspoon gelatine* · ½ *level teaspoon meat extract*

*Gives best result

Make pastry and keep warm in basin until ready to use. Remove pastry from basin and with two-thirds of the dough line a loaf tin, moulding the pastry to fit. Wash and dry the meats, removing any skin, and cut into cubes. Roll the meats together in seasoning and lemon rind. Place half the meat in the bottom of the pastry-lined tin, cut the eggs into halves, place on top of the meat, cover with remaining meat. Pour into the pie 3 tablespoons of the water or stock. Turn the top edge of pastry in over the meat, damp it all round, roll out remaining third of pastry to make a lid. Press down well all round the edge and flute the edge. Make a hole in the centre, brush over with beaten egg, decorate with pastry 'leaves' and again brush with beaten egg. Bake in centre of a moderate oven, 350°F, 180°C, Gas Mark 4, for 2–2½ hours. Leave to cool. Melt the gelatine in remaining *very hot* water or stock and stir in the meat extract. When the pie is cool and the gelatine mixture just setting, pour into the pie through the hole in the centre and leave to set before serving.

626 HERRING ROE VOL-AU-VENT

200g/8oz *puff pastry* (Recipe No. 588)* · 25g/1oz *butter*
100g/4oz *button mushrooms, chopped* · *juice 1 lemon*
200g/8oz *canned or fresh soft herring roes* · *seasoning*
parsley to garnish

*Or use ½kg (1lb) frozen puff pastry

Make the pastry; roll out and cut out vol-au-vent cases (Recipe No. 624). Cook in a very hot oven, 475°F, 240°C, Gas Mark 8 or 9, for about 10 minutes. Heat the butter in a saucepan, add the mushrooms and lemon juice, cover with a lid and cook for 2 minutes shaking the pan occasionally. Add the herring roes and cook canned roes for a further 2–3 minutes; fresh roes for 6–8 minutes, stirring well. Add the seasoning. If serving hot, spoon the filling into the hot vol-au-vent cases. If serving cold, allow to cool, then spoon into cooled pastry cases. Garnish with parsley.

Herring roe vol-au-vent

Sausage roly-poly

Steak and kidney pudding

627   **SAUSAGE ROLY-POLY**

225–250g/8–9oz *suet crust pastry (Recipe No. 603)*
½kg/1lb *sausage meat* · ½ *teaspoon mixed herbs* · 1 *egg*
small knob fat · 2 *tablespoons milk*
3 *tablespoons soft breadcrumbs*

Make the suet crust as Recipe No. 603. Roll out on a floured board to an oblong shape. Mix the sausage meat, herbs and egg together and spread over the suet crust pastry. Roll up like a Swiss roll. Put on to a baking sheet or tin which should be greased lightly with the melted fat. Brush with the milk then press the crumbs firmly over the roll. Bake in the centre of a hot oven, 425°F, 220°C, Gas Mark 6–7, for 20–25 minutes then lower the heat to very moderate, 325°F, 170°C, Gas Mark 3, for a further 40–45 minutes. If the roll appears to brown too quickly cover with greaseproof paper. Serve with brown sauce, Recipe No. 685.

628   **LIVER AND ONION RING**

200g/8oz *liver* · 1 *level teaspoon salt*
¾ *level teaspoon celery salt*
½ *level teaspoon marjoram* · *good pinch pepper*
3 *tablespoons tomato ketchup* · ½ *teaspoon Worcestershire sauce*
1 *medium-sized onion*
200g/8oz *American biscuit crust pastry (Recipe No. 619)*
egg or milk to glaze
426ml/¾pint *tomato soup or tomato sauce (Recipe No. 656)*

Place the liver in a small saucepan and just cover with water. Season and simmer for approximately 15 minutes. Drain. Mince or chop finely, adding salt, celery salt, marjoram, pepper, tomato ketchup and Worcestershire sauce. Chop the onion finely and boil for a few minutes in salted water. Strain and add to the other ingredients. Make the pastry. Roll out to a rectangle, 23-cm by 28½-cm (9 by 11-inches), and spread with the liver mixture. Roll up, starting from the longer side. Seal the edge. Place on a greased baking sheet and shape into a ring. Join the ends together. Take a pair of scissors and cut through the pastry at 5-cm (2-inch) intervals to within 2½ cm (1 inch) of the ring centre. Brush with egg or milk. Bake in centre of a hot oven, 425°F, 220°C, Gas Mark 7, for 20–30 minutes. Serve hot with tomato soup or sauce.

629   **HAM HORSESHOES**

200g/8oz *flaky pastry (Recipe No. 604)*
200g/8oz *sliced cooked ham* · *egg or milk to glaze*

Make pastry and leave covered for 30 minutes in a cool place. Roll out to an oblong 39-cm (15-inches) by 26-cm (10-inches) with the edges trimmed. Divide into 6 equal-sized squares. Cut across each square to form triangles. Place a piece of ham on each triangle, and rolling from the longest edge towards a point, roll up the pastry with the ham inside. Damp the corner and secure. Shape gently into horseshoe shapes, place on a baking sheet. Brush with beaten egg or milk and cook in a very hot oven, 475°F, 240°C, Gas Mark 8, for 15–20 minutes.

630   **STEAK AND KIDNEY PUDDING**

200g/8oz *suet crust pastry (Recipe No. 603)*
½kg/1lb *stewing steak* · 100g/4oz *ox kidney*
2 *tablespoons seasoned flour* · 2 *tablespoons stock or water*

Turn suet crust pastry on to a lightly floured board. Roll out two-thirds and with it line a well greased ¾litre (1½ pint) size pudding basin. Put in the steak and kidney – cut into small pieces and rolled in the seasoned flour – and add the cold stock or water. Roll out the remaining pastry to form a topping, cover the pudding and seal the edges with cold water. Cover with greaseproof paper or foil. Steam for 3–3½ hours.

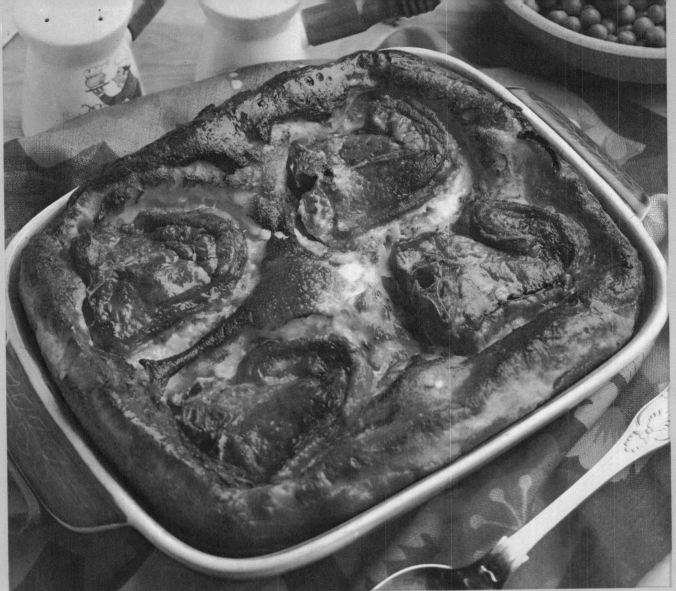

Chops in batter

631 CHEESE AND ONION QUICHE OR FLAN

rolled oat pastry (Recipe No. 632) · 1 large onion
50g/2oz butter · 1 tomato, sliced · 75g/3oz cheese, grated
2 eggs · 284ml/½pint milk · seasoning

Make the pastry, roll out and line an 18 or 20-cm (7 or 8-inch) flan ring. Slice the onion thinly and fry in the hot butter. Add the tomato and fry for 2–3 minutes. Lift out a little onion and the tomatoes and reserve for garnish. Mix the rest of the onions with the grated cheese, beaten eggs, milk and seasoning. Pour into pastry case and bake in centre of moderately hot oven, 375–400°F, 190°C, Gas Mark 5, for about 35 minutes until filling is firm and set and pastry crisp. Garnish with the reserved onion and tomatoes.

632 ROLLED OAT PASTRY

100g/4oz plain flour · pinch salt
25g/1oz quick-cooking rolled oats · 25g/1oz margarine
25g/1oz lard or cooking fat · 1 egg yolk · cold water

Sieve the flour and salt. Add the oats and rub in the margarine and lard or cooking fat. Mix to a firm dough with the egg yolk and a little cold water. Roll out on a floured board to about ½-cm (¼-inch) thick. Bake as for short crust pastry (Recipe No. 566).

633 CHOPS IN BATTER

4 loin chops · 25g/1oz butter or fat
284ml/½pint pancake batter (Recipe No. 636)

Trim the chops into a neat shape. Melt the butter or fat in an ovenproof dish or a Yorkshire pudding tin until hot. Put in chops and cook in a moderately hot oven, 400°F, 200°C, Gas Mark 6, for about 15 minutes. Pour in the batter and return to a hot to very hot oven, 450–475°F, 230–240°C, Gas Mark 7–8, for about 30 minutes. If using very hot oven, lower heat slightly after 10–15 minutes so the batter does not get too brown before being cooked.

OTHER PASTRY RECIPES

Many more pastry recipes, both sweet and savoury, will be found in other parts of this book. They are all listed in the index.

634 PILCHARD AND MUSHROOM FLAN

150g/6oz *short crust pastry (Recipe No. 566)*
40g/1½oz *butter* · 1 *medium-sized onion, sliced*
150g/6oz *button mushrooms*
1 *heaped tablespoon flour* · *seasoning* · 284ml/½pint *milk*
200g/8oz *can pilchards* · 2 *tablespoons milk* · 1 *egg yolk*
beaten egg to glaze · *tomato wedges and parsley to garnish*

Make the pastry, roll out and line a deep flan ring. Heat the butter and fry the onion and mushrooms for 3–4 minutes. Stir in the flour and seasoning and cook without browning, for a further 2–3 minutes. Gradually add the milk; stirring, bring to the boil and cook for 2–3 minutes. Remove from the heat and stir in the flaked pilchards, 2 tablespoons milk and egg yolk. Cool slightly, then spoon into the flan case. From the pastry trimmings, cut strips and make a lattice work over the top. Brush with beaten egg and bake in a moderately hot oven, 400°F, 200°C, Gas Mark 6, for 20–30 minutes. Garnish with tomato wedges and parsley and serve.

Flaked corned beef or finely chopped cooked ham or ham and chicken may be used in place of pilchards.

635   STEAK AND KIDNEY PIE
(Illustrated in colour on the jacket)

½kg/1lb *stewing steak* · 100g/4oz *kidney* · *seasoned flour*
water or stock · about 200g/8oz *pastry**
milk or beaten egg to glaze

*This can be puff as in picture, flaky or short crust

Cut the steak and kidney into cubes and toss in seasoned flour. Put a pie funnel or egg cup (not plastic) in the centre of a pie dish and put in the meat. Pour in sufficient water or stock to come halfway up the meat. Make the pastry, roll out and cover the pie. From the pastry trimmings make leaves and place in the centre of the pie. Brush all over with milk or beaten egg and bake in the centre of a hot to very hot oven (depending on type of pastry) until this is well risen and golden (approx. 25–35 minutes). Reduce the heat to very moderate, cover the pastry with a piece of greaseproof paper, and cook for a further 1½–2 hours.

Alternatively, simmer the prepared steak and kidney in water or stock until nearly tender. Thicken the gravy and transfer to a pie dish. Allow the meat to cool so there is no steam to spoil the pastry. Cover with pastry as method above. Bake in the centre of a hot to very hot oven, depending upon type of pastry, for 45–60 minutes lowering the heat as necessary.

Pilchard and mushroom flan

SWEET PANCAKES

Raspberry pancakes

636 PANCAKE OR YORKSHIRE PUDDING BATTER

110g*/4oz *flour, preferably plain* · *pinch salt* · 1 *egg***
284ml/½pint *milk or milk and water****

**Gives best result*
***For a richer mixture use 2 eggs*
****For a light batter use ⅓ water (iced water is excellent) and ⅔ milk or use instant milk – 3 tablespoons to 284ml (½ pint) water. A little melted butter or olive oil can be added to the pancake batter. It gives a good flavour and prevents sticking*

Sieve flour and salt together into a basin. Drop in egg and beat mixture well. Gradually beat in just enough liquid to make stiff, smooth batter. Be sure there are no lumps. Allow to stand for a few minutes, then gradually whisk or beat in the rest of the liquid. This mixture can be allowed to stand some time before cooking. If possible put into a refrigerator or really cool place. Give final beat or whisk before using.

637 FRENCH PANCAKES

110g*/4oz *butter or margarine* · 110g*/4oz *castor sugar*
2 *eggs* · 110g*/4oz *plain flour, sieved* · 284ml/½pint *milk*
apricot jam, heated · *lemon juice*

**Gives best result*

Cream together butter or margarine and sugar till light and fluffy, beat in the egg yolks, then stir in the flour. Add the milk gradually to form a thick batter, and beat till smooth. Leave to stand for 30 minutes in a cool place, then quickly and lightly fold in the stiffly beaten egg whites. Cover 8 *strong* greased saucers with the mixture and cook in moderately hot oven, 400°F, 200°C, Gas Mark 6, for 15 minutes. Remove from oven, turn out on to greaseproof paper dredged with castor sugar, spread each with heated apricot jam and fold over. Transfer to a warm serving dish and sprinkle with lemon juice. Serve at once.

638 RASPBERRY PANCAKES

284ml/½pint *pancake batter (Recipe No. 636)*
fat or oil for frying
300g/12oz *can raspberries or equivalent in fresh or frozen fruit*
sugar to taste · *about* 142ml/¼pint *water*
1 *level tablespoon cornflour*

Make the batter and cook the pancakes as Recipe No. 644. Put each pancake on to a square of greaseproof paper on a heat resisting plate and keep hot in the oven or over a pan of boiling water. Drain the canned or frozen raspberries, measure the liquid and make up to 284ml (½ pint) with water, add sugar to taste. (If using fresh raspberries poach for 5 minutes in 284ml (½ pint) water and 75g (3 oz) sugar). Blend the cornflour with a little of the cold raspberry liquid; bring the rest of the liquid to the boil, pour over the cornflour mixture. Return to the pan and boil, stirring until thickened. Cool slightly then add raspberries. Fill each hot pancake with a portion of raspberries and sauce and fold over. Keep hot on an uncovered dish in the oven until ready to serve.

SAVOURY PANCAKES

639 SURPRISE PANCAKES

284ml/½pint *pancake batter (Recipe No. 636)*
fat for frying · generous 30g/1¼oz *butter or margarine*
generous 30g/1¼oz *flour* · 284ml/½pint *milk*
50g/2oz *cheese, grated* ·
100g/4oz *ham, chopped* · *seasoning to taste*

Heat a small quantity of fat or oil in a frying pan, pour in a
little of the batter. Fry quickly on both sides then turn out
on to greaseproof paper. Use up all the batter in this way,
making 12 pancakes in all. Keep warm. Make a white sauce
with the butter or margarine, flour and milk. When thick,
add the cheese, ham and seasoning to taste. Reheat gently
and spread a dessertspoonful in the centre of each pancake,
fold over like an envelope, then put on to a warm dish. Serve
with sprouts and carrots.

640 SHRIMP AND ASPARAGUS PANCAKES

100g/4oz *shelled shrimps** · 1–2 tablespoons cream*
284ml/½pint *white sauce (Recipe No. 663)*
250g/10oz *can asparagus tips***
284ml/½pint *pancake batter (Recipe No. 636)*
fat or oil for frying · 50g/2oz *mushrooms*

*Fresh or frozen prawns could be used instead
**Or use freshly cooked asparagus tips

Stir shrimps and cream into hot sauce and keep warm. Heat
asparagus tips. Make pancakes (Recipe No. 644) and spread
with shrimp mixture and asparagus tips. Roll up and keep hot
on a dish over a pan of boiling water. Meanwhile fry mushrooms in the heated fat or oil, drain and serve with pancakes.

641 SAVOURY PANCAKE LAYER

165g*/6oz *flour* · ¼ teaspoon *salt*
1 *whole egg and 1 egg yolk or 2 small eggs*
426ml/¾pint *milk* · 25g/1oz *dripping* · ¾kg/1½lb *minced beef*
1 *onion, chopped* · 2 *carrots, grated*
426ml/¾pint *stock made from a cube*
1 teaspoon *tomato purée* · *seasoning* · 50g/2oz *flour*
fat or oil for frying

*Gives best result

The picture shows a newer and easier way to serve filled pancakes. Instead of rolling each pancake round a filling you
sandwich the pancakes together with the sweet or savoury
mixture – in this case an interesting minced beef mixture.
Make the pancake batter as Recipe No. 636 and let this stand
while preparing the meat mixture. Heat the dripping and fry
minced beef and onion for 10 minutes. Add the grated carrots,
stock, tomato purée and seasoning. Simmer for 30 minutes.
Skim off surplus fat. Mix flour with a little cold water until
smooth. Blend some of mince liquid with the flour mixture,
return to the pan, bring to the boil and allow to thicken. Keep
hot while making the pancakes. Heat a small quantity of oil
or fat in a frying pan, pour in a little of the batter. Fry quickly
on either side until cooked then put on to a warmed serving
dish. Cover with some of the filling. Cook the next pancake
and continue in this way until the batter and filling are used,
ending with a pancake. Serve quickly after making.
Makes 6–7 servings.

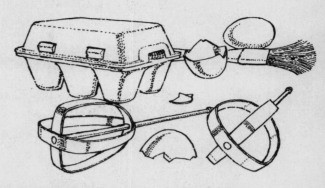

Savoury pancake layer

642   **CAPRICE PANCAKES WITH
RUM SAUCE**

(Illustrated in colour on opposite page)

284ml/½pint *pancake batter (Recipe No. 636)*
284ml/½pint *rum sauce (Recipe No. 643)*
3 pears, peeled, cored and sliced
200g/8oz *canned pineapple or diced fresh pineapple*

Make the pancakes (Recipe No. 644). Place on a plate, with
greaseproof paper between each pancake, and keep warm over
a saucepan of hot water. Make the rum sauce and keep hot.
Keep a few pear slices and pineapple pieces aside for decoration; mix the remainder together. Place some fruit mixture in
each pancake and roll up. Arrange on a serving dish, spoon over
a little of the sauce and decorate with the reserved fruit. Serve
the remaining sauce separately.

643   **RUM SAUCE**

1 tablespoon *cornflour* · 284ml/½pint *milk* · 50g/2oz *sugar*
2 tablespoons *rum*

Blend the cornflour with 3 tablespoons of the cold milk. Bring
the rest of the milk to the boil; pour this over the cornflour,
stirring well. Return to the pan, add the sugar and cook until
thickened, stirring well. Add the rum and heat for 1–2
minutes.

644   **TO MAKE PANCAKES**

Put a little oil, cooking fat or butter into a frying pan. Heat
until a faint blue haze is seen. Meanwhile transfer the pancake
batter to a jug for easy pouring. Pour enough of the batter
into hot pan to give a paper-thin layer. Cook quickly on one
side until golden brown – if you lift edge with a palette knife
you can soon see if it is ready. Toss or turn and cook on the
second side.
For filled pancakes put hot filling on to pancake. Roll away
from handle. Put on to hot dish and keep hot in a low oven or
stand dish over pan of boiling water.
For sweet pancakes lift or tip pancake on to sugared paper.
Roll and transfer to hot dish.

645   **YOUR PAN FOR PANCAKES**

Look after the pan in which you cook pancakes just as you do
your omelette pan. The same pan can be used for both
omelettes and pancakes if liked.
See Recipe No. 375 for directions on looking after an omelette
pan.

646   **BACON AND MUSHROOM
PANCAKES**

284ml/½pint *pancake batter (Recipe No. 636)*
4 rashers streaky bacon
100g/4oz *canned sweetcorn or cooked fresh or frozen corn*
seasoning · 50g/2oz *butter* · 100–150g/4–6oz *mushrooms, sliced*
3 tablespoons double cream · 4 eggs

Make the batter and leave to stand. Chop the bacon rashers
and fry until crisp. Mix in the sweetcorn and heat for a few
minutes. Season to taste. Transfer to a dish and keep warm.
Heat the butter and fry the sliced mushrooms. Remove from
the heat and stir in the cream. Transfer to a dish and keep
warm. Either make the pancakes (Recipe No. 644), in a small
frying pan or grease large pastry cutters, heat in a large pan;
pour the batter into the cutters. Spread hot bacon filling over
four pancakes, cover each with another pancake. Make
another layer with mushroom filling and cover with remaining
pancakes. Top each with a fried egg. Serve at once.

Caprice pancakes with rum sauce

647   **FRITTER BATTER**

100g/4oz *plain flour* · pinch salt · 1 egg *
142ml/¼pint *milk or milk and water***

*For a richer mixture use 2 eggs
**For a light batter use ⅓ water (iced water is excellent) and ⅔ milk

Sieve flour and salt together in a basin. Drop in egg and beat
mixture well. Gradually beat in just enough liquid to make
stiff, smooth batter. Be sure that there are no lumps. Allow to
stand for a few minutes then gradually whisk or beat in the
rest of the liquid. This mixture can be allowed to stand for
some time before cooking. If possible put into a refrigerator
or really cool place. Give final beat or whisk before using.
For a very light fritter put yolk only into the batter and fold in
stiffly beaten egg white just before coating the fruit or other
filling.
The fritter batter will make an excellent thick pancake. Drop
in spoonfuls into a little hot fat and cook steadily until brown
on the under side – turn and brown on the second side. Serve
with maple or glucose syrup. This same mixture cooked on
a flat hotplate or girdle makes a good SCOTCH PANCAKE
for tea.

648   **FRUIT-FILLED PANCAKES**

284ml/½pint *pancake batter (Recipe No. 636)*
3 tablespoons raspberry jam
3 tablespoons juice, from canned pineapple
2 teaspoons *cornflour* · squeeze lemon juice
1 teaspoon *Kirsh, optional* · 1 small can pineapple pieces

Make the pancake batter. Boil jam and pineapple juice
together for 5 minutes, stirring from time to time. Strain and
return to the pan. Mix the cornflour smoothly with 1 tablespoon pineapple juice and add to the syrup. Stir until boiling
and boil for 3 minutes. Add lemon juice and Kirsch, if used.
Stir in the pineapple pieces and reheat. Make small pancakes,
spread with the fruit filling and roll up.

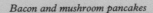

Bacon and mushroom pancakes

Toad-in-the-hole

649   TOAD-IN-THE-HOLE

284ml/½pint *pancake batter (Recipe No. 636)*
4 *large pork sausages* · 4 *rashers streaky bacon*
little made mustard · 50g/2oz *lard* · *parsley to garnish*

Make the batter and leave to stand. Wrap each sausage in a
bacon rasher. Spread with a little mustard. Heat the lard in
a roasting tin or ovenproof dish. Add the sausages and cook
in a hot oven, 450°F, 230°C, Gas Mark 7, for 10 minutes.
Remove from the oven, turn the sausages over and pour in the
batter. Return to a hot to a very hot oven, 450–475°F, 230–
240°C, Gas Mark 7–8, for approximately 30 minutes. Serve
garnished with parsley.
The traditional Toad-in-the-Hole is made with all sausages.
Use 6–8 large sausages and cook as above.

650   TIERED PANCAKES WITH CHEESE AND TOMATOES

284ml/½pint *pancake batter (Recipe No. 636)*
200g/8oz *Cheddar cheese, grated* · 4 *tomatoes, thinly sliced*
salt and pepper

Make the batter and leave to stand for at least 1 hour in a cool
place. Cook thin pancakes (Recipe No. 644) and pile as made
on a warm dish. Sprinkle grated cheese and arrange the tomato
slices between each layer. Season each layer and keep hot in
a moderate oven; build up layer by layer until all the batter is
used. Top the last pancake with grated cheese and serve hot,
cutting into wedges like a cake.

651 CHEESE AIGRETTES

25g/1oz butter · 4 tablespoons water · 50g/2oz plain flour
2 eggs · 75g/3oz Cheddar cheese, grated
1 level teaspoon finely chopped onion · salt and cayenne pepper
fat or oil for deep frying · little grated cheese to garnish

These are a type of fritter made with a mixture similar to choux pastry.
Bring butter and water to boiling point, and remove from heat. Add flour all at once. Beat mixture well for several minutes until smooth, when it will form a ball in the pan. Cool slightly, then beat in eggs gradually. Add cheese, onion and seasonings. Mix well. Drop small teaspoonfuls of mixture into deep fat or oil, heated to 350°F, 180°C, and fry until golden brown, about 7–10 minutes each. Drain on absorbent paper and serve sprinkled with a little grated cheese.

652 NUTTY CHEESE AIGRETTES

Follow the recipe for cheese aigrettes, above, but mix in 15g (½ oz) salted chopped almonds with the grated cheese.

653 FRITTERS

For sweet fritters use fresh or canned pineapple rings, apples (peeled, cored and sliced) or bananas.
For savoury fritters use slices of corned beef, canned meat, cheese, etc. coated with seasoned flour, then the batter or, if preferred flaked into the batter.

To cook fritters

Coat the prepared food in flour, then dip in fritter batter (Recipe No. 647). Use cooking fat, and it can be deep or shallow fat. Heat until very faint blue haze is seen. *Do not fry too quickly,* particularly with raw fruit as it is essential to cook the fruit through to the middle. Drain on absorbent paper and serve at once; sprinkle with sugar for sweet fritters and a little pepper and salt for savoury fritters.

To turn a pancake

Cheese aigrettes

Tuna fritters

654 TUNA FRITTERS

142ml/¼pint fritter batter (Recipe No. 647)
175g/7oz can tuna fish · seasoning · deep fat for frying
tomato sauce (Recipe No. 656)

Make fritter batter and add the flaked tuna fish. If wished make fritter batter with the egg yolk and fold in the stiffly beaten egg white after adding fish. Drop tablespoonfuls of the mixture into deep fat which is lightly smoking and fry until golden brown. Drain thoroughly on absorbent paper and transfer to a serving dish. Serve with tomato sauce.

655 PANCAKE HINTS

To toss a pancake

When the pancake is cooked on the underside it can be tossed. However, remember that the really delicate, very thin pancakes are better turned. Hold the pan loosely in your hand, keeping your wrist very flexible. Flick sharply upwards. With practice it will twist in the air and come down in the pan with the cooked side uppermost.

To turn a pancake

When cooked on the underside put a small fish slice or palette knife under the pancake. Get the knife right to the centre of pan. Lift carefully and then flick over to turn. Illustrated is an ideal 'flipper-lifter' for pancakes. It can also be used for fish, eggs, etc.; as it is perforated it allows any fat to drain back into the pan.

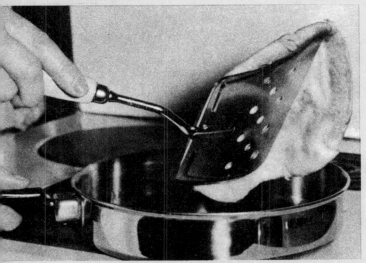

SAUCES

In this chapter you will find the classic sauces which can be served with a variety of dishes. A good sauce is NOT difficult to make. It does however take both time and care and careful measuring of ingredients. Always taste sauces during cooking to adjust seasonings.

656   TOMATO SAUCE

25g/1oz butter · 1 small onion, chopped · 1 carrot, chopped
1 rasher bacon, chopped
200g/8oz can tomatoes or 5 large fresh tomatoes · bay leaf
15g/½oz flour · 284ml/½pint liquid from can or stock
salt and pepper · good pinch sugar

Heat the butter and toss the onion, carrot and bacon in this; do not brown. Add tomatoes and bay leaf and simmer for a few minutes. Blend the flour with the stock, add to the ingredients and simmer gently for about 30 minutes. Stir from time to time. Rub through a sieve, add seasoning and sugar and reheat.

657   SPAGHETTI WITH MEAT BALLS AND SPEEDY TOMATO SAUCE

½kg/1lb minced beef · 4 heaped tablespoons soft breadcrumbs
seasoning · 1 egg, beaten · little flour
25g/1oz butter or margarine · 284ml/½pint stock

Tomato sauce
25g/1oz butter or margarine · 1 small onion, chopped
1 small apple, peeled, cored and chopped
4 tablespoons tomato purée (from can or tube)
2 level teaspoons cornflour · 284ml/½pint water · seasoning
pinch sugar

approx. 300g/12oz spaghetti · grated Parmesan cheese
knob butter · parsley to garnish

Mix the minced beef, breadcrumbs and seasoning together. Bind with the beaten egg. Shape into balls and toss in flour. Heat 25g (1 oz) butter or margarine in a saucepan and fry the meat balls until just brown, then add the stock and simmer steadily for 10–15 minutes. Meanwhile heat second 25g (1 oz) butter or margarine in another pan and fry the onion and apple for 2–3 minutes. Add the tomato purée, cornflour, blended with the water and seasoning. Bring to the boil and stir until smooth. Add the pinch of sugar, cover and simmer for about 10 minutes. Cook the spaghetti in boiling salted water until just tender. Strain thoroughly and put on to a heated serving dish. Top with the well drained meat balls, tomato sauce and sprinkle with Parmesan cheese and top with a knob of butter. Garnish with parsley.

Spaghetti with meat balls and speedy tomato sauce

Individual ham and apple curries

658 INDIVIDUAL HAM AND APPLE CURRIES

curry sauce (Recipe No. 659) · 300g/12oz cooked ham, cubed
saffron rice (Recipe No. 140) · chopped apple to garnish

Make the curry sauce and stir in the cubed ham. Cover and leave on a low heat. Cook the rice and arrange in a border in individual serving dishes. Spoon the curry mixture in the centre. Serve garnished with chopped apple.

659 CURRY SAUCE

1 medium-sized onion · 1 small green pepper · 1 cooking apple
25g/1oz butter · 1 level tablespoon curry powder
1 teaspoon curry paste · salt · 1 level tablespoon cornflour
284ml/½pint stock or water · 1 dessertspoon chutney
1 tablespoon desiccated coconut · 1 dessertspoon sultanas
1 teaspoon lemon juice · 1–2 tablespoons milk or single cream*

*This can be omitted with meat curries

Chop the onion, pepper and cooking apple and sauté in the butter. Then add curry powder, paste, salt and cornflour. Stir until blended, cook a few minutes and then stir in stock. Bring to the boil, stirring all the time. Add chutney, coconut and sultanas. Cover and simmer for at least 1 hour. Stir in the lemon juice, add seasoning and the milk or cream if used.

660 CHEESE SAUCE MADE WITH EVAPORATED MILK

100–150g/4–6oz cheese, grated · salt and pepper
1 small can evaporated milk · little made mustard

Put all the ingredients into a saucepan, the top of a double saucepan or a basin placed over a pan of hot water. Heat gently, stirring, until cheese dissolves, then cook until thick. Serve at once. Delicious with vegetable dishes.

COLD SAUCES

Mayonnaise, salad dressing and French dressings are in the salad section (Recipe Nos. 398, 408–412, 416, 418, 419, 427).

661 TARTARE SAUCE

Make mayonnaise (Recipe Nos. 408, 412) and add little chopped parsley, gherkins, capers. If available add a little chopped fresh tarragon or a few drops tarragon vinegar.

662 HORSERADISH SAUCE

pinch dry mustard · good pinch sugar · salt and pepper
284ml/½pint double cream
2 good tablespoons grated horseradish
1 tablespoon white vinegar

Mix all seasonings with the cream, and whisk slightly. Add the horseradish and the vinegar.

663 WHITE SAUCE

25g/1oz butter or margarine · 25g/1oz flour
284ml*/½pint milk for coating consistency, i.e. sauce
142ml*/¼pint milk for panada or binding consistency
568ml*/1pint milk for thin white sauce for soups

*If easier to measure use a generous ¼ litre instead of ½ pint; a generous ½ litre instead of 1 pint; 25g is slightly less than 1 oz flour but the very slight difference in consistency will be adjusted in cooking

Heat the butter or margarine gently, remove from the heat and stir in the flour. Return to the heat and cook for a few minutes, so that the 'roux', as the butter and flour mixture is called, does not brown. Again, remove the pan from the heat and gradually blend in the cold milk. Bring to the boil and cook, stirring with a wooden spoon, until smooth. Season well. If any small lumps have formed whisk sharply.

Variation	Method	To accompany
664 Anchovy Sauce	Stir in 1 teaspoon anchovy essence or a few chopped anchovies when the sauce has thickened	Fish
665 Cheese sauce	Stir in about 100g (4 oz) grated cheese when sauce has thickened, and add a little mustard	Vegetable, meat, fish and savoury dishes
666 Caper sauce	Use 142ml (¼ pint) milk and 142ml (¼ pint) stock. Add 2 teaspoons capers and a little caper vinegar when the sauce has thickened	Boiled lamb
667 Fish sauce	Use 142ml (¼ pint) fish stock and 142ml (¼ pint) milk	Fish
668 Egg sauce	Add 1 chopped hard-boiled egg when the sauce has thickened	Boiled chicken
669 Onion sauce	Boil 3 onions, chop or slice and add when the sauce has thickened	Lamb, mutton or sausages
670 Parsley sauce	Add 1–2 teaspoons chopped parsley when the sauce has thickened	Fish
671 Creamed tomato sauce	Whisk a thick tomato purée (which should be hot but not boiling) into the hot sauce. Do not boil together	Fish, meat and savoury dishes
672 Cucumber sauce	Whisk about 142ml (¼ pint) thick cucumber purée into the hot sauce. Add little lemon juice, green colouring and cream	Fish and vegetable dishes
673 Horseradish sauce (hot)	Whisk about 1 dessertspoon vinegar and 2 tablespoons grated horseradish into the hot sauce. Add a little double cream and a pinch of sugar	Beef, hot trout
674 Mushroom sauce	Simmer 50–100g (2–4 oz) chopped mushrooms in the milk until tender. Strain and use this to make the sauce	All types of savoury dishes
675 Béchamel sauce	Simmer pieces of finely chopped onion, carrot, celery in milk. Strain and use to make the sauce.	In place of white sauce
676 Economical Hollandaise sauce	Make white sauce, remove from heat and whisk in 1 egg, 1 dessertspoon lemon juice or vinegar. Cook gently without boiling for a few minutes	Fish
677 Maître d'hôtel sauce	Use 142ml (¼ pint) fish stock and 142ml (¼ pint) milk. Add 2 teaspoons chopped parsley and 3 tablespoons double cream just before serving	Fish
678 Oyster sauce	Make Béchamel sauce, add about 12 oysters and a little single cream just before serving	Fish
679 Prawn or shrimp sauce	Make white sauce, add 50g (2 oz) chopped prawns and a little anchovy essence just before serving. If using fresh prawns simmer shells and use 142ml (¼ pint) stock instead of the same amount of milk	Fish
680 Tartare sauce (hot)	Make Béchamel sauce; remove from the heat and whisk in 2 egg yolks, 1 tablespoon single cream, 1 teaspoon capers, 1 teaspoon chopped gherkin, 1 teaspoon chopped parsley and a squeeze of lemon juice. Cook gently for a few minutes without boiling	Fish, vegetable and some meat dishes; excellent with veal
681 Mustard cream sauce	Add 1 dessertspoon dry mustard with the flour. Just before serving stir in a little single cream	Herrings, mackerel, trout

HOLLANDAISE SAUCE

2 egg yolks · pinch cayenne pepper · salt and pepper
1–2 tablespoons lemon juice or white wine vinegar
50–100g/2–4oz butter

If possible use a double saucepan for Hollandaise and similar sauces. Put the egg yolks, seasoning and lemon juice or vinegar into the top of the pan. Whisk over hot water until sauce begins to thicken. Add the butter in very small pieces, whisking in each pat and allowing it to melt before adding the next. DO NOT ALLOW TO BOIL otherwise it will curdle. If too thick, add a little single cream.

Variations on Hollandaise sauce	Method	To accompany
683 Béarnaise sauce	Add finely chopped shallot and extra pepper to ingredients for Hollandaise sauce. Add little chopped parsley and tarragon vinegar. A more economical Béarnaise sauce can be made by adding vinegar, chopped shallot and pepper to a white sauce	Steak
684 Mousseline sauce	Use only 25g (1 oz) butter to the 2 egg yolks and add a little double cream and grated nutmeg	Asparagus, broccoli and other vegetables

685 BROWN SAUCE
(Coating consistency)

25g/1oz cooking fat or dripping · 25g/1oz flour
salt and pepper · 284ml/½pint brown stock

Follow the method for white sauce (Recipe No. 663), but cook the roux until a light brown colour. For a better flavour fry a little chopped onion and other vegetables in the fat or dripping first, using 50g (2 oz) of this. Strain if liked.

Variations on brown sauce	Method	To accompany
686 Espagnole sauce	Add a few mushrooms, piece of bacon, onion and carrot with the stock. Simmer until tender and sauce very thick. Sieve and reheat. Add little tomato pulp and sherry	Meat dishes
687 Madeira sauce	As Espagnole sauce, but add Madeira instead of sherry	Ham, tongue and game
688 Poivrade sauce	Add about 12 peppercorns to brown or Espagnole sauce. Sieve and reheat. Add a little brandy	Grilled steak
689 Orange or bigarade sauce	Add grated rind of orange (bitter Seville if possible) to brown sauce. Strain and reheat with orange and lemon juice and little claret or port wine. Add sugar as well as seasonings	Duck, goose

690 SWEET WHITE SAUCE

1 tablespoon cornflour · 284ml/½pint milk · 15g/½oz butter
25g/1oz sugar · little vanilla essence

Blend the cornflour with a little cold milk. Bring the rest of the milk to the boil, pour over the cornflour and return to the pan with the butter and sugar and continue to cook steadily, stirring, until smooth and thick. Add the essence. Serve with steamed puddings.

691 SWEET MOUSSELINE SAUCE

2 large eggs, separated · 50g/2oz sugar
4 tablespoons double cream · little sherry or white wine

Beat the egg yolks and sugar together in a double saucepan until thick and smooth. Remove from the heat, add the cream and the stiffly beaten egg whites. Heat gently without boiling. Stir in sherry or white wine and serve with rich steamed puddings.

692 CUSTARD SAUCE

2 eggs or egg yolks · 568ml/1pint milk · 25–50g/1–2oz sugar

Put all the ingredients together in the top of a double saucepan, and cook over a very gentle heat until thick and smooth. Do NOT allow to boil, or mixture will curdle.
To flavour either infuse vanilla pod or lemon rind with milk or add a few drops essence to the custard.

693 FLUFFY EGG SAUCE

Follow the recipe for custard sauce (Recipe No. 692) but use 2 egg yolks. Remove from the heat and fold in 2 stiffly beaten egg whites. Alternatively make the sauce with custard powder. Blend in 2 egg yolks until smooth (do not allow sauce to boil) then fold in 2 stiffly beaten egg whites. Serve with sweets, fruit, on trifles, etc. If liked the sauce can be flavoured with any essence, rum or sherry.

OTHER SWEET SAUCES
will be found in various sections. They are all listed under SAUCES in the index.

CAKES NEW RECIPES AND OLD FAVOURITES

In this chapter are over one hundred recipes for cakes, biscuits and icings. You will find family cakes, small cakes and cakes for all special occasions.

694 SUCCESS IN CAKE MAKING

Follow recipes very carefully – weigh or measure the ingredients, for the correct balance between fat, sugar, eggs etc. is essential.

All recipes in this book have both metric and Imperial measurements. If the accepted conversion of 25g to 1oz is used throughout you produce a smaller cake so in many recipes you will find a less 'rounded' amount given, e.g. instead of 100g for 4oz I have given 110g where I find it gives a better result. In other cases where 100g = 4oz will be quite satisfactory I have retained this measurement which is generally accepted as the most convenient conversion.

When a recipe specifically states plain flour do use this for it will give a better result.

Cooking temperatures are given in these recipes – but as stated in the table at the beginning, ovens vary and you must at all times be guided by your manufacturer's recommendations.

Where reference is made to icings etc., in recipes without stating any amount, it means the quantity of icing in the original recipe.

695 TINS FOR CAKES

Buy good tins and look after them well. If possible wipe with kitchen roll or soft paper after using, while the tins are warm. This is much better than washing them. The tins shown with the cakes in Recipe No. 720 are excellent as they are seamless, long-lasting and give good results.

696 DARK GINGER CAKE

(Illustrated in colour on the opposite page)

½ teaspoon bicarbonate of soda · 4 tablespoons milk
110g*/4oz butter or margarine · 110g*/4oz moist brown sugar
170g*/6oz black treacle or golden syrup
225g*/8oz plain flour · 2 teaspoons ground ginger
1 teaspoon grated lemon rind · 1 egg

*This gives best result

Blend the bicarbonate of soda with 1 tablespoon of the milk. Put the butter or margarine, sugar and treacle or syrup in a saucepan. Heat gently until the fat has melted. Sieve the flour and ground ginger together. Pour the melted ingredients into the sieved flour, etc. Beat with a wooden spoon until thoroughly mixed. Heat the remaining milk in the saucepan in which the treacle or syrup was melted. Add to the flour, etc., with the bicarbonate of soda liquid, lemon rind and beaten egg and beat again. Pour the mixture into a lined 18–19-cm (7–7½-inch) round cake tin and bake in the centre of a cool oven, 300°F, 150°C, Gas Mark 2, for 1 hour 10 minutes–1½ hours. Test by pressing gently in the centre of the cake. If no impression is left, the cake is cooked. Leave in the tin for 15 minutes, then turn out and finish cooling on a wire tray.

This cake can be iced and topped with sliced preserved ginger, or pieces of preserved ginger pressed firmly on to the cake as in the picture.

697 TIPSY CAKE

*Victoria sandwich (Recipe No. 700) · jam · sherry
568ml/1pint custard sauce (Recipe No. 692)
double cream, whipped*

Split each half of the Victoria sandwich through the centre and spread with jam. If possible use different flavoured jams. Put on to a plate or dish and soak lavishly in sherry. Make the custard sauce, and pour over the cake. Decorate with cream.

698 PINEAPPLE LAYER CAKE

*Victoria sandwich (Recipe No. 700)
butter icing (Recipe No. 751) · pineapple essence
glacé pineapple · glacé cherries
glacé icing (Recipe No. 747)*

Make the Victoria sandwich, and when cooked and cool put the two halves together with the butter icing, flavoured with a little pineapple essence. Add a layer of chopped glacé pineapple and cherries on top of the butter icing. Cover the cake with glacé icing, again flavoured with pineapple essence. Pipe a border of pineapple-flavoured butter icing at the bottom and decorate with pieces of glacé pineapple and glacé cherries.

699 SHORTBREAD CRISPS

Use the recipe for rich shortbread (No. 801). Add a few drops of vanilla or almond essence. Roll the mixture into balls the size of a walnut and put on to ungreased baking sheets, allowing room for them to spread during cooking. Decorate with a glacé cherry or nut and cook in the centre of a moderate oven, 375°F, 180°C, Gas Mark 4, for about 14 minutes. Cool on the baking sheets. If liked, 25g (1 oz) desiccated coconut can be substituted for 25g (1 oz) flour.

Dark ginger cake (Recipe No. 696)

700 VICTORIA SANDWICH

Quantities of ingredients are often written as the weight of eggs in fat, sugar and flour. If you wish you can still continue to weigh in this manner, putting the eggs – still in their shells – on the scales in place of weights. You are fairly safe, though, in assuming that the weight of an average egg is 50g (2 oz), so that you would use the following ingredients to make a 20-cm (8-inch) sandwich cake. Use half quantities for 15-cm (6-inch) sandwich tins or 170g (6 oz) flour, etc., for 18–19-cm (7–7½-inch) tins. Although one assumes an egg is 50g – when you use 4 medium eggs it is wiser to use 225g of flour, etc., or if you would rather use only 200g of flour, etc., then choose smaller eggs.

225g/8oz flour (with plain flour use 2 level teaspoons baking powder) · 225g/8oz soft margarine or butter 225g/8oz castor sugar · 4 medium-sized eggs (if the eggs are unusually small, add a dessertspoon water to make up the extra liquid)

Sieve flour and baking powder, if used, together. Cream the fat and sugar until light and fluffy. Break the eggs into a cup to ensure each one is fresh before beating them in a basin. Add a little of the beaten egg to the creamed mixture and stir carefully. Add a little flour and stir gently. Continue in this way, adding egg and flour alternately until thoroughly mixed. Grease and flour two 20-cm (8-inch) sandwich tins carefully and divide the mixture equally between them. Spread slightly away from the centre, so that the two halves will be flat. Bake for 20 minutes in a moderate oven, 350–375°F, 180–190°C, Gas Mark 4–5. If using a gas oven either put the tins side by side on a shelf just about two rungs from the top of the oven, or put one under the other. With an electric oven or solid fuel put one about the second rung from the top and one the second rung from the bottom, or have them side by side on the same shelf. Test by pressing gently but firmly on top and if no impression is left by the finger the cake is ready to come out of the oven. Turn out of the tins on to a wire tray. It is quite a good idea to give the tins a sharp tap on the table before attempting to turn out the cakes, so loosening the cake away from the sides and bottom of the tin. When cold sandwich together with jam and sprinkle the top with a little sieved icing sugar.

701 CHOCOLATE-FLAVOURED VICTORIA SANDWICH

Use 150–175g (6 oz), see above, flour and 50g (2 oz) chocolate powder or 175–200g (7 oz), see above, flour and 25g (1 oz) cocoa.

702 CHOCOLATE AND VANILLA MARBLE CAKE

170g/6oz butter or margarine · 170g*/6oz castor sugar 3 eggs · 225g*/8oz flour (with plain flour use 1 teaspoon baking powder) · 1 heaped tablespoon cocoa or chocolate powder · few drops vanilla essence icing sugar*

*Best result

Cream together fat and sugar till light and fluffy, then gradually add the beaten eggs. Divide the mixture equally in two. To one half gently fold in half the flour sieved with the cocoa powder and to the other half fold in the remaining sieved flour, together with the vanilla essence. Drop the mixtures, in alternate spoonfuls, into a well greased fluted cake mould or 18-cm (7-inch) round cake tin and bake in the centre of a moderate oven, 350°F, 180°C, Gas Mark 4, for 40–50 minutes. Cool on a wire tray then dust with icing sugar before serving.

Victoria sandwich

Marble cake

703 MARBLE CAKE

*170g**/6oz self-raising flour and 2 level teaspoons baking powder* 110g**/4oz castor sugar · 110g**/4oz whipped-up cooking fat 2 eggs · 1 tablespoon milk · ½ teaspoon vanilla essence few drops cochineal · 1 rounded dessertspoon cocoa glacé icing (Recipe No. 747) · little plain chocolate, melted*

*Or plain flour and 4 level teaspoons baking powder
**Best result

Sieve flour, baking powder and sugar into a bowl. Add cooking fat, eggs, milk and essence, and mixing all ingredients beat for 1 minute only. Divide the mixture into three. Colour one pink with cochineal, to the second add cocoa, leaving the third plain. Place alternate spoonfuls of the mixture in a 15-cm (6-inch) cake tin, lined with greaseproof paper and brushed with melted fat. Bake in the centre of a moderate oven, 325°F, 170°C, Gas Mark 3, for 1–1¼ hours. Cool on a wire tray. When cold, spread most of glacé icing over the top of the cake (a band of greaseproof paper, placed round the cake will prevent the icing from running down the side). Beat a little melted plain chocolate into the remaining icing and pipe lines across the white icing. Quickly draw a skewer across the lines to give a 'feather' effect. Leave to set.

704 BLOW-AWAY SPONGE CAKE

4 eggs · 50g/2oz plain flour · 50g/2oz cornflour
1 level teaspoon baking powder · pinch salt
110g**/4oz castor sugar · dash Angostura bitters*
orange filling (Recipe No. 705), using 150g/6oz butter, etc.

*This gives a lovely flavour to the cake
**Best result

Separate the eggs. Sieve the flour, cornflour, baking powder
and salt together. Beat egg whites until stiff and peaky,
gradually add sugar, whisk until thick and smooth then whisk
in egg yolks and Angostura. Quickly and lightly fold in sieved
ingredients with a metal spoon and divide mixture evenly
between 2 well greased 20-cm (8-inch) sandwich tins. Bake in
a moderately hot oven, 400°F, 200°C, Gas Mark 6, for 15
minutes. Cool on a wire tray then sandwich together with some
of the filling. Spread remainder over the top and sides.

Blow-away sponge

705 ORANGE FILLING

75g/3oz butter · 150g/6oz icing sugar, sieved
finely grated rind 1 orange · 1 dessertspoon orange juice
¼ teaspoon Angostura bitters

Cream together butter and sugar until light and fluffy. Beat in
the orange rind, juice and Angostura. For special occasions
decorate with halved rings of pineapple and glacé cherries.

706 CHOCOLATE SPICE CAKE

225g*/8oz plain flour · 3 level teaspoons baking powder
2 level tablespoons cocoa · ½ level teaspoon nutmeg
½ level teaspoon mixed spice · 1 level teaspoon cinnamon
170g*/6oz butter or soft margarine · good 125g/5oz castor sugar
2 level tablespoons golden syrup · 3 eggs
75g/3oz dates or nuts, finely chopped
1 teaspoon Angostura bitters · ½ teaspoon vanilla essence
4 tablespoons milk · Port o' Spain frosting (Recipe No. 707)
almonds and glacé cherries to decorate

*Gives best result

Sieve together flour, baking powder, cocoa and spices. Cream
butter or margarine and sugar until light and fluffy, add syrup,
then the eggs, one at a time, beating thoroughly after each
addition to prevent curdling. Stir in nuts or dates, Angostura
and vanilla essence, then fold in the flour mixture alternately
with the milk. Bake in two well greased 20-cm (8-inch) sandwich tins in moderate oven 350°F, 180°C, Gas Mark 4, for 30
minutes. When cold sandwich together and cover with the
Port o' Spain frosting and decorate the top with almonds and
glacé cherries.

Peppermint cake

708 PEPPERMINT CAKE

170g*/6oz flour (with plain flour use 1½ teaspoons
baking powder) · 170g*/6oz butter or soft margarine
170g*/6oz castor sugar · 3 eggs · few drops vanilla essence
peppermint cream (Recipe No. 709)
chocolate buttons to decorate

*Gives best result

Sieve the flour and baking powder, if used. Cream the butter
or margarine and sugar together until light and fluffy then
add the eggs, one at a time, beating thoroughly after each
addition to prevent curdling, and a few drops of vanilla
essence. Lightly fold in the flour, then spoon the mixture
into two well greased 20-cm (8-inch) sandwich tins. Bake in a
moderately hot oven, 400°F, 200°C, Gas Mark 6, for 20–25
minutes. Leave to cool on a wire tray. Sandwich the two cakes
together with a layer of peppermint cream, then cover
top with remaining cream, swirling it on with a knife. Decorate
with chocolate buttons and leave the cake in a cool place for
the icing to set.

707 PORT O' SPAIN FROSTING

generous 250g/10oz icing sugar, sieved · 125g/5oz butter
1 teaspoon Angostura bitters · 1 dessertspoon milk

Cream together icing sugar and butter until very light and
fluffy, then beat in the Angostura and milk.

709 PEPPERMINT CREAM

100g/4oz soft margarine · 200g/8oz icing sugar, sieved
1 tablespoon milk · few drops peppermint essence
green colouring

Beat the margarine then cream thoroughly with the icing
sugar. Beat in the milk and sufficient peppermint essence to
give a delicate flavour. Colour pale green.

Date and apple tea bread

710   DUNDEE CAKE

170g*/6oz *margarine* · 170g*/6oz *castor sugar* · 3 *eggs*
225g*/8oz *plain flour* · 1 *teaspoon mixed spice*
1½ *level teaspoons baking powder*
50g/2oz *blanched almonds, chopped*
50g/2oz *glacé cherries, chopped* · ½kg/1lb *mixed dried fruit*
50g/2oz *candied peel, chopped* · 2 *tablespoons milk*
50g/2oz *blanched almonds, split* · *little egg white to glaze*

*Gives best result

Cream the margarine and sugar together until soft and light.
Add the beaten eggs. Sieve dry ingredients together. Mix the
chopped almonds, floured cherries, fruit and peel together.
Stir in the flour and enough milk to make a slow dropping
consistency; lastly put in the fruit. Put into a greased and
floured 20-cm (8-inch) cake tin. Cover the top with the split
almonds and brush with a little egg white to glaze. Bake in the
centre of a very moderate oven, 325–350°F, 170°C, Gas Mark
3, for 2–2¼ hours, reducing the heat after 1½ hours if wished.
Cool slightly in tin before turning on to a wire tray to finish
cooling.
For a more economical Dundee Cake see Recipe No. 724.

711   RICH ROCK BUNS

225g*/8oz *flour (with plain flour use* 2½ *teaspoons baking
powder)* · 140g*/5oz *margarine*
140g*/5oz *sugar* · 1 *egg, beaten* · *milk to mix*
150g/6oz *dried fruit* · 50g/2oz *candied peel*

*Gives best result

Sieve flour and baking powder, if used, together. Rub in
margarine, add sugar, the beaten egg and enough milk to make
a stiff consistency. Be careful not to make the mixture too wet,
or the buns will spread, particularly in this richer recipe. Add
the fruit and peel. Grease and flour baking sheets and put
small heaps of the mixture on these, dusting lightly with sugar.
Bake for 10 minutes near the top of a hot to very hot oven,
450–475°F, 220–230°C, Gas Mark 7–8. If the oven is inclined
to be rather fierce, lower the heat after the first 5 minutes.

712   CHERRY BUNS

Follow the recipe for rich rock buns (Recipe No. 711), but
omit the dried fruit and candied peel and use 100–150g (4–6 oz)
chopped glacé cherries.

713   JAM BUNS

Follow the recipe for rich rock buns (Recipe No. 711), but
omit the dried fruit. Place in heaps on the baking sheets. Make
a small hole in the centre of each and put in a spoonful of
apricot or raspberry jam.

714   SAFFRON BUNS

Follow the recipe for rich rock buns (Recipe No. 711), but
omit the mixed fruit and candied peel and use small ½ teaspoon
powdered saffron and a few drops yellow colouring.

715   ECONOMICAL ROCK BUNS

Follow the recipe for rich rock buns (Recipe No. 711), but
use 75–100g (3–4 oz) margarine, 75–100g (3–4 oz) sugar, or
75g (3 oz) dried fruit only.

716   DATE AND APPLE TEA BREAD

2 *large cooking apples* · 2 *tablespoons water*
75g*/3oz *butter* · 140g*/5oz *castor sugar* · 2 *eggs*
275g*/10oz *self-raising flour (with plain flour use* 2¼ *level
teaspoons baking powder)* · *pinch salt*
110 *or* 100g/4oz *crystallised ginger, chopped*
50g/2oz *walnuts, chopped*
110 *or* 100g/4oz *stoned dates, chopped*
2 *tablespoons apricot jam, melted*
walnut halves to decorate

*Gives best result

Peel, core and slice the apples. Cook gently with the water
until tender then sieve or beat until a *thick* purée. If the apples
are particularly juicy the purée must be simmered in an open
pan until it is *very thick*. Allow to cool.
Cream the butter and sugar together until light and fluffy.
Gradually beat in the eggs. Fold in the sieved flour and salt,
and mix to a soft consistency with the apple purée. Fold in
the ginger, nuts and dates. Spoon the mixture into a large
greased loaf tin and bake in a moderate oven, 350°F, 180°C,
Gas Mark 4, for 1–1¼ hours. Cool on a wire tray then brush
the top with melted apricot jam and decorate with walnut
halves.

THREE CAKES WITH YEAST

717 SAVARIN

scant 10g/¼oz *fresh yeast or* ½ *teaspoon dried yeast*
110g*/4oz *plain flour* · 50g/2oz *butter, melted* · 2 *eggs, beaten*
1 *teaspoon sugar* · 4 *tablespoons tepid milk*
Syrup
142ml/¼pint *water* · 50g/2oz *golden syrup* · *juice 2 lemons*
1 *tablespoon rum* · *double cream, whipped*
and selection of fruit to decorate

*Gives best result

Cream the yeast and sugar together; add the milk and a sprinkling of flour. If using dried yeast follow directions in Recipe No. 808. Put in a warm place for 20 minutes, then work in the rest of the flour. Add the melted butter and eggs and beat well. Turn the mixture into a greased plain or fluted ring tin and allow to 'prove' for about 25 minutes in a warm place. Bake in the centre of a hot oven, 425°F, 220°C, Gas Mark 7, for 15 minutes. Lower the heat to 400°F, 200°C, Gas Mark 6, and bake for about a further 10–15 minutes, until firm to the touch. Cool in the tin for a few minutes, then turn out and finish cooling on a wire tray.

To make the syrup, boil the water, golden syrup and lemon juice for a few minutes. Remove from the heat and add the rum. Prick the savarin and soak with the syrup. If liked, the centre of the savarin can be filled with fresh or canned fruit before serving and piped with whipped double cream.

If you wish to bake a savarin in a 20–23-cm (8–9-inch) fluted or plain cake tin (as shown in the picture) then use exactly double all ingredients. Allow to 'prove' for 35 minutes, then bake for 15 minutes in the centre of a hot oven, as above; lower the heat and cook for a further 25 minutes.

Savarin

718 CRUMBLE CAKE

Dough
20g/¾oz *fresh yeast** · 50g/2oz *sugar*
5 *tablespoons tepid milk* · 225g**/8oz *plain flour*
50g/2oz *margarine* · 2 *egg yolks or* 1 *egg*
¼ *teaspoon salt* · 50g/2oz *quick-cooking rolled oats*
Crumble
25g/1oz *quick-cooking rolled oats* · 40g/1½oz *flour*
50g/2oz *margarine* · 50g/2oz *brown sugar*
1½ *teaspoons cinnamon*

*Or use dried yeast, see Recipe No. 808
**Gives best result

Cream yeast with 1 teaspoon sugar and add 1 tablespoon of the milk. Add 1 tablespoon flour and leave to stand until bubbles appear. Cream margarine and sugar. Add egg yolks or egg and gradually mix in flour, salt and oats. Stir in yeast mixture together with rest of milk, beat well. Cover and allow to rise in a warm place. Meanwhile prepare the crumble. Toast rolled oats and add to flour. Rub in fat and mix in remaining ingredients. Knead dough and transfer to a greased and floured 18 or 20-cm (7 or 8-inch) cake tin. Sprinkle crumble over the cake and leave to rise in a warm place. Bake in a hot oven, 450°F, 220°C, Gas Mark 7, for 15 minutes. Reduce heat to 350°F, 180°C, Gas Mark 4, and cook for a further 40–45 minutes. Turn out and cool on a wire tray.

719 POPPYSEED ROLL

225g*/8oz *plain flour* · ¼ *teaspoon salt* · 75g/3oz *sugar*
50g/2oz *margarine* · 15g/½oz *fresh yeast***
about 2 *tablespoons tepid milk* · 1 *egg*
Filling
25g/1oz *poppyseeds* · 25g/1oz *quick-cooking rolled oats, toasted*
½ *teaspoon cinnamon* · 50g/2oz *sultanas or raisins*
grated rind 1 *orange*

*Gives best result
**Or use dried yeast, see Recipe No. 808

Prepare poppyseeds: put in a basin and cover with boiling water. Cool and strain. Repeat twice more. Mix with other ingredients for filling.

Sieve the flour and salt. Add most of the sugar and rub in the margarine. Cream the yeast with the remaining sugar and add 1 tablespoon warm milk. Pour into a well in the centre of the rubbed-in mixture. Leave, in a warm place, until bubbles appear in the yeast. Mix in the egg and remaining milk to form a soft dough. Knead well and leave, covered, in a warm place to rise. Knead again and roll to a rectangle, 31-cm (12-inches) by 40-cm (16-inches). Spread the filling over the dough; roll up and transfer to a greased and floured roasting tin, form the dough into a horseshoe shape. Cover and leave in a warm place to rise. Brush with milk and bake in a hot oven, 425°F, 220°C, Gas Mark 7, for 15 minutes, then reduce heat to 350°F, 180°C, Gas Mark 4, and bake for a further 30–40 minutes. Cool on a wire tray.

Madeira cake

720   MADEIRA CAKE

100 or 110g*/4oz margarine · 100 or 110g*/4oz sugar
200 or 225g*/8oz flour (with plain flour use 2 level teaspoons
baking powder) · 2 eggs · 1 teaspoon grated lemon rind
milk to mix · little sugar · few strips candied peel

**I have given a choice of metric weights here for you automatically have
the correct consistency by the amount of milk used in blending to a soft
consistency. If you use the smaller amount, i.e. 100g as 4 oz margarine
then the economical cake will be cooked within about 1 hour and the
richer cake within about 1¼ hours*

Cream together the margarine and sugar until light and fluffy.
Sieve flour and baking powder, if used, together. Beat eggs.
Add eggs and flour alternately to margarine mixture, with
lemon rind and enough milk to make a soft consistency. Put
into a greased and floured 18-cm (7-inch) cake tin; sprinkle
a little sugar on top and put on a few strips of candied peel.
Bake in the centre of a moderate oven, 350°F, 180°C, Gas
Mark 4, for 1¼ hours. For a richer cake use 150 or 170g (6 oz)
butter, 150 or 170g (6 oz) sugar and 3 eggs. Bake in a very
moderate oven, 325°F, 170°C, Gas Mark 3, for 1½–1¾ hours.

721   MADELEINES

100g/4oz flour · 4 eggs · 100g/4oz castor sugar
100g/4oz butter or soft margarine, melted
few drops vanilla essence · apricot jam, heated and sieved
desiccated coconut · glacé cherries and angelica leaves
to decorate

Sieve flour. Whisk eggs and sugar together over hot water
until mixture is thick, pale in colour and will hold its own
weight. Very lightly – with a metal spoon – fold in flour and
then melted butter or margarine and vanilla essence. Three-
quarters fill 16–18 well greased dariole moulds with mixture,
and cook near the top of a moderately hot oven, 400°F, 200°C,
Gas Mark 6, for 10–15 minutes. Turn out on to a wire tray to
cool. When cold brush each madeleine with apricot jam and
roll in desiccated coconut. Decorate top of each with half a
glacé cherry and angelica leaves.

Madeleines

722   ALMOND CAKE

200 or 225g*/8oz flour (with plain flour use 2 level teaspoons
baking powder) · 100 or 110g*/4oz soft margarine
100 or 110g*/4oz castor sugar · 2 eggs
50g/2oz ground almonds · milk to mix

*See comments under Madeira cake, Recipe No. 720

Sieve the flour and baking powder together. Cream the
margarine and sugar together until light and fluffy. Beat in the
eggs, one at a time, adding a little of the sieved flour mixture
with the second. Using a metal tablespoon, fold in the remaining flour and the ground almonds. Add sufficient milk to make
a soft consistency. Spoon the mixture into a lined 18-cm
(7-inch) tin and bake in the centre of a moderate oven, 350°F,
180°C, Gas Mark 4, for about 1¼ hours. Turn out and cool on
a wire tray.

Almond cake

Economical Dundee cake

723   GENOA CAKE

200 or 225g*/8oz flour (with plain flour use 2 level teaspoons baking powder) · 100 or 110g*/4oz margarine 100 or 110g*/4oz sugar · 2 eggs · 150 or 175g*/6oz dried fruit 50g/2oz candied peel, chopped · 1 teaspoon grated lemon rind milk to mix · little sugar

*See comments under Madeira cake, Recipe No. 720

Sieve the flour and baking powder, if used, together. Cream the margarine and sugar together until light and fluffy. Beat in the eggs, one at a time, adding a little of the sieved flour with the second. Using a metal tablespoon gently fold in the remaining flour, the fruit, candied peel and lemon rind. Add enough milk to make a soft consistency. Put the mixture in a lined 18-cm (7-inch) cake tin and bake in the centre of a moderate oven, 350°F, 180°C, Gas Mark 4, for just over 1¼ hours.

For a richer cake use 150g (6 oz) butter, 150g (6 oz) sugar, 3 eggs and 200g (8 oz) fruit. Bake in a very moderate oven, 325°F, 170°C, Gas Mark 3, for 1¾ hours.

724   ECONOMICAL DUNDEE CAKE

Follow the recipe for Dundee Cake (Recipe No. 710), but reduce sugar and margarine to 100g (4 oz), the fruit to 250g (10 oz) and the eggs to 2. Bake the mixture in a 20-cm (8-inch) tin in a moderate oven, 350°F, 180°C, Gas Mark 4, for 1¼ hours.

Chelsea ring

725   JAPONNAISE CAKES

4 egg whites · 225g*/8oz castor sugar 225g*/8oz ground almonds or 170g*/6oz ground almonds and 50g/2oz ground rice · almond essence coffee butter icing (Recipe No. 751) small amount almond paste (Recipe No. 744) green and red colouring

*Gives best result

Grease two baking sheets and lightly sprinkle with flour. Whisk egg whites with half sugar until stiff, fold in rest of sugar, the almonds, ground rice, if used and a few drops of essence. Spread mixture on the baking sheets evenly about a ¼-cm (⅛-inch) thick. Cook in a cool oven, 300°F, 150°C, Gas Mark 2, until almost set. Mark with a 3½-cm (1½-inch) cutter into rounds. Return to oven and cook until golden and crisp. Cool on a wire tray. Crush trimmings with a rolling pin and sieve. Put some coffee butter icing in centre of half the biscuits. Place the other rounds on top and press together. Spread remaining butter icing round sides and top. Coat in prepared crumbs. Decorate by piping with butter cream and topping with small cut-out shapes of green and red marzipan.

726   CHELSEA RING

225g*/8oz flour (with plain flour use 2 level teaspoons baking powder) · pinch salt · 50g/2oz margarine · 1 egg 4 tablespoons milk · 4–5 tablespoons mincemeat glacé icing (Recipe No. 747) · glacé cherries and angelica to decorate

*Gives best result

Sieve the flour, salt and baking powder, if used. Rub in the margarine until mixture resembles fine breadcrumbs. Add the beaten egg and milk. Mix to a soft dough. Knead gently until smooth. Roll out, on a lightly floured surface, into an oblong about 26-cm (10-inches) by 18-cm (7-inches). Spread the mincemeat over the dough, leaving a narrow margin round the edges, and roll up lengthways. Shape the roll into a circle and join the ends by damping with water and pressing together; place on a greased baking sheet. Make 6 cuts in the top. Bake in the centre of a moderately hot oven, 400°F, 200°C, Gas Mark 6, for 30 minutes; cool on a wire tray. When cold pour over the glacé icing, decorate the top with cherries and angelica and leave to set.

727   CHOCOLATE CRISPIES

25g/1oz margarine · 2 tablespoons golden syrup
25g/1oz drinking chocolate · 7 tablespoons cornflakes
or other crisp ready-cooked breakfast cereal

Melt fat and syrup slowly in a saucepan. Add the drinking chocolate and heat thoroughly. Remove from heat and using a metal spoon, fold in cereal until coated. Spoon into 9 or 10 portions, or fill paper cases, and leave to set.

728   CHOCOLATE FANCIES

75g/3oz flour (with plain flour use 1 level teaspoon
baking powder) · 1 heaped tablespoon cocoa
100g/4oz butter or margarine · 100g/4oz sugar · 2 eggs
1 tablespoon warm water to mix · glacé icing (Recipe No. 747)
butter icing (Recipe No. 751) · glacé cherries to decorate

Sieve the flour, baking powder, if used and cocoa. Cream the butter or margarine and sugar until light and fluffy. Gradually add the beaten eggs. Fold in the sieved flour mixture. Mix with the warm water to give a soft, dropping consistency. Transfer the mixture into a lined Swiss roll tin and cook in a moderate oven, 350°F, 180°C, Gas Mark 4, for about 20 minutes. When cold cut into fancy shapes. Coat with glacé icing and pipe a border of butter icing round the edge. Decorate with glacé cherries.

729   SPONGE CAKE WITHOUT FAT

3 large eggs (at least day old) · 100g/4oz castor sugar
75g/3oz flour (with plain flour ½ level teaspoon baking powder
can be used) · 1 tablespoon hot water
25g/1oz melted butter or margarine if the cake is to be kept
for a day or two

Put the eggs and sugar into a basin and whisk until thick. You will get a lighter result if NOT whisked over hot water. Sieve the flour and baking powder, if used. FOLD in the flour carefully and gently with a metal spoon. FOLD in water and the butter or margarine, if used; divide the mixture between two greased and floured 18-cm (7-inch) sandwich cake tins and bake near the top of a really hot oven – with gas it is a good idea to heat the oven on 8 then turn to 6 or 7 when the cakes go in. With electricity heat to 450–475°F, 230–240°C, then re-set oven to 425°F, 220°C, when the cakes go in. Test by pressing gently in the centre of the cakes and if firm they are cooked. Remove from the oven, leave for a minute, tap tins sharply then turn on to a wire tray. COOL AWAY FROM A DRAUGHT.

For a chocolate sponge, omit 25g (1 oz) flour and add 25g (1 oz) chocolate powder.

730   SWISS ROLL

Follow the recipe for sponge cake (Recipe No. 729). Cook the mixture in a lined Swiss roll tin for about 7 minutes. Turn on to greaseproof paper, sprinkled with castor sugar, trim the edges and make a dent with the back of a knife about 1-cm (½-inch) from the edge on one short side. Quickly spread with warm jam or lemon curd. Place two flake bars along the dent and roll up the Swiss roll. Cool on a wire tray. When cold decorate the top with whipped double cream and 2–3 halved flake bars. For a smaller roll use 2 eggs, 50g (2 oz) flour, etc.

Swiss roll

Locomotive cake

731 COFFEE ROLL

Follow the recipe and method for Swiss roll (Recipe No. 730). Instead of spreading with jam or lemon curd, cover with a sheet of greaseproof paper and roll up. When cold, unroll, spread with coffee butter icing (Recipe No. 751) and roll up again. Coat with coffee glacé icing (Recipe No. 747) and leave to set.

732 CHOCOLATE YULE LOG

40g/1½oz plain flour · 1 level tablespoon cocoa · 2 eggs
50g/2oz sugar · 1 tablespoon warm water
butter icing (Recipe No. 751), made with
100g/4oz butter, etc.

Sieve the flour and cocoa together. Whisk the eggs and sugar until thick and creamy. Fold in the sieved flour mixture. Gently add the warm water. Pour the mixture into a lined Swiss roll tin. Bake in a hot oven, 425°F, 220°C, Gas Mark 7, for 7 minutes. Turn out on to sugared paper, cover with piece of greaseproof paper and roll up firmly. When cold unroll, spread with some of the butter icing and re-roll. Pipe or spread the remaining butter icing over the log. Mark with a fork. If liked decorate with holly, etc.

733 MOCHA SANDWICH

100g/4oz flour (with plain flour use 1 level teaspoon
baking powder) · 1 tablespoon cocoa
100g/4oz butter or margarine · 100g/4oz sugar · 2 eggs
warm water to mix · coffee-flavoured butter icing
(Recipe No. 751), made with 100g/4oz butter, etc.
glacé cherries to decorate

Sieve the flour and cocoa together. Cream the butter and sugar until light and fluffy. Gradually add the beaten eggs. Fold in the flour and cocoa and mix to a soft dropping consistency with a little warm water. Put mixture into two greased 18-cm (7-inch) sandwich tins and cook in a moderate oven, 350°F, 180°C, Gas Mark 4, for 20–25 minutes. When cold, sandwich together with some of the coffee butter icing. Cover the top with the remaining butter icing and decorate with glacé cherries.

734 LOCOMOTIVE CAKE

Swiss roll (Recipe No. 730)
butter icing (Recipe No. 751), made with 100g/4oz butter, etc.
5 marshmallows · chocolate vermicelli
1 red-skinned eating apple · 1 tablespoon lemon juice

Make the Swiss roll, but omit the flake bars, and when cold, spread with most of the butter icing. Sandwich 3 of the marshmallows together with butter icing. Coat sides in butter icing then roll in chocolate vermicelli. Place on top of Swiss roll to represent a funnel. Core and slice the apple, dip in lemon juice to keep it white. Place 4 slices in position to represent wheels. Finally decorate with remaining marshmallows and a small piece of apple peel as shown in the photograph.

*yeast dough as fruit buns (Recipe No. 826) but omit
dried fruit and peel · jam · fat or oil for deep frying
castor sugar*

Allow dough to 'prove' as described in Recipe No. 806, knead
well and form into the various shapes for the doughnuts.
Round doughnuts Form into balls – remembering they will
double their size in cooking. Make a deep hole and put in jam,
re-roll the balls to cover the jam.
Crescents Form into half-moon shapes – if wished these can
be cut thinly and two halves sandwiched together with jam.
Ring doughnuts Roll out dough and cut into rings with a
pastry cutter. With a smaller cutter, make a hole in the centre.
Put the shapes on to a warmed baking sheet to 'prove' again
for 15 minutes. Meanwhile heat the fat or oil to 350°F, 180°C.
– it should turn a small cube of bread golden brown within 1
minute – no sooner. Put in the doughnuts and cook for 5–10
minutes – the ring doughnuts will cook more quickly. Lift out,
drain for one minute on absorbent paper, then roll in castor
sugar.
If liked, the doughnuts can be split when cold and filled with
whipped double cream.

Doughnuts

Linzer torte

736   LINZER TORTE

*150g/6oz plain flour · ½ level teaspoon cinnamon
75g/3oz butter · 50g/2oz sugar · 50g/2oz ground almonds
grated rind 1 lemon · 2 egg yolks · lemon juice
200–300g/8–12oz raspberry jam*

Sieve the flour and cinnamon into a bowl. Rub in butter until
mixture resembles fine breadcrumbs. Add sugar, ground
almonds and lemon rind. Beat egg yolks and add to flour
mixture with sufficient lemon juice to bind to a pliable dough.
Knead lightly and leave in a cool place for 30 minutes. Place
two-thirds of the pastry into an 18-cm (7-inch) fluted flan ring
on a baking sheet. Press out and mould to the shape of the
ring, making sure that it is of even thickness. Fill with raspberry jam. Roll out remaining pastry and cut into 1-cm (½-
inch) strips with a pastry wheel or knife. Use to make a lattice
design over the jam. Bake in the centre of a moderately hot
oven, 375°F, 190°C, Gas Mark 5, for 25–30 minutes. Leave to
cool before removing the flan ring. Serve with cream.

Gingerbread

737   GINGERBREAD

110g*/4oz *cooking fat* · 110g*/4oz *soft brown sugar*
110g*/4oz *black treacle* · 110g*/4oz *golden syrup*
225g*/8oz *plain flour* · ½ *level teaspoon salt*
1 *level teaspoon bicarbonate of soda*
2 *level teaspoons ground ginger* · 1 *level teaspoon mixed spice*
2 *eggs* · 6 *tablespoons milk*

*Gives best result

Put fat, sugar, treacle and syrup into a pan. Heat gently until the fat melts. Cool slightly. Sieve dry ingredients into a bowl. Make well in centre. Slowly pour in syrup and milk and beat thoroughly. Warm the milk in the saucepan so no treacle, etc. is wasted. Stir, without beating, till well blended. Lastly stir in the beaten eggs. Pour mixture into a 20-cm (8-inch) lined square cake tin. Bake in the centre of a very moderate oven, 325°F, 170°C, Gas Mark 3, for about 1 hour. Cool in the tin for 15 minutes, then turn out and finish cooling on a wire tray. Leave at least 1 day before cutting.

Ginger parkin An excellent parkin can be made if you use 110g (4 oz) plain flour and 110g (4 oz) fine or medium oatmeal in place of 225g (8 oz) plain flour.
To weigh treacle: Either weigh empty saucepan, put treacle in this and weigh in pan or allow a tablespoon for each 25–28g (1 oz).

738   PRESERVED GINGER CAKE

5 *medium-sized eggs*
generous ½kg (575g*)/1¼lb *golden syrup, warmed*
140g*/5oz *sugar* · 170g*/6oz *butter, softened*
25g/1oz *ground ginger* · bare ½kg/1lb *plain flour*
grated rind 2 *lemons*
100 or 110g/4oz *preserved ginger, chopped*

* This gives best result

Beat the eggs well. Add the warmed syrup gradually, beating all the time. Add the sugar, then the butter. Add the ground ginger to the flour and sieve the two together. Add the syrup mixture to the sieved flour and beat until bubbles appear in the batter, then add the grated lemon rind and the preserved ginger. Bake in a shallow 23–26-cm (9–10-inch) lined square tin in the centre of a cool oven 300°F, 150°C, Gas Mark 2, for about 2 hours. When cold, store in a tin to mature before using.
If liked, spread glacé icing (Recipe No. 747) over the top and decorate with slices of preserved ginger.

739   KOEKSISTERS

(*South African recipe*)

Syrup
½kg/1lb *granulated sugar*
284ml/½pint *water* · 1 *stick cinnamon*

225g*/8oz *flour (with plain flour use* 2 *level teaspoons baking powder*) · *pinch salt* · 25g/1oz *margarine* · 1 *egg*
4–5 *tablespoons milk* · *fat or oil for deep frying*

*Gives best results

Put ingredients for the syrup into a small strong pan and stir over the heat until sugar dissolves. Bring to the boil and boil rapidly for 1 minute. Leave to cool.
Sieve the flour, baking powder and salt. Rub in margarine. Add the egg and enough milk to form a dough. Roll out to a rectangle about ½-cm (¼-inch) in thickness and from this cut strips 7½-cm (3-inches) by 2½-cm (1-inch). Cut each strip into 3 lengthways, not completely cutting through to the end, and plait, pinching together at the end. Fry a few at a time in the fat or oil heated to 350°F, 180°C, (see Recipe No. 735) until golden brown. Drain, on absorbent paper then dip at once into cold syrup; cool on a wire tray. Koeksisters keep well but must be kept apart in the tin.

740   STRAWBERRY SHORTCAKE

200g/8oz *flour (with plain flour use* 2 *level teaspoons baking powder*) · ½ *teaspoon salt*
75g/3oz *sugar* · 100g/4oz *butter* · *grated rind* 1 *lemon*
2 *egg yolks* · *about* 6 *tablespoons milk*
½kg/1lb *fresh strawberries*
284ml/½pint *double cream, lightly whipped*

To make the shortcake sieve the flour, baking powder, salt and sugar together. Work in butter and lemon rind using a knife. Add egg yolks, a little at a time then gradually add the milk, stirring, until the mixture holds together, but is still soft. Turn into a greased and floured 20-cm (8-inch) square cake tin and bake in a hot oven, 425°F, 220°C, Gas Mark 7, for 15 minutes. Lower heat to moderate and bake for a further 15 minutes. Cool on a wire tray. Cut strawberries in half. To serve, split shortcake in half and fill with half the strawberries and cream. Spread top with remaining cream and arrange strawberries on top.

Strawberry shortcake

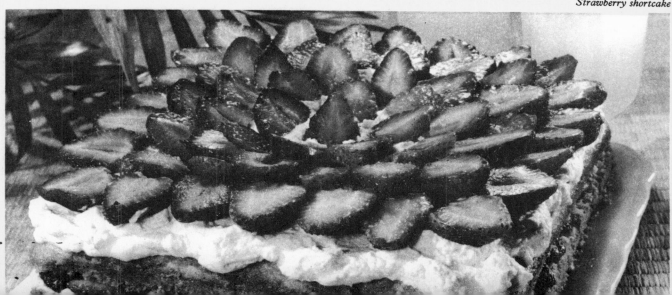

Humpty Dumpty cake

741 HUMPTY DUMPTY CAKE

chocolate-flavoured Victoria sandwich (Recipe No. 701)
1 pear · 50g/2oz plain chocolate, melted · lemon juice
2 cloves · angelica · glacé cherry · 2 sugar-coated sweets
glacé icing (Recipe No. 747), made with 100g/4oz icing
sugar, etc.

Make the Victoria sandwich and bake the mixture in a greased loaf tin in the centre of a very moderate oven for 50 minutes – 1 hour. Turn out and cool on a wire tray. When cold place the cake on its side on a serving dish. Peel the pear and dip the pointed end in the melted chocolate. When the chocolate has set stand the pear on the cake. Brush the pear with a little lemon juice to prevent it turning brown. Insert the 2 cloves for 'eyes', a small piece of angelica for a 'nose' and a glacé cherry for a 'mouth'. Place 2 sugar-coated sweets at the base of the pear. Put the glacé icing in a small piping bag, fitted with a writing pipe and pipe lines on the cake as shown in the picture.

742   CROWN CAKE

170g*/6oz *flour (with plain flour use 1½ teaspoons baking powder)*
110g*/4oz *butter or margarine* · 110g*/4oz *castor sugar*
2 eggs · *few drops vanilla essence* · 2 tablespoons milk
3 tablespoons apricot jam, heated and sieved
almond paste (Recipe No. 744)
lemon glacé icing (Recipe No. 747)
glacé cherries and silver balls to decorate

Gives best result

Sieve the flour and baking powder, if used, together. Cream fat and sugar until light and fluffy then add eggs, one at a time, beating thoroughly after each addition. Add vanilla essence, then fold in flour alternately with the milk. Turn mixture into a well greased 20-cm (8-inch) ring tin and bake in centre of moderate oven, 350°F, 180°C, Gas Mark 4, for 30–40 minutes. Cool on a wire tray, then brush all over with melted and sieved apricot jam. Divide almond paste into 8 pieces, shape into pyramids and stand, at equal intervals on top of the cake. Coat cake and pyramids with lemon glacé icing, leave for about 10 minutes to set, then decorate points of crown with glacé cherries. Decorate sides and lower edge with silver balls.

743   LAZY DAISY CAKE

3 egg whites · 140g*/5oz *sugar* · 75g/3oz *butter*
2 teaspoons baking powder · *pinch salt* · 2 tablespoons milk
170g*/6oz *plain flour* · *few drops almond essence*
butter icing (Recipe No. 751) · *satin icing (Recipe No. 750)*
glacé icing (Recipe No. 747) · *yellow colouring*

This gives best result

Beat egg whites until stiff. Beat in half sugar a little at a time. Cream together butter and remaining sugar. Sieve together the dry ingredients and add alternately with milk to the butter mixture. Lastly, fold in the beaten egg whites and almond essence. Divide mixture between three greased and floured sandwich tins and bake in a moderate oven, 350°F, 180°C, Gas Mark 4, for about 30 minutes until sponge feels firm to light pressure. Cool on a wire tray. Sandwich layers together with butter icing. Cover top and sides of cake with satin icing. Make up glacé icing, and tint one dessertspoonful a pale yellow. Pipe daisy shapes over top of cake with white glacé icing. Use the yellow icing for the daisy centres.

MARZIPAN AND ICING

744   ALMOND PASTE OR MARZIPAN

100g/4oz *ground almonds* · 50g/2oz *icing sugar*
50g/2oz *castor sugar* · *few drops almond essence*
egg yolk to mix

Mix all the ingredients together, adding enough egg yolk to make a firm mixture. Knead thoroughly. This is enough to cover the top of a 15–18-cm (6–7-inch) cake. For a 20–23-cm (8–9-inch) cake use 150g (6 oz) ground almonds, etc. To cover the top and sides of a cake use at least double quantities.

745   ALMOND PASTE

(With semolina)

340g*/12oz *finest semolina* · 420g*/15oz *castor sugar*
3 teaspoons almond essence · *little cold water* · 3 egg yolks

This gives best result

Mix semolina and sugar together. Add almond essence and a little cold water to the egg yolks and beat well. Gradually add this to the dry ingredients.
NOTE: Care must be taken not to make the paste too wet.

746   ROLLED OAT MARZIPAN

225g*/8oz *quick-cooking rolled oats*
110g*/4oz *butter or margarine* · 4 tablespoons water
225g*/8oz *castor sugar* · 2 teaspoons vanilla essence
2 teaspoons almond essence

This gives best result

Rub the rolled oats between your hands (or put them through a mincer) until they are fine – like flour. Beat the fat, hot water, sugar and essences together until the sugar has dissolved. Add the rolled oats and work with a wooden spoon until the mixture is cool enough to knead by hand.

747   WATER ICING or GLACE ICING

225g/8oz *icing sugar** · about 1½ *dessertspoons warm water*

To cover the top of a 15-cm (6-inch) cake use 125g (4 oz) icing sugar; for an 18-cm (7-inch) cake 175g (6 oz); a 20–23-cm (8–9-inch) cake 225g (8 oz). If covering top and sides use at least double quantities. Metric quantity exactly the same with 225g icing sugar

If the icing sugar seems rather lumpy you can sieve it, but if you add the water and let it stand for some time it will become smooth by itself. Gradually add the water and beat with a wooden spoon until smooth and glossy.
For chocolate glacé icing add 1 dessertspoon cocoa to the icing and then beat in a knob of melted butter.
For coffee glacé icing mix with either strong coffee or coffee essence instead of water.
For lemon glacé icing mix with lemon juice instead of water.
For orange glacé icing mix with orange juice instead of water.
For vanilla glacé icing add a few drops of vanilla essence.

748   VANILLA ICING

40g/1½oz *margarine*
75g/3oz *icing sugar, sieved* · *few drops vanilla essence*

Soften the margarine, then beat in the icing sugar and vanilla essence.

749   GLACE FUDGE ICING

50g/2oz *table margarine* · 2½ *tablespoons milk or water*
225g*/8oz *icing sugar, sieved* · *flavouring*

Gives best result

Put the table margarine and milk or water into a saucepan. Stir over a low heat until the margarine has melted. Remove from the heat and stir in icing sugar and flavouring.
For orange or lemon fudge icing use orange or lemon squash instead of milk or water.
For coffee fudge icing use diluted coffee essence or strong coffee instead of milk or water.
For chocolate fudge icing use 200g* (7 oz) icing sugar and 25g (1 oz) chocolate powder.
This icing can be moulded into flowers etc. or can be piped.

750 SATIN ICING

2 lemons · 50g/2oz table margarine
½kg/1lb icing sugar, sieved
100–200g/4–8oz icing sugar, sieved, for thickening and
kneading

Squeeze the juice from the lemons. Put table margarine and juice into a saucepan and stir over a low heat until the margarine has melted. Add half the icing sugar and stir until dissolved. Cook for 2 minutes only – timing is most important as if the icing is over-boiled it will be difficult to manipulate. Add the rest of the ½kg (1lb) icing sugar and beat hard. Allow to cool slightly, then work in enough of the rest of the icing to make a pliable dough. To coat cakes with this icing roll out and use like an almond paste (see illustration). The flowers are made by moulding small pieces of the icing. Flavouring and colouring can be kneaded in. The satin icing will keep well if wrapped in foil or waxed paper.

For small cakes cut rounds of the icing with a pastry cutter, spread cakes with jam and press satin icing rounds on top or round the sides.

751 BUTTER ICING

50g/2oz butter
75–110g*/3–4oz icing sugar, sieved (to make a firmer icing use the higher amount of sugar) · flavouring, see below

*To give right proportion

Cream the butter until very soft and white – it is essential not to warm it. Work in the sugar and flavouring.
For coffee butter icing work in 1 dessertspoon coffee essence. Do this gradually to prevent the mixture from curdling.
For lemon butter icing add 2 teaspoons finely grated lemon rind and gradually beat in 1 dessertspoon lemon juice.
For orange butter icing add 3 teaspoons finely grated orange rind and gradually beat in 1 dessertspoon orange juice.
For vanilla butter icing add ½ teaspoon vanilla essence.

752 ROYAL ICING

1 egg white · about 225g*/8oz icing sugar
1 dessertspoon lemon juice · few drops glycerine, optional

*Gives best result

Beat the egg white lightly. Sieve the icing sugar. Add this and the lemon juice to the egg white. If this is a little small you may need just under the 225g (8 oz) icing sugar. Beat until the mixture is very white, and firm enough to stand up in points. If the icing is soft do not add more sugar. It is an indication that it has not been sufficiently beaten, so beat the icing again until very smooth and the correct consistency. A few drops of glycerine, beaten in when the icing is smooth, prevent it from becoming too hard.

753 TO PIPE CAKES

Use an icing pipe and syringe or pipe and paper bag. The best icings for piping are butter and royal. Make sure they are the right consistency – firm enough to stand up in peaks in the bowl but soft enough to handle. There is a wide range of icing pipes available – those illustrated are a small proportion, but show the various effects which can be obtained. The numbers are those on the pipes. The cake shows that simple piping can look just as effective as more elaborate piping. For superb examples of piping see the pictures accompanying Recipe No. 1065.

Satin icing

Examples of piping

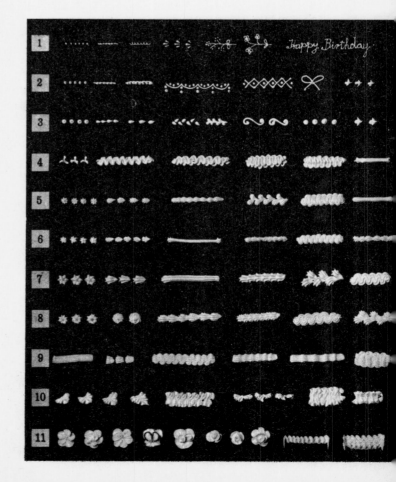

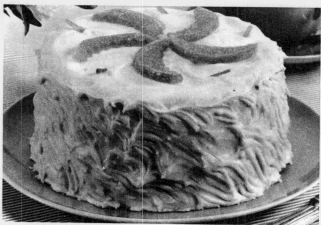
White chiffon cake

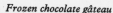
Orange and grape gâteau

754 WHITE CHIFFON CAKE

200g**/7oz self-raising flour · pinch salt
1 level teaspoon baking powder*
½ level teaspoon cream of tartar
140g**/5oz whipped-up cooking fat · 140g**/5oz castor sugar
3 egg whites · 3 tablespoons milk
glacé fudge icing (Recipe No. 749), using 100g/4 oz fat etc.
angelica and crystallised orange slices to decorate

*With plain flour use 3 level teaspoons baking powder
**Gives best result

Brush two 18-cm (7-inch) sandwich tins with melted cooking fat and line the bottoms with rounds of greaseproof paper brushed with melted fat. Sieve the flour, salt, baking powder and cream of tartar together. Cream the fat and sugar in a bowl until light and fluffy. Add the egg whites one at a time and beat thoroughly. Fold in the sieved flour and the milk. Divide the mixture between the two tins and smooth over the tops. Bake in the centre of a moderately hot oven, 375°F, 190°C, Gas Mark 5, for 25–30 minutes. Turn out to cool on a wire tray. When the cakes are cool sandwich them together with some of the icing and smooth the remainder over the top and sides. Fluff up the icing round the sides with a fork. Decorate the top with angelica and crystallised orange slices.

755 ORANGE AND GRAPE GATEAU

110g**/4oz self-raising flour · 1 level teaspoon baking powder*
2 oranges · 110g**/4oz soft margarine · 75g/3oz castor sugar
2 eggs · 142ml/¼pint double cream, whipped
approx. 100g/4oz each, green and black grapes, halved and
pips removed
4 tablespoons apricot jam, heated and sieved

*With plain flour use 2 level teaspoons baking powder
**Gives best result

Grease and flour two 18-cm (7-inch) sandwich tins. Sieve flour and baking powder into a bowl. Grate rind from the oranges and add to flour with margarine, sugar and eggs. Beat with wooden spoon until smooth, about two minutes. Place in tins and bake, just above the centre, in a moderate oven, 350°F, 180°C, Gas Mark 4, for approximately 25 minutes. Turn out and cool on a wire tray. Remove all pith from oranges with a sharp knife and cut between sections to remove segments. Spread one sandwich with cream and cover with some of the grapes, cover with other sandwich. Spread top with half the jam and arrange segments and remaining halves of grapes on top. Glaze with remaining apricot jam.

Frozen chocolate gâteau

756 FROZEN CHOCOLATE GATEAU
(Uncooked)

about 24 sponge fingers · 3 tablespoons sherry or orange squash
200g/8oz block plain or milk chocolate
4 tablespoons castor sugar · 4 tablespoons water
4 eggs · 142ml/¼pint double cream, whipped
walnuts to decorate

Put the sponge fingers on to a flat dish and sprinkle with the sherry or orange squash. Break up the chocolate. Put either into a basin or the top of a double saucepan and stand over boiling water until melted. Add the sugar, water and egg yolks and cook gently until smooth and thick. Allow to cool. Fold in the stiffly beaten egg whites. Line an 18–20-cm (7–8-inch) cake tin with waxed or greaseproof paper. Place sponge fingers at the bottom and at regular intervals round the sides of the lined tin. Pour in half the chocolate mixture. Cover with a layer of sponge fingers and then add the rest of the chocolate mixture. Top with sponge fingers and cover with waxed or greaseproof paper. Place in the refrigerator for several hours. Turn out carefully. Smooth the cream over the top and decorate with walnuts.

Mississippi show boat

757 MISSISSIPPI SHOW BOAT

Victoria sandwich (Recipe No. 700), using
225g*/8oz flour, etc.
butter icing using 170g/6oz butter, etc. (Recipe No. 751)
75g/3oz nuts, chopped · 50g/2oz glacé cherries, halved
thin strips angelica · 50g/2oz glacé orange slices, halved
2 brandy snaps (Recipe No. 786) · cotton wool
1 small flag · cocktail sticks
2 thick slices red-skinned apple · lemon juice

*You need this amount to give adequate quantity for this recipe

Make the Victoria sandwich cake mixture. Bake two-thirds of the mixture in a lined Swiss roll tin towards the top of the oven for 15–20 minutes and the remaining one-third in a 15-cm (6-inch) sandwich tin for approximately 20–25 minutes, temperature as Recipe No. 700. Make the butter icing. Cut one thin slice from the oblong piece of cake and put on one side for the 'canopy', cut the remainder of the cake into three equal pieces. From the round cake cut out an oval (as large as possible) and shape it to a point at either end. Sandwich the three equal cake layers together with butter icing, then coat completely with butter icing and chopped nuts. Place in position in centre of shaped cake. Fix glacé cherries along side of base layer with a little more butter icing. Mark division of sponge layers with thin strips of angelica, and fix orange slices along the top and bottom layer. Place two brandy snaps in position as funnels, with a little cotton wool as smoke. Support the 'canopy' on top of the 'show boat' with four cocktail sticks. Top with a small flag. Remove one-third of the apple slices and discard, brush larger portions with lemon juice. Use thin strips of angelica for wheel spokes and attach to each side of 'show boat' with a cocktail stick topped with glacé cherry.

Note: The pieces of sponge removed from the 15-cm (6-inch) round can be used in a small trifle.

758 STRAWBERRY SHORTCAKE RING

175g/7oz flour (with plain flour use 2 level teaspoons
baking powder) · 25g/1oz cornflour · pinch salt
25g/1oz butter · 25g/1oz sugar
about 142ml/¼pint milk to mix · strawberries
cream

Sieve together flour, baking powder, if used, cornflour and salt. Rub in butter to form a mixture resembling coarse crumbs, the add sugar. Mix to a smooth, elastic dough with milk and roll out thinly into an oblong shape. Damp the edges and roll up like a Swiss roll. Place on a baking sheet and form into a ring. Make 10–12 slits across the roll and twist each section, or slice, a little to its side. Brush with milk and dredge with sugar. Bake just above the centre of a hot oven, 450°F, 225°C, Gas Mark 7, for 15–20 minutes. When cold, fill the centre of the ring and the slits with strawberries and serve with cream.

759   MERINGUES

2 egg whites · 110g/4oz castor sugar or half castor sugar
and half icing sugar, sieved*

*This ensures meringues keep crisp

Whisk egg whites until stiff, fold in the sugar gradually or beat
in half the sugar and fold in rest. Then pipe or pile small spoonfuls on to a well oiled or buttered baking tin or oiled or buttered
paper on a baking tin. Bake in a very cool oven, 225°F, 110°C,
Gas Mark 0, for 2–3 hours depending on size, until crisp, but
still white. Remove from the baking sheet with a warmed
palette knife; cool, then store in an airtight tin. Before serving,
sandwich together with cream, ice cream or fruit and cream.

760   ALMOND MERINGUE FINGERS

3 egg whites · 170g/6oz sugar, half castor sugar and half
icing sugar, sieved · 50g/2oz almonds, chopped
double cream, whipped*

*This ensures meringues keep crisp

Make the meringue mixture (Recipe No. 759), then pipe the
mixture in finger shapes on to oiled baking sheets. Sprinkle
with the chopped almonds and bake in the centre of a very cool
oven, 225°F, 110°C, Gas Mark 0, until firm, about 1½ hours.
When cold, sandwich together with whipped double cream.

761   MUSHROOMS

2 egg whites · 110g/4oz sugar, half castor sugar and half
icing sugar, sieved · chocolate powder
small quantity marzipan (Recipe No. 744)*

*This ensures meringues keep crisp

Make the meringue mixture (Recipe No. 759), pipe in tiny
rounds on to oiled baking sheets and shake on a little chocolate
powder. Bake in a very cool oven, 225°F, 110°C, Gas Mark 0,
for about 1½ hours. The chocolate powder will melt slightly
and form a layer of icing. Cool on a wire tray. Make small
stalks of marzipan and stick these on to the meringue tops.

762   COFFEE MERINGUES

*2 level teaspoons soluble coffee powder
170g*/6oz sugar, half castor sugar and half icing sugar, sieved
3 egg whites*

*This ensures meringues keep crisp

Mix the coffee powder and sugars together then follow the
recipe for meringues (Recipe No. 759).

763   CHOCOLATE MERINGUES

*1 tablespoon cocoa
170g*/6oz sugar, half castor sugar and half icing sugar, sieved
3 egg whites · double cream, whipped or
chocolate-flavoured butter icing (Recipe No. 791)*

*This ensures meringues keep crisp

Mix cocoa with the sugars, then follow the recipe for almond
meringue fingers (Recipe No. 760), omitting the almonds.
When cold sandwich together with cream or butter icing.

764   NUT MERINGUES

*75g/3oz nuts, chopped
170g*/6oz sugar, half castor sugar and half icing sugar, sieved
3 egg whites*

*This ensures meringues keep crisp

Mix the nuts with the sugars and fold into the beaten egg
whites. Continue as for meringues (Recipe No. 759).

765   PEAR PAVLOVA

225g/8oz castor sugar · 25g/1oz cornflour
3 egg whites · 142ml/¼pint double cream · 2 fresh pears, sliced
little apricot jam, heated and sieved · grated chocolate
to decorate*

*This ensures meringue keeps crisp

Draw a circle, about 20-cm (8-inches) in diameter, on greaseproof paper placed on a greased baking sheet. Sieve the castor
sugar and cornflour together, twice. Whisk the egg whites
until foamy, then add half the sugar mixture and beat until
the egg white stands in peaks. Add the rest of the sugar mixture
and beat only until the sugar is well blended. Spoon the
mixture into a piping bag fitted with a large star pipe. Pipe
round the circle and over the entire centre. Pipe round the
edge, building it up to form a wail. Bake in a very slow oven,
200°F, 110°C, Gas Mark 0–¼ for 2–3 hours, until dry and
crisp. Remove from the paper while still warm and place on a
wire tray. Whip the cream until thick and spoon into the
meringue case. Arrange the pear slices on top of the cream.
Brush the pear slices with a little apricot jam. Decorate with
grated chocolate. The meringue case can be made in advance
and stored in a tin until required.

Pear pavlova

CAKES FOR SPECIAL OCCASIONS

766   SIMNEL CAKE
(For Mothering Sunday or Easter)

Use the recipe for Dundee cake (Recipe No. 710), but omit the chopped and split almonds. Make up twice the amount of marzipan given in Recipe No. 744. Roll out some of the marzipan in a round a little smaller than the diameter of the cake. Place half the cake mixture in the prepared tin, cover with the round of marzipan, then the remainder of the cake mixture. Bake as directed, but leave in the oven a little longer because of the marzipan. When cooked and cool, brush the top of the cake with egg white or sieved apricot jam. Roll out most of the remaining marzipan to a round large enough to cover the top of the cake. Place on the cake; if liked, mark the marzipan with a knife. Form the remaining marzipan into small balls and a circle for the centre. Place the balls round the edge and the circle in the centre. Brush with egg white and brown under a low grill, taking care not to burn the edges. Decorate with an Easter chick, small Easter eggs, etc.

Simnel cake

767   CHRISTENING CAKE

Use the recipe for Dundee cake (Recipe No. 710), but omit the split almonds. Cover the cake with marzipan (Recipe No. 744) and either royal or satin icing (Recipe Nos. 752, 750). Pipe the cake (using royal icing) with a border of rosettes and pipe in the same way round the base of the cake. Using a plain writing pipe, pipe the baby's name on top of the cake. With the same tube, pipe small dots as shown in the photograph. Put a stork decoration on top of the cake and tie a pale blue or pale pink ribbon round the sides.

Christening cake

768   EASTER BONNET CAKE

Victoria sandwich cake (Recipe No. 700), using 100g/4oz flour, etc. · satin icing (Recipe No. 750) 4 tablespoons apricot jam · ribbon · Easter chicks and artificial flowers to decorate

Make the sandwich cake, put into one 20-cm (8-inch) sandwich tin. Bake as Recipe No. 700. Leave to cool on a wire tray. Make the satin icing. Boil and sieve the apricot jam. Brush the top and sides of the cake with apricot jam. Roll out one third of the satin icing into a circle large enough to cover the top of the cake. Place on top and trim off any surplus. Roll out a long strip of icing for the sides. Roll up like a bandage, then cover the sides of the cake. Roll out the remainder of the icing into a long strip and trim on long side with a pastry wheel. Pleat or fold it round the outside edge of a cake board or flat plate. Lift the cake on to the centre of the board or plate. Tie the ribbon round the edge of the cake and decorate the top with Easter chicks and flowers.

Easter bonnet cake

769 CHOCOLATE VALENTINE CAKE

200 or 225g/8oz *plain flour · 4 level teaspoons baking powder*
1 tablespoon cocoa · 150 or 175g/6oz butter or margarine
150 or 175g/6oz castor sugar · 3 eggs · little milk or water
butter icing, made with 110g/4oz butter, etc. (Recipe No. 751)
1 dessertspoon cocoa · few drops vanilla essence
little cochineal · glacé icing made with 110g/4oz
icing sugar, etc. (Recipe No. 747)

Sieve the flour, baking powder and cocoa. Cream the fat and
sugar until light and fluffy. Beat in the eggs. Fold in the sieved
flour mixture and enough milk or water to form a soft dropping
consistency. Divide the mixture between two fairly large
greased heart-shaped tins and bake above centre in a moderate
oven, 350°F, 180°C, Gas Mark 4, for 30–35 minutes. Turn
out and cool on a wire tray. Make the butter icing. Add the
cocoa and vanilla essence to a quarter of it. Colour the remainder
a pale pink colour with a little cochineal. Make the glacé icing.
Sandwich the cakes together with some of the pink butter
icing. Spread the glacé icing over the top of the cake and allow
to set. Pipe a heart shape on top of the cake with chocolate
butter icing then pipe in the small dots. With the remaining
pink butter icing, pipe stars round the top edge, the centre and
the bottom edge.

Chocolate valentine cake

770 MOTHERS' DAY CAKE
(Uncooked)

½kg/1lb *wholemeal biscuits*
generous 200g/8oz *icing sugar, sieved*
½kg plus 100g/1¼lb *milk or plain chocolate*
generous 200g/8oz *table margarine*
glacé fudge icing (Recipe No. 749) · 1 rounded teaspoon cocoa
crystallised violets · ribbon

Crumble biscuits in a basin, and mix with icing sugar. Break
up chocolate, and melt with table margarine over low heat.
Stir well together, then pour over biscuit crumbs. Mix
thoroughly. Brush 20-cm (8-inch) square or 23-cm (9-inch)
round cake tin with melted margarine. Press chocolate mixture
in tin, smooth top. Leave to become firm for 2–3 hours or
overnight in a cool place. Turn out. Make the icing; take out
about a tablespoonful of icing and blend with the cocoa
powder. Cover cake with glacé fudge icing and allow to set.
Pipe the word 'MOTHER' with chocolate icing, and decorate
with crystallised violets. Tie ribbon round the outside of the
cake.

Mothers' day cake

Butterfly cake

771 BUTTERFLY CAKE
(For a birthday or special occasion)

Use the Dundee or Christmas cake recipe (Recipe Nos. 710,
777). Cover with rolled oat marzipan (Recipe No. 746) and
royal icing (Recipe No. 752). Pipe flowers round edge.
To make the butterfly, place some fairly stiff royal icing, tinted
a pale blue colour, in a piping bag fitted with a petal pipe.
Place a small square of waxed or greaseproof paper on an icing
nail and secure with a little icing. Holding the pipe horizontally, with the wider end towards you, force out some icing to
form a wing. Repeat for the opposite wing. Make the body of
the butterfly by rolling a small piece of stiff royal icing into a
long thin strip. Allow to set completely before removing from
the paper. Place on either side of the 'body' then arrange on
the cake. Make 'feelers' with icing. If liked, paint markings
on the butterfly wings with edible colouring and a fine paint
brush.

772 RICH CHOCOLATE CAKE

110g*/4oz margarine · 110g*/4oz castor sugar
1 tablespoon golden syrup (measure this carefully)
few drops vanilla essence
140g*/5oz flour (with plain flour use 1½ teaspoons
baking powder) · 40g/1½oz chocolate powder or
25g/1oz cocoa · 2 eggs · little milk to mix

*Gives best result

Cream together the margarine and sugar. Beat in the golden
syrup and vanilla essence. Sieve together the dry ingredients.
Beat the eggs well. Stir the eggs and dry ingredients alternately into the creamed mixture, add just enough milk to make
it a soft consistency. Be careful not to make the mixture too
soft, for if you do, the weight of the golden syrup will cause it
to sink in the middle. Bake in the centre of a moderate oven,
350°F, 180°C, Gas Mark 4, for 1¼ hours. Cool on a wire tray.
If liked sprinkle with icing sugar. This cake keeps well.

773 MOCHA GATEAU
(Illustrated in colour on the jacket)

Make up the Victoria sandwich mixture (Recipe No. 700),
using 200g (8 oz) flour, etc. and cook in two 20-cm (8-inch)
sandwich tins. When cold sandwich together with chocolate
butter icing (Recipe No. 791). Coat the top and sides with
mocha fudge icing (Recipe No. 775); decorate the top with
blanched almonds and mimosa balls and leave to set.

774 CHOCOLATE WALNUT SANDWICH

Make up the chocolate-flavoured Victoria sandwich mixture
(Recipe No. 701), using 200g (8 oz) flour, etc., and cook it in
two 20-cm (8-inch) sandwich tins. When cold, sandwich the
two layers together with chocolate butter icing (Recipe No.
791), made with 150g (6 oz) butter, etc. Spread chocolate
butter icing round the sides of the cake and roll in chopped
nuts. Smooth more chocolate icing over the top and pipe
round the top edge. Decorate the top with walnut halves.

775 MOCHA FUDGE ICING

100g/4oz butter or margarine · 75g/3oz granulated sugar
4 tablespoons milk · 1 tablespoon coffee essence
generous 200g/8oz icing sugar
3 level dessertspoons cocoa

Melt the butter or margarine in a saucepan. Add the granulated sugar, stir until dissolved and then bring to the boil. Add
milk and coffee essence. Stir until bubbling, then remove from
the heat and cool. Sieve the icing sugar and cocoa into a bowl.
Pour on the liquid and beat well until smooth and glossy.
Leave covered until cooled to a coating consistency.

Chocolate walnut sandwich

CAKES WITH WHOLEMEAL FLOUR

776

Any recipes in the cake or pastry sections can be made with
wholemeal flour. As wholemeal flour absorbs a little extra
liquid the cakes will take a slightly longer time to cook.
Wholemeal flour can vary in texture and it is a good idea to
reserve a little of the flour before adding to the liquid, so that
you can control the consistency of the dough or cake mixture.
The very coarse varieties of wholemeal flour can be mixed
with a proportion of white flour.
It is advisable to buy wholemeal flour in small quantities and
store it in a cool place. Try to use it fairly quickly, as the fat it
contains may go rancid if it is kept too long.

Christmas cake

777   CHRISTMAS CAKE
(This mixture makes a 23-cm (9-inch) round or 20-cm (8-inch) square cake)

340g*/12oz *plain flour* · 1 *teaspoon cinnamon*
1 *teaspoon mixed spice* · ½ *teaspoon salt*
100 or 110g*/4oz *candied peel*
100 or 110g*/4oz *glacé cherries, chopped* · 1kg/2lb *dried fruit,
preferably* ½kg/1lb *currants,* 225g*/8oz *sultanas,*
225g*/8oz *raisins*
100g/4oz *blanched almonds, chopped*
finely grated rind 1 *lemon* · 4 *eggs*
4 *tablespoons milk, sherry or brandy*
225g*/8oz *margarine or butter* · 225g*/8oz *Demerara sugar*
1 *tablespoon black treacle*

*This gives exactly the same sized cake as Imperial measurements

Sieve together all the dry ingredients. Mix peel, cherries, fruit, chopped almonds and lemon rind. Whisk the eggs and milk, sherry or brandy together. Cream the fat, sugar and black treacle until soft. Add the flour and egg mixtures alternately to the creamed mixture – do not overbeat when mixing. Lastly, stir in the fruit mixture. Put into the cake tin, lined inside with double thickness of greased paper round the sides and brown paper and greased greaseproof paper at the bottom. Tie a double band of brown paper round the outside of the tin, standing well above the top of it. Put in the middle of a very moderate oven. Bake for 3¼–3½ hours – at Gas Mark 3 for the first 1½ hours, then Gas Mark 2 for the remainder of the time. In electric oven put the cake in at 300–350°F, 150–180°C, and after 1½ hours reduce the heat to 275–300°F, 150°C. Cool in cake tin, then store in airtight tin. For a very moist cake prick the cold cake and pour over a little sherry at intervals before icing. Make this cake at least 3 weeks before Christmas. Cover with marzipan (Recipe No. 744) and royal icing (Recipe No. 752) about a week before Christmas.

Almond slices

Macaroon biscuits

778 ALMOND SLICES

200g/8oz *short crust pastry (Recipe No. 566)* · *apricot jam*
100g/4oz *castor sugar* · 100g/4oz *icing sugar*
100g/4oz *ground almonds* · 50g/2oz *semolina* · 1 *whole egg*
1 *egg white* · *few drops almond essence* · *blanched almonds*

Make the pastry, roll out and cut into two strips, approximately 26-cm (10-inches) by 7½-cm (3-inches). Transfer to a greased baking sheet and pinch up the long edges to form a thick band along both sides of each strip. Spread the base thinly with apricot jam. For the topping, mix dry ingredients together. Stir in the eggs and essence. Spread over the jam carefully. Decorate the top with the blanched almonds. Cook on second shelf from the top of a moderately hot oven, 400°F, 200°C, Gas Mark 6, for 25–30 minutes. Cool on a wire tray and when cold cut into fingers.

779 MACAROON BISCUITS

1 *egg white* * · *few drops almond essence*
65–75g/2½–3oz *castor sugar* · 65–75g/2½–3oz *ground almonds*
blanched almonds · *rice paper*

*1 egg white will make about 6 biscuits

Whisk the egg white until very stiff. Add the almond essence, then sugar and ground almonds. If the egg white is exceptionally large then work in a little more ground almonds. Roll the mixture into rounds and place, well spaced out, on baking sheets lined with rice paper. Put an almond on top of each biscuit. Bake for 20–25 minutes in the centre of a moderate oven, 350°F, 180°C, Gas Mark 4. When nearly cold, remove from the tin and tear or cut round the rice paper.

780 CHOCOLATE MACAROONS

To each egg white allow 25g (1 oz) ground almonds, 25g (1 oz) grated chocolate or chocolate powder, 15g (½ oz) ground rice. Use 75g (3 oz) sugar. Bake as for macaroons.

781 COCONUT MACAROONS

To each egg white allow 40g (1½ oz) ground almonds, 25g (1 oz) desiccated coconut and 65g (2½ oz) sugar. Bake as for macaroons.

782 CORNFLAKE MACAROONS

To each egg white allow 40g (1½ oz) ground almonds, 25g (1 oz) crushed cornflakes and 65g (2½ oz) sugar. Bake as for macaroons.

783 VIENNA FINGER MACAROONS

Follow the recipe for macaroons, but work in sufficient ground almonds to make a mixture which can be rolled out. Cut into fingers and cook as for macaroons. When cold cover with glacé icing (Recipe No. 747), flavoured with a few drops of almond essence and decorate with chopped nuts.

Chocolate cream shells

784 CHOCOLATE CREAM SHELLS

140g*/5oz *flour* · 1 *dessertspoon cocoa* · 85g*/3oz *butter*
85g*/3oz *castor sugar* · 1 *small egg*
butter icing (Recipe No. 751)

*This keeps correct proportions between flour and butter, etc.

Sieve the flour and cocoa together. Cream the butter and sugar until light and fluffy. Beat in the egg. Fold in the sieved flour mixture. Spoon the mixture into a piping bag fitted with a large star pipe. Pipe the mixture on to greased baking sheets and bake in the centre of a moderate oven, 350°F, 180°C, Gas Mark 4, for 15 minutes. Cool on a wire tray. When cold sandwich together with butter icing.

785 BRANDY SNAPS

50g/2oz flour · 50g/2oz margarine · 50g/2oz sugar
2 level tablespoons golden syrup
½ level teaspoon ground ginger

Take a teaspoon of flour away, so the scales do not give quite 50g (2 oz). Put margarine, sugar and syrup into a saucepan. Sieve flour and ginger together. Allow margarine to melt slowly, then take pan off heat and stir in the sieved flour. Grease 2 or 3 baking tins very well – do not flour. Put tea-spoonfuls of mixture on the tins, allowing about 7½ cm (3 inches) all round. As rolling the brandy snaps takes several minutes put one tray in the oven to begin with. The biscuits take 8–12 minutes to cook in a very moderate oven, 325–350°F, 170–180°C, Gas Mark 3, but you can look into the oven half-way through and again a little later. They are ready to remove when they are a uniform golden brown colour. Put a second tin in the oven after about 5 minutes, and the third after about 10 minutes. Keep trays as near the middle of the oven as possible. When the first tray comes out of the oven do not touch the biscuits for about 2 minutes, since they are very soft. Test after 2 minutes; if a palette knife can be slipped under the biscuits they are ready to roll. Grease the handle of a wooden spoon, lift biscuit from tray, and press round spoon. Hold in position for a few seconds to give the biscuit a chance to set. Slip out the handle of the spoon and put the biscuit on a wire tray. Do the same with the next biscuit. Try to work quickly with each tray as when the biscuits start to harden they cannot be removed from the tin. If this does happen to the last one or two, put the baking tin back into the oven for a minute and start testing again when you bring it out. Store, *away from all other biscuits or cakes*, in airtight tin. If liked biscuits can be filled with whipped double cream just before serving.

Brandy snaps

Oatmeal biscuits

786 VIENNESE TARTS

(Sometimes known as Swiss tarts)

100g/4oz margarine · 40g/1½oz icing sugar, sieved
50g/2oz flour · 50g/2oz cornflour
glacé icing (Recipe No. 747) or raspberry jam

Cream together margarine and icing sugar. Work in flour and cornflour then pipe into small paper cases. Bake for approximately 45 minutes in centre of a very moderate oven, 325°F, 170°C, Gas Mark 3, until pale brown. Fill centres with glacé icing or raspberry jam. If liked, dust with icing sugar.

787 OATMEAL BISCUITS

100g/4oz flour (with plain flour use 1 level teaspoon baking powder)
½ level teaspoon salt · 100g/4oz rolled oats
50g/2oz castor sugar · 75g/3oz black treacle
100g/4oz butter or margarine · coarse oatmeal to sprinkle

Sieve the flour, baking powder, if used, and salt together. Stir in the rolled oats. Put the sugar, black treacle and butter or margarine into a saucepan and heat gently until just melted. Cool slightly then add to the sieved ingredients and mix well. Press the mixture into a greased sandwich cake tin and sprinkle the surface with coarse oatmeal. Bake in the centre of a moderate oven, 350°F, 180°C, Gas Mark 4, for 20–25 minutes. Cool slightly, cut into wedges, then lift out carefully and complete cooling on a wire tray.

Flapjacks

791 CHOCOLATE BUTTER ICING or BUTTER CREAM

75g/3oz butter or margarine · 75g/3oz icing sugar, sieved
25g/1oz chocolate powder

Cream fat well. Beat in the icing sugar and chocolate powder.

792 MELTING MOMENTS

75g/3oz butter · 50g/2oz icing sugar · 50g/2oz plain flour
50g/2oz cornflour · chocolate butter cream (Recipe No. 791)
little melted chocolate, optional

Cream together butter and sugar until very soft and light.
Sieve flour and cornflour together. Work into the butter and
sugar mixture, put into a piping bag, fitted with a large star
pipe. Pipe in neat shapes, on to a greased baking sheet. Bake in
the centre of a very moderate oven, 350°F, 180°C, Gas Mark
4, for 15 minutes. Cool on the baking sheet. When cold sandwich together with butter cream. If liked, dip the ends in
melted chocolate.

793 CHOCOLATE MELTING MOMENTS

Follow the recipe for melting moments, but replace half the
flour with cocoa.

794 PENNY WISE MACAROONS

50g/2oz flour · 50g/2oz quick-cooking rolled oats
100g/4oz sugar · 2 egg whites · 100g/4oz icing sugar, sieved
juice ½ lemon

Mix flour, rolled oats and sugar together. Work in 1 egg white.
Roll out, on a board sprinkled with sugar, to about ½-cm (¼-
inch) thick. Cut into fingers or rounds. Mix the icing sugar
with the remaining egg white and the lemon juice. Beat until
smooth. Cover biscuits with thin layer of the icing and transfer
to a greased baking sheet. Bake in a cool oven, 300°F, 150°C,
Gas Mark 2, for 10–15 minutes. Allow to cool on the baking
sheet.

795 LOLLIPOPS

190g*/7oz self-raising flour (with plain flour use 1½ level
teaspoons baking powder)
pinch salt · ½ teaspoon bicarbonate of soda
75g/3oz soft brown sugar · 65g/2½oz margarine
½ teaspoon vanilla essence · 3 tablespoons milk
50g/2oz quick-cooking rolled oats
greengage, strawberry and apricot jam
wooden skewers or lollipop sticks · glacé icing (Recipe No. 747)

*Gives right consistency

Mix flour, salt, bicarbonate of soda and sugar together. Rub in
the margarine; add the vanilla essence and milk. Knead for
about 2 minutes. Add oats and knead well. Roll out to ¼-cm
(⅛-inch) thick on a floured board. Cut into 12 rounds with an
8½-cm (3½-inch) fluted cutter. Place on baking sheets and
spread with a thin layer of jam. Press skewers lightly into the
jam. Roll out the trimmings and cut into small rounds. Press
one on to each jam-covered round. Bake in a moderate oven,
350°F, 180°C, Gas Mark 4, for 10–12 minutes. Remove from
tin and cool on a wire tray. Decorate with glacé icing.

788 FLAPJACKS

150g/6oz butter or margarine · 150g/6oz Demerara sugar
200g/8oz quick-cooking rolled oats · pinch salt

Melt the fat in a saucepan over a very gentle heat. Mix in the
sugar, oats and salt. Stir well and turn the mixture into a well
greased Swiss roll tin and press lightly together. Smooth the
surface with a knife and bake in the centre of a moderate oven,
350°F, 180°C, Gas Mark 4, for 30–35 minutes. Leave in the
tin for a few minutes, then cut into squares or fingers. Leave
in the tin until quite cold.
For a more moist flapjack use 75g (3 oz) Demerara sugar and
3 tablespoons golden syrup instead of all sugar.

789 SPICED WALNUT FLAPJACKS

Follow the recipe for flapjacks, but add 50g (2 oz) chopped
walnuts and 1 teaspoon mixed spice with the oats.

790 ACE BISCUITS

75g/3oz flour · 25g/1oz cornflour · ½ teaspoon baking powder
pinch salt · 50g/2oz margarine · 50g/2oz sugar
1 level tablespoon cocoa · 1 teaspoon coffee essence
milk to mix · glacé icing (Recipe No. 747)
chocolate butter icing (Recipe No. 791)

Sieve flour, cornflour, baking powder and salt. Rub in the
margarine. Mix in the sugar and cocoa. Add the coffee
essence and enough milk to form a stiff dough. Knead lightly
and roll out on a floured board. Cut into heart, diamond and
other card shapes and place on a greased baking sheet. Bake
in the centre of a moderate oven, 350°F, 180°C, Gas Mark 4,
for 10–15 minutes. Cool on a wire tray. When cold decorate
with various coloured glacé icings and pipe with chocolate
butter icing.

Cherry and walnut cookies

796 CHERRY AND WALNUT COOKIES

75g/3oz flour (with plain flour use ¾ teaspoon baking powder)
40g/1½oz margarine · 40g/1½oz soft brown sugar
40g/1½oz granulated sugar · few drops vanilla essence
1 small egg · 25g/1oz walnuts, chopped
25g/1oz glacé cherries, chopped

Sieve the flour and baking powder, if used. Cream the margarine and sugars together. Beat in the vanilla essence and egg. Fold in the sieved flour, walnuts and cherries. Place teaspoonfuls of the mixture, well apart, on greased baking sheets. Bake in the centre of a moderate oven, 350°F, 180°C, Gas Mark 4, for 10–12 minutes, until crisp and golden brown. Remove and cool on a wire tray. Store in an airtight tin or jar.

797 ALMOND ROSETTES

50g/2oz butter · 75g/3oz castor sugar
50g/2oz icing sugar, sieved · 50g/2oz flour
few drops almond essence · 100g/4oz ground almonds
1 egg, beaten · glacé cherries or chopped nuts to decorate

Cream together butter and sugars. Work in the flour, almond essence and ground almonds; add enough egg to give a consistency soft enough to pipe. Spoon the mixture into a piping bag fitted with a large star pipe. Pipe into rosette shapes on to a lightly greased baking sheet. Decorate with tiny pieces of cherry or nut, and bake in the centre of a very moderate oven, 325°F, 170°C, Gas Mark 3, for about 15 minutes. Cool on the baking sheet.

Waffle biscuits

Chocolate crisps

Jelly biscuits

798 JELLY BISCUITS

50g/2oz quick-cooking rolled oats · 100g/4oz flour
50g/2oz castor sugar · 50g/2oz butter or margarine · jelly
sieved icing sugar

Mix rolled oats, flour and sugar on a pastry board. Work in the butter or margarine. Roll out to about ½-cm (¼-inch) thick and cut into oval shapes. From half of the oval shapes cut out two small ovals. Place on an ungreased baking sheet and bake in centre of a moderately hot oven, 375°F, 190°C, Gas Mark 5, for 10–12 minutes. Cool on the baking sheet. When cool, spread the ovals with redcurrant, bramble, black grape or some other jelly; dredge the biscuits with the cut-out shapes with icing sugar. Place these on top of the ovals.

799 WAFFLE BISCUITS

200g/8oz rich flan pastry (Recipe No. 576)
200g/8oz almond paste (Recipe No. 744) · 1 egg white
125g/5oz icing sugar, sieved · 3–4 tablespoons jam

Make the pastry, roll out and line a Swiss roll tin. Bake 'blind' (Recipe No. 560) for about 30 minutes in a very moderate oven, 325°F, 170°C, Gas Mark 3. Meanwhile break the almond paste up and place in the top section of a double saucepan with boiling water underneath. Stir with a wooden spoon over the heat until soft and pliable. Remove, stir in the egg white and sieved icing sugar. Return to the heat and stir over the boiling water for 2–3 minutes longer. Remove and beat well. Put into a large piping bag fitted with a small star pipe. Pipe a lattice pattern all over the pastry in diamond shapes keeping the lines of almond paste mixture about ⅓-cm (⅛-inch) apart. Return to a moderately hot oven, 400°F, 200°C, Gas Mark 6, and cook for 10 minutes. Remove and cool. Boil the jam for 2–3 minutes, sieve if necessary, and cool. Put into a piping bag fitted with a small, plain pipe, and pipe into the empty spaces on the biscuits. If jams of different flavours and colours are used pipe separately into alternate spaces, or use for separate sections of the biscuits. Leave until cold and firm, then with a sharp knife, cut into fingers.

800 CHOCOLATE CRISPS

100g/4oz margarine · 75g/3oz castor sugar
few drops vanilla essence
125g/5oz self-raising flour (with plain flour use 1¼ level
teaspoons baking powder)
50g/2oz chocolate dots · 1 egg
3–4 tablespoons crushed cornflakes

Cream the margarine, sugar and vanilla essence together until light and fluffy. Add the flour and chocolate dots, stir well, then gradually add enough beaten egg to give a soft rolling consistency. Form the mixture into approximately 12–14 small balls: if slightly sticky damp your fingers. Toss in the crushed cornflakes. Place, well apart, on greased baking sheets and bake near the centre of a moderate oven, 350°F, 180°C, Gas Mark 4, for 15 minutes. Cool on a wire tray.

Shortbread

801   SHORTBREAD
(Rich recipe)

75g/3oz butter or soft margarine · 40–50g/1½–2oz sugar
75g/3oz plain flour · 25g/1oz cornflour or rice flour

Cream butter or margarine and half sugar, work in flour and cornflour or rice flour, then the remaining sugar. Knead well, then press into a flan ring placed on an ungreased baking sheet or into a floured shortbread mould; or roll thinly and cut into fingers or rounds. Cook for 40 minutes, if in a round, in centre of a slow oven, 300–325°F, 150–170°C, Gas Mark 2. For shortbread fingers or rounds cook for about 20 minutes in the centre of a moderate oven, 350°F, 180°C, Gas Mark 4. Cool on tin.

802   PEACH SUNFLOWER

Cover a round of cooked shortbread (Recipe Nos. 801, 805) with ice cream and sliced peaches. Decorate with chopped nuts and serve at once.

803   SUNFLOWER SHORTCAKE

100g/4oz table margarine · 75g/3oz castor sugar
150g/6oz plain flour · 1 medium-sized can peach halves
4 strawberries · 2 rounded teaspoons arrowroot
284ml/½pint fruit juice · yellow colouring
few blanched almonds

Cream together margarine and sugar until light and fluffy. Beat in sieved flour until smooth. Brush a 20-cm (8-inch) sandwich tin with melted margarine. Press mixture into tin, and smooth top. Bake in a moderate oven, 350°F, 180°C, Gas Mark 4, for 25–30 minutes. Remove and cool on a wire tray. Drain peaches (reserve 284ml (½ pint) fruit juice) and slice thinly, keeping a half uncut for centre. Arrange peach slices around the edge of the shortcake, overlapping each other. Place the uncut half peach in the centre. Cut the strawberries in quarters and arrange round centre with pointed ends upwards in a ring. Blend arrowroot with fruit juice in a saucepan, bring to the boil, and boil for 2–3 minutes, stirring continuously. Remove and stir in a little yellow colouring. Coat fruit with arrowroot glaze. Slice almonds thinly lengthways and stick into centre peach.
Makes 6–8 servings.

Raisin shortbread

804   RAISIN SHORTBREAD

4 tablespoons orange squash or canned orange juice
100g/4oz seedless raisins · 150g/6oz plain flour
50g/2oz castor sugar · 100g/4oz butter

Put the orange squash or juice and raisins in a saucepan and bring slowly to the boil. Turn into a bowl and leave to cool, preferably overnight. Sieve the flour into a bowl, add sugar and rub in the butter until the mixture resembles fine breadcrumbs. Knead the dough thoroughly and divide into two. Form into equal sized rounds and roll lightly to give a neat shape. Place one round on a baking sheet; spread raisins over surface, and top with second round, pressing down firmly. Pinch edges together; prick the surface. Bake in the centre of a very moderate oven, 325°F, 170°C, Gas Mark 3, for about 45 minutes, until crisp and golden brown. Mark into segments and leave on baking sheet to cool.

805   ECONOMICAL SHORTBREAD

50g/2oz margarine · 25g/1oz sugar · 100g/4oz flour

Slightly melt margarine, then work in other ingredients. Proceed as for Recipe No. 801, but bake for 25 minutes only at 325°F, 170°C, Gas Mark 3.

BREAD & SCONES

In this chapter you will find recipes for breads with yeast and also recipes for breads and scones not using yeast as the raising agent. Do not be frightened by the mention of yeast if you have not used it before, as it is very straightforward and enables you to produce economical buns as well as breads.

806 WHITE BREAD

½kg/1lb *plain flour* · 3–7 *level teaspoons salt*
50g/2oz *margarine* · 15g/½oz *fresh yeast*
284ml/½pint *tepid milk and water*
melted margarine, milk or egg and water for brushing

Sieve the flour and salt into a mixing bowl. Rub in the margarine. Blend the yeast into the milk and water. Mix dry ingredients with yeast liquid using a wooden spoon. Work to a firm dough, adding extra flour if needed, until sides of bowl are clean. Turn dough on to a lightly floured table and knead thoroughly until it is firm, elastic and no longer sticky. It will take about 10 minutes. Shape dough into a ball and place in a lightly greased large polythene bag, loosely tied, or leave in a mixing bowl and cover lightly with a cloth. Allow to rise until doubled in size and dough springs back when pressed with a floured finger. Choose rising time to fit in with the day's plan, 45–60 minutes in a warm place, 2 hours at average room temperature; up to 12 hours in a cold larder or room; up to 24 hours in a refrigerator. Return refrigerator-risen dough to room temperature 1 hour before shaping. Turn risen dough on to a lightly floured surface, flatten to knock out air bubbles and knead to make firm. Form into loaves and put into warmed and lightly greased loaf tins, half filling them. To give a crisp crust, brush over with a little melted margarine, milk or egg and water. Leave in a warm place to prove for about 20 minutes. Bake in the centre of a hot oven, 425–450°F, 220–230°C, Gas Mark 6–7, for 10 minutes. Then lower the heat to 350°F, 180°C, Gas Mark 4 and bake for a further 35–40 minutes. When cooked the loaves should sound hollow when tapped underneath. Cool on a wire tray, away from a draught.

This is a basic recipe for bread. If you are using brown flour (i.e. equal quantities of white and wholemeal flour) you will find you need a little more liquid – with wholemeal flour, even more. The amount of salt varies a great deal according to personal taste. For the first time try the smaller quantity. Do not be alarmed by the terms used in bread making. 'Proving' simply means allowing the dough to rise; this must not be done too quickly or at too high a temperature otherwise the yeast (which is a living organism), unlike baking powder and other raising agents, will be killed.

807 SUCCESS WITH BREAD MAKING

This depends on correct handling of the dough and using really fresh yeast (unless using the dried variety, in which case use half the amount indicated for fresh yeast). If yeast is fresh it should be crumbly, have a pleasant smell and be a pale putty colour. Keep all the ingredients and utensils warm, BUT NOT too hot.
Kneading should be done lightly, but firmly. The dough is sufficiently kneaded if, when pressed firmly the finger mark comes out. If the impression stays in the dough, then continue kneading.
Obviously a correct metric conversion is important to give the same result. Where ½kg is given as the equivalent of 1lb (it is really 1·1lb) you will need a little extra liquid to compensate for the extra flour, *but* no recipe using yeast can be too dictatorial about the amount of liquid required as flours vary in the quantity they absorb.
Where grammes are given in place of ounces I have indicated when a better result is obtained by using a conversion other than 25g = 1oz.

808 BREAD WITH DRIED YEAST

Use half the amount indicated for fresh yeast. Mix with 1 teaspoon sugar and a little tepid liquid. Allow to stand in warm place until frothy – about 20 minutes. Continue after this as for fresh yeast.

809 SHAPING BREAD

After you have tried ordinary tin loaves, i.e. cooking in loaf tins, you will be anxious to make more ambitious shapes. The approximate weights refer to the dough (i.e. weight of flour plus water, etc.). In the picture opposite you will find the following:

Crown loaf (*Top left hand corner*)
Take just *under* a quarter of the bread dough and divide it into 6 pieces about 50g (2 oz) each. Work each piece to form a smooth ball. Place five to form a ring in a greased 15-cm (6-inch) sandwich tin and place the sixth in the centre. Brush with beaten egg and milk and sprinkle with poppy seeds. To prevent outside becoming too firm place tin inside a lightly greased large polythene bag or cover lightly with a cloth and allow to rise until doubled in size and dough springs back when pressed with a floured finger. Remove polythene bag or cloth and bake the bread at 450°F, 230°C, Gas Mark 8, for 30–40 minutes; reduce heat to moderate after 15–20 minutes when the bread starts to brown. Turn out and cool on a wire tray.

Bumpy loaf (*Top right hand corner*)
Take a third of the remaining dough, approx. ½kg (1lb) made with half white flour and half wholemeal flour – and divide into four. Roll into rounds using palm of one hand. Press down hard at first and then ease up. This is best done on an unfloured board with a little flour on palm of hand only. Place the four rolls side by side in a well greased ½kg (1lb) loaf tin. Put inside a lightly greased large polythene bag or cover lightly with a cloth and leave to rise until dough comes to top of tin and springs back when pressed with a floured finger. Remove the polythene bag or cloth. Bake in the centre of a

Crown loaf, bumpy loaf, flower pot loaf, lattice coburg, poppy seed twist (Recipe No. 809)

hot oven, 450°F, 230°C, Gas Mark 8, for 30–40 minutes, lowering the heat to moderate after 15–20 minutes. Turn out and cool on a wire tray.

Flower pot loaf (*Centre left*)

Take just under a quarter of the dough (made with half white flour and half wholemeal flour). Shape to half fill a well greased 13-cm (5-inch) new earthenware flower pot.* Brush the top with salt and water and sprinkle with crushed corn-flakes or cracked wheat. Put inside a greased polythene bag or cover lightly with a cloth and leave to rise until the dough has doubled in size and springs back when lightly pressed with a floured finger. Remove polythene bag or cloth. Bake in the centre of hot oven, 450°F, 230°C, Gas Mark 8, for 30–40 minutes, lowering the heat to moderate after 15–20 minutes. Turn out and cool on a wire tray.

To prevent the loaf from sticking, grease the flower pot well before using and bake it empty in a hot oven.

Lattice coburg (*Centre right*)

Take ½kg (1lb) of dough and divide into two. Shape each half into a round and place in two greased 15-cm (6-inch) sandwich tins Slash the surface with a sharp knife to form a lattice. Place in lightly greased polythene bags or cover lightly with a cloth and allow to rise until doubled in size and dough springs back when pressed with a floured finger. Remove the cover from the dough or take out of the polythene bags. Bake in the centre of a hot oven, 450°F, 230°C, Gas Mark 8, for 30–40 minutes, lowering the heat to moderate after 15–20 minutes, until the loaves sound hollow when tapped underneath, and are golden brown. Cool on a wire tray.

Poppy seed twist (*Centre bottom*)

Take ½kg (1lb) of dough, divide into two equal pieces, and roll into two strands about 36 cm (14 inches) long. Arrange the two strands in a cross on the board. Take the two opposite ends of the bottom strand and cross them over in the centre. Repeat this with the other strand. Cross each strand alternately until all the dough is used up. Finally gather the short ends together and lay the plait on its side. Place the plait on a lightly greased baking sheet, brush with beaten egg and milk and sprinkle with poppy seeds. Put inside a lightly greased polythene bag or cover lightly with a cloth and allow to rise until doubled in size. Remove the cover or polythene bag. Bake in the centre of a hot oven, 450°F, 230°C, Gas Mark 8, for 30–40 minutes, lowering the heat to moderate after 15–20 minutes when the bread starts to brown. Cool on a wire tray.

FANCY YEAST BREADS

810 ORANGE BREAD

15g/½oz *fresh yeast* · 1 *level teaspoon sugar*
2 *tablespoons tepid water* · 50g/2oz *lard* · 1 *teaspoon salt*
2 *level tablespoons golden syrup* · 25g/1oz *brown sugar*
75g/3oz *quick-cooking rolled oats* · *grated rind* 1 *orange*
6 *tablespoons boiling water* · *juice* 1 *orange*
350g*/12oz *plain flour* · *crystallised orange slices
to decorate*

In this particular recipe gives better result than 300g

Cream yeast and sugar; add the tepid water. Set in warm place until bubbly. Mix lard, salt, syrup, brown sugar, oats and grated orange rind in a large bowl. Measure the boiling water and orange juice and if necessary add cold water to give a total of 142ml (¼pint). Pour into the rolled oats, etc., then blend in the yeast mixture. Add flour gradually and mix to soft dough. You may require just a little extra liquid. Knead dough on floured board until smooth. Place in greased bowl and brush with melted fat. Cover and leave to rise in warm place until doubled in size, about 1 hour. Shape dough into a loaf and place in greased loaf tin. Leave to prove until doubled in bulk. Sprinkle a few oats on the top and bake in the centre of a hot oven, 425–450°F, 220–230°C, Gas Mark 6–7, for 15 minutes, reduce temperature to moderate, 350°F, 180°C, Gas Mark 4, and bake for a further 30 minutes. Remove from tin and cool on a wire tray. Decorate the top with crystallised orange slices.

811 RICH FRUIT LOAF

100g/4oz *margarine* · 1kg/2lb *plain flour* · *pinch salt*
125g/5oz *currants* · 125g/5oz *sultanas*
75g/3oz *candied peel* · 50–75g/2–3oz *sugar*
really good 25g/1oz *fresh yeast* · 2 *eggs*
approx. 426ml/¾pint *tepid milk or milk and water*
2 *tablespoons sugar and water to glaze*

Rub margarine into the sieved flour and salt; add fruit and all but a teaspoon of the sugar. Cream yeast with the teaspoon of sugar; add to the beaten eggs and warm milk. Set aside in a warm place for about 10 minutes, until frothy. Add to the rest of the ingredients and mix to form a dough. Turn on to a floured board and knead. Put to rise until doubled in size. Put into two large loaf tins and allow to prove in a warm place for 20 minutes. Bake in centre of hot oven, 425–450°F, 220–230°C, Gas Mark 6–7, reducing the heat after the first 10 minutes to moderately hot, 375°F, 190°C, Gas Mark 5, for 40–50 minutes. Brush with a glaze made with the sugar and water as soon as the loaves come out of the oven. Cool on a wire tray.

Orange bread

812 BREAKFAST ROLLS

Batter
125g/5oz *plain flour* · 1 *level teaspoon sugar*
15g/½oz *fresh yeast* · scant 284ml/½pint *tepid milk*

Dough
. 275g/11oz *plain flour* · 1 *level teaspoon salt*
50g/2oz *margarine* · 1 *egg* · *little beaten egg to glaze*

Although you use the usual proportions etc. here, this method gives a good result; you have two mixtures, a 'batter' and then the dough.

Blend the batter ingredients together in a large bowl. Set aside until frothy – 20 minutes in a warm place, longer in a cool one. Mix the remaining flour with salt and rub in margarine. Add egg and flour mixture to the batter and mix well to give a fairly soft dough that leaves sides of bowl clean. Turn dough on to a lightly floured surface and knead until smooth and no longer sticky – about 10 minutes. No extra flour should be necessary. Place dough in a lightly greased polythene bag, loosely tied, or cover lightly with a cloth and allow to rise until doubled in size and dough springs back when pressed gently with a floured finger. Rising times can be varied to suit your convenience: for a quick rise 45–60 minutes in a warm place, for a slower rise 2 hours at average room temperature or for an overnight rise up to 12 hours in a cold room, larder or refrigerator. Refrigerated dough must be returned to room temperature 1 hour before shaping. Turn dough on to a floured surface and knead lightly. Divide into 50g (2 oz) pieces and shape into plaits, round rolls, crescents and miniature cottage loaves. (To make cottage loaves, form the dough into 2 rounds – one considerably smaller than the other. Press the small round on top of the larger and make a deep thumb mark in the middle of the top round). Place on greased baking sheets and leave in a warm place for 15–20 minutes. Brush with beaten egg and bake above the centre of a hot oven, 425°F, 220°C, Gas Mark 7, for 15–20 minutes.

Breakfast rolls

813 PLAITED TEA LOAF

Make up the breakfast roll dough (Recipe No. 812) and form into 3 long strips and plait loosely. Place on a greased baking sheet, leave to rise in a warm place for 20–25 minutes, then bake in the centre of a hot oven, 425–450°F, 220–230°C, Gas Mark 6–7, for 5 minutes, then lower the heat to 375°F, 190°C, Gas Mark 5, and bake for a further 20 minutes. Cool on a wire tray.

BREADS & MUFFINS WITHOUT YEAST

Cheese and walnut loaf

814 CHEESE AND WALNUT LOAF

225g*/8oz *flour (with plain flour use 2 teaspoons baking powder)*
1 *level teaspoon dry mustard* · 1 *level teaspoon salt*
good pinch pepper · *generous* 100g/4oz *butter or margarine*
generous 100g/4oz *Cheddar cheese, finely grated*
25g/1oz *walnuts, chopped* · 2 *eggs*
approx. 142ml/¼pint *milk*

* Gives best result

Sieve together flour, baking powder, if used, mustard, salt and pepper, then rub in butter or margarine until mixture resembles fine breadcrumbs. Add cheese and walnuts, then mix to a soft dropping consistency with beaten eggs and milk. Turn into well greased loaf tin and bake in moderate oven, 375°F, 190°C, Gas Mark 5, for about 1 hour. Turn out and cool on a wire tray. When cold, cut in slices and spread with butter. Serve with cheese and salad.

815 ORANGE HONEY TEA BREAD

25g/1oz *margarine* · 150g/6oz *honey* · 1 *egg*
150g/6oz *self-raising flour (with plain flour use 2½ teaspoons
baking powder)* · 1 *level teaspoon baking powder*
1 *level teaspoon salt* · 6 *tablespoons milk*
1 *heaped tablespoon finely chopped nuts*
grated rind 1 large orange*
2 *teaspoons extra honey to glaze bread*

* *Use the zest of fruit only, i.e. coloured part of rind, not the bitter pith*

Cream margarine, gradually adding honey and mixing
together thoroughly. Add the egg and beat until bubbles
appear. Sieve together flour, baking powder and salt. Add to
creamed mixture alternately with milk. Stir in chopped nuts
and ⅔ of the orange rind. Line a loaf tin about 20 cm (8 inches)
by 10 cm (4 inches) with greaseproof paper, and spoon in the
mixture. Smooth the top and bake in centre of a moderate
oven, 350°F, 180°C, Gas Mark 4, for 45 minutes – 1 hour.
Then brush top with 2 teaspoons melted honey and sprinkle
with remaining orange rind, and bake for another 5–7 minutes
until the glaze is set. Remove from oven, leave for 5 minutes,
remove from tin and allow to become quite cold on a wire tray
before cutting. If wrapped in greaseproof paper, the loaf will
keep moist for a week.

816 HOT FRUITY MUFFINS

225g*/8oz *flour (with plain flour use 3 level teaspoons baking
powder)* · ½ *level teaspoon mixed spice*
50g/2oz *cooking fat* · 25g/1oz *margarine* · 25g/1oz *sugar*
50g/2oz *sultanas* · 1 *egg* · 1 *medium-sized cooking apple*

* *Gives best result*

Sieve together flour, baking powder, if used, and spice. Rub
in fats and add sugar and sultanas. Mix to a soft dough with
egg and peeled and finely grated apple. Turn on to a lightly
floured board, knead quickly and roll out to 1-cm (½-inch)
thickness; cut into rounds 9 cm (3½ inches) in diameter and
place on well greased baking sheets and bake above the centre
of a hot oven, 425–450°F, 220–230°C, Gas Mark 6–7, for 15
minutes. Split open, spread with butter and sprinkle with
brown sugar. Serve hot.

817 CREAM MUFFINS

Use above recipe but bind with egg and a little single cream
instead of egg and grated apple.

818 CHEESE AND RAISIN MUFFINS

50g/2oz *Cheddar cheese* · 50g/2oz *seedless raisins*
225g*/8oz *flour (with plain flour use 2 teaspoons baking
powder)* · ½ *level teaspoon salt* · ½ *level teaspoon dry mustard
pinch pepper* · 100g/4oz *soft margarine* · 1 *egg*
6–8 *tablespoons milk*

* *Gives best result*

Grate cheese and chop raisins, if large. Sieve flour, baking
powder, if used, salt, mustard and pepper into a bowl. Rub in
the margarine until mixture resembles fine breadcrumbs. Stir
in cheese and raisins. Mix to a fairly soft dough with the egg
and milk, beating with a wooden spoon. Put the mixture in 18
well greased bun tins. Bake in a moderately hot oven, 400°F,
200°C, Gas Mark 6, for 15–20 minutes. Split open while still
warm; spread with butter and serve immediately.

Orange honey tea bread

Hot fruity muffins

Cheese and raisin muffins

819   BILBERRY BREAD

300g/10oz *plain flour* · 1 *level teaspoon baking powder*
1 *level teaspoon bicarbonate of soda* · *pinch salt*
50g/2oz *quick-cooking rolled oats* · 75g/3oz *butter*
100g/4oz *light brown sugar* · 2 *eggs*
284ml/½pint *buttermilk** · 100g/4oz *walnuts, chopped*
100g/4oz *fresh or frozen bilberries***
142ml/¼pint *THICK apple purée****

* Or use fresh milk with a few drops of vinegar or lemon juice added
** These are often called blueberries or whortleberries
***Made by baking, not stewing, apples

Sieve the flour, baking powder, bicarbonate of soda and salt
together. Mix in the oats. Cream together the butter and sugar.
Beat in the eggs and buttermilk. Make a well in the centre of
the flour mixture and pour in the egg mixture. Mix with a
wooden spoon until well blended. Fold in the nuts, bilberries
(allow frozen ones to defrost and *drain well*) and apple purée.
Pour into a greased large loaf tin and bake in the centre of a
moderate oven, 325°F, 170°C, Gas Mark 3, for about 1 hour,
until golden brown and firm to the touch. Cool for a while in
the tin before turning out on to a wire tray. When cold, slice and
spread with butter.

Bilberry bread

820   BANANA BREAD

200g/8oz *flour (with plain flour use 3 level teaspoons
baking powder)* · *pinch salt*
50g/2oz *margarine or vegetable shortening* · 1 *egg*
50g/2oz *sugar* · *grated rind 1 lemon*
3 *medium-sized bananas, mashed* · *milk*

Sieve the flour, baking powder, if used, and salt together. Rub
in the margarine then add the egg, sugar, lemon rind and
mashed bananas. Mix thoroughly. If necessary add sufficient
milk to give soft consistency. Put into greased and floured loaf
tin and bake in centre of moderate oven, 350°F, 180°C, Gas
Mark 4, for about 45 minutes. Leave in the tin for about 5
minutes, then turn out and cool on a wire tray.

821   DATE AND WALNUT BREAD

225g*/8oz *flour (with plain flour use 2 teaspoons baking powder)*
1 *level teaspoon bicarbonate of soda* · 50g/2oz *sugar*
25g/1oz *margarine* · 350g*/12oz *dates, chopped*
142ml/¼pint *water* · 1 *egg* · 100g/4oz *walnuts, chopped*

* Gives best result

Sieve the dry ingredients. Put the sugar, margarine and dates
into a basin. Boil the water and pour over the sugar, etc. Allow
to cool. Stir in the dry ingredients, egg and nuts. Put into
20-cm (8-inch) greased cake tin or small loaf tin and bake in
centre of moderate oven, 350°F, 180°C, Gas Mark 4, for about
50 minutes. Cool on a wire tray. When cold, slice and spread
with butter.

822   ORANGE BANANA BREAD

Follow the recipe for banana bread (Recipe No. 820), but
instead of lemon rind add the grated rind of 2 oranges and mix
with a little orange juice instead of milk.

823   RAISIN BREAD

Follow the recipe for date and walnut bread (Recipe No. 821),
but add 200g (8 oz) large raisins, chopped, instead of dates.
Nuts can be added if liked.

824   SODA BREAD

about 25g/1oz *margarine** · 225g**/8oz *plain flour*
pinch salt · 1 *level teaspoon bicarbonate of soda*
1 *level teaspoon cream of tartar* · 142ml/¼pint *milk****

* This is not essential, but helps to keep the bread moist
** Gives best result
***Use buttermilk or sour milk if available but omit the cream of tartar

Rub the margarine into the flour. Add the salt, dissolve the
bicarbonate of soda and cream of tartar in the milk, add to the
flour. Knead lightly and form into a round loaf. Place on a
baking sheet and bake in the centre of a very hot oven, 475°F,
240°C, Gas Mark 8, for 15 minutes, then lower the heat to
moderately hot, 375°F, 190°C, Gas Mark 5, and bake for a
further 10–15 minutes.

BUNS & SCONES

Chelsea buns

825   BATH BUNS

15g/½oz *fresh yeast* · 50g/2oz *sugar*
scant 142ml/¼pint *tepid milk* · scant 350g*/12oz *plain flour*
100g/4oz *margarine* · *good pinch salt*
100g/4oz *mixed dried fruit* · 50g/2oz *candied peel*
2 *eggs or* 3 *egg yolks, beaten* · 4 *or* 5 *sugar lumps*

* *Gives best result*

Cream yeast with 1 teaspoon of the sugar. Add the milk and a sprinkling of flour. Put into a warm place for about 20 minutes for the 'sponge to break through'. Meanwhile rub margarine into flour and salt; add sugar, fruit and peel. Work in yeast liquid and eggs. The mixture should be just firm enough to handle, but definitely softer than most buns, bread or rolls. It may be necessary to add a little more tepid milk. Allow to prove for 1 hour, then knead again and form into 12 round shapes. Put on to warmed, greased baking sheets, allowing room to spread. Break lumps of sugar with a rolling pin and sprinkle on top of buns. Prove for 15 minutes in a warm place, then bake above the centre of a hot oven, 425–450°F, 220–230°C, Gas Mark 6–7, for 15 minutes.

826   FRUIT BUNS

15g/½oz *fresh yeast* · 25–50g/1–2oz *sugar*
generous 142ml/¼pint *tepid water, milk and water or milk*
350g*/12oz *plain flour* · *pinch salt* · 25g/1oz *margarine*
50–100g/2–4oz *mixed dried fruit* · 25–50g/1–2oz *candied peel*
25g/1oz *sugar and* 1 *tablespoon water for glaze*

**Gives best result*

Cream yeast with 1 teaspoon of the sugar. Add tepid liquid and a sprinkling of flour. Put into a warm place for about 20 minutes. Meanwhile sieve flour and salt into a warm bowl, rub in margarine; add sugar, fruit and peel. Then work in yeast liquid and knead thoroughly. Put into a warm place for about 1 hour, until doubled in size. Form into round buns, place on warmed, greased baking sheets and prove for 15 minutes. Bake near the top of a very hot oven, 450°F, 230°C, Gas Mark 8, for 10 minutes. Mix the sugar with the water and glaze the buns immediately they come out of the oven.

827   HOT CROSS BUNS

350g*/12oz *plain flour* · *good pinch salt*
1 *teaspoon mixed spice* · 15g/½oz *fresh yeast*
25–50g/1–2oz *sugar*
about 200ml*/generous ¼pint *tepid water, milk and water or milk* · 25g/1oz *margarine*
100g/4oz *mixed dried fruit* · 50g/2oz *candied peel*
25g/1oz *sugar and* 1 *tablespoon water for glaze*

* *Gives best result*

Sieve the flour, salt and mixed spice together. Proceed as for fruit buns (Recipe No. 826), proving for 15 minutes. The cross should be marked before proving. Do this with the back of a knife or by cutting thin strips of pastry and arranging on the top. Bake near the top of a very hot oven, 450°F, 230°C, Gas Mark 8, for 10 minutes. If buns are to be eaten straight away dissolve the 25g (1 oz) sugar in the tablespoon of water, and use to glaze the buns. If, as so often happens, they are to be reheated on Good Friday, glaze the buns after reheating.

828   CHELSEA BUNS

15g/½oz *fresh yeast* · 100g/4oz *sugar*
142ml/¼pint *tepid milk or milk and water*
scant 350g*/12oz *plain flour* · 100g/4oz *margarine*
pinch salt
1 *egg (this can be omitted and a little more milk used)*
75–125g/3–5oz *mixed dried fruit* · 25g/1oz *candied peel*
25g/1oz *sugar and* 1 *tablespoon water for glaze*

* *Gives best result*

Cream yeast with 1 teaspoon of the sugar. Add tepid milk or milk and water and a sprinkling of flour. Leave in a warm place for about 20 minutes. Rub half the margarine into flour and salt; add 25g (1 oz) sugar and the egg. Work in yeast liquid, knead lightly then prove for about 1 hour or until doubled in size. Knead dough again and roll out to oblong shape. Spread with the remaining margarine, warmed; sprinkle over sugar, fruit and peel. Roll up like a Swiss roll, then cut into 12 equal pieces and place in a greased and warmed square tin. Prove for 15 minutes, then bake near the top of a hot oven, 425–450°F, 220–230°C, Gas Mark 6–7, for 15 minutes. Either sprinkle buns with castor sugar or glaze them immediately they come out of the oven with the sugar mixed with the 1 tablespoon of water.

Hot cross buns

Brown scones

829   BROWN SCONES

100g/4oz *wholemeal flour* · 100g/4oz *plain white flour*
good pinch salt · 1 *level teaspoon bicarbonate soda*
2 *level teaspoons cream of tartar* · 25g/1oz *margarine*
milk to mix

Sieve together dry ingredients; rub in fat, then mix to a soft, but not sticky, dough with milk. Turn on to a lightly floured surface, knead quickly and roll out to 1-cm (½-inch) thick. Cut into rounds, put on to greased baking sheets and bake near the top of a hot oven, 425°F, 220°C, Gas Mark 7, for 15–20 minutes. When cold, split open and spread with butter. Top with jam or jam and cream; for a change try cottage cheese and strawberry jam. Brown scones should be a little more moist than white scones.

830   RICH SCONES

200g/8oz *flour (with plain flour use 3 level teaspoons baking powder)* · 1 *level teaspoon baking powder*
good pinch salt · 50g/2oz *butter or margarine**
15–25g/½–1oz *castor sugar* · 1 *egg*
about 142ml/¼pint *milk*

* *Use either unsalted butter or soft margarine for a creamy taste*

Sieve flour, baking powder and salt into a bowl. Rub in butter or margarine. Add sugar. Mix to a soft dough with beaten egg and milk. Turn on to a lightly floured board and knead quickly. Roll to 1–1½-cm (½–¾-inch) thickness. Cut with knife or floured cutter. Place on greased baking sheets and brush with milk. Bake near the top of a hot oven, 450°F, 230°C, Gas Mark 8, for 12–15 minutes.
Delicious with jam, fruit or cheese.
To make PLAIN SCONES use the above recipe, but omit the egg and use 25g (1 oz) margarine only.

831   COTTAGE CHEESE SCONES

Follow the recipe for rich scones (Recipe No. 830), but reduce the fat to 25g (1 oz) and add 100g (4 oz) sieved cottage cheese and a pinch of nutmeg. Use 200g (8 oz) plain flour sieved with 1 level teaspoon bicarbonate of soda and 1 level teaspoon cream of tartar. Mix with sour or fresh milk.

Sultana scones, scone rings

832   SULTANA SCONES

Follow the recipe for rich scones (Recipe No. 830), but add 50g (2 oz) sultanas with the sugar.

833   SCONE RINGS

Follow the recipe for rich scones (Recipe No. 830). Roll out the scone dough and cut out with a floured cutter. With a smaller cutter, remove a circle from the centre, then bake as Recipe 830.
This dough can however be used for a type of doughnut (shown in picture). Prepare as Recipe No. 830, then fry the rings, a few at a time, in fat or oil heated to 350°F, 180°C, and turning once during cooking. Drain on absorbent paper and toss in castor sugar.

SWEETS

Home-made sweets are not difficult to make, if the following rules are remembered:

1. Always make sure the sugar has dissolved by stirring the mixture well, before it comes to the boil.
2. To prevent the ingredients drying against the sides of the pan during cooking, brush frequently round the inside of the pan with a pastry brush dipped in cold water.
3. Test quite early – if making sweets often it is worth while investing in a sugar thermometer.
4. Use a really strong saucepan, as sweet mixtures reach a very high temperature.

834   **MARZIPAN FRUITS**
(Illustrated in colour on the opposite page)

marzipan (Recipe No. 744) · castor sugar
1 small eating apple, peeled, cored and grated
colouring · cloves

Make the marzipan, turn on to a board dusted with sugar and knead in the grated apple. Cut the marzipan into 4 pieces. Leave one portion plain and work in a few drops of green, orange and red colouring into each of the remaining portions. Mould the plain marzipan into lemon and banana shapes, the green and red into apple shapes and the orange marzipan into orange shapes. Decorate the apples with cloves and sprinkle all fruits with castor sugar.
The apple in the above recipe gives an excellent flavour, but it does prevent the sweetmeats from keeping. If you wish to store for more than a few days then omit the apple.

835   **COCONUT ICE**
(With condensed milk)

4 tablespoons full cream condensed milk
350g*/12oz icing sugar, sieved · 175g*/6oz desiccated coconut
1 drop cochineal

*Gives best result

Mix together the full cream condensed milk and icing sugar. Stir in the coconut (the mixture should be very stiff) and divide into two parts. Tint one half of the mixture pale pink with cochineal. Shape the mixture into two identical bars and press firmly together. Dust a plate or tin with icing sugar and leave the coconut ice on this until firm, then cut into squares.

836   **APPLE AND CHERRY FUDGE**
(Illustrated in colour on the opposite page)

½kg/1lb granulated sugar · 284ml/½pint milk
50g/2oz butter · 1 teaspoon glucose
50g/2oz glacé cherries, quartered
1 eating apple, peeled, cored and chopped

Place the sugar and milk in a pan and heat gently to dissolve the sugar. Stir in the butter and glucose. Bring to the boil and boil steadily until a temperature of 238°F, 115°C, is reached, or until a little of the mixture forms a soft ball when dropped into cold water. During cooking, brush the inside of the pan with cold water, to prevent graining. Remove from the heat and leave to cool for a minute. Add the cherries and apple and then beat with a wooden spoon until thick and creamy. Pour into a well greased shallow tin. When cool and set cut into small squares.
Although the apple adds flavour to the fudge it is advisable to omit this when you wish the sweetmeat to keep for more than a few days.

Marzipan fruits, apple and cherry fudge (Recipe Nos. 834, 836)

Fruit and nut fudge

Coconut ice

837 FRUIT AND NUT FUDGE

284ml/½pint *milk* · 1kg/2lb *granulated sugar*
100g/4oz *soft margarine or butter* · ½ *teaspoon vanilla essence*
50g/2oz *raisins or sultanas*
50g/2oz *almonds, coarsely chopped*

Mix the milk and sugar together and leave to stand for 1 hour, then cook very slowly until sugar dissolves. Add the margarine or butter in small pieces and when melted bring the mixture to the boil. Boil steadily until a temperature of 238°F, 115°C is reached or until a little of the mixture forms a soft ball when dropped into cold water, this will take about 1 hour. During cooking brush the inside of the pan with cold water to prevent graining; stir frequently especially when nearing 238°F, 115°C, to prevent burning. Remove from heat and add the vanilla essence, fruit and almonds. Beat until the fudge is thick and creamy, then pour into a well greased tin. When cool and set cut into small squares.

838 WALNUT FUDGE

½kg/1lb *granulated sugar* · 142ml/¼pint *water*
1 *large can full cream condensed milk*
50g/2oz *soft margarine or butter* · 50g/2oz *walnuts, chopped*

Place the sugar and water in a pan and heat gently to dissolve the sugar. Add the condensed milk and margarine or butter. When the fat has melted bring the mixture to the boil and boil steadily until a temperature of 238°F, 115°C is reached or until a little of the mixture forms a soft ball when dropped in cold water. During cooking, brush the inside of the pan with cold water to prevent graining. Stir very carefully throughout to prevent burning. Remove from heat and add the chopped walnuts. Beat until the fudge is thick and creamy, then pour into a well greased tin. When cold and set cut into small squares.

839 COCONUT ICE

1kg/2lb *granulated sugar* · 142ml/¼pint *milk*
142ml/¼pint *water* · 200g/8oz *desiccated coconut*
few drops cochineal

Very slowly dissolve sugar in the milk and water over a low heat, stirring from time to time. Bring to the boil and cook until mixture reaches a temperature of 238°F, 115°C, or until a little forms a soft ball when dropped in cold water. Remove from the heat, add coconut and beat until mixture is thick and creamy. Quickly pour half into a well greased shallow tin. Add few drops cochineal to remainder and pour on to first half. When cold and set, mark and cut into squares.
NOTE *It is essential to work quickly after the coconut ice has been beaten as it sets fairly rapidly. See Recipe No. 835 for coconut ice which does not require cooking.*
To vary the flavour add a little grated lemon or orange rind to the white coconut ice and a few drops Angostura bitters to the pink.

840 TOFFEE

½kg/1lb *sugar, preferably brown* · 142ml/¼pint *water*
1 *tablespoon golden syrup* · 50g/2oz *butter*
pinch cream of tartar · 1 *teaspoon vinegar*

Put all the ingredients into a saucepan, stir until the sugar has dissolved, then boil steadily, stirring from time to time until 290°F, 144°C, is reached or until a little of the mixture forms a very brittle thread and is firm enough to crack when dropped in cold water. Pour into a well greased tin, mark with a knife before quite set, and break into pieces when hard. Wrap each piece in waxed or greaseproof paper.
To vary the flavour, stir in 50g (2 oz) chopped walnuts before pouring the mixture into the tin, or use maple syrup or treacle instead of golden syrup.

841 MARZIPAN SURPRISE BOX

100g/4oz *almond paste with semolina (Recipe No. 745)*
colouring · stoned dates · walnut halves · cocoa
desiccated coconut · halved glacé cherries · angelica leaves

Make the semolina marzipan. Care must be taken that the paste is not made too wet. Divide into 5 equal portions and use in the following ways:

Colour pale green and use to stuff stoned dates
Colour pink and use to sandwich walnut halves together
Work in some cocoa, divide into balls and roll in cocoa
Shape into balls, roll in desiccated coconut and top with halved glacé cherries
Colour yellow, shape into diamonds and decorate with angelica leaves

Place in sweet paper cases and arrange in a fancy box.

Marzipan surprise box

Cream candy, French truffles

842 CREAM CANDY

2 teaspoons *Angostura bitters* · 284ml/½pint *milk*
1kg/2lb *granulated sugar* · 100g/4oz *margarine*

Add the Angostura to the milk, dissolve the sugar in it, over a low heat, then add the margarine. Bring the mixture to the boil and boil steadily until temperature of 255°F, 124°C is reached or until a little of the mixture dropped in cold water forms a fairly hard ball. During cooking brush the inside of the pan with cold water to prevent graining. Stir carefully throughout to prevent burning. Remove from heat, beat until thick and creamy, then very quickly spread into a well greased tin. When cool and set cut into small squares.

843 FRENCH TRUFFLES

100g/4oz *plain chocolate* · 50g/2oz *margarine*
6 level tablespoons *icing sugar, sieved* · 2 *egg yolks*
½ teaspoon *Angostura bitters* · *cocoa* · *desiccated coconut*

Gently melt the chocolate in a basin over a pan of boiling water. Cream together the margarine, icing sugar and egg yolks and stir in the melted chocolate. Add the Angostura, beat thoroughly, then leave in a cool place for the mixture to thicken and set. Form into balls and roll half the quantity in cocoa and half in desiccated coconut. Place in sweet paper cases.

Satin candies, peppermint creams

844 SATIN CANDIES

Make up satin icing (Recipe No. 750) and either mould into various shapes or cut out with tiny cutters. Decorate with nuts, cherries etc. and use to stuff dates. Place in sweet paper cases.

845 PEPPERMINT CREAMS

Make up royal icing (Recipe No. 752) and flavour with a few drops of peppermint essence. Roll out and cut into tiny rounds. Allow to dry in the air before putting into boxes.

BREAKFAST DISHES

A nourishing breakfast makes a good start to the day. The modern trend is for light breakfasts, but it is wise to have some kind of well balanced meal in the morning.

As a first course fruit juice or grapefruit is a good choice, or perhaps one of the ready-cooked cereals with milk, or try the Swiss dish, muesli.

Porridge is an excellent breakfast dish; it gives a feeling of warmth and well being. If using quick-cooking oats follow directions on the packet and serve with hot or cold milk.

846   MUESLI

I tablespoon quick-cooking rolled oats · 3 tablespoons water
I large eating apple · I tablespoon sweetened condensed milk
juice ½ lemon, optional

Soak oats in the water overnight. Wash and grate the apple and mix with the oats. Add condensed milk and lemon juice, if used. Muesli can be varied by adding chopped nuts, various kinds of fruit and by topping with yoghourt.
Makes I serving.

847   SAUSAGE AND APPLE PANCAKES

(Illustrated in colour on the opposite page)

284ml/½pint pancake batter (Recipe No. 636)
200g/8oz small pork sausages
2 eating apples, peeled, cored and sliced
25–50g/1–2oz sugar · 4 tablespoons water

If wished cook the pancakes the night before or make the batter and keep in cool place.
Grill or fry the sausages and cook the apples with the sugar and water until just tender and not mushy. Cook or reheat the pancakes. Place some cooked apple slices on each pancake and roll up. Serve with the sausages.

848   COOKING BACON

Bacon can be grilled or fried – be careful not to over-cook it. Cut the rind off rashers and, if frying, arrange in pan so that fat and lean overlap – in this way the lean part of the bacon is kept moist.

849   SAUSAGE AND BACON

Cook sausages first – either by grilling or frying. Then grill or fry the bacon.

850   BACON AND TOMATOES

Cook tomato halves after bacon and eggs, as they tend to make the pan sticky. When grilling, the tomatoes can be put in the pan under the bacon. Canned peeled tomatoes are excellent with bacon – these can be heated in a saucepan.

851   BACON AND EGGS

Cook the bacon first and lift on to a hot dish. If necessary add a little extra fat – melt this, but do not get it too hot or there will be a hard skin on the egg. Break eggs into a saucer and slide into pan. Tilt pan slightly as each egg goes in to keep the white a good shape.

852   BACON AND MUSHROOMS

Fry bacon first. Add a little extra fat if necessary before cooking mushrooms. When grilling the mushrooms can be put in the pan under the bacon. Make sure there is plenty of fat in the pan so the mushrooms do not dry.

853   BREAKFAST BURGERS

(Illustrated in colour on the opposite page)

300g/12oz streaky bacon rashers or
200g/8oz bacon pieces and ·100g/4oz streaky rashers
200g/8oz sausage meat · seasoning
2 teaspoons chopped parsley · I egg yolk · 25g/1oz cooking fat
I large or 2 smaller eating apples, cored and cut into 6 slices
parsley to garnish

Cook 200g (8 oz) of the bacon, mince or chop finely. Mix with the sausage meat, seasoning and parsley. Bind together with the egg yolk. With floured hands form the mixture into 6 rounds. Remove rinds from the remaining rashers of bacon and form into bacon rolls, secure with wooden cocktail sticks. Fry the burgers and bacon rolls on each side until cooked through. Keep hot then heat the apple rings in any fat remaining in the pan. Arrange the burgers and bacon rolls on a serving dish, top with the apple rings. Serve garnished with parsley.
Makes 6 servings.

Sausage and apple pancakes (Recipe No. 847)

Breakfast burgers (Recipe No. 853)

Scrambled eggs

854   SCRAMBLED EGGS

Allow 1–2 eggs per person and up to 1 tablespoon of milk or double cream. Lightly beat the eggs and milk. Add seasoning. Heat a knob of butter in a saucepan, pour in the eggs and cook quickly, stirring well from the bottom until the mixture starts to thicken. Turn the heat very low and continue cooking until as firm as you like. Serve on slices of hot buttered toast or with grilled or fried sausages and tomatoes. Garnish with parsley.

855   POACHED EGGS

If you have an egg poacher, put a piece of table margarine or butter into each cup, wait until this is melted, then carefully slide an egg into each cup, adding a pinch of salt if liked. Put on the lid and allow the water in the pan underneath to boil steadily for 3½–4 minutes. Slide the egg on to buttered toast. A second method is to bring a good 284ml (½ pint) water to the boil in either a saucepan or frying pan. Add a dessertspoon vinegar, for this prevents the egg whites from spreading, and a good pinch salt. Slide the eggs into the gently boiling water, leave for about 3 minutes, or until egg white is set. Lift carefully on to hot buttered toast.
Poached eggs can be used in interesting savoury dishes; the picture accompanying the introduction to the salad section shows a delicious supper dish:

Poached eggs Alexandra

Fry 50g (2 oz) sliced mushrooms and make 284ml (½ pint) white sauce (Recipe No. 663). Blend 2 tablespoons cream and ½ teaspoon curry powder with the sauce. Toast and butter 4 crumpets or rounds of bread, top with most of the mushrooms, a slice of ham and lightly poached eggs. Coat with the sauce and garnish with the remaining mushrooms.

856 TOMATO OMELETTE AND BACON

Details for cooking omelettes are given in Recipe No. 376. Make a plain omelette and fill it with slices of cooked or raw tomato. Serve with a gammon rasher, grilled for 5–7 minutes on each side or grilled rashers of bacon.

857   BOILED EGGS

Put enough water into a small saucepan to cover the eggs. Bring this to the boil, then gently lower the eggs into the boiling water. Time carefully, allowing 3–4 minutes for a soft-boiled egg; for a firmer egg allow 7–10 minutes.

858   QUICK PIZZA

4 slices white bread · 50g/2oz butter · 4 tomatoes, sliced
4 cooked sausages · 6 rashers streaky bacon, halved
100g/4oz mushrooms

Remove the crusts from the bread and spread the slices with butter. Place on a baking sheet. Arrange tomato slices, one sausage split lengthways and 3 pieces of bacon on each piece of bread. Garnish with whole mushrooms, spread lightly with butter. Cook in a moderately hot oven, 375°F, 190°C, Gas Mark 5, for 15 minutes until bacon is crisp.

Quick pizza

859   KEDGEREE

about 150g/6oz *cooked smoked haddock · 1 hard-boiled egg*
about 200g/8oz *cooked long grain rice · pinch salt*
pinch cayenne pepper · parsley to garnish

A cooked smoked haddock makes a good breakfast dish.
Poach in hot milk or milk and water in the oven or in a pan
until tender. Drain and top with butter and a poached egg, if
liked, for each person. Another way of serving haddock, and
an excellent way of using any left over, is as a *kedgeree*.
Flake cooked fish coarsely with a fork. Chop egg white, sieve
yolk and put on one side for garnishing. Mix flaked fish,
chopped egg white, cooked rice and seasoning in a saucepan
over moderate heat until hot. Pile mixture into a heated
serving dish and garnish with parsley and the sieved egg yolk.
If liked about 100g (4 oz) grated cheese can be stirred in just
before serving.

Kedgeree

860   HAWAIIAN BREAKFAST GRILL

fat for frying · ½kg/1lb pork sausages · 100g/4oz mushrooms
200g/8oz *can pineapple rings · little Demerara sugar*
parsley to garnish

Melt sufficient lard or cooking fat to grease a shallow frying
pan. As soon as the fat has melted but before it is hot, add
pricked sausages and fry very slowly for about 20 minutes,
turning as necessary, until browned. Put on one side to keep
hot. Add mushrooms to the pan. Drain pineapple rings and
dip in Demerara sugar. Fry these with mushrooms until
tender and lightly browned. To serve, place a sausage through
each pineapple ring and garnish with the mushrooms and
parsley.

861   SPECIAL FISH CAKES

1 egg, *separated · squeeze lemon juice · pepper*
1 tablespoon *soft breadcrumbs*
142ml/¼pint *thick white sauce (Recipe No. 663)*
175g/7oz *can tuna fish · browned breadcrumbs*
fat or oil for frying

Beat egg yolk, lemon juice, pepper and breadcrumbs into
sauce. Flake the tuna finely and mix in. Turn on to floured
board, shape into 8 rolls. Dip in beaten egg white and coat
with browned breadcrumbs. Fry in fat or oil heated to 350°F,
180°C, until golden brown. Drain on absorbent paper and
serve at once.
For variations try any of the following:
  In place of the white sauce use 100g (4 oz) creamed potatoes
  Add 1 tablespoon grated cheese to the mixture
  Whip in 75g (3 oz) sweet corn kernels
  Add a little finely chopped celery to the mixture
  Add 2 tablespoons finely chopped cooked bacon to the mixture
  Add 1 tablespoon chopped parsley or chives or a pinch of
  marjoram to the mixture.

862   BREAKFAST SANDWICH

2 slices *white bread · 50g/2oz butter · 1 thick slice ham*
1 *tomato · few drops Worcestershire sauce*

Spread one side of the bread slices with half the butter.
Sandwich together with the slice of ham in between. Slice the
tomato. Heat the remaining butter in a frying pan. Add the
sandwich and tomato slices. Cook the sandwich for about 2
minutes on each side, until golden brown and crisp (remove
the tomato slices after just 1 minute's cooking and keep warm).
Arrange tomato slices on top of the sandwich, sprinkle with
a few drops of Worcestershire sauce and serve at once.
Makes 1 serving.

Breakfast sandwich

HOT & COLD DRINKS

In this chapter are recipes for some of the many delicious beverages which can be made at home.

Hot chocolate drinks

863 MILK SHAKES

(With ice cream)

Put ½litre (1 pint) milk and 1 dessertspoon ice cream and flavouring into a liquidiser and switch on for about 30 seconds, until light and fluffy. If a liquidiser is not available whisk the mixture in a basin until light and fluffy.

864 ORANGE MILK SHAKE

Use orange squash or flavouring syrup and vanilla ice cream; top with sliced oranges. If using a liquidiser peeled fresh oranges can be used.

865 COFFEE MILK SHAKE

Use very strong coffee, 1 teaspoon coffee powder or coffee essence and vanilla ice cream. Top with grated chocolate.

866 STRAWBERRY MILK SHAKE

Use strawberry-flavoured syrup and strawberry ice cream. Blend fresh strawberries and milk in an electric liquidiser.

867 ICE CREAM SODAS

Put fruit juice and ice cream into tall glasses and top with soda water. Decorate with fruit slices and serve with a long spoon. For a more elaborate ice cream soda put a very little ice cream into the bottom of tall glass. Half fill glass with milk, add fruit and more ice cream. Top with soda water, ice cream and fruit.

868 MILK WITH HONEY

Add 1 teaspoon honey and a few drops of lemon juice to a glass of warm milk.

869 HOT CHOCOLATE DRINKS

*scant 284ml/½pint hot milk · 2 teaspoons drinking chocolate
2 marshmallows, preserved ginger, grated lemon rind or
chocolate, 4 ratafia biscuits or 1 cinnamon stick and pinch
cinnamon*

Pour the hot milk into a cup or beaker and quickly whisk in the drinking chocolate. Top with:
a) marshmallows
b) chopped preserved ginger
c) grated lemon rind or chocolate
d) ratafia biscuits
e) cinnamon stick or pinch cinnamon

870 ICED FRUIT CUPS

Mix together canned and fresh fruit juices. Pineapple and fresh orange juice, or juice from canned raspberries with fresh orange and lemon juice, are two excellent mixtures. Pour over crushed ice and top with orange or lemon slices.

871 ICED COFFEE

Put a little crushed ice in a tall glass – half fill with cold coffee and then add cold milk. Sweeten to taste and top with whipped double cream, if liked.
Coffee ice cubes make a pleasant addition to coffee milk shakes, iced coffee etc. Pour cold black coffee into an ice tray and place in the freezing compartment. Leave until frozen.

872 COFFEE AND CREAM

Make coffee as directed in Recipe No. 874, pour into cups and top with double cream.

Iced coffee

873   TO MAKE GOOD TEA

Everyone has a pet theory about the perfect tea pot – silver, china, metal, but whatever your taste, these points are important:
1. Always warm the pot.
2. Fill the kettle with fresh water from the main water supply and bring just to the boil before pouring over the tea.
3. Allow to infuse for 3–4 minutes before pouring.
4. Quantities of tea will vary according to personal taste, but the old ruling, one teaspoon for each person and one for the pot, is a good average amount.

874   TO MAKE GOOD COFFEE

Whether coffee is made in a percolator or saucepan certain points are very important:
1. Coffee loses its flavour quickly, so do not buy too much at a time, and store it in air-tight tins or screw topped jars.
2. Buy the correct grinding of coffee for your particular coffee maker. A very finely ground coffee, for example, is quite unsuitable for a percolator though it will be excellent for an Italian espresso coffee pot.
3. Do not allow coffee to boil; just bring the water to the boil, then pour on to the coffee. For a good flavour, percolate coffee gently or simmer gently in a pan.
4. Warm the coffee jug before pouring in the coffee.
5. Use the right amount of coffee – most people will like coffee made from 4 dessertspoons coffee to 568ml (1 pint) water – although this may be a little strong if drinking black coffee.

Irish coffee: serve in warmed glasses or beakers rather than cups. Pour a measure of whiskey into each glass. Add 4–6 tablespoons strong black coffee and sugar to taste; stir. Very slowly pour 1 tablespoon double cream over the back of a spoon into the coffee. It should form a thick layer of cream resting on the coffee. Sip the coffee through the layer of cream. Alternatively float a teaspoonful of whipped double cream on top of the coffee. If liked, decorate with finely grated orange rind.

Irish coffee

Milk shakes

875   MILK SHAKES

(Without ice cream)

Instead of using ice cream, add 1–2 teaspoons of flavoured instant whip powder to 284ml (½ pint) milk and whisk until frothy. Pour into glasses and top with fresh or canned fruit.

876 GOSSAMER FLIP

284ml/½pint *milk* · 1 *egg* · 50g/2oz *sugar*
142ml/¼pint *pineapple juice* · 1 teaspoon *Angostura bitters*
mint leaves and fruit to decorate

Whisk together milk, egg yolk and half the sugar. Blend in pineapple juice and Angostura. Whisk egg white to a stiff froth with rest of sugar and fold in. Pour into glasses, decorate with mint leaves and pieces of fruit and serve at once.

877 SUMMER TOMATO JUICE COCKTAIL

Chill tomato juice. Put into a jug with a few drops of Tabasco sauce, a little lemon juice and Worcestershire sauce, adjusting amounts to taste. Stir well. Pour into small tumblers and garnish with sprigs of fresh mint.

878 SUMMER FRUIT COOLER

284ml/½pint *fresh or canned orange juice*
284ml/½pint *fresh or canned grapefruit juice*
2 tablespoons *lemon juice* · *few Maraschino cherries*
ice cubes · 2–3 *sprigs mint*

Blend the orange and grapefruit juice together, add lemon juice, cherries and ice cubes. For long drinks dilute with extra ice or chilled water and decorate with sprigs of mint. For short drinks add a measure of gin.

879 EGG NOG

Whisk egg and hot or cold milk together, add brandy or whisky to taste and sweeten as liked.

880 MERRY-GO-ROUND

(A punch for the younger generation)

100g/4oz *lump sugar* · 1 *orange* · 3 *lemons*
generous litre/2pints *hot strong tea* · 1 can *pineapple juice*
3 *cloves* · dash *Angostura bitters* · 1 ripe *banana, sliced*

Rub sugar lumps on the skin of the orange and lemons to absorb oil. Put sugar in a large bowl, add the hot strained tea, pineapple, orange and lemon juices, cloves; add Angostura just before serving. Stir with a wooden spoon until all the sugar granules have dissolved. Stir in the sliced banana. For a festive brew, float thick orange and lemon slices on the surface.

881 CHRISTMAS PUNCH

300g/12oz *sugar* · poor ½litre/¾pint *lemon juice*
thin pieces orange rind · generous litre/2pints *white wine*
¼litre/½pint *pineapple juice* · generous ½litre/1pint *tea*
1 tablespoon *Angostura bitters* · *orange and apple slices*

Heat together sugar, lemon juice and orange rind. Stir in wine and pineapple juice. Just before serving add freshly brewed strained tea and the Angostura. Pour into warmed punch bowl or jug. Stir in the orange and apple slices.

Gossamer flip

Summer tomato juice cocktail, summer fruit cooler

Christmas punch

PRESSURE COOKING

The colour pictures on these two pages give some idea of the scope of cooking in a modern pressure cooker. You will find detailed instructions in your own recipe book, but I have selected in this section some of the recipes and types of cooking which save you time and very often produce better results than when cooked by ordinary methods. Unless stated to the contrary use 15lb pressure.

882

SOUPS

Undoubtedly a pressure cooker is quite wonderful for making stock and soups. You retain all the flavour of the ingredients and the soup is cooked in a very short time. If adapting an ordinary recipe use about half the amount of liquid as there is almost no loss of liquid by evaporation.

FISH

Although fish cooks quite quickly under normal conditions it is even quicker in a pressure cooker. You keep a very good flavour and the smell of fish in your kitchen is avoided. The fish can be cooked in a pressure cooker together with any vegetables, without there being any intermingling of flavours.

MEAT

A few recipes are included in this section. For stews the saving of time is enormous. As with soup, you must cut down the amount of liquid in an ordinary recipe. Meats, such as tongue and ham, which normally take a long time to cook are ready in a short time and wonderfully tender.

PUDDINGS

A variety of puddings can be cooked in a pressure cooker. Egg custards will not curdle, steamed puddings are cooked in a much shorter time and it is also possible to have a creamy rice pudding.

VEGETABLES

Possibly one of the most popular of all uses of a pressure cooker is for vegetables. It has been found that vegetables correctly cooked in a pressure cooker retain as much, and often even more, vitamins than when cooked by ordinary means. To keep green vegetables green, put into boiling water in pressure cooker. Root and dried vegetables are made exceptionally tender, and have a first-class flavour.

PRESERVES AND BOTTLING

A section has been devoted to this as here again there is much saving of time with fruit bottling, and with softening the fruit for jam. Vegetable bottling can, of course, only be done in a pressure cooker.

Soup making can be done much more quickly in a pressure cooker. In addition, bone stock (which forms the basis of so many soups) is worth making, even with a small quantity of bones, for it does not take longer than 45 minutes. The quicker cooking does not spoil the flavour – in fact, as with most foods cooked under pressure, there tends to be an improvement. It is very important, when making soups in pressure saucepans to see that the cooker is not more than half filled. You will notice that very much less liquid than usual is given in the following recipes – this is because there is almost no evaporation of liquid in a pressure cooker. As so much less liquid is added, be sparing with the amount of seasoning. Any recipe in the soup section can be used, but reduce the amount of liquid by about half. Use 15lb pressure.

884 MINESTRONE SOUP
(Cooking time : 3 minutes at 15lb pressure)

25g/1oz *dripping or fat* · 1 *onion, peeled and chopped*
1 *stick celery, chopped* · 200g/8oz *tomatoes, skinned and chopped*
200g/8oz *cabbage, chopped*
1 *medium-sized can butter or haricot beans*
50g/2oz *cooked macaroni* · *seasoning*
284ml/½pint *stock or water* · *grated cheese, optional*

Melt the fat in the pan, fry the onion and celery for 5 minutes. Add the tomatoes, cabbage, drained butter or haricot beans, macaroni and seasoning. Pour in the stock or water, put the lid on the cooker; bring to pressure and cook for 3 minutes. Allow the pressure to drop and take off the lid. If liked, serve the soup sprinkled with grated cheese. This is a thick soup.
Note If using dried instead of canned beans use 75g (3 oz). Soak for 24 hours in cold water. Drain, then cook for 25 minutes at 15lb pressure with 426ml (¾ pint) water. Allow pressure to drop, remove beans and save 284ml (½ pint) of the liquid then follow recipe above.

885 ONION SOUP
(Cooking time : 3 minutes at 15lb pressure)

50g/2oz *butter* · ¾kg/1½lb *onions, sliced*
generous ½litre/1pint *stock or water* · *seasoning*
4 *small slices toast* · 50g/2oz *cheese, grated*

Melt the butter in the cooker and fry the onions until pale golden brown. Remove a few rings and keep aside for garnish. Add the liquid and seasoning. Put on the lid, bring steadily to pressure. Lower heat and cook for 3 minutes. Allow pressure to drop. Arrange toast on heated soup plates. Pour the soup over, garnish with reserved onion rings and sprinkle with grated cheese. For a creamy soup blend 25g (1 oz) flour with 142ml (¼ pint) milk and stir into soup to thicken.

886 STOCK
(Cooking time : 45 minutes at 15lb pressure)

1kg/2lb *bones, large marrow bones if possible*
generous litre/2pints *water* · 1 *carrot* · 1 *turnip*
1 *onion* · 1 *teaspoon salt*

Break the bones and put into the cooker with all the other ingredients. Bring slowly to the boil and remove the scum from the top. Fix the lid and bring steadily to pressure. Reduce the heat and cook for 45 minutes. Allow pressure to return to normal before removing lid. When the stock is cold lift off any fat from top. Do not add potatoes or green vegetables to this stock as it will not then keep. In hot weather store in a refrigerator *for a few days* or re-boil every other day.

887 LENTIL SOUP
(Cooking time : 15 minutes at 15lb pressure)

100g/4oz *lentils* · 2–3 *sticks celery, chopped*
2 *medium-sized potatoes, peeled and chopped*
2 *onions, peeled and chopped* · generous ¾litre/1½pints *water*
seasoning · *bunch mixed fresh herbs or pinch dried herbs*
142ml/¼pint *milk*

Put all the ingredients except the milk into the pressure cooker. Bring steadily to pressure. Lower the heat and cook for 15 minutes. Allow pressure to drop. Rub through a sieve return to cooker with milk and reheat.

888 OXTAIL SOUP
(Cooking time : 40 minutes at 15lb pressure)

Use ingredients in Recipe No. 68, but halve the amount of liquid. Cook for 40 minutes.

Minestrone soup

889 CHRISTMAS PUDDING
(Cooking time : 2 hours at 15lb pressure)

100g/4oz *mashed potato* · 50g/2oz *flour*
100g/4oz *shredded suet or melted butter*
100g/4oz *sugar, preferably brown sugar* · 1 *small carrot, grated*
½kg/1lb *mixed dried fruit*
2 *level tablespoons golden syrup or black treacle*
2 *level tablespoons marmalade* · 1 *teaspoon cinnamon* · 2 *eggs*
6–8 *tablespoons ale, beer, stout, brandy or whisky*
1 *teaspoon mixed spice* · 1 *teaspoon vanilla essence*
1 *teaspoon almond essence* · 1 *teaspoon lemon essence*
1 *small apple, grated*

Remember that 100g is slightly less than 4 oz, so if you wish to make a slightly larger pudding add about 10g to each 4 oz; but the cooking time will be 1½–2½ hours – 1½ for 2 smaller puddings – 2½ for 1 large pudding. The 2 hours at the top is a general indication.
Mix all the ingredients together. Put into one or two greased basins. Cover with 2 layers of greased greaseproof paper or foil. Put puddings on the rack in the cooker. Pour in a generous litre (2½pints) boiling water. Fix the lid, but do not put on the pressure weight. Steam rapidly for 30 minutes. Put on the weight, bring to pressure. Lower the heat and cook for 1½–2 hours. Reduce pressure gradually. Take off the paper or foil and when cold cover with clean paper before storing. The mashed potato gives a softer, more spongy texture than bread-crumbs. The Christmas pudding recipe given in Recipe No. 1017 can also be cooked in a pressure cooker.

890 POT-ROASTING IN A PRESSURE COOKER

A pressure cooker can be used for pot-roasting. Any meat that can be roasted in the normal way is suitable, and if by chance you have a less tender piece of meat, then try pot-roasting. The method is simple:

1. Put a little fat at the bottom of the cooker and heat this.
2. Brown the meat well in the fat, then lift the meat out of the cooker, insert the rack, replace the meat and add the water.
3. Allow 284ml (½ pint) water for a joint that takes up to 15 minutes pressure cooking time, and add an additional 142ml (¼ pint) water for each 15 minutes over this, e.g. for a joint taking 45 minutes use generous ½ litre (1 pint) water.
4. Beef needs 10 minutes per ½ kg (1 lb) at 15lb pressure. Lamb, veal, pork, need 12 minutes per ½ kg (1 lb). Roasting chicken needs 5 minutes per ½ kg (1 lb).
5. Allow pressure to drop at room temperature. The liquid in the cooker makes excellent gravy.
6. If liked the pressure can be allowed to drop and vegetables put in at the right time, so that all the meal is cooked together in the one pressure cooker.

Pot-roast of topside

Nut and raisin bread

891 SILVERSIDE WITH VEGETABLES

(Cooking time: 10 minutes per ½ kg (1lb) at 15lb pressure)

(Illustrated in colour on the jacket)

Soak a piece of salted silverside in cold water for several hours. Drain off the water. Weigh the meat and calculate the amount of water and cooking time (notes 3 and 4 opposite). Stand the meat on the rack in the cooker, add the water. Bring to pressure and cook for the calculated time. Allow the pressure to drop at room temperature. Place the silverside on a serving dish and surround with a selection of vegetables in season. Carrots and white cabbage go particularly well with silverside. Garnish with watercress.

892 CAKES IN A PRESSURE COOKER

Cakes and bread can be cooked in a pressure cooker. This is an ideal arrangement for people living in bedsitting rooms who have no oven. Also there may be occasions when it might not be convenient to use an oven, in which case a pressure cooker can be used.

Remember:

1. Use 5lb pressure.
2. Use seamless or watertight cake or loaf tins.
3. If using glassware allow an extra 10 minutes cooking time.
4. Have at least a generous ¾ litre (1½ pints) BOILING water in the cooker – add some vinegar to prevent the cooker discolouring.
5. Cover with a pleated double thickness of greased greaseproof paper or foil.
6. Steam without the weight in position for 15 minutes, then bring to pressure and cook for required time. Allow pressure to drop to room temperature.
7. For a brown top on the cake or loaf put it under a moderate grill for a few minutes.

893 NUT AND RAISIN BREAD

(Cooking time: 30 minutes at 5lb pressure)

*200g/8oz flour (with plain flour use 2 level teaspoons baking powder) · pinch salt · 75g/3oz margarine
¼ teaspoon grated nutmeg · 50g/2oz sugar
50g/2oz walnuts, chopped · 100g/4oz raisins · 1 egg, beaten
milk to mix*

Grease loaf tin well. Sieve flour, baking powder, if used, and salt into a basin. Rub in margarine, add nutmeg, sugar, nuts, raisins. Add the beaten egg and enough milk to give a very stiff consistency – this is important. Beat well, and put into the tin. Cover as directed in note 5 above, then steam for 15 minutes; bring to pressure and cook for 30 minutes at 5lb pressure. Allow the pressure to drop at room temperature. If liked put under a moderate grill for a few minutes to brown the top.

894 COOKING STEWS IN A PRESSURE COOKER

1. Adapt any stew recipe in the meat section, but use only half the quantity of liquid as there is almost no loss by evaporation. Use 15lb pressure.
2. DO NOT over-cook the meat; this will toughen it. If the meat is not quite cooked, put on the lid, bring to pressure again and cook for a further few minutes. You will notice 15 minutes is given as the cooking time for the goulash; if the meat is rather tough it may take 20 minutes, but it is better to cook for the shorter time, then cook again if needed.
3. Stews with beef take 15–20 minutes to cook. Stews with lamb or veal take about 12 minutes to cook.
   Boiling chicken takes about 9 minutes per ½kg (1lb) when whole, or 8–9 minutes when jointed.

895 HUNGARIAN GOULASH
(Cooking time: 15 minutes at 15lb pressure)

50g/2oz *fat*
½kg/1lb *beef, mutton or pork, cut into cubes*
1 *clove garlic, crushed, optional* · ½kg/1lb *onions, sliced*
100g/4oz *mushrooms, optional* · 2 *teaspoons salt*
4 *teaspoons paprika* · *pinch allspice* · 200g/8oz *can tomatoes*
142ml/¼pint *water* · 6 *medium-sized potatoes, peeled and chopped*
25g/1oz *flour blended with 4 tablespoons cold water*
1 *small carton soured cream and paprika to garnish*

Melt fat in cooker, add meat, garlic, if used, onions and mush-rooms, if used, and brown lightly. Add seasoning, spice, tomatoes and water. Place potatoes on top of meat. Cover, bring to pressure and cook for 15 minutes. Reduce pressure with cold water. Thicken liquid with blended flour. Cook until smooth and thick, stirring all the time. Spoon into a serving dish and serve garnished with warmed soured cream and paprika.

Hungarian goulash

896 HAM OR BACON
(Cooking time: 12 minutes per ½kg (1lb) at 15lb pressure)

Soak ham in cold water for several hours. Weigh the ham and calculate the amount of water and cooking time – allow 12 minutes per ½kg (1 lb) and 284ml (½ pint) water for every 15 minutes cooking time or fraction of 15 minutes. Place the ham on the rack in the cooker. Bring to pressure and cook for the calculated time. Reduce pressure at room temperature. If vegetables are to be served as well, reduce pressure and add these 15 minutes before end of cooking time, bring up to pressure again and continue cooking. Shown in the picture on the right is collar of bacon served with carrots, onions and dumplings. Add the vegetables. Bring to pressure and cook for a further 5 minutes, cool the cooker under cold water. Make the dumplings (Recipe No. 218), drop these into the boiling liquid and steam for about 7–10 minutes depending upon size. Refix the lid, bring to 5lb pressure and cook for 8 minutes. Cool under cold water. If wished press browned breadcrumbs around the outside of the joint before serving.

897 OX TONGUE
(Cooking time: 1 hour at 15lb pressure)

about 2kg/4lb *salted tongue* · generous ½litre/1pint *hot water*
1 *tablespoon vinegar* · 4 *cloves* · 6 *peppercorns*
1 *bay leaf* · *parsley to garnish*

Soak the tongue in cold water for several hours. Put the tongue into cooker, barely cover with water and bring to the boil. Simmer 5 minutes. Discard this water. Add the hot water, vinegar, cloves, peppercorns and bay leaf; cover and bring to pressure. Pressure cook, allowing 15 minutes per ½kg (1 lb) of tongue. Reduce pressure at room temperature, remove tongue, skin, take off bones and root ends. Serve hot with vegetables or glaze to serve cold. Roll tongue and fit into mould or cake tin – a tight fit ensures a neat professional result. Boil stock in open cooker until 142ml (¼ pint) remains. Strain over tongue. Put a saucer and weight on top and leave until firm. Turn out and serve garnished with parsley. Always try to carve from the same end, as the glaze helps to keep tongue moist.

Ox tongue

Collar of bacon with dumplings

898 STEAMED PUDDINGS IN A PRESSURE COOKER

1. The best results are obtained by using metal basins.
2. If glass or china basins are used allow an extra 10 minutes cooking time.
3. In order to produce a light pudding always STEAM without the weight in position for the first 15 minutes.
4. Light sponge and suet puddings are best cooked at 5lb pressure. Christmas puddings (Recipe Nos. 889, 1017) can be cooked at 15lb pressure.
5. Cover puddings in the usual way with greased greaseproof paper or foil.
6. Stand on the rack in the pressure cooker, and allow 142ml (¼ pint) BOILING water for each 15 minutes cooking time.
7. Allow pressure to drop at room temperature.

899 FRUIT SUET PUDDING

Make up suet crust pastry (Recipe No. 603), roll out thinly and use two-thirds to line a pudding basin. Fill with fresh fruit sweetened to taste. Roll out remaining pastry, dampen the edges and place over the fruit. Cover with greased grease-proof paper or foil, stand on the rack in the pressure cooker. Add the water (see note 6, above), steam for 15 minutes; bring to 5lb pressure and cook for 35 minutes. Cool at room temperature. Turn the pudding on to a plate and serve with custard.

900 PEAR CONDE

rice pudding (Recipe No. 908) · little double cream, optional
4 canned pear halves · 1 teaspoon cornflour or arrowroot
142ml/¼pint pear syrup · 2–3 tablespoons redcurrant jelly
little double cream, whipped to decorate (optional)

Make rice pudding and allow to cool. Mix in cream, if used. Spoon into individual serving dishes. Place a drained pear half in each dish. Make a glaze by blending cornflour with the pear syrup. Pour into a saucepan and add the redcurrant jelly. Stirring, bring to the boil and cook until thick and clear. Cool slightly then coat each pear with the glaze. If liked, decorate each serving with whipped cream.

901 DRIED FRUIT

Dried fruit is wonderfully tender if you use a pressure cooker. Soak for 5–10 minutes in boiling water before cooking, then allow the following times. Add sugar and flavouring to taste. If you like plenty of syrup to serve with the fruit, use double the amount of liquid given below.

Fruit	Amount of water per ½kg (1lb) fruit	Minutes at 15lb pressure	Flavouring
Apple rings*	284ml (½ pint)	10 minutes	grated lemon rind or 1 or 2 cloves
Figs	284ml (½ pint)	10–15 minutes	grated lemon rind or 1 or 2 cloves
Prunes**	284ml (½ pint)	10–15 minutes	grated lemon rind or 1 or 2 cloves
Apricots	284ml (½ pint)	5–6 minutes	little orange juice
Peaches	284ml (½ pint)	5–6 minutes	little orange juice

*Add a little lemon juice
**Excellent cooked in coffee

With dried fruit salad all the fruit can be cooked for 10 minutes or the pressure can be reduced half way through the cooking time and the apricots and peaches added.

Fruit suet pudding

Pear condé

902 JAM, CHUTNEYS AND MARMALADES IN A PRESSURE COOKER

A pressure cooker is ideal for softening fruit for jam and vegetables for chutney. This can be done in a very short time and makes quite certain the skins are really soft before the sugar is added.

Here are a few simple rules to remember.

1. If using any of the recipes in the ordinary jam making section – reduce liquid to half quantity. This is because in a pressure cooker there is almost no loss of liquid due to evaporation as in a preserving pan.
2. Use 10lb pressure for jam making.
3. Be sure not to fill the cooker more than half full.
4. Pressure cook the fruit only, as instructed in the recipe.
5. Cook jam in open cooker after the sugar has been added, treating the pressure cooker as an ordinary preserving pan. Test as directed in Recipe No. 959.
6. Remove rack when making preserves.

Ladling marmalade into warmed jars

903 BLACKCURRANT JAM

1kg/2lb *blackcurrants* · 284ml/½pint *water*
1kg/2lb *sugar*

Remove stalks and wash fruit if necessary. Pour water into cooker and add blackcurrants. Cover, bring to 10lb pressure and pressure cook for 1 minute. Reduce pressure with cold water. Remove cover and add sugar, stir until sugar has dissolved. Bring to the boil without the cover and boil rapidly until setting point is reached. Pour into warmed jars and cover in the usual way. This has slightly different proportions from Recipe No. 968 and gives a softer jam. If preferred use Recipe No. 968 with half quantity of water or use any of the recipes – cutting liquid to *half* quantity given for ordinary methods, but using *same* amount of sugar.

904 ORANGE MARMALADE

½kg/1lb *Seville oranges* · generous ½litre/1pint *water*
1kg/2lb *sugar* · *juice 1 lemon*

Slice oranges and leave to soak in the water for 24 hours. Pips should be put in a muslin bag and left to soak with fruit. Pour soaked fruit and water into cooker. Cover, bring to 10lb pressure, and cook for 10 minutes. Reduce pressure with cold water. Take out pips. Add sugar and lemon juice and stir until dissolved. Boil in the open cooker until setting point is reached. Ladle into warmed jars and seal in usual way. Alternatively use Recipes Nos. 1001–1005 with *half* quantity of water but *same* amount of sugar.

905 GREEN TOMATO CHUTNEY

about 1½kg/3lb *tomatoes* · ½kg/1lb *cooking apples*
200g/8oz *onions* · 15g/½oz *root ginger* · 200g/8oz *sultanas*
1 teaspoon *salt* · 284ml/½pint *vinegar* · 200g/8oz *sugar*

Remove skins of tomatoes, peel and core apples and cut into very small pieces, chop onions, tie ginger in muslin bag. Put all ingredients except sugar into cooker. Stir well, cover, bring to 10lb pressure and pressure cook for 10 minutes. Reduce pressure with cold water. Stir in sugar and simmer without lid of cooker until chutney is of a thick consistency. Remove ginger. Ladle into warmed jars and seal.

906 APPLE AND MARROW CHUTNEY

1kg/2lb *apples* · ½kg/1lb *marrow* · ½kg/1lb *onions*
100g/4oz *crystallised ginger* · ¼ teaspoon *cayenne pepper*
2 *cloves garlic* · 1 *dessertspoon salt* · 284ml/½pint *vinegar*
pinch allspice · ¾kg/1½lb *brown sugar*

Peel, core and chop the apples; peel and chop the marrow into small pieces and slice onions finely. Put all ingredients except sugar into cooker. Stir well, cover and bring to 10lb pressure. Pressure cook for 15 minutes. Reduce pressure with cold water. Stir in sugar and simmer in open cooker until the chutney is of a thick smooth consistency. Ladle into warmed jars and seal.

907 APRICOT MARSHMALLOW

100g/4oz *dried apricots* · 284ml/½pint *boiling water*
2 *tablespoons sugar* · 2 *tablespoons orange juice*
12 *marshmallows* · 2 *egg whites* · *blanched almonds*
or crystallised orange slices to decorate

Wash apricots, pour over boiling water, leave to soak 10 minutes. Lift out rack, put apricots, water and sugar into cooker, cover, bring to 15lb pressure and cook for 6 minutes. Reduce pressure at room temperature. Remove apricots and chop coarsely. Put apricots, 2 tablespoons cooking liquid, orange juice and marshmallows into saucepan, heat slowly, stirring, until marshmallows are half melted. Remove from heat, continue to stir until mixture is smooth and spongy. Fold in stiffly whisked egg whites. Pour into freezing tray of refrigerator and freeze until smooth, beating well when half frozen. Cut into individual portions with knife dipped in hot water and decorate with blanched almonds or crystallised orange slices. If refrigerator is not available, put mixture at once into individual dishes and decorate when cold.

908 RICE PUDDING

(Cooking time: 10–15 minutes at 15lb pressure)

knob butter · generous ½litre/1pint *milk* · 50g/2oz *rice*
50g/2oz *sugar* · *little grated lemon rind or*
few drops vanilla essence

Melt butter in bottom of cooker, add milk, bring to boil in open cooker, then add rice, sugar and flavouring. Stir well, cover, bring to 15lb pressure slowly over low heat; pressure cook for 10–15 minutes then reduce pressure at room temperature. Other cereals, tapioca, etc., can be cooked in the same way.

909 FRUIT BOTTLING IN A PRESSURE COOKER

This not only saves a great deal of time, but the fruit remains an excellent colour and texture. Special instructions for your own make of cooker should be followed, but below is a general guide to bottling by this method.

1. For preparation of fruit before bottling see Recipe No. 1006. Special preserving jars are recommended. Scald jars and invert them on a clean folded cloth. Scald lids and rings by pouring boiling water over them. Do not boil but keep them in water until ready for use. Choose fruit of even size. Pack tightly without damaging the fruit, to within 1 cm (½ inch) of top of jar. Tap jar on folded cloth. Adjust rings and lids. If using screw top jars, screw band tightly, unscrew ¼ turn.

2. Pour generous ½litre (1 pint) hot water into cooker, add 1 tablespoon vinegar to prevent cooker staining. Stand jars on inverted rack. Do not allow jars to touch one another or side of cooker. Use paper between jars if they are likely to touch. If using ordinary jam jars, put cloth or layers of newspaper on rack to prevent breakage. Add extra 142ml (¼ pint) water to allow for absorption by cloth or paper. When using electricity, bring to pressure on low heat.

3. Fix cover, place on heat and bring to 5lb pressure in usual way. Process for time stated in table opposite.

4. Turn off heat and leave cooker on stove to reduce pressure at room temperature. If using an electric stove, gently move the pressure cooker away from heat. Do not reduce pressure with cold water as sudden cooling will crack jars. Open cooker, remove jars one at a time on to a cloth or wooden surface. Tighten screw band and allow to cool. Test seal after 24 hours by inverting jars. If seal is not perfect re-process.

TIMETABLE FOR BOTTLING FRUIT

Fruit	Minutes at 5lb pressure	Fruit	Minutes at 5lb pressure
Apples	3–4 minutes	Peaches	7 minutes
Apricots	3–4 minutes	Pears	3–4 minutes
Blackberries	3–4 minutes	Plums	3–4 minutes
Blackcurrants	7 minutes	Raspberries	3–4 minutes
Cherries	7 minutes	Redcurrants	7 minutes
Damsons	3–4 minutes	Rhubarb	3–4 minutes
Gooseberries	3–4 minutes	Tomatoes	7 minutes
Loganberries	3–4 minutes		

910 VEGETABLE BOTTLING IN A PRESSURE COOKER

Remember it is UNSAFE to bottle vegetables other than in a pressure cooker. Always follow the special instructions for your own make of pressure cooker. Below are the points to remember.

1. Wash vegetables thoroughly to remove all traces of soil. Pre-cook or blanch by immersing in boiling water for the time stated in the table below, then drop into cold water. Drain well and pack into clean jars to within an inch of top. Do not pack too tightly.

2. Still leaving 2½cm (1 inch) at top, cover vegetables with a hot brine solution, made by dissolving 50–75g (2–3 oz) salt in a scant 5litres (1 gallon) water, boiled before using. Work out air bubbles by quickly twisting the jar from side to side. Adjust rings and lids.

3. Process jars of hot food immediately. Pour generous ½litre (1 pint) hot water into cooker, add 1 tablespoon vinegar. Stand jars on inverted rack. Do not allow jars to touch each other or the sides of the cooker. Use paper between jars if necessary. Fix cover, place on LOW heat. Do not put on pressure control; allow air to be expelled through centre vent for 5 minutes. Put on 10lb pressure control valve and, still at low heat, bring to pressure. Process for the time stated below. See that there is always a steady flow of steam from the pressure control as pressure must not drop below 10lb.

4. As point 4 in fruit bottling (Recipe No. 909).

5. The loss of liquid does not interfere with the keeping quality of the food. Jars should never be opened, after processing, to replace liquid that has boiled out. When opening a jar of bottled vegetables do not taste the cold food. If the contents of the jar do not smell right and the food is soft and mushy, discard it at once. As a safeguard, heat bottled vegetables at boiling temperature for 10–15 minutes before tasting or using.

TIMETABLE FOR BOTTLING VEGETABLES

Vegetables	Preparation	Minutes to blanch in boiling water	Minutes to process at 10lb pressure
Asparagus	Wash, trim, cut into even lengths, tie in bundles, pack upright	2–3 minutes	40 minutes
Beans, broad	Pod. Choose very young beans	5 minutes	55 minutes
Beans, runner	Wash, string and slice	5 minutes	40 minutes
Beetroot	Cut off tops. Blanch before slicing or dicing	15–20 minutes	40 minutes
Carrots	Wash, scrape, slice or dice. Leave new carrots whole	10 minutes	45 minutes
Corn	Strip from cob	2–3 minutes	50 minutes
Celery	Wash, cut in even lengths	6 minutes	40 minutes
Peas	Wash, shell and grade	2–3 minutes	50 minutes
Potatoes, new	Wash, scrape carefully or peel thinly	5 minutes	50 minutes

TELEVISION SNACKS & SANDWICHES

The advent of television has changed catering habits in many homes. Instead of an evening meal the family enjoy a substantial snack while watching their favourite programmes. Choose food that is easy to serve and eat on a tray.

911 DISHES TO CHOOSE FOR TELEVISION SUPPERS

It is an excellent idea to base the meal on one delicious main dish. Pasta dishes are particularly good as they are easy to serve and eat. Macaroni cheese (Recipe No. 352) would be a good choice, or any of the recipes in this section.

912 AUTUMN RISOTTO

(Illustrated in colour on the opposite page)

25g/1oz butter · 1 onion, peeled and chopped
2 rashers streaky bacon, chopped · 1 green or red pepper, sliced
300g/12oz long grain rice · ¼ teaspoon saffron powder or strands
generous ½litre/1pint chicken stock or water and 1 chicken stock cube
200g/8oz pork luncheon meat, cubed
50g/2oz sultanas, optional · 1 eating apple, cored and sliced
seasoning · parsley to garnish

Heat the fat in a frying pan and cook the onion, bacon and red pepper until tender. Stir in the rice and mix with the onion, etc. Blend the saffron powder with the stock; if using saffron strands infuse in the stock for about 30 minutes, strain and discard the saffron. Pour the stock into the pan with the rice and vegetables, bring to the boil, stir well, cover and cook for 15 minutes. Add the luncheon meat, sultanas and apple. Mix well together and leave on a low heat for 5–10 minutes, until hot. Season to taste. Spoon into a serving dish and serve garnished with parsley.
If liked 4–8 chopped chicken livers can be fried with the onion. Add a little extra butter if necessary.
Makes 6 servings.

913 PRAWN RISOTTO

Prepare risotto as above, but fry 100g (4 oz) prawns with the onion. Omit the luncheon meat and stir in the contents from a 200g (8 oz) can tomatoes. Continue as above recipe.

914 SWEET CORN AU GRATIN

1 large can creamed sweet corn or large packet frozen corn off cob, cooked
100–150g/4–6oz cheese, grated · 4 potatoes · 2 onions
seasoning

Arrange the canned or cooked frozen sweet corn in layers in casserole with cheese and thinly sliced potatoes and onions. Season each layer. Top with grated cheese and cook in a moderately hot oven, 375–400°F, 190–200°C, Gas Mark 5, for about 45 minutes.

Sausage twists

915 SAUSAGE TWISTS

generous 200g/8oz short crust pastry (Recipe No. 566)
½kg/1lb large pork sausages · beaten egg
284ml/½pint sweetened apple purée
25g/1oz pickled cucumber, sliced · pinch dry mustard
seasoning · parsley to garnish

Make the pastry, roll out thinly and cut into strips 30 cm (12 inches) by ½ cm (¼ inch). Twist each strip around a sausage and brush the pastry with beaten egg. Place on a greased baking sheet and bake in a hot oven, 425°F, 220°C, Gas Mark 7, for 20 minutes.
Heat apple purée with sliced cucumber, mustard and seasoning. Arrange sausages on a heated serving dish and garnish with parsley. Serve the sauce separately. If liked the sausage twists can be served cold.

916 TELEVISION GRILL

Fry rashers of bacon and then heat pineapple rings and halved bananas in the bacon fat. Serve with tiny potato croquettes (Recipe No. 297) and salad.

Autumn risotto (Recipe No. 912)

Eggs in a nest

917   EGGS IN A NEST

Mash approximately ½kg (1 lb) potato and form into 4–6 flan shapes on a well greased baking tin or ovenproof serving dish. Fork neatly as in picture.

Cook above the centre of a moderate oven, 350°F, 180°C, Gas Mark 4, for about 10 minutes, remove from the oven. Break an egg into each potato 'flan', season well and return to the oven for a further 10 minutes. Lift on to a heated serving dish (if necessary), sprinkle with chopped parsley or chives and garnish with sprigs of parsley.

918   MUSHROOM BAKED EGGS

75g/3oz *cooking fat* · 100g/4oz *mushrooms, sliced* · *seasoning*
4 *eggs* · 4 *tablespoons double cream*

Divide 50g (2 oz) cooking fat between 4 small ovenproof dishes. Place these on a baking sheet and heat for a few minutes in a moderate oven, 375°F, 190°C, Gas Mark 5, to melt the fat. Remove from the oven, add the mushrooms and seasoning; cook for 10 minutes. Break one egg over the mushrooms, top with the cream, the rest of the fat in small pieces, and season lightly. Return to the oven for a further 10–12 minutes until the eggs are set.

Mushroom baked eggs

Sausage burgers

919   SAUSAGE BURGERS

40g/1½oz *butter* · 1 *medium-sized onion, chopped*
200g/8oz *sausage meat*
2 *heaped tablespoons white breadcrumbs*
1 *cooking apple, peeled, cored and chopped* · *seasoning*
pinch dried sage · 1 *egg* · 50g/2oz *fat for frying* · 4 *soft rolls*
little made mustard, optional · *watercress to garnish*

Melt 25g (1 oz) of the butter in a frying pan and fry the prepared onion until tender. Mix together the sausage meat, breadcrumbs, onion, apple, seasoning and sage. Bind with egg. On a floured board form the mixture into 4 rounds. Heat the fat and fry the sausage burgers for about 7 minutes on each side. Split the rolls, spread with remaining butter and the mustard, and place a burger in each. Garnish with watercress and serve with a green salad.

920 POTATO AND BACON SAVOURY

100g/4oz raw potato, grated · 100g/4oz bacon, chopped
100g/4oz flour (with plain flour use 1 level teaspoon baking powder)
50g/2oz canned sweet corn · 2 eggs · seasoning
25g/1oz lard · tomato slices to garnish

Choose a very heavy frying pan in which to fry this, so the mixture cooks without burning on the bottom. If you have no heavy pan, then see the note below.

Mix together the potato, bacon, flour and sweet corn. Beat the eggs and add to the potato mixture. Season to taste. Heat the lard in a frying pan and spread the mixture evenly over the pan. Cook gently until brown and crisp on the base. Turn over and cook the other side. Turn on to a serving dish and garnish with tomato slices. To serve, cut in wedges.

NOTE

In a lighter pan it is better to fry spoonfuls of the mixture in hot lard until brown, turn and brown on the second side, then lower the heat and cook more gently for a few minutes.

Potato and bacon savoury

921 FINNAN HADDIE NIPS

4 slices bread · 150g/6oz cooked smoked haddock
4 tablespoons condensed cream of mushroom soup · 2 egg yolks
1 teaspoon lemon juice · seasoning
tomato and parsley to garnish

Toast the bread, remove the crusts, cut each slice into triangles and keep hot. Flake the fish and place in a saucepan with the soup. Stirring, heat gently add the egg yolks, lemon juice and seasoning. Stir over a gentle heat until the mixture thickens – do not allow to boil. Spoon the haddock mixture on to the toast triangles and serve garnished with tomato and parsley.

Finnan haddie nips

Salad Niçoise

922 BACON PUDDING

426ml/¾pint milk · 50g/2oz fresh breadcrumbs · 2 eggs, beaten
100g/4oz cooked bacon or ham, minced · 15g/½oz butter
little grated cheese, optional

Heat the milk and pour over the breadcrumbs; leave to soak for 20–30 minutes, add the beaten eggs, bacon or ham and butter. Pour into a greased ovenproof dish, sprinkle with grated cheese if liked and bake in the centre of a moderate oven, 375°F, 190°C, Gas Mark 4–5 for about 45 minutes until golden brown and firm. Serve at once.

923 SALAD NICOISE

200g/8oz cooked French beans
200g/8oz cooked potatoes, cubed
vinaigrette dressing (Recipe No. 419) · 1 lettuce
4 tomatoes, quartered · 2 hard-boiled eggs, quartered
½ cucumber, sliced · few black olives · few anchovy fillets

Toss the French beans and potatoes in the dressing; arrange in a salad bowl lined with lettuce leaves. Arrange the tomatoes, eggs and cucumber slices on top. Garnish with black olives and anchovy fillets.

924　PILCHARDS SPANISH STYLE

1 tablespoon oil · 1 small onion, chopped
1 small green pepper, chopped · 200g/8oz long grain rice
½litre/generous ¾pint water · seasoning
100g/4oz cooked peas · 1 large can pilchards, flaked
parsley to garnish

Heat the oil in a saucepan and fry the onion and green pepper
for 2–3 minutes. Add the rice, water and seasoning. Bring to
the boil, stir well, cover, lower the heat and cook until all the
liquid has been absorbed and the rice is tender. Stir in the
peas and flaked pilchards and allow to heat through. Spoon
into a serving dish and serve garnished with parsley.
Use diced cooked ham, chicken or other meat in place of
pilchards.

Pilchards Spanish style

Egg and bacon flan

925　SPAGHETTI BOLOGNESE

150–225g/6–8oz spaghetti · grated Parmesan cheese

Bolognese sauce

25g/1oz butter · 1 tablespoon oil
1 clove garlic, crushed, optional · 1 onion, finely chopped
50g/2oz mushrooms, chopped · 1 carrot, chopped
150g/6oz minced beef
350g/14oz can tomatoes or small can tomato purée or
4 fresh tomatoes, chopped
stock, see method · 4 tablespoons red wine · seasoning

Heat the butter and oil in a pan and fry the garlic, if used,
onion, mushrooms and carrot for several minutes. Add the
meat and the rest of the ingredients. If using canned tomatoes
add 284ml (½ pint) stock; with tomato purée and fresh tomatoes add 284ml (½ pint) plus 4 tablespoons. Simmer for about
25 minutes.
Meanwhile cook the spaghetti in boiling salted water (quick-
cooking variety takes only 7 minutes) until just tender. Drain
and place on a serving dish. Pour the sauce on top and serve
with grated Parmesan cheese.

926　EGG AND BACON FLAN

100g/4oz puff pastry* (Recipe No. 588) · 3 rashers bacon
1 eating apple, peeled, cored and chopped · 2 eggs
284ml/½pint milk or milk and single cream · seasoning
parsley and stuffed olives to garnish

*Or use 200–225g/8oz frozen pastry

Make the pastry, roll out thinly and line a round, fairly shallow
ovenproof dish. Chop the bacon and fry lightly; place the
bacon and apple over the pastry. Lightly beat the eggs and
milk or milk and cream together. Mix in seasoning. Carefully
pour into the pastry case and bake in a hot to very hot oven,
450–475°F, 230–240°C, Gas Mark 8–9 for 20 minutes, then
lower heat to moderate, 350°F, 180°C, Gas Mark 4, to set the
filling, and bake for a further 35–45 minutes. Garnish with
parsley and slices of stuffed olive.
This egg and bacon flan or quiche is often called Quiche
Lorraine.

927 SAUSAGE AND APPLE GRILL

8 sausages · 2 large cooking apples, cored and cut into rings
knob butter · mixed spice · creamed potatoes (Recipe No. 303)
parsley to garnish

Grill sausages until cooked; keep warm. Fry apple rings in
butter until tender, remove to a warm plate and sprinkle with
mixed spice. Pipe the edges of 4 individual dishes with a
border of mashed potato, and place under a hot grill to brown.
Place cooked sausages in centre of the dishes, and place on
large serving plates. Arrange apple rings along side of the
dishes and garnish with parsley.
Fried apple rings are excellent with either bacon or sausages.
Core, but do not peel, dessert or fairly sweet cooking apples
and fry in the bacon or sausage fat until tender.
The picture shows an interesting way of serving the homely
'sausage and mash'.

928 BACON AND TOMATO CASSEROLE

150g/6oz spaghetti or macaroni · 8 large ripe tomatoes
1 medium-sized onion, sliced · 1 clove garlic, chopped
bouquet garni · 1 teaspoon cornflour · 25g/1oz butter, melted
salt and pepper · pinch sugar · 6 rashers bacon, chopped
50g/2oz cheese, grated

Cook spaghetti or macaroni in boiling salted water until just
tender. Cut up tomatoes and crush them with a wooden
spoon in a thick saucepan. Add the onion, garlic and bouquet
garni. Simmer gently for 10 minutes until soft. Press through
a sieve to make a purée. Mix the cornflour with the melted
butter, add to the purée, return to the pan and simmer for 15
minutes. Season with salt and pepper and a pinch of sugar.
Fry the bacon until crisp. Mix together the sauce, bacon and
cooked, drained spaghetti or macaroni and place in a casserole
or ovenproof dish. Sprinkle grated cheese on top and place in
a moderate oven, 375°F, 190°C, Gas Mark 5, for 5–10 minutes.

Sausage and apple grill

Pilchards Mornay

929 PILCHARDS MORNAY

4 hard-boiled eggs · 200g/8oz can pilchards · seasoning
6 tomatoes, sliced · 284ml/½pint cheese sauce (Recipe No. 665)
25g/1oz cheese, grated
chopped parsley and a sprig of watercress to garnish

Cut the eggs in half lengthways and scoop out the yolks. Mix
the yolks with the pilchards; season well and spoon back into
the egg whites. Place in an ovenproof dish with the tomato
slices. Pour the cheese sauce over the eggs and sprinkle over
the grated cheese. Place in a moderately hot oven, 400°F,
200°C, Gas Mark 6, for about 20 minutes. Garnish with
chopped parsley and a sprig of watercress.

Cheese life-savers

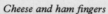
Cheese and ham fingers

930   CHEESE LIFE-SAVERS

sliced white bread (day-old) · butter · cheese, finely grated
pinch cayenne pepper · 1 large carrot

Cut circles from the sliced bread using a 4-cm (1¾-inch) pastry cutter and remove the centres using a 2½-cm (1-inch) cutter. Melt a little butter in a frying pan, dip the bread rings in the butter then toss in the finely grated seasoned cheese until well coated. Use Cheddar to which a little Parmesan may be added for extra flavour. Place the cheese-coated bread on a baking sheet and brown in a moderately hot oven, 375–400°F, 190–200°C, Gas Mark 5, for about 10 minutes. Serve at once. Trim the base of a large clean carrot and stand it upright with cocktail sticks prodded diagonally into the top part – hang the life-savers on the sticks.

931   CHEESE AND HAM FINGERS

6 slices white bread · butter · 2 slices ham
little made mustard · 100g/4oz cheese, grated

Toast the slices of bread and spread with butter. Arrange ham on 2 slices of toast, spread with mustard then cover with another slice of toast. On top of that put the cheese. Top with the remaining slice of toast. Cut into fingers and serve.
Makes 2 servings.

932   BEAN CLUB SANDWICH

½kg/16oz can baked beans
4 teaspoons chopped spring onion tops or pickled onions
2 teaspoons Worcestershire sauce · 8 rashers bacon, cut in half
lettuce leaves · 24 slices toast · parsley to garnish

Mash baked beans with a fork. Mix in onion and Worcestershire sauce. Fry bacon until crisp. Arrange lettuce and bacon on eight slices of toast. Cover with a slice of toast. Spread with bean mixture. Cover with remaining slices of toast. Cut diagonally and garnish with parsley.
Makes 8 servings.

933 SAUSAGE SNACKS

4 sausages · 4 thick slices bread · butter
2 tomatoes, sliced · watercress and radishes to garnish

Grill or fry the sausages, cut in half lengthways and leave to cool. Spread the slices of bread with butter. Place 2 sausage halves on each slice of bread; arrange tomato slices down the centre and garnish with watercress and radishes.

934 KIPPER CROQUETTES

200g/8oz cooked kipper, without skin or bones*
250g/10oz mashed potato · 1 egg · seasoning
2 teaspoons lemon juice · 2 tablespoons water
3 tablespoons crisp breadcrumbs for coating
oil or fat for frying · lemon and parsley to garnish

*Kipper fillets save removing bones

Blend the flaked kipper flesh, potato and egg yolk together. Season lightly with salt and more generously with pepper. Add the lemon juice and form into 8–12 finger shapes. Blend the egg white with the water, brush the croquettes with this and then coat in the crisp crumbs. If possible allow to stand in a cool place for a short time before frying. Heat either deep fat or oil, (see Recipe No. 735 for advice on testing this), or 50–75g (2–3 oz) fat or oil in a frying pan and cook the croquettes until crisp and brown. Drain on absorbent paper and garnish with twists of lemon and parsley.

Sausage snacks

Kipper croquettes

935 TOMATO CHEESE TOASTS

25g/1oz butter · 25g/1oz flour · 284ml/½pint milk
good pinch salt · ½ teaspoon made mustard
pinch cayenne pepper · 200g/8oz Cheddar cheese, grated
4 tomatoes, skinned and sliced · 4 slices buttered toast
2 rashers bacon, halved and grilled to garnish

Melt the butter in a small saucepan. Add the flour and cook for 1 minute. Gradually add the milk, stirring, and bring to the boil. Add the seasonings and grated cheese and stir over a gentle heat until the cheese has melted. Arrange the tomato slices on the toast and put under a moderate grill to heat through. Pour over the hot cheese sauce and serve at once garnished with crisp bacon rashers.

Tomato cheese toasts

Savoury eccles

936 SAVOURY ECCLES

200g/8oz puff pastry (Recipe No. 588)
100–125g/4–5oz Cheddar cheese, grated
100–125g/4–5oz cooked ham, chopped
6 level tablespoons tomato pickle or ketchup · 1 egg

Roll out the puff pastry to ¼-cm (⅛-inch) in thickness and cut into six 14-cm (5½-inch) rounds. Blend the cheese, ham and tomato pickle or ketchup together then place the mixture in the centre of the pastry rounds. Brush the edges of the pastry with water, then gather these together until you have a round ball. Turn each pastry ball over so the joins are underneath. Roll gently to form a neat oval shape and put on to a baking sheet or tin. Leave in a cool place for at least 15 minutes then make 3 slits on top with a sharp knife or kitchen scissors. Brush with the beaten egg. Bake above the centre of a hot to very hot oven, 425–450°F, 220–230°C, Gas Mark 7–8, for 15–20 minutes. Lower the heat after about 10 minutes if necessary, to prevent the pastry becoming over brown. Serve hot or cold with salad.

SUBSTANTIAL SANDWICHES FOR HUNGRY FOLK

937   PARTY LAYER SANDWICH

½kg/1lb *cottage cheese* · 2 *tablespoons whipped double cream*
1 *tablespoon mayonnaise (Recipe No. 408)*
seasoning to taste · 1 *dessertspoon gelatine, see method*
1 *large unsliced loaf* · *various sandwich fillings**
fruit and salad garnish**

*Minced ham mixed with made mustard, a little chopped gherkin and mayonnaise; flaked tuna fish and capers mixed with mayonnaise; chopped hard-boiled eggs, a little chopped anchovy and mayonnaise; lamb's brains and chopped walnuts with salad dressing lightly seasoned with mustard
**Peach halves or pineapple slices, clusters of grapes or fresh cherries, radish, cucumber or tomato slices, olives, cress or lettuce

Rub the cottage cheese through a sieve and blend with the cream and mayonnaise. Season to taste and chill. (If the weather is very hot add 1 dessertspoon gelatine dissolved in 1 tablespoon boiling water). Slice the crusts off loaf and cut along the loaf lengthways in 3 or 4 slices. Sandwich with various fillings; (only butter the bread if the filling needs the blandness and moisture of butter). Place on serving dish and spread the creamy cheese mixture over top and sides. Garnish attractively.

938   BACON BURGERS

½kg/1lb *minced beef* · 3 *tablespoons fresh breadcrumbs*
1 *egg, beaten* · *seasoning* · 8 *rashers streaky bacon*
cocktail sticks · *fat for frying* · *butter* · 8 *round soft rolls*
tomato ketchup · *French mustard*

Mix together the minced beef, breadcrumbs, egg and seasoning. On a floured board, form the mixture into 8 rounds. Wrap a rasher of bacon round each, secure with cocktail stick. Heat the fat in a frying pan and fry the burgers for about 4 minutes on each side, until cooked through; remove the cocktail sticks. Put the burgers between the buttered rolls, top with tomato ketchup and serve with French mustard.

Party layer sandwich

939   PILCHARD AND CUCUMBER SANDWICHES

200g/8oz *can pilchards in oil* · 1 *teaspoon grated onion*
1 *teaspoon tomato ketchup* · *pepper* · 4–6 *slices buttered bread*
watercress · *slices of cucumber*

Mash the pilchards and mix with the onion, tomato ketchup and pepper to taste. Spread on slices of buttered bread, top with a little watercress and 1 or 2 thin slices of cucumber. Minced ham and tongue or chicken and ham or other meats may be used as a change from pilchards. Blend either with mayonnaise or a little chutney and mayonnaise.

Pilchard and cucumber sandwiches

Cottage cheese and fruit layers

940 COTTAGE CHEESE AND FRUIT LAYERS

Sandwich slices of brown, wholemeal or rye bread together in threes with cottage cheese, canned drained mandarin oranges and pear slices, dipped in lemon juice. Garnish with cottage cheese and toasted almonds.

941 BACON WEDGES

Top thick slices of fresh bread with plenty of butter and with crisp bacon rolls. Allow 2–3 per person.

942 BANANA SURPRISE

thick slices French bread · banana butter (Recipe No. 943)
bananas

Make a hole in the middle of each piece of French bread. Spread with banana butter, and put a portion of banana through. Children love these.

943 BANANA BUTTER

50g/2oz butter · 1 large banana · squeeze lemon juice

Cream the butter in a small basin and gradually mash the banana into this. Add a squeeze of lemon juice.

944 OPEN SANDWICHES

Spread slices of brown bread with savoury butter (Recipe No. 945). Arrange a lettuce leaf on each slice and top with a mixture of any of the following: slices of tomato, hard-boiled egg, apple (dipped in lemon juice or coated with dressing or oil), salami, cheese or ham. Garnish as shown in the picture below with prawns sprinkled with paprika pepper, slices of apple, cucumber or radish or halved black grapes.

945 SAVOURY BUTTER

50g/2oz butter · squeeze lemon juice
good pinch celery salt · good pinch cayenne pepper

Mix all the ingredients together.

Open sandwiches

946   DANISH SANDWICHES

While small dainty open sandwiches can be served, the real Danish sandwiches are a meal in themselves. Cut reasonably thin bread, and vary this as much as possible – use brown, white, wholemeal and if possible look for rye bread, etc. in shops selling continental specialities. Make your open sandwiches look as colourful as possible. If prepared beforehand, cover them with damp cloths or damp paper so that they keep fresh.

947   DANISH SANDWICH SELECTION

The picture on the right shows a selection of Danish open sandwiches.

Thin slices of Samsoe cheese garnished with black grapes and parsley.

Slices of smoked pork fillet (ham can be used instead) on a lettuce leaf, topped with firm scrambled egg and garnished with parsley and a slice of tomato.

Slices of ham (boiled shoulder of bacon could be used) garnished with cucumber slices and parsley.

Slices of luncheon meat garnished with lettuce, a stoned prune and twist of orange.

Thin slice of Danish Blue cheese garnished with halved black grapes.

Slices of salami garnished with lettuce and raw onion rings.

Slices of brawn garnished with raw onion rings and parsley.

Scrambled egg on a lettuce leaf garnished with crisp bacon rashers and parsley.

948   DANISH LUNCHEON

1. Cover buttered bread with a lettuce leaf, top with slices of tomato and hard-boiled egg. Garnish with a piping of mayonnaise (Recipe No. 408) and chopped parsley.
2. Cover buttered bread with a slice of pâté; top with grilled bacon rashers and cucumber slices.
3. Cover buttered bread with a lettuce leaf, top with slices of tongue. Garnish with mayonnaise (Recipe No. 408) and a slice of green pepper.
4. Cover buttered bread with a lettuce leaf; top with scrambled egg then slices of salami. Garnish with cress and onion rings.
5. Cover buttered bread with a lettuce leaf; top with slices of brawn. Garnish with parsley and strips of green pepper.
6. Cover buttered bread with slices of luncheon meat; top with cream cheese. Garnish with black olives and a twist of orange.
7. Cover buttered bread with a lettuce leaf; top with slices of smoked ham and cream cheese. Garnish with slices of radish.
8. Cover buttered bread with slices of ham; top with a lettuce leaf and a little shredded cabbage tossed in mayonnaise (Recipe No. 408). Garnish with parsley and slices of cucumber.

949   MANHATTAN LAYER LOAF

1 *small round white loaf* · 50g/2oz *butter*

Bottom slice

1 *lettuce* · 2 *tomatoes, sliced*
2 *teaspoons chopped chives or spring onion tops*

Middle slice

2 *tablespoons mayonnaise (Recipe No. 408)*
¼ *teaspoon curry powder* · 100g/4oz *cold chicken*

Top slice

3 *teaspoons mango chutney* · 3 *slices cooked ham*
9 *stuffed olives* · 2 *spring onions, finely chopped*

Cut loaf into 4 slices horizontally. Discard the top crust slice. Butter 3 remaining slices.
Bottom slice: cover with small lettuce leaves and tomato rings. Sprinkle with chopped chives or spring onion tops.
Middle slice: mix together mayonnaise with curry powder and stir in chicken cut into 1-cm (½-inch) cubes. Spread over bread.
Top slice: place a teaspoon of mango chutney on each slice of ham. Fold in half diagonally then fold again making a triangle. Arrange on bread with points of triangle at the centre. Re-assemble loaf. Place stuffed olives between ham triangles and a little chopped spring onion on top of each ham triangle. To serve, cut into wedges.
Makes 6 servings.

Danish sandwich selection

Danish luncheon

Manhattan layer loaf

Luncheon salad sandwiches

Savoury sandwich gâteau

950 LUNCHEON SALAD SANDWICHES

These sandwiches have a topping with a new flavour.

Curried prawn sandwich

1 *slice white or brown bread, about 1-cm (½-inch) thick · butter*
few small lettuce leaves · good pinch curry powder
2 tablespoons soured cream or natural yoghourt
50g/2oz prawns, peeled · 1 slice lemon

Spread the bread with butter. Arrange lettuce leaves on bread. Blend curry powder into soured cream or yoghourt, then mix in prawns, leaving 4 for garnishing. Place prawn mixture on lettuce, then garnish with the remaining prawns and the lemon slice.
Makes 1 serving.

Devilled ham sandwich

2 slices cooked ham · 1 tablespoon mayonnaise (Recipe No. 408)
mixed with 1 teaspoon made mustard
1 slice wholemeal or caraway seed bread, about 1-cm (½-inch) thick
butter · 8 thin slices cucumber
3 wedge-shaped slices Edam cheese

Spread ham slices with mayonnaise and mustard mixture and roll up. Spread the bread with butter. Place cucumber slices, slightly overlapping, along edges of bread slice, then place on ham rolls meeting in the centre and finally top ham with slices of cheese. Serve with extra mayonnaise, if liked.
Makes 1 serving.

Salami salad sandwich

½ bap or soft roll · butter · 1 lettuce leaf · 3 slices salami
3 raw onion rings · ¼ tomato · 2 black olives

Spread the bap or soft roll with butter. Cover with lettuce leaf. Arrange salami, onion rings, tomato and olives on top.
Makes 1 serving.

951   SAVOURY SANDWICH GATEAU

1 round loaf, all crusts removed and cut into 4 layers

Fillings

Top and bottom layers
100g (4 oz) cream cheese blended with 50g (2 oz) butter and either left plain or flavoured to taste with tomato purée, chopped chives or anchovy paste.

Centre layer
1 small can sardines, drained and mashed with seasoning to taste and 1 dessertspoon lemon juice or 100g (4 oz) liver pâté blended with a little fried chopped bacon or 100g (4 oz) minced cooked meat or poultry blended with a little mayonnaise (Recipe No. 408) or 2 hard-boiled eggs, chopped and blended with seasoning and a little top of the milk or single cream.

Coating and Garnish

100g/4oz cream cheese blended with 50g/2oz butter
chopped salted peanuts · radish 'rose' · sprigs of watercress
tomato wedges

Sandwich together the layers of bread with prepared fillings. Spread cream cheese mixture over top and sides. Press peanuts firmly against the sides, transfer to a serving dish and pipe lines of cream cheese mixture over the top. Garnish with watercress sprigs and a radish 'rose' in the centre. Place tomato wedges round the edge of the dish and serve with a mixed salad.

TIME-CONTROLLED COOKING

The introduction of time-controlled cookers is an enormous boon to the families of career housewives where there are children, or when entertaining.

The following menu and facts will help you to get the most successful results with your timer.

The complete family meal illustrated was left to 'cook itself' and all the housewife had to do was to make a very few simple last-minute adjustments.

MENU

Chicken soup

Roast beef and roast potatoes

Peas and onion rings

Plum pie and cream

952 FAMILY MENU USING THE TIMER

Before cooking

Prepare soup as Recipe No. 70, put into ovenproof dish and cover with foil – do not over-fill the dish as the soup could boil over. The foil was removed before taking the picture, opposite. Place on bottom shelf.

Wash and dry meat, add little fat if you feel this necessary, but the potatoes will be coated in fat, see below. Meat in picture weighs about generous 1½kg (3½ lb).

Roll the raw peeled potatoes in well melted fat, so keeping them from discolouring in the oven. Arrange round beef and put into centre of oven.

Shell fresh peas or use frozen peas (do not defrost). Put into a casserole with rings of thinly sliced onion, butter and seasoning. Add a little water with fresh peas. Cover tightly with foil (this was removed before taking the picture, opposite). Put beside soup on bottom shelf.

Make the plum pie (this pie had short crust pastry). If the fruit is very juicy stand on a baking tin, so any juice cannot boil into the oven. Lay a piece of greaseproof paper over the pastry so it does not become over-brown. (This was removed before taking picture). Put on top shelf.

Oven set at

375–400°F, 190–200°C,
Gas Mark 5–6, for 1¼ hours.

After cooking

Make gravy for main course. Stir soup and serve. Dish up meat and potatoes, strain peas and serve. Dish up pie and serve with cream.

953   COOKING BY THE TIMER

Many women still think that cooking by the timer must involve lengthy preparation and careful selection of food. This is not, in fact, the case – it is a way of cooking that gives greater leisure and convenience without spoiling the food.

Modern research has shown that nearly all food can be cooked by the timer and that, with the exception of a few recipes that are cooked in a very short time, the results are as good as those obtained by the more orthodox methods.

The oven of a good, modern cooker fitted with a timer can be used in three different ways.

First of all it can be used in the orthodox fashion, by putting the food in a pre-heated oven and removing it when it is cooked. This method does not involve using the timer.

Secondly the food can be put in the cold oven, the timer set for the oven to switch on later in the day and to switch off again when the food is cooked. This method is usually referred to as 'cooking *from* cold', and while most food can be cooked in this way, the obvious great value to the busy housewife lies in the fact that a complete meal can be put in the oven hours ahead of the time it is to be served, and forgotten about until it is time to serve it.

Thirdly, food can be put in a hot oven and the timer set to switch off at an appropriate time, leaving the cooked food to cool in the oven. This method is called 'cooking *to* cold', and is of most value with rich cakes and baked ham, or long-cooking meat dishes to serve cold. A busy woman can put such food in the oven last thing at night and set the timer so that the food will be cooked in the morning.

Stuffed breast of lamb served with duchesse potatoes (Recipe No. 168)

954   USE OF THE TIMER

The value of a time-controlled cooker is immediately obvious to any housewife, but as I feel that many housewives do not use them as much as they might, here is a short list of the types of food that can be cooked by this method.

1. The complete meal, to be served hot. Either lunch or dinner can be ready without attention and, as the cooker switches off when the food is cooked, it can be safely left for children to help themselves. Roast joints as well as casseroles are excellent, so are sweet and savoury pies.

2. In hot weather, the food, which is nearly always to be eaten cold with a salad, can be cooked at night when the house-wife is in bed. She can prepare the meal (say a round of beef or stuffed breast of lamb, see picture above and Recipe No. 168, to be served with a salad and a fruit pie) in the cool of the evening, and serve it the following day.

3. Picnic and packed luncheon food can also be cooked over-night.

4. In households where the whole family is in a hurry first thing in the morning, breakfast can be put in the oven at night, and the timer set to switch on 30 minutes or so before the food will be wanted – in fact while the family are getting up, the breakfast is cooking itself. For details of temperatures, timing and oven positions consult your manufacturer's instruction book.

Most foods need no more preparation than is required if they are cooked by orthodox methods, but there are a few exceptions listed below:

1. Food that discolours while standing must be protected. Potatoes, for example, if waiting in the meat pan after peeling, will oxidise before the oven switches on. The best prevention is to coat such foods in fat so that they are not in contact with the air. With vegetables to be roasted this serves the double purpose of ensuring that they will brown without basting, which, of course, cannot be done if the meal is to cook without any attention.

2. Fruit and vegetables can be 'boiled' in the oven. They should be prepared in the usual way, placed in an ovenproof dish and covered with a very well-fitting lid or, better still, a piece of foil folded over the side of the dish to ensure a good seal. (As the whole point of cooking by the timer is to save the housewife staying in the kitchen to attend to the food, it is important that the seal should be good enough to prevent the food from boiling dry). This foil can be used again.

Here again some food has to be protected against discoloura-tion before cooking, and it is advisable to toss root vegetables in melted butter. Some fruit, such as apples and pears, will also look unsightly, and since a coating of fat is hardly suitable, it is usually suggested that the discolouration is concealed by mixing with another, coloured, fruit or even a spoonful of jam. Baked apples (see picture below and Recipe No. 450) for example, are ideal as the skins form a protective layer.

3. Puddings can be steamed in the oven, by making the pudding in the usual way, placing the mixture in a basin and covering with foil. The basin should then be stood on a rack or pastry cutter in another larger basin or suitable container, which should be half-filled with cold water. This larger basin must then be sealed with aluminium foil, giving the effect of a steamer.

4. A very few recipes are unsuitable for cooking by the timer. Any foods that cook in less time than it takes to heat the oven, such as scones, Swiss rolls and small cakes have to be cooked by orthodox methods. A soufflé mixture is spoiled if it stands in the oven even for a short time before it cooks and the vitamins, colour and flavour of green vegetables would be destroyed by standing in the oven or prolonged oven cooking.

Baked apples stuffed with mincemeat (Recipe No. 450)

JAMS & PRESERVING

956 **CERTAIN SUCCESS WITH JAM MAKING**

1. Choose firm, ripe but NEVER over-ripe fruit. Over-ripe or damp fruit will frequently prevent the jam from setting, will cause it to go mouldy or ferment. Very under-ripe fruit lacks flavour, but slightly under-ripe fruit can be used.
2. Do not imagine that 1kg of sugar to each 1kg fruit (1lb sugar to 1lb fruit) is ideal for *all* jams. The pectin content, i.e. the setting quality of fruit varies a great deal, e.g. blackcurrants set very well, so this jam is made with *less* fruit than sugar. On the other hand cherry jam sets less well so use *more* fruit than sugar to give a greater quantity of pectin. In addition also add lemon or redcurrant juice.
3. *Simmer* the fruit very gently to extract the pectin and soften the skin or peel. NEVER add sugar until the skins or peel are tender, as fruit will tend to toughen rather than become softer when sugar is put in.
4. Stir over a *low heat* to dissolve the sugar; when once the sugar has dissolved, increase the heat so the jam boils rapidly. Do not stir the jam as it boils for this would lower the temperature and prevent it reaching setting point quickly.
5. Make jam in a really large preserving pan, saucepan or pressure cooker so there is plenty of space for the fruit and sugar to boil, without fear of it boiling over.
6. Start testing the jam early for setting point (see Recipe No. 959) for the time jams or marmalades take to set varies a great deal – with some preserves it is a few moments only after the sugar has been dissolved and the jam starts to boil. OVER-BOILING will give a jam lacking in flavour, and it might be too stiff, on the other hand you may go *past* setting point in which case the jam will *never* set.
7. Ladle most jams into hot jars immediately and cover with waxed circles. With whole fruit jam or marmalade, in order to distribute the peel or fruit evenly allow the jam or marmalade to cool slightly in the pan, and start to thicken, stir briskly, then ladle into warmed jars. This stops fruit or peel rising in jars. Fill to within ½ cm (¼ inch) of the top of the jar.
8. Though the waxed circle is put on the jam immediately, cool slightly before adding the top cover. Always cover jam thoroughly, and store in a cool, dry and preferably dark place.
9. Use preserving or loaf sugar if possible or if not available then choose granulated sugar.
10. Where recipes give 'redcurrant juice' this is obtained by crushing and straining redcurrants. Approximately 100g (4 oz) fruit should yield 2–3 tablespoons juice.

---

957 PEAR, APRICOT AND ALMOND JAM

(Illustrated in colour on the opposite page)

½kg/1lb *dried apricots* · generous 1½litres/3pints *water*
200g/8oz *pears, peeled, cored and thickly sliced*
1½kg/3lb *sugar* · *juice 2 lemons* · 75g/3oz *blanched almonds*

Wash the apricots and soak in the water for at least 24 hours. After soaking, put the apricots and water with the pears in a saucepan and simmer for 30 minutes. Add the sugar and lemon juice. Stir until the sugar has dissolved. Boil rapidly until the setting point is reached, then stir in the almonds. Allow to cool slightly, stirring occasionally to prevent fruit rising. Ladle into warmed jars and cover.

958 APPLE AND PLUM CHEESE

(Illustrated in colour on the opposite page)

1½kg/3lb *apples* · 1½kg/3lb *plums* · *sugar, see method*

This is a good preserve if you have windfalls; you must of course cut away any damaged part of the fruit. Rinse in cold water. Cut up the apples without peeling. Halve the plums, and put all the fruit into a preserving pan. Just cover with water and stew till pulpy. Rub through a sieve. Measure the pulp – allow ½kg sugar to each 590ml (1lb sugar to each 1 pint). Place the sugar and pulp in a pan. Stir until the sugar has dissolved. Bring to the boil and boil rapidly until thick. Ladle into warmed jars and cover.

A selection of preserves

959 HOW TO TELL IF JAM HAS REACHED SETTING POINT

1. Test with a sugar thermometer; jam (if the correct recipe is used) sets at 220°F, 104–105°C. Make sure the thermometer is registering correctly before use by putting it into boiling water, when it should register 212°F, 100°C.
2. Put a little on to a cold saucer – allow jam to cool, then push with your finger or teaspoon. If the jam has set it wrinkles.
3. Stir the preserve round thoroughly with a wooden spoon, then allow jam to cool slightly on the spoon. Hold the spoon over the preserving pan horizontally – if the jam has set it will hold a firm drop or flake on the edge of the spoon. If it drops off into the pan it is not set. Remember, though, you must wait and allow the jam to cool on the spoon.

Ladling apricot jam into warmed jars

960 YIELD OF JAM

Correctly made jam should contain 60% sugar. That means:
½kg sugar should produce ⅚kg jam and 1lb sugar should produce 1⅔lb jam.
1kg sugar should produce 1⅔kg jam and 2lb sugar should produce 3lb jam.
1½kg sugar should produce 2½kg jam and 3lb sugar should produce 5lb jam.
Jam made with commercial pectin often has a different yield and in the recipes where this is used the yield is given at the bottom of each recipe.

961 USING COMMERCIAL PECTIN

Many fruits are lacking in natural setting quality – pectin – and commercial pectin enables the jam to set quickly without prolonged boiling, which spoils flavour and colour.

962 YOUR PAN FOR JAM

Try to invest in a proper preserving pan – strong enough to prevent scorching and wide enough to encourage *rapid boiling*, which is one of the secrets of good-flavoured jam. The pans illustrated here are ideal for making jams and preserves.

963 APPLE GINGER

½kg/1lb *cooking apples, weight after peeling and coring**
½kg/1lb *sugar*
1 *teaspoon ground ginger or* 25–50g/1–2oz *crystallised ginger, chopped*

**Save both the peel and cores*

Cut the apples into neat cubes, sprinkle over the sugar and let it stand overnight with the peel and cores, also in the bowl, but tied in a muslin bag. Put into a saucepan or preserving pan, (with the muslin bag), simmer gently, stirring all the time until the sugar has thoroughly dissolved, add ginger, then boil steadily until the cubes of apple look transparent and the syrup has set. Discard the muslin bag then ladle the jam into warmed jars and cover.

964 APRICOT JAM

(With fresh fruit)

½kg/1lb *apricots*
2 *tablespoons water, unless the fruit is under-ripe, then use 4 tablespoons*
½kg/1lb *sugar · juice* ½ *large lemon*

Cut the fruit into pieces. If liked crack the stones and take out the kernels. Put kernels into a preserving pan with the fruit and water and simmer until the fruit is soft. Add the sugar and lemon juice and stir until the sugar has dissolved. Boil rapidly until set. Ladle into warmed jars and cover.

965 APRICOT JAM
(With dried fruit)

½kg/1lb *dried apricots* · generous 1½litres/3pints *water*
1½kg/3lb *sugar* · *juice* 1½ *lemons*

Soak the fruit in water for 48 or even 72 hours. Simmer gently until the fruit is soft. Add the sugar and lemon juice; stir until the sugar has dissolved, then boil rapidly until set. Ladle into warmed jars and cover.
DRIED PEACH JAM can be made in the same way.

966 DRIED APRICOT JAM
(With commercial pectin)

225g*/8oz *dried apricots* · generous ¾litre/1½pints *water*
3 *tablespoons lemon juice* · 1½kg/3lb *sugar*
1 *bottle commercial pectin*

*Gives best result

Wash fruit and leave to soak for at least 48 hours in the water. Simmer, covered for about 30 minutes to break up the fruit. Measure generous ¾litre (1½ pints) prepared fruit pulp, making up the amount with water if necessary. Add lemon juice and sugar and heat slowly, stirring occasionally until the sugar has dissolved. Bring to a full rolling boil and boil rapidly for 1 minute, stirring occasionally. Remove from heat, stir in commercial pectin. Skim if necessary then ladle into warmed jars and cover.
Makes 2½kg (5 lb).

967 BLACKBERRY AND APPLE JAM

½kg/1lb *cooking apples, weight after peeling and coring*
4 *tablespoons water* · ½kg/1lb *blackberries* · 1kg/2lb *sugar*

Put the apples and water into the preserving pan, cook gently until the apples have softened. Add the blackberries, and continue cooking until all the fruit is soft. Stir in the sugar and continue stirring until dissolved. Boil rapidly until jam has set then ladle into warmed jars and cover.

968 BLACKCURRANT JAM

½kg/1lb *blackcurrants* · 426ml/¾pint *water*
½kg plus 100g*/1¼lb *sugar*

*Gives best result

Put the fruit and water into a pan, simmer until the blackcurrants are quite soft. Stir in the sugar and allow to dissolve thoroughly, then boil rapidly until set. Ladle into warmed jars and cover.

969 CHERRY JAM
(With commercial pectin)

1¼kg/2½lb *Morello cherries, stoned* · 142ml/¼pint *water*
3 *tablespoons lemon juice* · 1½kg/3lb *sugar*
1 *bottle commercial pectin* · ¼ *teaspoon almond essence, optional*

Simmer the cherries in the water and lemon juice in a covered pan for about 15 minutes. Add the sugar and heat slowly, stirring occasionally, until sugar has dissolved. Bring to a full rolling boil and boil rapidly for 3 minutes. Stir in the commercial pectin and continue boiling for 1 minute. Remove from heat and skim if necessary. Cool slightly, ladle into warmed jars and cover in the usual way. For a stronger cherry flavour stir in ¼ teaspoon almond essence before ladling the jam into jars.
Makes 2½kg (5lb).
For other jams see Recipe Nos. 980–993

Dried apricot jam

970 BLACK CHERRY JAM
(With commercial pectin)

1¼kg/2½lb *black cherries, stoned* · 142ml/¼pint *water*
juice 2 *lemons* · 1½kg/3lb *sugar* · 1 *bottle commercial pectin*

Put prepared fruit in pan with water and lemon juice. Cook gently with lid on for 15 minutes, remove lid. Add sugar, stir over low heat until dissolved. Bring to rolling boil, boil rapidly for 3 minutes. Remove from heat, add pectin, stir well, cool for 15 minutes, stirring occasionally to prevent fruit rising. Ladle into warmed jars and cover.
Makes 2½kg (5lb).

971 CHERRY JAM

½kg/1lb *cherries*, stoned (this is about* 600g/1¼lb *before stoning)*
350g**/12oz *sugar*
juice ½ *lemon or* ½ *teaspoon citric or tartaric acid*

*If using red Morello cherries use only half the quantity of acid. Use black cherries for Swiss jam
**Gives best result

Put the fruit, and stones tied in muslin, into a pan, simmer until the fruit is soft. Remove the bag of stones and stir in the sugar and lemon juice or acid and continue stirring until the sugar has dissolved. Boil rapidly until set. Cool for 15 minutes, stirring occasionally to prevent fruit rising. Ladle into warmed jars and cover.

Cherry jam

972 SUCCESSFUL PICKLES

Use a good malt vinegar and follow directions carefully for preparing vegetables. Do not use iron pans. Cover carefully. Make sure metal lids do not come in contact with vinegar contents; put waxed paper or wax between lids and contents.

973 PICKLED ONIONS

Onions or shallots must be peeled with stainless knives and left for 48 hours in brine (Recipe No. 977). Remove from brine, rinse well under cold, running water then drain thoroughly. To each generous ½litre (1 pint) malt or white malt vinegar use 1 level tablespoon pickling spice. Boil for 15 minutes then strain. To give a slightly sweet flavour, which some people like, add 200g–½kg (8 oz–1 lb) sugar to each generous litre (2 pints) vinegar. The vinegar must be cold. Pack in jars with vinegar and seal carefully.

974 PICKLED RED CABBAGE

Shred cabbage, put it in a basin with a good sprinkling of salt between layers, and leave for 24 hours. Drain thoroughly – pack into jars and pour over cold spiced vinegar, see recipe below.
Cold spiced vinegar: to each generous ½litre (1 pint) vinegar allow 1 level tablespoon mixed pickling spice. Boil together for 15 minutes – strain and cool. To give a slightly more piquant flavour, blend 1 teaspoon dry mustard with the vinegar.

975 MUSTARD PICKLE

1 *small cauliflower* · 1 *small unpeeled cucumber*
300–350g/12oz *marrow, peeled* · 100g/4oz *shallots, peeled*
25g/1oz *salt* · 15g/½oz *dry mustard* · 1 *teaspoon ground ginger*
1 *teaspoon turmeric* · 40g/1½oz *flour* · 50g/2oz *sugar*
generous ½litre/1pint *malt vinegar*

Divide cauliflower into small sprigs and cut cucumber and marrow into cubes. Cover raw vegetables with salt, leave for 24 hours, then drain. Mix together mustard, ginger, turmeric, flour and sugar, and blend to a smooth paste with a little of the vinegar. Bring remaining vinegar to the boil, pour over the paste, then return all to the pan. Bring to the boil, stirring carefully and cook for 3 minutes. Add prepared vegetables and simmer gently for 10 minutes. Cool slightly, then ladle into warmed jars. Cover when cold.

976 PICKLED WALNUTS

Make sure the nuts are not over-ripe. Prick them deeply with a silver fork in two or three places. Then soak in brine (Recipe No. 977) for at least 3 days. Remove from brine and place on a tray or cloth in the sun, turning occasionally. In about 2 or 3 days they will turn black (if *very* hot 24 hours may suffice). When quite black, pack into jars and cover with spiced vinegar. Cover and mature for at least 1 month before using.
Spiced vinegar: to each generous ½litre (1 pint) vinegar allow 1 level tablespoon mixed pickling spices.

977 BRINE FOR PICKLES

50g/2oz *kitchen salt* · generous ½litre/1pint *cold water*

Mix the salt and water together.

CHUTNEYS

978 TOMATO CHUTNEY

1 *teaspoon pickling spice* · 2 *large onions, finely chopped*
284ml/½pint *malt vinegar*
generous 200g/8oz *apples, peeled, cored and chopped*
1kg/2lb *tomatoes, green or red, sliced* · ½ *teaspoon salt*
¼ *teaspoon pepper* · 1 *rounded teaspoon dry mustard*
½ *teaspoon ginger* · 200g/8oz *sultanas* · 200g/8oz *sugar*

First put the pickling spice into a piece of muslin. Put the onions into a saucepan with 4 tablespoons of the vinegar and simmer gently until nearly soft. Add the prepared apples, tomatoes, spice, salt, pepper, mustard, ginger and sultanas. Simmer gently until the mixture is quite soft, stirring from time to time. Add the remaining vinegar and the sugar. When the sugar has thoroughly dissolved boil steadily until the chutney is the consistency of jam. Remove the bag of spice. Pour the hot chutney into warmed jars and cover at once. It is a mistake to put metal directly on top of the chutney – use paper or melted wax, THEN the paper or metal cover.

Variation
SHARP APPLE CHUTNEY

Follow the recipe above for tomato chutney but use ½kg (1 lb) tomatoes and ¾kg (1½ lb) apples. Increase ground ginger to 2 teaspoons.

A selection of chutneys

979 APPLE AND BANANA CHUTNEY

½kg/1lb *cooking apples* · 284ml/½pint *water*
2 *large onions, chopped* · 200g/8oz *raisins, chopped*
100g/4oz *crystallised ginger* · 350g*/12oz *brown sugar*
3 *large bananas* · 25g/1oz *salt* · ½–1 *teaspoon cayenne pepper*
¾litre/1¼pints *malt vinegar*

**Gives best result*

Peel, core and chop the apples and put in a large saucepan
with the water. Add the chopped onions, raisins, ginger and
sugar. Simmer until soft. Add the chopped bananas, salt,
cayenne pepper and vinegar and simmer slowly, uncovered
until thick. Stir frequently to prevent the mixture burning.
Pour into warmed jars and cover at once.

Variation
APPLE AND RED PEPPER CHUTNEY

In place of bananas use 2 chopped red peppers.

MORE JAM RECIPES

980   DAMSON JAM

½kg/1lb *damsons* · 4 *tablespoons water if fruit is ripe*
½kg/1lb *sugar*

If fruit is very under-ripe use the following quantities:

½kg/1lb *damsons* · 284ml/½pint *water*
½kg plus 100g/1¼lb *sugar*

Put the fruit and water into a pan. Simmer until soft. Add
sugar, stir until dissolved, then boil rapidly until set. Ladle
into warmed jars and cover.

981   DAMSON CHEESE

Use the same quantity of fruit and water as for damson jam
(Recipe No. 980) and simmer until soft. Rub through sieve.
Measure pulp and add ½kg (1 lb) sugar to each 600ml* (1 pint)
pulp. Continue as for jam.

Gives best result

982   GOOSEBERRY JAM

½kg/1lb *gooseberries* · 4 *tablespoons water if fruit is ripe*
½kg/1lb *sugar*

If fruit is very under-ripe use the following quantities:

½kg/1lb *gooseberries* · 284ml/½pint *water*
½kg plus 100g/1¼lb *sugar*

Put the fruit and water into a pan. Simmer until soft. Add the
sugar and stir until dissolved, then boil rapidly until set.
Ladle into warmed jars and cover.

983   GREENGAGE JAM

½kg/1lb *greengages, weight after stoning*
4 *tablespoons water, if fruit is very under-ripe;*
none if fruit is ripe · ½kg/1lb *sugar*

The stones of the fruit can be cracked and the kernels in
cluded. Simmer fruit until soft, adding water if necessary.
Stir in the sugar and continue stirring until dissolved. Boil
rapidly until set. Ladle into warmed jars and cover.

984   MARROW GINGER JAM

½kg/1lb *prepared marrow, weight after peeling and cutting*
into cubes
½kg/1lb *sugar*
1 *teaspoon ground ginger or* 25–50g/1–2oz *crystallised ginger*
juice 1 *large lemon*

Follow the method for apple ginger (Recipe No. 963).

985   PLUM JAM

½kg/1lb *plums*
4 *tablespoons water, if fruit is very under-ripe;*
none if fruit is ripe · ½kg/1lb *sugar*

Method as for greengage jam (Recipe No. 983). If whole fruit
jam is required cut the plums into halves, put into a bowl,
sprinkle over the sugar and leave overnight. The next day
proceed as usual.

Plum jam ·

986   PLUM JAM
(With commercial pectin)

2½kg/5lb *plums* · 284ml/½pint *water* · *juice* 1 *lemon*
scant 3¼kg/6½lb *sugar* · ½ *bottle commercial pectin*

Wash the plums and cut into pieces, removing as many of the
stones as liked. Put the fruit and water into a large pan. If the
fruit is ripe or sweet add the juice 1 lemon. Bring to the boil.
Cover and simmer for 15 minutes stirring occasionally. Add
sugar, heat slowly until the sugar has dissolved, stir occasionally, then bring to a full rolling boil. Boil rapidly for 3 minutes,
stirring occasionally, then remove from the heat and stir in
commercial pectin. Skim if necessary. Allow to cool slightly
to prevent fruit rising. Ladle into warmed jars and cover.
Makes about 6kg (11lb).

987   QUINCE JAM

½kg/1lb *quinces* · 4 *tablespoons water* · ½kg/1lb *sugar*
juice ½ *lemon*

Peel, core and cut up the fruit (alternatively, the fruit can
be grated). Simmer with the water until soft. Add the sugar
and lemon juice and heat slowly, until the sugar has dissolved;
then boil rapidly until set. Ladle into warmed jars and cover.

988   RHUBARB AND DRIED FIG JAM

½kg/1lb *dried figs* · 568ml/1pint *water* · 1kg/2lb *rhubarb*
1½kg/3lb *sugar* · *juice* 1 *large lemon*

Soak the figs in the water for at least 48 hours. Simmer until
the fruit is nearly soft. Add the rhubarb and continue cooking
until the mixture forms a thick pulp. Add the sugar and lemon
juice, stir until dissolved, then boil rapidly until set. Ladle
into warmed jars and cover.

989   RHUBARB AND GINGER JAM

Follow the method for marrow ginger jam (Recipe No. 984).

990 RASPBERRY JAM

½kg/1lb *raspberries* · ½kg/1lb *sugar*

Place the fruit in a pan and bring to the boil. Stir in the hot sugar – heated for a few minutes in the oven. Allow the sugar to dissolve then boil rapidly until set. If the fruit is firm and fresh this should only take about 3 minutes. Ladle into warmed jars and cover.

991 STRAWBERRY JAM

generous ½kg/1lb *strawberries* · scant ½kg/1lb *sugar*
juice 1 lemon or 4 tablespoons redcurrant juice

Simmer the fruit until soft. Add the sugar and lemon or redcurrant juice and stir until dissolved. Boil rapidly until set. Ladle into hot jars and cover.

992 STRAWBERRY JAM
(Whole fruit jam)

Put the sugar and fruit into pan. Heat very gently until sugar has dissolved, add lemon juice or redcurrant juice and boil steadily until set.

993 TOMATO JAM

1kg/2lb *tomatoes* · 1kg/2lb *sugar* · 4 *tablespoons lemon juice*
1 *teaspoon ground ginger, optional*

Cut the tomatoes in quarters, sprinkle over the sugar and leave to stand overnight to draw out the juice. Simmer gently in the juice stirring well until sugar has dissolved, then continue simmering until tomatoes are soft. Add lemon juice and boil rapidly until set. If liked, add ground ginger. Ladle into warmed jars and cover.

RECIPES FOR JELLIES

994 APPLE JELLY (1)
(With commercial pectin)

1½kg/3lb *apples* · generous litre/2pints *water*
1½kg/3lb *sugar* · ½ *bottle commercial pectin*

Wash the apples and remove any bad parts or bruises. Cut into small pieces but do not peel or core. Put into a saucepan with the water, cover and simmer until the fruit is soft enough to mash. Place the mashed fruit in a jelly bag and leave to drain. Measure generous litre (2 pints) drained apple juice into a large saucepan, add 1½kg (3 lb) sugar and heat slowly, stirring occasionally until the sugar has dissolved. Bring quickly to a full rolling boil and boil rapidly for 1 minute. Stir in the commercial pectin, return to the boil and continue boiling for 30 seconds. Remove from the heat. Skim if necessary; ladle into warmed jars and cover.
Makes 2½kg (5 lb).
If liked the fruit pulp left in the jelly bag can be used for making apple butter (Recipe No. 996).

995 APPLE JELLY (2)

Use either cooking apples or crab-apples and allow generous ½litre (1 pint) to ½kg (1 lb) fruit. Simmer the fruit until a pulp; there is no need to peel or core the fruit. Put the pulp into thick muslin or through a jelly bag and leave hanging overnight. Measure the juice and allow to each 600ml* (1 pint) of juice ½kg (1 lb) sugar; heat until the sugar has dissolved then boil rapidly until set. Ladle into warmed jars and cover.

* This gives best result

996 APPLE BUTTER

1kg/2lb *apple pulp* · *juice 2 lemons*
finely grated rind 3 lemons · 100g/4oz *butter*
1kg/2lb *sugar*

Heat the apple pulp with the lemon juice, rind and butter. Stir in the sugar, allow to dissolve, then boil steadily until thick. Ladle into warmed jars and cover.

997 MINT JELLY
(Also illustrated in colour at the beginning of this section)

Ingredients as for apple jelly (Recipe No. 995), but allow a few drops of green colouring and 3 tablespoons chopped mint to each ½kg (1 lb) jelly. Stir the colouring and mint into jelly when setting point is reached. Cool slightly, stir again to distribute the mint then ladle into warmed jars. A more savoury jelly can be made by adding 1–2 tablespoons white wine or white malt vinegar to each ½kg (1 lb) apple jelly just before it sets. Boil for a few minutes *then* stir in mint and colouring and proceed as before. Alternatively use Recipe No. 994 and stir in chopped mint when setting point is reached. *Straining pulp for jelly*: leave pulp in jelly bag for some hours, preferably overnight. Jelly bags, made of flannel, are obtainable from ironmongers or use several thicknesses of muslin.

Mint jelly

Apple jelly, apple butter

998 BLACKBERRY OR BRAMBLE JELLY

½kg/1lb *blackberries* · 4 *tablespoons water*
1 *medium-sized cooking apple*, chopped* · *sugar, see method*

**Instead of using an apple, you can use juice of a lemon to each ½kg (1lb) blackberries. Add this with sugar*

Put blackberries, water and apple into a pan and simmer until soft. Put the pulp through a jelly bag. Measure juice and allow ½kg (1 lb) sugar to 600ml** (1 pint). Stir in sugar and continue stirring until dissolved, then boil rapidly until set. Ladle into warmed jars and cover.

***Gives best result*

For BLACKBERRY AND APPLE JELLY (*Illustrated in colour at the beginning of this section*)
Follow the above recipe but use 2 medium-sized cooking apples.

999 MEDLAR JELLY

½kg/1lb *medlars* · 142ml/¼pint *water*
½ *teaspoon citric or tartaric acid or juice* ½ *lemon*

Simmer fruit in the water until soft. Put through a jelly bag, then measure juice and allow ½kg (1 lb) sugar to each 600ml* (1 pint). Stir in sugar and acid or lemon juice and continue stirring until dissolved. Boil rapidly until set. Ladle into warmed jars and cover.

**Gives best result*

1000 REDCURRANT JELLY

½kg/1lb *redcurrants* · 142ml/¼pint *water*

Follow the method for apple jelly (Recipe No. 995).

MARMALADES

1001 ORANGE MARMALADE, No. 1
(Coarse cut and bitter)

½kg/1lb *Seville or bitter oranges (3 medium-sized oranges)*
generous litre/2pints *water* · 1kg/2lb *sugar*

Wash oranges thoroughly and put into a pan with the water. Cover and simmer slowly for about 1½ hours or until a blunt wooden skewer will pierce the skin of the fruit easily. Remove oranges from liquid, allow to cool, then cut up neatly. Put pips into liquid and boil steadily for 10 minutes to extract the pectin from them, then remove and replace the cut up oranges. Bring to the boil, then stir in the sugar, warmed for a few minutes in the oven. Continue stirring until sugar has dissolved, then bring to the boil and boil rapidly without stirring until setting point is reached. Start testing the marmalade after about 15 minutes. Allow to cool slightly, stirring occasionally to prevent fruit rising. Ladle into warmed jars and cover.

1002 THREE-FRUIT MARMALADE

1 *Seville orange or grapefruit** · 1 *sweet orange** · 1 *lemon*
scant 1¼ litres/2¼pints *water* · 1kg plus 75g/2¼lb *sugar*

*All medium-sized
Follow the method for Recipe No. 1001.

1003 ORANGE MARMALADE, No. 2
(A sweeter variety)

½kg/1lb *Seville or bitter oranges*
generous 1½litres/3pints *water* · 1½kg/3lb *sugar*
juice 1 *lemon or* 1 *teaspoon citric or tartaric acid*

Cut or mince oranges finely, removing pips. Soak peel and pulp overnight in the water, together with the pips, which should be tied up in a piece of muslin. Then put fruit, water and pips into a covered pan and simmer slowly until peel is quite soft. This should take about 1½ hours. Remove the bag of pips and stir in the sugar, warmed for a few minutes in the oven, and lemon juice or acid. Stir until the sugar has dissolved, then bring to the boil, and boil rapidly in an uncovered pan until setting point is reached. This will take about 20 minutes. Allow to cool slightly, stirring occasionally to prevent the fruit rising. Ladle into warmed jars and cover.

1004 SWEET ORANGE MARMALADE

½kg/1lb *sweet oranges* · generous litre/2pints *water*
1kg/2lb *sugar* · *juice* 1 *lemon*

Follow the method for Recipe No. 1003.

1005 LEMON MARMALADE

½kg/1lb *lemons (4 medium-sized or 3 large lemons)*
1¼litres/2½pints *water* · 1¼kg/2½lb *sugar*

Follow the method for Recipe No. 1001.

A selection of marmalades

1006 BOTTLING BY THE OVEN METHOD

Prepare the fruit. To do this, wash and dry the fruit, or wash and drain soft fruit. Be careful not to use fruit that is bruised or over-ripe. Certain fruits require more complicated preparation and methods for these are given below:

Apples: peel, core and slice and immediately place into a bowl of salted water (1 level tablespoon kitchen salt to each generous litre (2 pints) cold water). Let the apples stay there for 10 minutes, with a plate on top of them if desired, but this is not really necessary. This prevents them from turning brown.

Peaches: immerse the peaches in boiling water and leave for ½–1 minute. Remove and put into cold water then skin them. Leave in cold water until ready to pack into the jars. This prevents discolouration.

Pears: preparation of pears is similar to apples. If using hard cooking pears, simmer these until soft. If pears are ripe, then remove from the salt water and put for 1 minute only in boiling water or boiling syrup. Pears treated in this way should remain absolutely white in colour.

Tomatoes: if liked skin the tomatoes, immersing them in boiling water for ½ minute, then put into cold water. The skins will immediately come off.

Put the prepared fruits into clean jars, packing as tightly as possible. As the fruit shrinks during sterilising the jars should be filled just above the top. Stand the jars on either an asbestos mat, several thicknesses of paper or cardboard, or a wooden board and put in a very cool oven 250°F, 130°C, Gas Mark ½; where pressure is extra good use Gas Mark ¼. Cover the tops of the jars with an old, clean tin lid. While the jars are in the oven, put the glass lids and rubber bands on to boil for 15 minutes. If using metal tops, just drop these for 1 minute into boiling water so that the lacquer is not damaged.

Length of time to leave the fruit in the oven:

Raspberries, loganberries	45 minutes
(do not pack these fruits too tightly, otherwise they form a solid block of fruit which is very difficult to sterilise)	
Rhubarb, redcurrants, blackcurrants	50 minutes
Plums, apples, blackberries, damsons, greengages, cherries	1 hour
Whole peaches, whole apricots	1¼ hours
Halved peaches, halved apricots, pears, tomatoes	1½ hours
Fruit salad	sterilise for time required by fruit needing maximum length of time

At the end of the given time, check that everything is handy, for the important thing about the oven method is speed when the jars are brought out. Have ready a kettle of boiling water or a pan of boiling syrup. Bring the jars out of the oven one at a time. Put on to a wooden surface, pour in the boiling liquid, tapping the jar as you do so, until it completely overflows. If using a screw top type of jar, put on the rubber ring first, put on the top, hold on to this tightly, then either screw down, clip down or put on weight. Do not handle the jars any more than necessary for 24 hours. After this time, remove the screw band or clip and test to see if the lid is firm. It should be possible to lift the jars by the lid. When the jars have sealed there is no need to replace either the clip or screw band.

If the screw band is put on the jar, do this only loosely, and it is advisable to lightly grease the inside of the band. The oven method is suitable for all fruits, but NOT FOR PULPED FRUIT (Recipe No. 1010) or TOMATOES BOTTLED IN THEIR OWN JUICE.

TOMATOES These are improved in flavour if salt and sugar are added. To each ½kg (1 lb) tomatoes allow ½ teaspoon salt, ½ teaspoon sugar. Sprinkle this into the jar before pouring on the boiling water.

1007   BOTTLING IN A STERILISER

Any deep container can be used as a steriliser, although a proper steriliser with a thermometer is obviously the most efficient to use.

Prepare the fruit and make the syrup. See instructions for doing this in Recipe Nos. 1006, 1008. Pack the fruit into the jars, as tightly as possible. Fill to the very top of the jars with cold water or cold syrup. Put on the boiled rubber bands and the lids. If using the screw band jars, turn these as tightly as possible, then unscrew for half a turn, so allowing for the expansion of the glass. If using the clip tops, put the clip into position. When using the skin covering, put this and the special string first of all into hot water for a few minutes, then tie on the skin as tightly as possible.

Put some sort of padding at the bottom of the steriliser. A wooden board, several thicknesses of paper or an old cloth will do. Stand the jars on this, being careful they do not touch the sides of the pan, or each other. It is always preferable to completely cover the jars in the steriliser with cold water, but if this is not possible, fill the steriliser with cold water up to the necks of the jars, then either put on the lid or cover with a board or tea cloth, so keeping in the steam. Take 1½ hours to bring the water in the steriliser to simmering, i.e. 165–175°F, 74–79°C, for all fruits except pears and tomatoes, when the water should be brought to 180–190°F, 82–87°C. With all fruits except pears, peaches and tomatoes maintain the temperature for 10 minutes. With pears, peaches and tomatoes maintain the temperature for 30 minutes. Before lifting out the jars scoop out a little water so that it is easier and safer to lift them out. Stand the jars on a wooden surface and, in the case of jars with screw bands, tighten these.

Leave the jars for 24 hours, then test by removing the clip or band and seeing if the lid is tight. If it is, and the jar can be lifted by the lid, then the jars have sealed. (See notes at end of Recipe No. 1006).

For bottling in a pressure cooker see Recipe No. 909.

1008 SYRUP FOR FRUIT

Heavy syrup: can be used for most fruits if people have a very 'sweet tooth'. Use particularly with peaches, pears and fruit salad.

350–450g* (12–16 oz) sugar to generous ½litre (1 pint).

Medium syrup: is most usually chosen for all fruits except perhaps apples.

170–225g* (6–8 oz) sugar to generous ½litre (1 pint).

Light syrup: is ideal for apples or when a slightly sharp flavour is required.

100–125g* (4 oz) sugar to generous ½litre (1 pint).

*Gives best result

Boil sugar and water together until sugar has dissolved.

1009 TO OPEN SCREW TOPPED JARS

Before putting screw topped jars away to store, oil the inside of the metal bands. If, in spite of this, they are difficult to remove there is a special screw cap opener available (illustrated).

1010 PULPED FRUIT

Pulping is a very good way of preserving, as pulped fruit takes up comparatively little space in the jars. Stew the fruit, adding little or no water, and sugar to taste. In the case of tomatoes, add ½ teaspoon sugar and ½ teaspoon salt to each ½kg (1 lb).

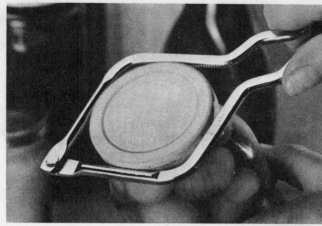

A screw cap opener

Skin the tomatoes, if liked. If a smooth pulp is required, rub the cooked fruit through a sieve and re-boil. Put tops of jars and rubber bands to boil, and boil for 10 minutes. Also put the glass jars to get VERY HOT. Pour the boiling pulp into very hot jars, seal down as quickly as possible, and immediately stand the jars in the steriliser filled with boiling water. Boil fruit pulp for a good 5 minutes and tomato pulp for a good 10 minutes. Screw bands should be loosened the half turn before going into the boiling water and tightened when they come out.

1011 MINCEMEAT

generous 100g/4oz *shredded suet or melted margarine*
generous 100g/4oz *apple, grated* · ½kg/1lb *mixed dried fruit*
generous 100g/4oz *sugar, preferably Demerara*
generous 100g/4oz *almonds, blanched and well dried*
generous 100g/4oz *mixed peel*
finely grated rind and juice 1 large lemon
1 *teaspoon mixed spice* · ½ *teaspoon cinnamon*
½ *teaspoon grated nutmeg* · 4 *tablespoons brandy, whisky or rum*

Mix all the ingredients together. Put into clean, dry jam jars and cover. Store in a cool dry place.

Do not cut down on the quantities of sugar, fat or spirit otherwise the mincemeat will not keep well. Make quite certain the fruit is dry. If this has been washed, let it dry for at least 24 hours before making mincemeat.

1012 LEMON CURD

rind 3 lemons · 200g/8oz *loaf or castor sugar*
juice 2 large lemons · 100g/4oz *butter* · 2 *eggs*

Grate the rind carefully, removing just the yellow 'zest' but none of the white pith. If using loaf sugar, rub this over the lemons until all the yellow has been removed. Squeeze the juice from 2 of the lemons. Put all ingredients, except eggs, into the top of a double saucepan or basin over hot water and cook, stirring from time to time, until the butter and sugar have melted. Add the well beaten eggs and continue cooking until the mixture coats the back of a wooden spoon. Pour into jars and seal down.

1013 ORANGE AND LEMON CURD

200g/8oz *loaf or castor sugar* · *grated rind 1 lemon*
grated rind 2 oranges · *juice 2 large oranges*
100g/4oz *butter* · 2 *eggs*

Follow the method for lemon curd (Recipe No. 1012).

1014 ORANGE JELLY

6 *oranges* · 1 *large lemon* · *water*
1kg plus 250g/2lb 10oz *sugar* · 1 *bottle commercial pectin*

Wash the oranges and the lemon, cut in halves and extract all the juice – about 426ml (¾ pint). Cover the orange peel with water. Bring to the boil, then simmer, covered for 10 minutes. Strain the liquid and add sufficient to the fruit juices to make generous ½litre (1 pint) in all. Place in a heavy saucepan with the sugar and stir over a low heat until the sugar has dissolved. Bring to a full rolling boil and boil rapidly for 2 minutes. Remove from heat. Stir in commercial pectin. Bring back to boil and boil for 30 seconds. Skim if necessary; cool then ladle into warmed jars and cover.

Makes about 2½kg (5 lb).

1015 GRAPE JELLY (1)

1½kg/3lb *slightly under-ripe grapes* · *juice 2 lemons*
142ml/¼pint *water*

Follow the method for medlar jelly (Recipe No. 999).

1016 GRAPE JELLY (2)

1½kg/3lb *ripe black grapes* · 142ml/¼pint *water*
generous 1½kg/3¼lb *sugar* · 3 *tablespoons lemon juice*
1 *bottle commercial pectin*

Use only fully ripe grapes. To prepare the juice, wash and crush the fruit thoroughly. Place in a saucepan with the water. Bring to the boil and simmer, covered, for 10 minutes. Place the fruit in a jelly bag and leave to drain. Measure the sugar, lemon juice and 710ml (1¼ pints) grape juice into a large saucepan. Heat slowly until the sugar has dissolved. Stir occasionally. Bring to the boil and stir in the commercial pectin – then bring to a full rolling boil and boil rapidly for 30 seconds. Remove from the heat, skim, cool, then ladle into warmed jars and cover.

Makes about 2¾kg (5½ lb).

ENTERTAINING

The secret of entertaining is to plan ahead to avoid last-minute panic. Throughout this book there are recipes which you will be proud to present to your friends, but in this section are special ideas for successful home entertaining.

CHRISTMAS TIME

Christmas fare is largely traditional and can so often be prepared beforehand. You will find the recipes for Christmas cakes, etc., in the cake section.

Christmas cake	— Recipe Nos. 777, 1066.
Christmas pudding and brandy butter	— Recipe No. 889 and opposite.
Mincemeat	— Recipe No. 1011.
Mince pies	— Recipe No. 564.
Roast turkey	— Recipe No. 262.
Mincemeat meringue pie	— Fill a flan case with mincemeat and crushed pineapple, top with meringue.
Meringue nests	— Follow the meringue recipe (Recipe No. 759). Pipe into neat shapes. Bake and store. When ready to serve fill with defrosted frozen or canned fruit.

1017   CHRISTMAS PUDDING
(Illustrated in colour on the opposite page)

110g*/4oz *flour* · 50g/2oz *breadcrumbs*
1 *teaspoon mixed spice* · 1 *level teaspoon cinnamon*
1 *level teaspoon nutmeg* · 110g*/4oz *shredded suet*
110g*/4oz *brown sugar* · 110g*/4oz *grated apple*
1 *small carrot, grated* · 110g*/4oz *mixed candied peel*
2 *eggs* · 110g*/4oz *currants* · 225g*/8oz *raisins*
110g*/4oz *sultanas* · 50g/2oz *prunes or dried apricots, chopped*
110g*/4oz *blanched almonds, chopped*
grated rind and juice ½ *lemon* · *grated rind* ½ *orange*
1 *tablespoon golden syrup or black treacle*
142ml/¼pint *ale, beer, stout or milk*

*This gives best result

Mix all ingredients together, stir well and leave overnight if possible. Place in one large or 2 smaller basins and cover securely with greased greaseproof paper and a cloth or foil. Steam or boil for 6–8 hours. Cool. Remove wet coverings. When cold put on dry covers. Steam for 2 hours on Christmas Day. To prevent the top of pudding becoming too wet it is a good idea to make flour and water paste. Mix about 200g (8 oz) flour with enough water to make a firm dough and roll into a round the size of the top of the basin. Place this mixture over greaseproof paper on the pudding; cover with more greaseproof paper, then cook.
For cooking a Christmas pudding in a pressure cooker see Recipe No. 889.

1018   BRANDY OR RUM BUTTER OR HARD SAUCE

100g/4oz *unsalted butter* · 150g/6oz *icing sugar, sieved*
4–8 *dessertspoons brandy or rum*

Cream the butter until white. Gradually add the sugar and the brandy or rum. Leave in the refrigerator or cool place to harden. Pipe or pile into a dish and if liked decorate with glacé cherries and angelica.

Christmas pudding with brandy butter (Recipe Nos. 1017, 1018)

Cooked gammon (Recipe No. 163)

1019 RICH CHARLOTTE RUSSE

284ml/½pint *sweet white wine* · 2 teaspoons *powdered gelatine*
75g/3oz *sugar* · approximately 18–20 *sponge* (*Savoy*) *fingers**
1 *egg white* · *few glacé cherries* · *small piece angelica*
284ml/½pint *double cream, whipped*

*If thick split through the centre and use 9-10 only

Heat most of the wine and soften the gelatine in the remaining
cold wine. Add to the hot liquid, with the sugar; stir until
dissolved. Allow to cool, but not to set. Meanwhile cut the
rounded ends from the biscuits and brush the sides with egg
white so they hold well. Arrange round the inside of a plain
mould, or cake tin without a loose base. The sponge fingers
must fit together tightly so the sweet is easy to turn out. Spoon
a little of the *cold* wine jelly into the base of the mould and
leave to stiffen. Make a design with cherries and angelica on
this. Fold the remainder of the cold wine jelly into the cream
and spoon into the mould. Leave to set firmly. Invert on to a
serving dish and tie a band of ribbon round the sweet.

Instead of the wine and gelatine use half or a whole packet of
lemon or other flavoured jelly. Dissolve in very hot water,
cool and use in place of the wine jelly.

Christmas tableaux

1020 CHRISTMAS TABLEAUX

200g/8oz *plain flour* · 150g/6oz *butter or margarine*
125g/5oz *castor sugar* · 50g/2oz *semolina*
1 *egg yolk mixed with 2–3 dessertspoons cold water*

Sieve flour, rub in butter or margarine until mixture resembles
fine breadcrumbs. Then add the sugar and semolina.
Divide the mixture into four portions and add:

To portion 1 (*Christmas wreaths*): 25g (1 oz) currants.

To portion 2 (*Star biscuits*): 25g (1 oz) ground almonds and a few drops almond essence.

To portion 3 (*Bell biscuits*): 1 level teaspoon cinnamon.

To portion 4 (*Christmas tree biscuits*): finely grated rind ½ lemon.

Mix each portion to a stiff dough with some of the egg yolk
mixture.

1021 CHRISTMAS WREATHS

Turn dough on to a lightly floured board. Roll out thinly and
cut into rings with fluted cutters. Place on a greased baking
sheet and bake in a moderately hot oven, 400°F, 200°C, Gas
Mark 6, for 10–12 minutes. Cool on a wire tray.

1022 STAR BISCUITS

Turn dough on to a lightly floured board. Roll out thinly and
cut into star shapes. Place on a greased baking sheet and bake
as for Christmas wreaths. When cold, ice with water icing
coloured green and put ½ glacé cherry in the centre of each.

1023 BELL BISCUITS

Turn on to a lightly floured board. Roll out thinly and cut
into bells. (The simplest method is to make a bell shape from
cardboard, put the shape on to the dough and then cut round
it.) Bake as above and when cold, sandwich together with
butter icing (Recipe No. 751). Outline the edges of the bells
with more butter icing and if liked decorate with silver balls.

1024 CHRISTMAS TREE BISCUITS

Turn dough on to a lightly floured board. Roll out thinly and
cut into tree shapes (use a cardboard shape as a guide). Bake
biscuits as above and when cold, sandwich together with jam.
Cover the tree part of each sandwich with more jam and
sprinkle with desiccated coconut.

FOR CHRISTMAS

1025 SCOTCH BUN

Pastry
350g*/12oz *flour* · *pinch salt* · ¾ teaspoon *baking powder*
175g*/6oz *cooking fat* · generous 25g/1oz *sugar*
water · *egg to glaze*

For the filling
about 2kg/4lb *dried fruit* · 100g/4oz *orange peel, chopped*
200g/8oz *almonds, chopped* · ½kg/1lb *flour*
generous 200g/8oz *sugar* · 40g/1½oz *mixed spice*
15g/½oz *cream of tartar* · 15g/½oz *bicarbonate of soda*
2 *eggs* · *little milk*

*You need this amount of pastry

This should be made several weeks before it is to be eaten
(by tradition at Hogmanay festival). Grease a 23-cm (9-inch)
square tin. Sieve the flour, salt and baking powder; rub in the
fat. Add the sugar and work into a stiff paste with water and
roll out thinly. Line the tin with this paste, reserving enough
to cover the top. For the filling, put all the ingredients into a
large bowl and use just enough milk to moisten, mixing with
the hands. Put the mixture into the lined tin, dampen the
edges of the pastry, and cover with the rest of the pastry.
Prick all over with a fork and brush with beaten egg. Bake in
the centre of a very moderate oven, 325°F, 170°C, Gas Mark
3, for 2 hours. Then lower the heat to 300°F, 150°C, Gas Mark
2, for 1–2 hours. For a smaller Scotch bun use half quantities
and bake the mixture in an 18-cm (7-inch) cake tin for 2¼–2½
hours.

CHEESE SAVOURIES FOR COCKTAIL PARTIES

1026 **CHEESE PASTRY**

100g/4oz plain or self-raising flour · pinch salt
pinch cayenne pepper · 50g/2oz whipped-up cooking fat
50g/2oz Cheddar cheese, finely grated · 1 egg yolk
1 tablespoon water

Sieve the flour, salt and cayenne pepper then rub in the cooking fat until mixture resembles fine breadcrumbs. Stir in the cheese and bind together with the egg yolk and water. Form into a firm dough.

1027 **CHEESE STRAWS**

Roll out the cheese pastry and cut into thin fingers ½-cm (¼-inch) wide; re-roll the pastry trimmings and cut into 7½-cm (3-inch) rings. Place on baking sheets and bake above centre in a hot oven, 425°F, 220°C, Gas Mark 7, for 7–10 minutes. Cool on the baking sheets then serve bundles of straws in the rings.

1028 **SACRISTANS**

Roll out the cheese pastry thinly, sprinkle with grated cheese and chopped nuts. Cut into finger-sized pieces. Twist and bake as for cheese straws.

Cheese straws

AND NEW YEAR

Scotch bun

Butterflies

1029 **BUTTERFLIES**

Roll out the cheese pastry thinly, cut into rounds and divide half of these to look like 'wings'. Bake as for cheese straws. When cold pipe bands of soft cream cheese on to rounds, press 'wings' in position. Garnish with parsley.

BUFFET PARTIES

1030

In these days of small houses and lack of domestic help a buffet or cocktail party is an excellent idea, as all the food can be prepared beforehand. As well as the recipes on these pages see fondue (Recipe Nos. 347, 358–9) and the many ideas in the hors d'oeuvre and salad sections.

1031 ROMAN BOAT

1 short French loaf · 1 large cucumber
½kg/1lb chipolata sausages, cooked · 200g/8oz cheese
175g/7oz can pineapple pieces
4 small slices white bread, crusts removed
cocktail sticks, 3 skewers, 3 paper flags

Cut a thin slice off the top crust of loaf to form a steady base for the boat. From the base of the loaf cut another horizontal slice which starts and finishes about 2½-cm (1-inch) in from ends, is thin at either end and about 1½-cm (¾-inch) thick in the middle. Cut half the cucumber into 16 thick slices. Place a cocktail stick through one end of each sausage and through a slice of cucumber. Secure other end of cocktail stick into sides of the boat so that cucumber slices slightly overlap. Use 8 sausages on either side.
Cut the cheese into cubes and mix with the drained pineapple pieces. Pile into centre of boat. For the sails take 2 skewers and secure two slices of bread on each, passing the skewer through opposite sides of bread so that the slices bow to look like sails. For the flags cut out three triangular pieces of paper and mark with a design. Secure on top of the skewers. Cut remaining cucumber into thin slices and arrange in a large oval or triangle on a wooden board. Place boat on top so that the 'oars' are placed over the cucumber slices.
Makes 4–6 servings.

Roman boat

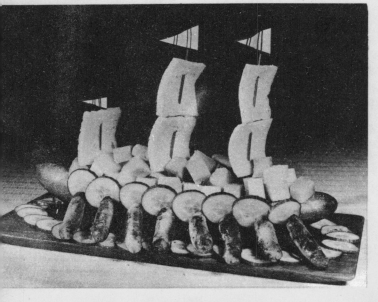

1032 MINCEMEAT AND WALNUT PLATE TART

300g/12oz short crust pastry (Recipe No. 566)
300g/12oz mincemeat (Recipe No. 1011)
50g/2oz walnuts, chopped · 1 dessertspoon rum
castor sugar to sprinkle

Make the pastry, divide the dough into two halves and roll out each half to a round large enough to cover a 20–23-cm (8–9-inch) ovenproof plate. Mix together the mincemeat, chopped walnuts and rum. Line the plate with half the pastry and cover with the filling. Moisten the edges and place remaining pastry on top, pressing edges together firmly with a fork. With a sharp knife make radiating slits from the centre. Bake in the centre of a moderately hot oven, 400°F, 200°C, Gas Mark 6, for about 35 minutes, lowering the heat to moderate after 20 minutes. Sprinkle with sugar and serve hot.

1033 COCKTAIL SAUSAGES WITH COCKTAIL SAUCE

Brown cocktail sausages in a little dripping or oil in the oven; insert a cocktail stick into each one. Serve with a sauce made by heating 3 tablespoons tomato sauce, 1–2 teaspoons Worcestershire sauce, squeeze lemon juice, seasoning and a few drops of Tabasco sauce together.

1034 ASSORTED CHEESE TRAY

Buy a well-balanced selection of cheeses, include Cheddar, Cheshire, Camembert, Danish Blue and Samsoe, etc. The picture shows the last two cheeses garnished with a selection of fresh fruit, thin slices of green pepper and walnut halves. For an attractive centre piece arrange cubes of cheese, black and green grapes and mandarin orange segments on cocktail sticks; then insert the cocktail sticks into an orange.

1035 DANISH SANDWICH PARTY

Open sandwiches make excellent dishes for a buffet party. Either cut into small fingers or serve with a knife and fork. Remove the crusts from thin slices of brown bread and spread with butter then top with the following:
1. Slices of salami, a slice of pear, dipped in lemon juice and rolled in a small slice of ham; garnish with cucumber and radish slices and an olive. (*illustrated*)
2. Potted shrimps held in place by a thick layer of butter.
3. Slices of cucumber and a small slice of ham, rolled; garnish with slices of stuffed olive. (*illustrated*)
4. Danish salami with scrambled egg and cucumber twists.
5. Slices of pear, dipped in lemon juice, cucumber and salami. Garnish with slices of stuffed olive. (*illustrated*)
6. Liver pâté (Recipe Nos. 20, 21) with crisp-grilled bacon rashers, button mushrooms and cucumber twists.
7. Cold chicken garnished with tomato and cucumber twists.
8. Grated cheese and slices of pear, dipped in lemon juice. Garnish with radish slices and small sprigs of parsley. (*illustrated*)
9. Tongue with curried Russian salad.
10. Slices of cucumber, salami and pear, dipped in lemon juice. Garnish with parsley or slices of stuffed olive. (*illustrated*) Arrange thin slices of salami on a serving dish and garnish with fruit, slices of gherkin and a sprig of parsley. Serve small bowls of olives, gherkins, nuts, etc.

1036 COCKTAIL PARTY SAVOURIES

Make these small and easy to eat as it is very difficult to balance a glass and try to hold food at the same time. The toppings, fillings, etc., must be firm. Cheese and other pastry cases can be made beforehand and kept in airtight tins.

1037 SAVOURY BOATS

Make cheese pastry (Recipe No. 1026), roll out thinly and line small boat-shaped tins. Bake above the centre in a hot oven, 425°F, 220°C, Gas Mark 7, for 10–12 minutes. When cold pipe with ham butter (Recipe No. 1038), garnish with thin strips of tomato or red pepper and coat with aspic jelly.

Assorted cheese tray

Danish sandwich party

1038 HAM BUTTER

50g/2oz *lean ham or cooked bacon*
50g/2oz *butter or margarine*

Chop finely or mince the ham or bacon. Work in the butter or margarine and mix to a smooth paste.

1039 HAM SAVOURIES

Make cheese pastry (Recipe No. 1026), roll out thinly and cut into small rounds. Bake above the centre in a hot oven, 425°F, 220°C, Gas Mark 7, for 10–12 minutes. When cold cover with a round of ham or cooked bacon, pipe with a little sieved cream cheese and garnish with a tomato slice coated with aspic.

1040 HAM BUTTERFLIES

Make cheese pastry (Recipe No. 1026) roll out thinly and cut into rounds; cut half the rounds in two to make wings. Bake above the centre in a hot oven, 425°F, 220°C, Gas Mark 7, for 10–12 minutes. When cold pipe with ham butter (Recipe No. 1038) and press in the pastry wings. Garnish with a sprinkling of cayenne pepper.

Salty savouries

1041 SALTY SAVOURIES

Make cheese pastry (Recipe No. 1026) roll out thinly and line small tartlet cases. Bake 'blind' (Recipe No. 560) at 425°F, 220°C, Gas Mark 7, for 10–12 minutes. When cold, fill with finely chopped smoked salmon, cooked kippers or mashed pilchards mixed with plenty of seasoning and a squeeze of lemon juice.

1042 BACON BOUCHEES

Make 200g (8 oz) puff pastry (Recipe No. 588) roll out and cut out 12–16 small vol-au-vent cases (Recipe No. 624). Bake as directed and when cold fill with chopped cooked lean bacon mixed with aspic jelly, pipe with sieved cream cheese and garnish with fancy shapes cut out of cucumber skin. Coat with aspic jelly.

1043 KEBABS

Arrange cooked bacon rolls or cubes of ham, pineapple pieces, cubes of cheese, slices of cooked sausage, gherkins and cocktail onions on cocktail sticks. Serve cold, or brush with melted butter and grill gently for 5 minutes.

1044 BACON TITBITS

Remove the rind from rashers of streaky bacon, cut the rashers in half and spread with a little made mustard or chutney. Roll round any of the following: a cube of cheese or pineapple; a cocktail sausage or a prawn; sweet gherkins or stuffed olives; a piece of banana or a date. Place on a cocktail stick, grill or bake until the bacon is cooked. Serve hot or cold.

1045 HAM BITES

Spread thin slices of ham or lean cooked bacon with cream cheese or peanut butter; cover with a little grated onion or horseradish sauce. Roll up tightly and leave in the refrigerator or a cold place for several hours. To serve, cut into bite-sized pieces.

MORE RECIPES FOR PARTY FARE

1048 BACON AND MUSHROOM ROLLS

50g/2oz soft breadcrumbs · 1 medium-sized onion, grated
50g/2oz mushrooms, finely chopped
1 tablespoon chopped parsley · 1 dessertspoon chopped chives
salt and pepper · 8 rashers streaky bacon

Mix together breadcrumbs, onion, mushrooms, herbs and seasoning. Stretch the bacon rashers, divide the mixture into 8 and spread evenly on each rasher. Roll up and secure with a cocktail stick. Grill under a moderate heat for 10–12 minutes, turning frequently to brown all over. If more convenient put ready in an ovenproof dish; just before the party begins cook for 15–20 minutes towards the top of a hot oven.

1049 THE DIP AND DUNK TRAY

This is a real party piece which is very quick to prepare. Fry or grill chipolata sausages until evenly browned and cooked. Drain on absorbent paper and cool. Place in a serving dish and spear the sausages with cocktail sticks. Fill small bowls with various chutneys, sweet and sour sauce (Recipe No. 202) etc., and arrange round the dish of sausages. To serve, let the guests dunk the sausages in the various dips.

1046 CHEESE PARTY

Cut Dutch or Cheddar cheese into cubes. Put nuts, grapes, pieces of orange, apple, etc., on each cube and secure with cocktail sticks.
Sandwich buttered biscuits together with thin slices of cheese. Put into a hot oven, 425°F, 220°C, Gas Mark 7, for a few minutes before serving.

1047 SALAMI CANAPES

knob butter · 1–2 eggs · seasoning
200g/8oz Danish salami, sliced · 125g/5oz can baked beans
200g/8oz can potato salad or home-made potato salad
(Recipe No. 433)
chopped chives or parsley to garnish

Heat the butter in a saucepan and scramble the eggs until lightly set. Add seasoning to taste. Arrange slices of salami (with skin in place) on rack and place under a hot grill for a few seconds only, when they will curl up round the edges forming small cups. Fill some of the salami cups with scrambled egg filling, some with baked beans and the remainder with potato salad. Arrange on a serving plate and garnish with chopped chives or parsley.

Bacon and mushroom rolls

The dip and dunk tray

1050 HERB SAUSAGE ROLLS

150g/6oz *flaky pastry (Recipe No. 604)*
200g/8oz *sausage meat · pinch mixed herbs*
beaten egg to glaze

Make the pastry and roll out thinly to a long strip. Mix together the sausage meat and mixed herbs and form the mixture into a long roll and place down one side of the pastry. Brush one edge with water, fold over and seal edges. Make slits across the top and cut into tiny rolls. Place on baking sheets and brush with beaten egg. Bake in the centre of a hot oven, 450°F, 230°C, Gas Mark 8, for 15–20 minutes.

1051 COCKTAIL PLATTER

Cheese canapés: make rich cheese pastry (Recipe No. 605), roll out thinly and cut into small circles with a fluted cutter. Bake towards the top of a hot oven, 425°F, 220°C, Gas Mark 7, for about 10 minutes. Cool on a wire tray, then spread with a mixture of cream cheese and chopped prawns. Garnish with prawns and a small slice of lemon.

Ham bouchées: make small vol-au-vent cases (Recipe No. 624) and fill with a mixture of thick white sauce (Recipe No. 663) and chopped ham.

Herb sausage rolls, cocktail platter

1052 TEENBURGERS

25g/1oz *lard · 1 onion, peeled and chopped*
½ *level teaspoon curry powder · 1 level tablespoon flour*
250g/10oz *can condensed vegetable soup · seasoning*
200g/8oz *minced beef · 4 baps or soft rolls*

Heat the lard in a saucepan and fry the onion until softened. Stir in the curry powder and flour and cook for 2–3 minutes. Add the soup and seasoning, bring to the boil. Put in the minced beef and stir until any lumps are broken. Cover the pan, simmer for about 30 minutes, stirring from time to time to prevent mixture from burning. Lift the lid for the last 5–8 minutes so the mixture may become really thick. Cool, enough to handle then form into 4 rolls. Heat under the grill. Split the baps or rolls and toast the cut sides. Fill with hamburger mixture and serve at once.

Teenburgers

Pizza

1053 PIZZA

(Italian tomato pie)

15g/½oz *dried yeast · ½kg/1lb flour · 4 tablespoons oil*
½kg/1lb *tomatoes or 350g/14oz can tomatoes*
1 *clove garlic, chopped · seasoning*
100g/4oz *Parmesan cheese, grated · 1 small can anchovies*
few black olives

Dissolve the yeast in a little tepid water. Mix the flour with 1 tablespoon of olive oil, then add the dissolved yeast. Knead until the dough is smooth. Leave, covered in a bowl in a warm place for 2 hours. Skin and chop the tomatoes, or drain canned tomatoes, and put them in a pan with the remaining oil and the garlic. Season with salt and pepper and simmer gently for 30 minutes. When the dough has risen, roll it out fairly thinly and place on an oiled baking sheet or in a large flan dish. Cover with the tomato mixture; sprinkle over the grated cheese and arrange anchovy strips and black olives on top. Bake in the centre of a hot oven, 425°F, 220°C, Gas Mark 7, for 15–20 minutes. Serve hot.

Quick party platter

PARTY FARE WITHOUT COOKING

1054 SANDWICHES WITH A DIFFERENCE

Never say sandwiches are dull. They can be prepared in various ways which are suitable even for the most special occasion.

   Sandwich cones: mould slices of fresh bread round cream horn cases. Fill with soft cheese mixed with nuts and sliced olives, and garnish with salami slices.

   Card sandwiches: cut bread into fancy shapes with a pastry cutter. Sandwich with various fillings.

   Sandwich gâteau: see Recipe Nos. 937, 951.

Make sure the bread is fresh, and the filling moist. Press top and bottom layer of bread firmly together so that the sandwich does not come apart.

By itself, a plate of sandwiches does not look very exciting, but garnishes can make all the difference. Instead of the conventional parsley try halved tomatoes, mandarin oranges, watercress, prawns, cocktail onions, radish 'flowers', etc.; with suitable sandwiches all these garnishes look attractive and can be eaten too. Serve a light wine or fruit cup with a sandwich meal.

1055 QUICK PARTY PLATTER

The picture above shows a selection of food which would be ideal to serve for a party or for a light luncheon dish.

Arrange the following on a serving dish:

Small sprigs of cauliflower garnished with paprika.

Strips of smoked salmon rolled up and the centres filled with cream cheese garnished with paprika pepper.

Slices of salami formed into horn shapes and garnished with sprigs of parsley.

Thick slices of cucumber topped with cream cheese garnished with paprika pepper.

Thin slices of eating apple dipped in lemon juice.

1056 MINIATURE PANCAKES

Fill tiny pancakes (Recipe No. 644) with creamed chicken or fish. Keep hot until ready to serve. Garnish with peeled shrimps.

1057 SAVOURY BEEF ROLLS

200g/8oz flaky pastry (Recipe No. 604)
175g/7oz corned beef · 2 cooking apples, peeled and cored
2 pickled walnuts, optional · 1 tablespoon horseradish cream
seasoning · little beaten egg · watercress to garnish

Make the pastry and roll out thinly in two long strips. Chop the corned beef, apples and walnuts, if used, finely. Mix together with the horseradish and seasoning. Bind with a little beaten egg. Form the mixture into two long rolls and place on the pastry strips. Brush one edge with water, fold over and seal edges. Make slits across the top and cut into small rolls. Place on baking sheets and brush with beaten egg. Bake in the centre of a hot to very hot oven, 450°F, 230°C, Gas Mark 8, for 15–20 minutes. Serve hot or cold garnished with watercress.

Savoury beef rolls

1058 BACON FRANKFURTERS

Wrap small pieces of streaky bacon round cocktail frankfurter sausages, or portions of large sausages. For variety place fingers of cheese or a small piece of crisp celery with the frankfurter sausages.

1059 CHEDDAR FINGERS

Wrap rashers of bacon round fingers of Cheddar cheese. Make sure the cheese is completely covered, secure with a wooden cocktail stick and cook under a moderate grill.

1060 DEVILS ON HORSEBACK

Wrap small rashers of bacon round stoned cooked prunes. Secure with a wooden cocktail stick and cook under a moderate grill. If liked put a small piece of liver pâté in the centre of each prune.

1061 ANGELS ON HORSEBACK

Wrap rashers of bacon round well seasoned oysters. Secure with a wooden cocktail stick and cook under a moderate grill.

1062 JAFFA ROLLS

Wrap rashers of bacon round segments of orange. Secure with a wooden cocktail stick, brush with melted butter and cook under a moderate grill.

1063 SALAMI AND PINEAPPLE ROUNDS

Arrange slices of salami on slices of fresh or canned drained pineapple. Garnish with slices of apple, dipped in lemon juice, and halved grapes. Place on a serving dish and for a centre piece skewer cubes of cheese, apple (dipped in lemon juice), luncheon meat, etc., on to cocktail sticks and press into an Edam cheese, whole cabbage, melon, etc.

Salami and pineapple rounds

FORMAL ENTERTAINING

When entertaining guests to a formal meal it is necessary to do quite a lot of planning beforehand. Make sure that the cutlery and glasses are sparkling and use the best china you have. If you are cooking for a dinner party with little, if any, domestic help, plan to have at least one cold course – perhaps the sweet or even the sweet and hors d'oeuvre so that they can be prepared beforehand and you are then free to attend to the main course.

Wedding cake

1064 BUFFET MEAL FOR A WEDDING

Allow the following quantities per person:

5 small cocktail savouries
75–100g/3–4oz cold meat or poultry off the bone, or salmon
2 small savouries (vol-au-vent) · 3 bridge rolls
100g/4oz potato salad · 75g/3oz other salads
100g/4oz fruit salad · 1 portion trifle or ice cream

The choice of drinks obviously depends on the amount you wish to spend, but the time to serve champagne is when the cake is being cut and the guests are drinking the health of the couple.

1065 WEDDING CAKE

The Christmas cake (Recipe No. 777) is sufficiently rich for a wedding cake, but if you want an even richer cake increase amount of fruit to 1½kg (3 lb). The cake will then take an hour longer to bake, and the recipe will make one 25-cm (10-inch) cake or smaller 13, 15 and 20-cm (5, 6 and 8-inch) cakes. Bake at least six weeks before the wedding. Above and left are examples of wedding cakes, decorated with a piping of royal icing and artificial flowers.

1066 CHRISTMAS CAKE

Here is another Christmas cake made from Recipe No. 777. The little house is made from wafer biscuits with a piping of icing on the roof. Notice how cleverly bright ribbon has been used round the sides. For a large number of people, a square cake is always more economical to cut, and another economy is to use the rolled oat marzipan (Recipe No. 746).

Casserole dishes are ideal to serve on most occasions especially when you do not want to be tied to the kitchen. Look in the wine section for help on wines. When planning a wedding reception it may be a formal meal or a buffet meal.

Christmas cake

EATING OUT OF DOORS

This can be a truly luxurious experience. However there are some wise rules to remember. Do not have sweets or cakes which become sticky in the hot sun. Keep salads, trifle, etc., in a cool place until the last minute. Always choose easy-to-serve dishes.

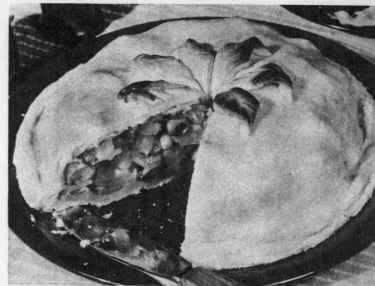
Cornish cheese pie

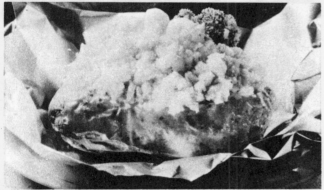
Picnic fare

1067   PICNIC FARE

All food on a picnic should be easy to carry. Try a selection of the following:

Sausage or savoury beef rolls (Recipe Nos. 1050, 1057) and lettuce – kept fresh in polythene bags

Stuffed baked potatoes – kept hot in foil

Individual trifles and jellies in waxed containers

Ice cold tomato juice – carried in a vacuum flask

Mincemeat and apple slices – make short crust pastry (Recipe No. 566) roll out thinly and with half line a Swiss roll tin. Cover with mincemeat and grated apple. Top with remaining pastry. Bake in a moderately hot oven, 400°F, 200°C, Gas Mark 6, for 35–40 minutes. Lower the heat slightly after 20 minutes. Carry in the tin and cut into slices just before serving.

1068   CORNISH CHEESE PIE

200g/8oz *cheese pastry (Recipe No. 605)*
200g/8oz *potato, cooked and chopped*
100g/4oz *carrot, cooked and chopped · 50g/2oz cooked peas*
1 *medium-sized onion, chopped · ½ level teaspoon mixed herbs*
salt and pepper to taste · beaten egg or milk to glaze

Make the pastry, turn on to a lightly floured board and divide in two. Roll out one half and line a greased 18-cm (7-inch) ovenproof plate. Moisten edges of pastry with water. Mix the remaining ingredients together and spread over the pastry-lined plate then cover with remaining pastry, rolled out into a circle slightly larger than the plate. Press edges well together to seal then knock up with the back of a knife. Brush top with beaten egg or milk and decorate with pastry leaves, rolled and cut from trimmings. Bake in the centre of a hot oven, 425°F, 220°C, Gas Mark 7, for about 35 minutes, reducing heat to moderate after 20 minutes.

The pastry in this recipe is rather fragile, so if carrying on a picnic keep in the tin or put into a polythene box.
Makes 6 servings.

1069   KIPPER PIZZA

200g/8oz *flour (with plain flour use 2 level teaspoons baking powder)*
½ *teaspoon salt · 50g/2oz butter · 142ml/¼pint milk*
100g/4oz *cheese, grated · 1 teaspoon dry mustard*
pinch dried oregano · pinch dried basil · 2 tomatoes, sliced
seasoning
200g/8oz *kipper fillets (if using frozen kipper fillets allow to thaw)*
6 black olives · little oil

Sieve flour, baking powder, if used, and salt. Rub in butter until mixture resembles fine breadcrumbs. Bind together with milk to form a soft dough. Roll out fairly thinly to a circle and place on greased baking sheet. Mix cheese, mustard and herbs together in a basin. Sprinkle evenly over the dough. Arrange tomatoes in a circle on top of the cheese and season. Arrange 6 kipper fillets in between the tomatoes. Divide each of the remaining two kipper fillets into 3 strips and curl around the olives. Place between the other kipper fillets. Brush kipper fillets lightly with oil. Bake in the centre of a moderately hot oven, 400°F, 200°C, Gas Mark 6, for about 30 minutes, until base is cooked and the cheese is bubbling and golden.
Makes 6 servings.

Kipper pizza

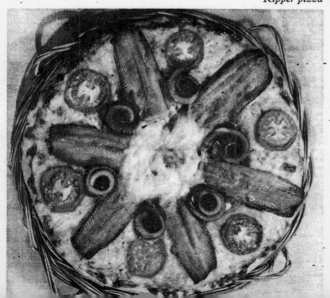

The picture on the left shows:
A cooked chicken, a melon and an Edam cheese.
A French loaf sliced lengthways and filled with a salmon filling and a cream cheese filling. The loaf is garnished with tomato and cucumber slices.
On the kebab skewers are cubes of Cheddar cheese, drained canned pineapple pieces and pieces of cooked sausage.
In the plastic container is fruit set in jelly, topped with a layer of custard and whipped double cream. The dish is decorated with cherries, angelica and mimosa balls.

Barbecue kebabs

1070   PLANNING A BARBECUE

Giving a barbecue out of doors has become a popular way of entertaining. You can purchase very luxurious equipment for cooking your barbecue food, but the handyman can produce a fire over which the food can be cooked out of doors. Cook gammon slices, kebabs (Recipe Nos. 187, 1071) sausages, chops, etc., or even jointed chicken. Serve with a well spiced tomato sauce (Recipe No. 656), rice and various salads. Beer, cider and hot coffee are the ideal drinks.

1071   BARBECUE KEBABS

Thread cubes of rump steak, tomato slices, pieces of green pepper, slices of aubergine and bay leaves on skewers. Sprinkle with salt and pepper, brush with oil or melted fat and cook over a barbecue, turning the skewers, so that the food becomes evenly browned.

USING A REFRIGERATOR FOR PARTY DISHES

A refrigerator is a help at all times, but particularly when entertaining, for it enables the food to be prepared in advance, and delicious iced or jellied sweets to be made. Illustrated in the picture are orange turn-abouts for which the refrigerator is especially helpful. Jellied sweets and ice cream sundaes are in the dessert section. Ice cream sodas are in the section on hot and cold drinks.
Pastry flans, etc., will be found in the pastry section.

Orange turn-abouts

1072 ORANGE TURN-ABOUTS

water · 1 orange-flavoured jelly
275g/11oz can mandarin oranges
1 small can evaporated milk, chilled · 1 flake bar, crushed
little double cream or evaporated milk, whipped
chocolate buttons to decorate

Rinse out 5 small moulds with cold water. Dissolve half the jelly in just under 284ml (½ pint) water and divide between each mould. Leave to set in the refrigerator. Dissolve remaining jelly in just under 142ml (¼ pint) of juice from the mandarins then cool until on the point of setting. Chop most of the mandarins. Whisk the evaporated milk (see instructions on can) until thick, stir into the jelly with the crushed flake and chopped mandarins. Pour mixture into the moulds on top of the jelly and leave in the refrigerator until set. To turn out, quickly dip the moulds into hot water and turn each serving on to a plate. Top with whirls of lightly whipped cream and decorate with reserved mandarin oranges and a chocolate button.
Makes 5 servings.

Apple party

1073 APPLE PARTY

Apples, cheese, salami, pâté and crisp biscuits make excellent party fare. Choose a variety of cheese – in the picture Danish Blue and Cheddar are shown. For a centre piece thread cubes of cheese, black and stuffed olives on to cocktail sticks, then secure the sticks into an apple.
A Beaujolais goes well with cheese and fruit.

FOOD FOR CHILDREN'S PARTIES

Chocolate pear bunnies

1074 COCONUT WHISPERS

1 large can condensed milk
225–250g*/9oz desiccated coconut · few drops cochineal
little rice paper

*See first sentence of method

Mix condensed milk with enough coconut to give firm mixture; colour half pale pink with a few drops of cochineal. Form into pyramid shapes and put on rice paper placed on a baking sheet. Put into a hot oven, 425–450°F, 220–230°C, Gas Mark 6–7, for 5–8 minutes to brown tips. Tear round rice paper.

1075 CHOCOLATE PEAR BUNNIES

4 firm dessert pears, peeled and cored but left whole
142ml/¼pint water · 1 teaspoon lemon juice
1 dessertspoon castor sugar
150g/6oz cooking or plain chocolate, melted in a basin placed over a saucepan of hot water
angelica, sugar-coated sweets and flaked almonds to decorate drinking straws

Poach the pears gently in the water, lemon juice and sugar for about 5 minutes, until tender. Remove from the liquid, pat dry, then coat each pear in the chocolate so that the whole pear is covered. When almost set insert the angelica, sweets and flaked almonds as shown in the picture. Make the whiskers from drinking straws or cardboard.

1076   CHOCOLATE BAR YACHTS

Cover chocolate ice cream bars with tiny sweets and press wafers, cut into triangles, on top of each bar. Serve at once.

Chocolate bar yachts

1077   ORANGE CLOWNS

8–12 small oranges · 1 orange-flavoured jelly
142–284ml/¼–½pint double cream, whipped
8–12 ice cream cornets · coloured sweets · glacé cherries
angelica

Cut a slice from the top of each orange to make sure they stand firmly. Remove fruit pulp. Put a few pieces of the fruit back in the orange cases, but put juice into a measure. Add enough water to the juice to give just over generous ½litre (1 pint) and dissolve jelly in this. When set, whisk jelly and pile into orange cases. Put a little cream on top and put ice cream cornets in position. Pipe cream on the cornets and press sweets in position, then pipe cream on the oranges to represent eyes and a mouth; press halved glacé cherries into the 'eyes' and use a small piece of angelica for the 'nose'.
Makes 8–12 servings.

1078   ORANGE SEGMENTS

1 orange-flavoured jelly · 1 raspberry-flavoured jelly
about 8 large oranges

Make the jellies and leave to cool. Cut the oranges in halves lengthways. Remove all the pulp which can be used in a fruit salad, etc. Cut away any surplus white pith but leave cases. Spoon the cold, but not set, jelly into the orange halves and leave until firm. To serve, cut into segments with a sharp knife dipped in hot water.
Makes 8–12 servings.

1079   SAILING SHIPS

1 greengage-flavoured jelly · few drops blue colouring
little double cream, whipped · 8 canned pear halves
8 ice cream wafers

Make the jelly and add a few drops blue colouring. Pour into shallow dishes or deep saucers and leave to set. When set pipe lines of cream to look like ripples on the sea. Put a halved pear on the jelly, cut side uppermost. Fill with a little cream and press wafers, cut into triangles on each halved pear.
Makes 8 servings.

Orange clowns, orange segments, sailing ships

Roman candles

1080   ROMAN CANDLES

142ml/¼pint double cream · 6 canned peach halves
6 chocolate-covered Swiss rolls · angelica*
little double cream, whipped, to decorate

*Softened in hot water to make it pliable

Whip the cream until stiff. Place each peach half, cut side uppermost, on a saucer. Put a spoonful of cream in the centre of each peach half and stand a Swiss roll upright in it, pressing into the cream to hold firm. Cut strips of angelica and form it to the shape of a handle and secure one end in the cream round the base of the Swiss roll and the other end underneath the peach half. Put a little cream on the top of each 'candle' and insert a small strip of angelica to form a 'wick'. Put a thin line of cream down the side to resemble a drip of wax.
Makes 6 servings.

1081 ALPHABET BISCUITS

200g/8oz plain flour · ¼ level teaspoon cinnamon · pinch salt
125g/5oz margarine · 50g/2oz castor sugar
1 tablespoon water · water and sugar to glaze
chocolate icing (Recipe No. 1082)

Sieve the dry ingredients together. Rub in the table margarine, until the mixture resembles fine breadcrumbs. Stir in the sugar and the water. Knead well, and roll out thinly. Cut into 5-cm (2-inch) squares. Place on baking sheets, brush with water and sprinkle with a little castor sugar. Bake in the centre of a very moderate oven, 325°F, 170°C, Gas Mark 3, for 15–20 minutes. Cool on baking sheet. Decorate, as shown in the picture, with chocolate icing.

1082 CHOCOLATE ICING

1 rounded dessertspoon cocoa · 2 tablespoons hot water
125g*/4oz icing sugar, sieved · 2 dessertspoons milk
40g/1½oz margarine

*Necessary for correct consistency

Blend the cocoa with the hot water. Cool slightly, then add to the rest of the ingredients and mix until smooth.

Parcel maypole

Alphabet biscuits

1083 PARCEL MAYPOLE

Make up generous ½litre (1 pint) instant pudding and pour into a shallow dish. Leave to set, then decorate with whipped cream. For small children use very little cream. Stand a coloured drinking straw in the centre. Decorate with bright ribbons and streamers to look like a maypole. At the end of each streamer or ribbon tie a small gift.

TEATIME SAVOURIES

Swiss roll sandwiches

1084 CHEESE BOATS

Make boat-shaped shells from short crust pastry – these may be either plain or cheese flavoured. Into these pipe a ripple of filling and decorate with capers, chopped walnuts or stuffed olives.
Filling: Mix to a smooth consistency 50g (2 oz) cream cheese, 1 dessertspoon horseradish cream and 1 dessertspoon salad cream or mayonnaise.

1085 SWISS ROLL SANDWICHES

Cut medium-thick slices of bread from the lower half of a small tin loaf and remove the crusts – new bread is essential. Spread generously with chicken and ham spread or paste blended with butter; sprinkle with a few drops of lemon juice and roll firmly. Dip one end of each sandwich in chopped parsley and arrange on a serving plate or a board. Serve garnished with cress.

WINES

1086

Many people are still slightly nervous of buying and serving wines as they feel they are entering the realm of the expert. There is no doubt that with a little knowledge you can enjoy a wide selection of wines, which add so much pleasure to meals. This knowledge can best be acquired by talking to a good wine merchant, who is generally an enthusiastic expert as well as a salesman, or by reading books on this subject. Do not be frightened by the people who say you MUST serve a white wine with fish and a red wine with game and meat. It is accepted that these are the best partners; food and wine should complement each other and neither should be overpowering. You might, however, prefer white wines at all times, in which case go ahead and enjoy them.

If you are faced with a formidable wine list and want to select your own wine you will find the various types of wines grouped together, i.e. all the Bordeaux wines, red and white (claret is the English name for red Bordeaux); all the Burgundies (Bourgogne is the French word); all the Rhone wines and the Hocks (Rhine wines); Moselles, Alsatians; the Chiantis and other Italian wines; the wines from Australia, South Africa, Cyprus, Portugal; the Champagnes and, of course, the sherries and ports. Choosing French wines always seems a complex business to the amateur, for there is such variety but the labels are not as bewildering as they seem. Cheap wines will have the name of the district only on them, for example 'Bordeaux superior'. In the Bordeaux area, however, there are over a dozen different districts and a slightly better wine may specify 'Haut Médoc', 'St. Emilion' etc. Inside these districts there are communes, for example 'Margaux', and in each commune a number of châteaux or vineyards, for example 'Château Talbot'. The better the wine of a year the more anxious the château or commune will be to sell it under its own name instead of under a general commune or district name. That is why commune wines are more valued than district wines and château wines in turn considered superior to commune wines. Other wine districts may have different systems of labelling. In Burgundy, châteaux are not normally distinguished. In Alsace the wine is labelled primarily after the type of grape from which it is made, and such descriptive labels are also found on German wines. A great deal is talked about vintage years; this simply means a year when the grapes were particularly fine and so produced outstanding wine of its type. Your wine merchant will tell you about these but remember vintage year wines are highly prized and will therefore be more expensive.

The wines listed below are reasonably safe choices if you are not absolutely certain what to ask for.

For a white wine, choose from:

White Burgundy – Chablis (very dry), Pouilly-Fuissé, Mâcon
White Bourdeaux – White Graves (dry), Sauternes (sweet), Barsac (sweet)
German wines – Moselle, Hock

For a good Vin Rosé which is an excellent 'in between' wine – not as heavy as red, choose from:

Rosé d'Anjou, de Touraine, de Lirac, Rosé des Côtes de Provence, Rosé d'Arbois or the best known and most easily obtainable rosé from Portugal called Mateus.
Red Burgundy – Beaune, Mâcon, Beaujolais
Red Bordeaux – various clarets, Médoc, St. Emilion, Margaux.

There are also sparkling wines which are less usual, but nevertheless very good – try a *sparkling* red Burgundy for a change.

For perfect results serve white wines (including Champagne) and a rosé at a cold temperature, NOT iced, between 45°F, 7°C, and 53°F, 11°C. Red wines on the other hand are better served at room temperature, i.e. approximately 60°F, 16°C, so leave in a warm room for a time before serving, and ideally one should remove the cork of red wine for about an hour so it can 'breathe'.

For a formal meal, where you wish to serve a number of wines, choose as follows:

Sherry – for a sweet sherry an Amorosa or brown; for a dry sherry a Fino, Amontillado or the very dry Tio Pepe
To serve with soup or hors d'oeuvre
  a dry white wine
To serve with meat, poultry
  for veal, sweetbreads – a white wine or Vin Rosé, which is also good with chicken
  for game poultry, red meat – a red wine
To serve with sweet
  a sweet white wine or Champagne
To serve with coffee
  port, Madeira or a liqueur.

Cocktail   Sherry   Burgundy   Claret   Sauternes   Graves   Hock   Moselle   Champagne   Liqueur   Port   Liqueur   Brandy

INDEX

(All references are to recipe numbers)

W

Y

Z

ACKNOWLEDGMENTS

The author and publishers would like to thank the following for their help and co-operation in supplying pictures for this book.

Angostura Aromatic Bitters: Colour pictures accompanying Recipe Nos. 51, 241, 563.
  Black and white pictures accompanying Recipe Nos. 43, 704, 839, 842–3, 876 881.
Australian Recipe Service: Colour picture accompanying Recipe No. 186.
  Black and white picture accompanying Recipe No. 221.
Baco Foil Advisory Bureau: Black and white picture accompanying Recipe No. 1067.
Batchelor's Foods Limited: Black and white pictures accompanying Recipe Nos. 74, 205, 423, 884.
Beechams Foods Limited: Colour pictures accompanying Recipe Nos. 227, 389, 463.
Birds Eye Frozen Foods Limited: Black and white pictures accompanying Recipe Nos. 60, 282, 321, 399.
Blue Band Bureau: Black and white pictures accompanying Recipe Nos. 59; 98, 147, 308, 333, 343, 555, 708, 721–2, 778, 801, 818, 837.
British Bacon Curers Federation: Colour pictures accompanying Recipe Nos. 198, 200, 299.
  Black and white pictures accompanying Recipe Nos. 29, 54, 235, 289.
British Egg Information Service: Colour picture accompanying Recipe No. 646.
  Black and white pictures accompanying Recipe Nos. 153, 368–9, 372, 386, 391, 512, 859.
British Meat Service: Colour pictures accompanying Recipe Nos. 167, 169, 187.
  Black and white pictures accompanying Recipe Nos. 175, 190, 208, 232, 248, 293, 627, 649, 920.
Brown and Polson: Colour pictures accompanying Recipe Nos. 273, 326, 407, 420, 433, 657.
  Black and white pictures accompanying Recipe Nos. 109, 182, 499, 542, 579, 600, 923, 1053.
H. P. Bulmer Limited: Colour picture accompanying Recipe No. 274.
  Black and white pictures accompanying Recipe Nos. 178, 877–8.
Butter Information Council: Colour picture accompanying Recipe Nos. 1017, 1018.
  Black and white pictures accompanying Recipe Nos. 53, 262, 309.
Cadbury Schweppes Foods Limited: Colour pictures accompanying Recipe Nos. 350, 589, 633, 730, 869, 1072.
  Black and white pictures accompanying Recipe Nos. 703, 769, 784.
California Raisin Bureau: Black and white picture accompanying Recipe No. 804.
Camp Coffee: Black and white pictures accompanying Recipe Nos. 470, 559.
Campbell's Soups Limited: Black and white pictures accompanying Recipe Nos. 12, 242, 244, 331, 921, 1052.
Carnation Milk Bureau: Black and white picture accompanying Recipe No. 615.

Cheese Bureau: Colour pictures accompanying Recipe Nos. 337, 361. Black and white pictures accompanying Recipe Nos. 112, 210, 246, 353, 355, 360, 385, 396, 651, 935.

Chicken Information Council: Black and white pictures accompanying Recipe Nos. 256, 397.

Christian Délu: Introduction to Marmalades.

Coffee Promotion Bureau: Introduction to Hot and Cold Drinks. Colour picture accompanying Recipe No. 871. Black and white picture accompanying Recipe No. 874.

Colman's Mustard: Black and white pictures accompanying Recipe Nos. 95, 203, 245, 295, 346, 609, 1068.

Colman's Semolina: Black and white pictures accompanying Recipe Nos. 537, 541, 841, 1020.

Cookeen: Black and white pictures accompanying Recipe Nos. 330, 556, 918, 1025.

Dairy Farmer: Black and white picture accompanying Recipe No. 306.

Danish Food Centre: Colour picture accompanying Recipe No. 896. Black and white picture accompanying Recipe Nos. 176, 947–8, 950, 953, 1034–5.

Dine Potato: Black and white picture accompanying Recipe No. 307.

Domestic Appliance Division of Tube Investments Limited (Radiation): Introduction to Time-Controlled Cooking.

Dutch Dairy Bureau: Colour picture accompanying Recipe No. 314. Black and white picture accompanying Recipe Nos. 8, 305, 342.

Eden Vale: Colour pictures accompanying Recipe Nos. 7, 13, 895, 937. Black and white pictures accompanying Recipe Nos. 27, 152, 366–7, 401.

Elders and Fyffes: Black and white picture accompanying Recipe No. 557.

Farmer and Stockbreeder: Black and white picture accompanying Recipe No. 564.

Findus Frozen Foods: Colour picture accompanying Recipe No. 107. Black and white picture accompanying Recipe No. 318.

Flour Advisory Bureau: Colour picture accompanying Recipes 468, 809. Black and white pictures accompanying Recipe Nos. 110, 135, 217, 451, 454–5, 458, 472, 478, 486, 571, 611–2, 628, 630, 641, 654, 736–7, 740, 755, 812, 814–6, 827–9, 858, 862, 919, 931, 949, 1031, 1085.

Fowlers West India Treacle: Black and white pictures accompanying Recipe Nos. 582, 787.

Fray Bentos: Colour picture accompanying Recipe No. 237.

J. W. French and Company Limited: Black and white picture accompanying Recipe No. 724.

Fruit Producers' Council: Colour pictures accompanying Recipe Nos. 22, 50, 106, 139–41, 166–7, 184–5, 201, 225, 329, 339, 393–4, 413, 417, 439, 450, 460, 469, 482, 492, 504–5, 518, 521, 534, 573, 577, 586, 592, 616, 622, 642, 658, 716–7, 734, 741, 757, 765, 819, 834, 847, 853, 912, 915, 926–7, 940, 944. Introduction to Jams and Preserving, Entertaining, 979, 1055, 1057, 1063, 1075. Black and white pictures accompanying Recipe Nos. 102, 428, 487.

General Foods Limited: Black and white pictures accompanying Recipe Nos. 585, 964, 966, 969, 986, 994, 996–7.

Green Giant Corn: Black and white pictures accompanying Recipe Nos. 304, 319.

Guernsey Tomato Marketing Board: Colour pictures accompanying Recipe Nos. 323, 373. Black and white pictures accompanying Recipe Nos. 290, 294.

Herring Industry Board: Colour picture accompanying Recipe No. 83. Black and white pictures accompanying Recipe Nos. 85, 89, 626, 934, 1069.

H. J. Heinz Company Limited: Black and white pictures accompanying Recipe Nos. 42, 72–3, 81, 219–20, 231, 358, 359, 726, 936, 955.

Kraft Foods Limited: Colour picture accompanying Recipe No. 796. Black and white picture accompanying Recipe No. 96.

Lard Information Bureau: Black and white pictures accompanying Recipe Nos. 1050, 1051.

Lea and Perrins: Black and white picture accompanying Recipe No. 69.

MacFisheries Limited: Black and white pictures accompanying Recipe Nos. 28, 131–2.

McDougalls Cookery Service: Black and white pictures accompanying Recipe Nos. 473, 483, 510.

Mushroom Information Service: Black and white pictures accompanying Recipe Nos. 11, 259, 336.

National Dairy Council: Black and white pictures accompanying Recipe Nos. 501, 509.

New Zealand Lamb Information Bureau: Colour pictures accompanying Recipe Nos. 215, 240. Black and white pictures accompanying Recipe Nos. 180, 189, 193, 195, 234, 236.

Oxo Meat Cookery Service: Black and white picture accompanying Recipe No. 229.

Pascalls Marshmallows: Black and white picture accompanying Recipe No. 568.

Pasta Foods Limited: Colour pictures accompanying Recipe Nos. 275, 352. Black and white picture accompanying Recipe Nos. 223.

Philips Electric Mixers: Black and white picture accompanying Recipe No. 558.

Pilchard Food Advisory Bureau: Colour pictures accompanying Recipe Nos. 634, 924, 929, 939. Black and white pictures accompanying Recipe Nos. 442–3, 1041.

Pol Roger: Black and white picture accompanying Recipe No. 1027.

Potato Marketing Board: Colour pictures accompanying Recipe Nos. 296, 306. Black and white pictures accompanying Recipe Nos. 310–1, 344, 917.

Prestige Group Limited: Introduction to Pressure Cooking. Colour picture accompanying Recipe No. 899. Black and white pictures accompanying Recipe Nos. 720, 893, 904, 1009.

'Pyrosil' – Jobling Housecraft Service: Colour pictures accompanying Recipe Nos. 119, 212, 325.

Quaker Oats Limited: Colour picture accompanying Recipe No. 788. Black and white pictures accompanying Recipe Nos. 500, 511, 602, 1066.

Rice Information Service: Colour picture accompanying Recipe No. 137. Black and white pictures accompanying Recipe Nos. 134, 192, 392, 432, 440.

Spanish Olive Oil: Colour picture accompanying Recipe No. 270.

Spillers Limited: Black and white picture accompanying Recipe No. 595.

Spry Cookery Centre: Black and white pictures accompanying Recipe Nos. 101, 111, 569, 623, 1029.

Stork Cookery Service: Black and white pictures accompanying Recipe Nos. 285, 750, 766, 767, 768, 770, 799, 844–5, 1081.

Summer County Margarine: Black and white picture accompanying Recipe No. 700.

Sunkist Growers: Black and white pictures accompanying Recipe Nos. 84, 279.

Symbol Polka Dots: Black and white picture accompanying Recipe No. 800.

Syndication International: Colour pictures accompanying Recipe Nos. 49, 213, 312, 603, 777, 1070, Introduction to Wines.

Tala Icing Equipment: Black and white pictures accompanying Recipe No. 753.

Taylor, Law and Company Limited: Black and white pictures accompanying Recipe No. 1065.

Uncle Ben's Rice: Black and white picture accompanying Recipe No. 143.

Unigate (Dairy Sales) Limited: Black and white picture accompanying Recipe No. 1080.

United Fresh Fruit and Vegetable Association: Black and white picture accompanying Recipe No. 890.

T. Wall and Sons (Ice Cream) Limited: Colour pictures accompanying Recipe Nos. 531, 551. Black and white picture accompanying Recipe Nos. 508, 513, 522, 524–8, 596, 1076.

T. Wall and Sons (Meat and Handy Foods) Limited: Black and white pictures accompanying Recipe Nos. 317, 933, 1048–9.

John West Foods Limited: Black and white pictures accompanying Recipe Nos. 144, 146, 854.

White Fish Kitchen: Colour pictures accompanying Recipe Nos. 93, 103, 116. Black and white picture accompanying Recipe No. 97.

Jacket photograph by Roy Rich of Angel Studios.

COOKERY IN COLOUR

© Copyright THE HAMLYN PUBLISHING GROUP 1960

LONDON · NEW YORK · SYDNEY · TORONTO

ASTRONAUT HOUSE · FELTHAM · MIDDLESEX · ENGLAND

First published 1960
Twelfth impression 1970
Revised edition 1972
Third impression 1974

Filmset in England by Filmtype Services Limited, Scarborough

Printed in Czechoslovakia by Svoboda

ISBN 0 600 31700 5

52010/13

COMPARISON OF WEIGHTS AND MEASURES

Imperial and metric weights and measures have been used throughout this book. In addition it is useful to note that 3 teaspoons equal 1 tablespoon; the average English teacup is ¼ pint; the average English breakfast cup is ½ pint. When cups are mentioned in recipes they refer to a B.S.I. measuring cup which holds ½ pint or 10 fluid ounces.

American equivalents are given in the conversion table. It should be noted that the American pint is 16 fluid ounces, as opposed to the British Imperial and Canadian pints which are 20 fluid ounces. The American ½-pint measuring cup is 8 fluid ounces and is therefore equivalent to ⅖ British pint.

In Australia the British Imperial pint, 20 fluid ounces, is used for liquid measures. Solid ingredients however are generally calculated in the American cup measure. In America, standard cup and spoon measurements are used and all measures in the table opposite refer to these standard units.

METRICATION

For quick and easy reference when buying food it should be remembered that 1 kilogramme (1000 grammes) equals 2·2 pounds (35¾ ounces) – i.e. as a rough guide, ½ kilogramme is about 1 pound. In liquid measurements 1 litre (10 decilitres or 1000 millilitres) equals almost exactly 1¾ pints (1·76), ½ litre is ⅞ pint. As a rough guide, therefore, one can assume that the equivalent of 1 pint is a generous ½ litre.

A simple method of converting recipe quantities is to use round figures of an exact conversion, and in this book a basic equivalent of 25 grammes to 1 ounce, and a generous ½ litre to 1 pint has been used. Since 1 ounce is exactly 28·35 grammes and 1 pint is 568 millilitres it can be seen that these equivalents will give a slightly smaller finished dish, but the proportion of liquids to solids will remain the same and a satisfactory result will be produced.

The following tables show exact conversions to the nearest whole number and alongside the recommended amount using the 25 grammes to 1 ounce and ½ litre to 1 pint equivalents.

SOLID AND DRY INGREDIENTS

Imperial	Exact conversion to nearest whole number	Recommended equivalent
Ounces	Grammes	Grammes
1	28	25
2	57	50
3	85	75
4	113	100
5	142	125
6	170	150
7	198	175
8	226	200

LIQUID MEASURE

Imperial	Exact conversion to nearest whole number	Recommended equivalent used only in *some* recipes
Pints	Millilitres	Litres
1 pint (20 fl oz)	568	½ litre – generous
¾ pint	426	⅜ litre – generous
½ pint	284	¼ litre – generous
¼ pint	142	⅛ litre – generous
1 fl oz	28·4	25 ml
B.S.I. tablespoon	—	18 ml
B.S.I. teaspoon	—	5 ml

In special cases, such as for pastries, it may be necessary to use more accurate quantities, and these are shown in the recipes.

A
Imperial weights

B
Accurate conversion

C
Recommended conversion –
25 grammes to 1 ounce